Annie Kennedy Bidwell

An Intimate History

Lois Halliday McDonald

STANSBURY
PUBLISHING
Chico Ca

ISBN 0-9708922-7-6
First Edition
Printed in the United States of America

Stansbury Publishing
An Imprint of Heidelberg Graphics
Chico, California 95928-9410
www.HeidelbergGraphics.com

Library of Congress Cataloging-in-Publication Data

McDonald, Lois Halliday.
   Annie Kennedy Bidwell: an intimate history / Lois Halliday McDonald.--1st ed.
      p. cm.
   Includes bibliographical references (p.) and index.
   ISBN 0-9708922-7-6
   1. Bidwell, Annie E. Kennedy. 2. Women pioneers--California--Biography. 3. Pioneers--California--Biography. 4. Bidwell, John, 1819-1900. 5. Frontier and pioneer life--California. 6. Frontier and pioneer life--California--Chico. 7. Chico (Calif.)--Biography. 8. Chico (Calif.)--History. I. title.

F864.B588M38 2004
979.4'3203'092--dc22
[B]   2004048232

Contents

Preface

*B*iography provides a portrait of a human being filtered through the eyes and mind of another person.

In this work I attempted to present the real and true life of Annie Kennedy Bidwell who was dead before I was born. I knew none of her family nor her companions, and though she left voluminous paper documentation of many of her life passions and activities, all of this evidence—both her own selected papers and the less personal reporting of contemporaries and newspapers—has been subjected to my own very biased point of view. I use the word "bias" in admitting to the values which I hold and the social code by which I live nearly a century after her death.

Still, I have tried to faithfully follow the evidence she gave as to the type of person she was and her actions as she related to the world in which she lived.

This meant breaking the code of Victorian thought and behavior. I am fortunate in that I was exposed to much feminine thinking akin to Annie's from my own family members reared with Victorian values. My grandmother's diaries, the stories of maternal great-grandparents, and the strict adherence to Victorian values with which my mother was inculcated and which rubbed off on me—all of this helped. I do not find that being an octogenarian has been a handicap to me, except perhaps in climbing stairs, or walking many blocks from my car or hotel to libraries where Annie K. Bidwell collections are deposited.

Preface

Writing about the life of Annie Bidwell meant identifying the great forces that drove her to become involved in converting others to her own overpowering belief in God's will, even when her efforts led to mental anguish. I think I have traced the passions that enabled her to bear what were to her physical discomfort, loneliness and rejection, and to understand how she was sustained by the love of God, her parents and her husband.

I understand that the same material I studied might bring another writer to a different interpretation. There is certainly more material to find and to use in interpreting the life of the wife of Chico's founder and leading citizen. I hope that others will be encouraged to have a go at it!

The work of many persons has been utilized in this biography. Though I was instrumental in getting the Bidwell diaries published on CD-ROMs, the way was laid out by Shirley Connelly, a Green Thumb worker at the Bidwell Mansion Historical Park, who typed out the diaries from copies of the originals in the park archives. The encouragement of park personnel has had a strong influence on me, from forming the idea of undertaking the biography a number of years ago to making the park archives accessible with papers and photographs when the writing began.

Gary F. Kurutz, director of Special Collections at the California State Library was very helpful with his suggestions made on the final draft, as well as with special research problems. I thank him.

Larry S. Jackson of Stansbury Publishing has my lasting gratitude for his support, ideas, and insistence on quality work in the many projects on which he and I have worked over a number of years. He was no less demanding of excellence with this biography of Annie Bidwell.

I thank especially Paul Holman, park ranger when I first served on the Bidwell Mansion Association Board of Directors: Ellen M. Clark, guide 1 at the park and now interpretive specialist for the Northern Buttes District of the California State Parks, and Judy Crain, guide 1 at the Bidwell Mansion State Historic Park at this time. Others who made an input include Shirley Kendall of the park staff and numerous guides and volunteers whose enthusiasm for the Bidwells and their home, and interesting conversations speculating on the nature of the couple's relationship to each other and the wider community amused and inspired me.

I am grateful to Joan Bidwell, genealogist for the family, and to Bernie Bidwell of Colbert, Washington, for their gracious assistance in the attempt to "unseal the envelope" of General John Bidwell's personal secret.

I thank my own family for supporting me in this effort and especially my daughter Satsie D. Veith, for her editing skills and comments. Others have made a significant input, including Craig D. Bates, curator of ethnography, Yosemite National Park, whose insightful study of the Mechoopda Indian Tribe has been shared with me through a number of letters.

It is necessary to make a disclaimer here. In spite of the considerable information about the residents of the Bidwell Rancheria given in this book, I do not claim to have written a definitive account of that interesting group. That is something for future authors to undertake—a complicated and worthwhile topic. My portrayal of the Mechoopda Indians comes through Annie Bidwell's eyes and by her pen.

Lois H. McDonald

Introduction

California was long a land of mythical enchantment, or of fearful dangers, depending on the mind-set of those who visualized it from afar—be they geographers, adventurers or dreamers. Sons and husbands departed to see for themselves whether promises hinted at by that golden island on the Pacific might be fulfilled. Annie Kennedy's grandfather, upon being invited in 1868 to her wedding wrote, "California! In my boyhood almost 'terra incognita.'"

Annie Kennedy became engaged to marry a Union general—the California pioneer and congressman, John Bidwell. He would take her west to Rancho Chico, away from the high society Washington, D.C., home of her parents. Though fearful of the West's savage Indians, Annie's parents nevertheless recognized that the marriage of their daughter to this man of presumed enormous wealth and high rank in California politics could scarcely be forbidden.

Some commentators still assume Annie's chief accomplishment was to bring social polish to Chico, the crude new town in Northern California founded by her husband. Not so, for though the Bidwells entertained many guests and were lavish in both the meals and entertainment provided to visitors to their mansion, Annie's focus came to be the causes that she welcomed as God's plan for her life. Lucky she was that her ambitions so neatly meshed with those of a lenient and loving husband. The two shared everything of themselves after meeting, both of their earlier lives and the frustrations and successes of their life together.

The year following her marriage to Bidwell, Annie traveled by herself on the newly opened transcontinental railway to visit her family. A year later Chico was hooked by rail to San Francisco, a frequent destination of the Bidwells. She traveled from coast to coast many times. She learned to combine her social obligations with participation at both state and national Indian associations, and attendance at Women's Christian Temperance Union conventions across the country.

Bidwell's dedication to education reminds one of Jane Stanford, Annie's contemporary who put so much of both her wealth and her ideas into forming a university. With the Bidwells, it was Chico Normal School built on land they donated, started with their suggestions for curriculum, and over a century later became a state university. Another nineteenth century supporter of education, Phoebe Apperson Hearst, was drawn to Annie with their similarity of ideas and willingness to work for them.

Annie began her role as educator with the Indians of Bidwell Rancheria, driven by both the need to bring these "savages" to Christ and to help prepare them to survive in the white man's world.

Prohibition and eradication of alcohol produced for human consumption became perhaps the most dedicated endeavor of the many that obsessed this little woman. She became a good friend of Susan B. Anthony and a great admirer and correspondent of Frances Willard. Annie worked tirelessly to achieve women's suffrage and the multifaceted program of the WCTU.

Annie went on camping trips. She toured Europe. She started businesses, supported friends and relatives in life and death, and she made plans for development and parks in Chico.

Annie Kennedy Bidwell's greatest achievement was providing leadership in the causes she prayed ceaselessly to win others to, and in so doing she gave Chico and all of California a female model of whom to be proud.

Annie Kennedy Bidwell

Annie Bidwell—one of her last photographs—taken probably after 1911. Courtesy of California State Parks.

Glimmerings
from childhood

While her railway car was shunted on a siding in western Pennsylvania preparatory to being transferred to another line that would take her to Chicago, Annie Bidwell glimpsed in the distance a large body of water.

With a burst of happy recollection, Annie realized that it was Conneaut Lake. She hastily reached for her traveling writing case to confide her feelings to her husband in a letter, a habit acquired in over twenty-five years of marriage. Separation from John was by no means a rare situation but they had never let down expectations that almost daily communication between them would occur. Writing from a bouncing train or lonely hotel was commonplace.

Putting in writing the news of the moment was as much joy as work. By 1895 her memories of childhood spent near Conneaut Lake had lain fallow for as much as fifty years. Now the "scene of childhood delight" overwhelmed her. Here, her family had come by wagon on many an outing from the farm that her father owned and worked between Meadville, Pennsylvania, and the large natural lake.

In the summer the Kennedy children and their cousins had waded in the water under the watchful eye of parents, aunts, and uncles sitting in the shade of hardwood trees along the bank. Crawdads and minnows fled before toy shovels and small fingers. Her castles had been built and flooded, Joey's forts built and destroyed under siege. Father Joseph Kennedy would have lost himself in the pages of one of his favorite Greek classics. Mother

Catherine Kennedy chatted gaily with her sisters-in-law about the upcoming style for bonnets that season.

Annie's sister Sallie, two years her junior, was the center of the fishing expeditions undertaken when the children were older and allowed to come to the lake on picnics of their own. Sally was extraordinarily lucky with a rod and hook, Annie recalled in her letter to John—written that September day of 1895—recalling how the other anglers flocked to Sallie's chosen spot for fishing. She always "hauled the fish in." When her pool became crowded with other lines, Sallie slipped away to another place along the bank and continued to show her skill and her luck with the laughing bravado that came to characterize her as an adult. Annie told John, "It was not my taste to fish but to enjoy the wildly beautiful scene of dashing water and islands."[1]

By 1895 Conneaut Lake had already begun to build up with vacation homes, and several small steamboats visible from Annie's passing railroad car plied the water for both sightseeing and providing transportation across the lake. Lake Conneaut is still today one of Crawford County's pleasure sites, with a state park set aside for recreation.

Childhood, as it shaped Annie Bidwell, was revealed in other letters to her husband. One written much earlier in her marriage, near the eve of their first Christmas, was sadder in tone. From her bedroom in the still not-quite-furnished mansion, she wistfully penned to "my dear husband" that she tried not to be hurt that he had departed for Oroville so hastily, that "you scarcely waited to give me a kiss."[2]

"My dear General, my husband," she wrote as she waited the coming of Christmas Day itself, "I do think of my old home where Santa Claus made the occasion so 'jubilant at this event.'" The Kennedy house had been decorated lavishly with tree and gifts. The merriment of gift exchange had given way to turkey and plum pudding.[3]

"I should not write you so sad a letter but am I not your wife? To whom else on earth am I to talk to as my heart bids?"

The carefully planned cheer of a Kennedy Christmas, especially for the children at both her Meadville and Washington, D.C., homes, came rushing back during her new husband's absence in December 1868. She could not resist reminding John Bidwell that she was almost marooned. She had wanted to drive to town, but without an escort could scarcely get in and out of the carriage. "And, oh, the mud!" for Chico was still a new town on the frontier.[4]

Perhaps she fleetingly recalled the letter of her step-grandfather, John Reynolds, age eighty-six at the time of her marriage. He had written in awe when explaining why he was no longer physically able to make the trip to her wedding in Washington, D.C., from Meadville. He had added, "California! in my boyhood almost 'terra incognita.'"[5]

When Annie was nine or ten years old, the Kennedy family residence was moved from the Pennsylvania farm to Washington, D.C., where Joseph C. G. Kennedy had been appointed as director of the U.S. Census. The ties with Crawford County and their Pennsylvania kinfolk remained strong. Return to the farm (still owned by Annie's father until his death but now rented out) took place often, especially in the summer months. Both of Annie's parents had siblings in Crawford County; they and their homes seemed always open to the Kennedys when they assumed temporary residence, though the ties with Catherine's family, the Morrisons, seem to have been more tenuous.

Most of what is known of Annie Kennedy's childhood comes from momentary flashbacks that overwhelmed her in her new life and were recorded in her letters.

One of the realities of Annie's girlhood stayed with her, however, as the move to Washington was accomplished. That was the frailty of her mother's emotional health. Catherine Kennedy was subject to spells of depression and anxiety. These became more obvious to Annie as she, the daughter, began to experience strong religious faith, and her mother felt that she personally lacked such assurance from God. At a time when Annie looked around her for ways to serve the Lord to whose service she had been converted, Catherine began to create of Annie an anchor to which she might attach herself and from which she could expect solace.

Annie was converted to Presbyterianism when she was fifteen. It was on her own initiative that she sought counseling from a Presbyterian pastor, possibly first during one summer spent in Meadville. She was admitted to membership in the Fifth Street Presbyterian Church in Washington, where the Reverend Dr. Gurley held open to her the new light that shone after her conversion.

Annie's parents were not irreligious exactly, but they felt their duty was done by occasional church attendance—usually Episcopalian in Annie's childhood—and more-or-less generous monetary support. Their children were given free rein to make such choices for themselves, should they wish. Joseph C. G. Kennedy was himself an irregular churchgoer at best.

In a letter tucked away for over sixty years Annie had written in confidence to favorite cousin Sallie Ellicott, "Mary [a mutual friend] is one of the most bigoted girls I ever knew. She says many things about the Presbyterians which hurt my feelings. I do not know whether she intends it. She likes Presbyterians and Baptist the least of any protestant denomination."[6]

The hurt to Annie's ego was not deep. Her letter went off into detailing her next task, "to put my laundry in a satchel and take to this woman," and describing a bonnet her mother was making for her, and the rush to dress for dinner upon her as she signed her girlish letter.

At a celebration of one of her teenage birthdays, Annie could boast freely to her cousin that "two parties have been given for me. And I cannot count the calls!"

Both Annie and sister Sallie Kennedy were sent in Washington, D.C., to Mrs. Breshaw Burr's private day school for young women, "finishing" them off to take their place in "Society."

French was one study at which Annie excelled and Mrs. Burr specialized in French instruction. Annie later pursued it on her own, often wishing to tackle German and Italian as well. It was not a heavy course of study at Madame Burr's. By sixteen Annie and Sallie attended courses more as they felt like it, and when Mrs. Kennedy decided which one should be favored by taking classes in any given year, based on the girls' interests and their needs as she saw them.

Mrs. Burr's school was evidently not a model for strict decorum. When she was sixteen Annie wrote to cousin Sallie Ellicott that she was taking fewer lessons this year. At one riotous recess, "the desks were shaking as we girls 'were dancing on the benches.'"[7]

Home parties were equally given to giggling, and to playing Old Maid, Truth or Consequences, and a game referred to as "Tommy come tickle me." During those years of the 1850s, when the whole of the Kennedy family had to adjust to the social demands of Washington, it was with relief that they fled in the summers back to Meadville.

In her teen years Annie, and often her sister Sallie, volunteered to help in a mission run by the Young Men's Christian Association in the poorer section of Washington. Those impressionable years were learning years of quite different dimension than the gaiety of the annual social season, but even the great civil conflict of the 1860s did little to dampen the festivities of the latter, or to ease the pain of poverty in the former.

Annie's father wrote long letters to his stepfather, John Reynolds, of the stresses of life in Washington. He emphasized the degree of importance placed on the social season, the three months beginning soon after Christmas, in which lavish entertaining was done by the families in the social set including the foreign embassies and the members of the U.S. government, up to and including successive Presidents Taylor, Fillmore, Pierce, Buchanan and Lincoln.

Joseph C. G. Kennedy moaned that for some evenings he and Mrs. Kennedy had three invitations! Rather than seeming to show preference, the Kennedys made a practice of appearing at all of them. This required hiring a carriage to wait near each entrance and hurry them on from reception to reception.[8]

Noted in one filial letter was the news that Annie had the mumps. Interesting, in that she repeated this disease in 1908— that is, if doctors' diagnoses can be trusted. But then, mumps do repeat on the reverse side of one's face.

Introducing
a family

$\mathcal{M}$ost of us are aware of the many generations that now separate us from the eighteenth century and the Thirteen American Colonies' assertion of independence from Great Britain, especially so if a forefather fought in the Revolutionary War. Annie Kennedy needed only to count back three generations, to her great-grandfather. And not just one great-grandfather, but three, had served under the command of General George Washington.[1]

Annie Kennedy Bidwell was over fifty years old before the significance of this made an impression. It was her own and her parents' generations that claimed her thoughts and molded her as a person. Still, the shadows of the past loomed over her shoulder and in time caught her up in them, in part due to her sister Sallie's close involvement with the Daughters of the American Revolution when that group formed in Washington in 1890.

But first—the arrival of Annie Ellicott Kennedy in the world. Both parents—her father, Joseph C. G. Kennedy, and her mother, Catherine Morrison—were born in Pennsylvania. By their time the center of population in the new nation was sweeping westward toward the Pennsylvania western frontier. Meadville, in Crawford County on the border with Ohio, is the point where both the Morrison and Kennedy families had settled and taken active roles in creating the city late in the eighteenth century. Names of Annie's forebears appear in connection with development of Meadville's domestic water supply, a community gas company, medical care, the justice system, and to the founding of

Allegheny College. These families appear also in the neighboring counties of Mercer and Franklin.

In the history of early Meadville,[2] the names of prominent settlers included Reynolds, Kennedy, Morrison, Craighead and Huidekoper, all of which appear in Annie's family tree.

Jane Judith Ellicott, of another prominent Pennsylvania and Delaware family, came as the bride of Dr. Thomas Kennedy to Meadville, he having set up to practice medicine there in 1795. Kennedy was said to have been the first practicing physician west of the Allegheny River.

Dr. Kennedy had two children by his marriage to Jane Julia Ellicott: Andrew and Joseph Calm Griffith Kennedy, the latter born in 1812 or '13. Andrew died in a stagecoach accident as a young man and Annie never learned of this uncle until she read a few details her father gave in a letter many years later.[3]

Dr. Thomas Kennedy died while Joseph C. G. Kennedy, Annie's father-to-be, was still an infant, so young that Jane Julia's second husband, John Reynolds, was the only father and grandfather the family was to remember. Joseph's stepbrothers and sisters were John Van Liew Reynolds, William Reynolds, Jane Maria Reynolds (Sergeant), and Lydia L. Reynolds (Craighead).

Jane Judith Ellicott Kennedy Reynolds was the daughter of George Washington's friend and fellow surveyor, Andrew Ellicott. Washington tapped Ellicott to survey the streets for the newly created District of Columbia, the site chosen for the U.S. government by a neophyte Congress after both earlier sites, New York City and Philadelphia, had been tried and rejected.

Ellicott's expertise had also taken him to the disputed border between Canada and the eastern colonies, and a final line had been drawn under Ellicott's guidance and marked with border monuments along its course.

Annie Ellicott Kennedy was born and lived her first ten years in Meadville, Pennsylvania. This childhood photo of her from a private collection was given to the Bidwell Mansion State Historic Park about 1994. Courtesy of Lois McDonald.

Joseph Calm Griffith Kennedy—a long name for a very short man—and Catherine Morrison were married in Meadville on October 22, 1834. They were young—he only twenty-one and Catherine but nineteen. The minister who united them at the altar liked to tell the story of his impression of that wedding—that he was marrying two mantel ornaments, they looked so pretty and handsome.[4]

Catherine was the daughter of Joseph Morrison and Anne McMillan, both early residents of western Pennsylvania. Joseph Morrison's name appears many times in early Crawford County history. He was a member of the bar (but did not practice), worked diligently for road and canal construction, for awhile cashiered in a bank he helped form, and was treasurer of Crawford County at the time his daughter Catherine married Kennedy.

Joseph C. G. Kennedy graduated from his hometown Allegheny College, a liberal arts institution which had been subscribed to by all of Meadville's prominent citizenry. Kennedy had shown initiative, when after graduation from Allegheny, and not yet twenty years old, he purchased the *Crawford Weekly Messenger.* This weekly was to go under financially fairly soon, largely because neither Kennedy nor its previous owner-editor, had figured out how to get subscribers to pay!

Joseph C. G. Kennedy actively involved himself in politics at an early age as a member of the Whig Party, a standard which had united those opposed to British rule. The party finally disappeared in 1852 when most of the Whigs, especially those opposed to slavery, went with the newly formed Republican Party.

Kennedy's political fervor led the young man to take over the editorship of the Franklin, Pennsylvania, *Intelligencer* after his own paper collapsed, but his disgust with the newspaperman's life led him soon to retire to farming at Hilltop Farm, between Meadville and Conneaut Lake, a farm he had owned since he was eighteen.

At heart though, Joseph Kennedy was a scholar. He continued his formal studies which brought him an M.A. degree in 1856 followed by an LL.D. in 1864.

It was said to be a common first impression of Joseph Kennedy—that of finding him with a book in hand, often a Greek classic or one of his beloved first editions of another of the great books. His love for reading aloud was something his children and wife reacted to with mixed feelings, often fretting over their inability to escape a long evening listening to the drone of father's voice as his lips mouthed words from *Petronius* or some other classic that held less fascination for them than for him.

The combination of strong political beliefs and a reputation for thorough scholarly research resulted in Kennedy's name coming before the Whig administration of President Zachary Taylor. Joseph Kennedy was appointed by Taylor to direct the U.S. Census for 1850. Hilltop Farm was leased; parents, aunts, uncles, and cousins were proud that one of their family should have so high a calling and wished him well. J. C. G. Kennedy with his family resettled in Washington, D.C., during the year 1849.

Significant changes in the census-taking procedure immediately were made as Congress approved of Kennedy's recommendations. These included methods for improving the reliability of the information gathered. To the joy of later genealogists, the censuses began listing the name, sex and age of every living person, not just that of the household head followed by a list of house-hold members by sex and by nonspecific age groupings as provided in the original 1790 legislation and in use for over half a century.

Kennedy was not replaced by Whig President Millard Fillmore, or by the administrations of Pierce, Buchanan and Lincoln. He used much of the time between overseeing the 1850 and 1860 censuses to complete his advance degrees, then to accept invitations abroad. From a presentation at the International Statistical Congress in Paris and Brussels in 1851, Kennedy became known as an authority on social statistics and was invited in later years to return to Europe to teach his methods.[5]

While family letters between members of the Kennedy family rarely mentioned the changes the War between the States had on their lives, either physical or emotional, one letter from her mother to Annie from Meadville in November 1862, described her husband's bout with war-related stress.

"Father is having a difficult time composing a letter connected with the removal of Gen. McClellan (from command of the Union forces). He says that the consequences will be fearful for our country. He suffers from pain in the bowels and diarrhea. He has had little appetite for a month."[6]

This item, plus other hints that are given in family correspondence suggests that Kennedy was a part of a cabinet of sorts, that counseled on many subjects. He told John Bidwell, his future son-in-law, of having been one of a group of government officials strongly recommending that Congress support a transcontinental railroad.

Washington's social whirl was welcomed by Catherine Kennedy, whose infatuation lay with the latest in ladies' styles and in acquiring sufficient elegant gowns for herself and her daughters to wear to teas, receptions, and dinner parties. This ambition was checked somewhat by the perceived miserliness of her husband.

Keeping a well-trained staff of house servants was a key to success in society, and Catherine Morrison Kennedy was up to the task and seemed to easily fill her obligations in Washington society, often by teasing her husband for the funds needed to dress his wife and daughters in a manner befitting their station.

Catherine Kennedy, like her husband, was a small person physically. She was loving to her children and not overindulgent. She made it a practice to have a small conspiracy going with her daughters against the small tyrannies of her husband whom she considered to be inconsiderate of his wife's needs and feelings.

Sallie advised her mother to say nothing to her husband when receiving a gift of cash, for example Bidwell's gift to her of $100 at the time of his marriage to Annie. As Sallie told her, "Pa will just expect you to use it to meet household expenses."[7]

It was Catherine Kennedy's fate to have her little world fall in pieces around her from time to time, and then she took to her couch with a throbbing headache, to brood mostly on the deep doubts she had of her reconciliation with impending death and of earning acceptance into heaven. Annie and Sallie were yet in their teens when they were sometimes made to change plans for the day and tend to their suffering mother. It was Annie who excelled in the role of comforter and nursemaid—thus perhaps earning, in fact, the status her siblings jokingly gave her of "mother's favorite."[8]

On July 31, 1836, Joseph and Catherine's first son was born in Meadville, Joseph Morrison Kennedy, named for his maternal grandfather. Joey or Joe, as he was called by his sister Annie much of his life, seemed admirably fitted to the life of a Pennsylvania farmer such as his father had given up. Like an unwatered plant, Joey drooped when penned in the confines of a large city residence.

Joey's nurturing of growing plants continued in Washington, D.C., where he grew his vegetables and roses in the garden, filling the rooms with bowls of the flowers in season. Joe spent much of his time in Meadville with his uncles' families, even after reaching adulthood. There was no business career to which Joe aspired.

Joe's career uncertainties were finally cut short by the outbreak of the War between the States. With early battles taking place close to the capitol itself, Joey sought a commission in the Union army, and with his father's influence, succeeded in being appointed as captain to a company of volunteers. His rank shifted from a brevet lieutenant colonel with the U.S. Volunteers in 1866 to first lieutenant in the regular U.S. Army, there being two distinct military organizations. He was promoted when he elected to stay with the military service after the end of active hostilities.[9]

From 1862 to 1869 Joey saw service from the Virginias into Florida and Pennsylvania. After the war he was for a while in Tennessee where former Confederate soldiers were carrying concealed arms and carrying on a form of undercover resistance.

During Joey's service in military surveillance which followed the surrender of the Confederacy, only few—and they were termed unsatisfactory—letters came to the family. There were, however, spottings of Joey coming out of bars and worse places—and word of this reached his father.

The army stresses were more than Joey seemed able to handle. Joseph C. G. Kennedy worked as assiduously to get his son discharged as he had done to get him a commission. He was discharged in about 1869 with the rank of colonel.

Annie Ellicott Kennedy was born on June 30, 1839, in Meadville, and was named for her grandmother Anne MacMillan Morrison and for her father's Ellicott forebears.

Her first ten years left behind little trace of either extraordinary performance or failure. She was a tiny girl as befit her diminutive parents. Of the family she was to grow in height the least. At four feet, eight inches, she did not look out of place with the Kennedys, of course, for none reached much above five feet in stature.

When John Bidwell became a part of the Kennedy's D.C. household it was a bit of a shock to both family friends and relatives to accept the General's six-foot-plus proportions. Mrs. Burr, who operated the finishing school Annie and Sallie had attended, remarked in mock horror to Catherine, "'What a monster Gen. Bidwell is—when did he become so large?' I told her he was not as large now as when he was married.

Annie Ellicott Kennedy as a school girl in Washington, D.C. Courtesy of California State Parks.

"I recalled then the General saying [to me], 'What a little woman Mrs. Burr is.' Is it not funny?"[10]

Another humorous comment passed on by Catherine was made by an elderly relative, that she feared the General might accidentally gobble Annie up!

Madam Burr's private school for young ladies was important, too, for Annie sought perfection in many ways. The worth of her father's scholarliness had not been lost on her. Nor had his fluency in languages. She determined to learn French to read and to speak fluently. It was a goal that she held to all her life in spite of her husband's scepticism. He believed that learning ought to have a practical application.

Many years later Annie met a former schoolmate in San Francisco and felt both embarrassed and pleased to be reminded in a large company of friends how all the other girls at Madame

Burr's were jealous of Annie's grades. "All the girls wished Annie to have a sore throat oftener so that she would not every day shine over them."[11]

What or who led Annie Kennedy first toward the Presbyterian Church is not known, but she was drawn instinctively toward the church and its teachings after being exposed. She analyzed carefully—using a teenager's standards of perfection, of course—how the church's teachings of redemption through confession of sin, followed by rededication to efforts to do God's will, can bring even the most grievous sinner salvation. The dedication demanded by God of his chosen workers to help sinners along this difficult path seemed quite clear to Annie. It seemed to her there was no sacrifice in following this path—that it would provide the only true joy.

There was a certain social chic in undertaking mission work, of course, as often happens in a social atmosphere where the danger of appearing too pleasure-loving is to be avoided. Annie and her sister doubtless learned of opportunities to work among the poorer element in Washington from other sources than the church. They were both more or less faithful in volunteering at the YMCA mission, teaching Sunday school, helping with children's reading classes, women's sewing classes, and making home visits when needed with distribution of food to households without a wage earner. The mission was supported through Annie's Presbyterian Church where moneymaking projects for the mission abounded.

There was great emphasis on the worthiness of the parents in such a household. Many were found to be women whose husbands had deserted them, often leaving a history of physical abuse. The mother in such a home would be urged to pray diligently for God's help in reforming such a husband, or if need be, pray that he might not return. A dissolute unremorseful woman might expect limited assistance.

In 1862 after the first military encounters between rebel and Union troops sent wounded Union soldiers into the city for shelter, Annie enlisted as a volunteer to take small edible dainties to the wounded in any of a number of small military hospitals in the city. Annie noted in her brief journal for 1862 that she had taken jelly water, toast, oranges and currant water to the men and engaged them in conversation in a sisterly way—something they desperately missed. She sang patriotic songs to the "boys," and gave them religious tracts from which she read in her gentle voice. She listened to their stories and sympathized with their fears.[12]

Annie went on some days to the hospital and found the bed of a badly wounded soldier empty. Annie would be given the task of gathering up his few belongings to send to his parents, with a few words describing his bravery and, if she knew them, his last words of home and mother. She was not a nurse and received no training in physical care of the wounded, yet her role was important. Sometimes a young soldier whose arm had been amputated could cheerfully say to Annie, "And I'd do it all again for my country, Miss!" implying that for such a beautiful lady as herself no sacrifice would be too great.[13] This was heartrending work and Annie sometimes missed days at the hospital when she lacked the courage to venture from her home into the sad atmosphere of suffering.

All throughout the war she wrote long cheering letters to her brother Joey and other friends in the military. Since Washington was on the borderline with the Confederacy, many of her friends in the South were lost to her for the war years, behind the curtain created by secession of the rebellious states from the government in Washington.

Although only examples of "kind" treatment of the black servants in the Kennedy household exist, it seems strange that Annie made no mention in her diaries or letters during those years of a personal consciousness of cases in which this was otherwise. The cause for the War between the States—the issue of slavery—did she ever view it as her mission to help rectify?

The Kennedy children were brought up in a society where a large proportion of the populace was black, including most of the servant class. There were no slaves in the District of Columbia, or at least they could not be openly owned, but Annie traveled extensively in the South and knew well that her friends' servants were not free to move from job to job. She doubtless realized that the fading of the shiny black visages of first-generation Africans in later generations was the result of white masters requiring female slaves to accept them into their beds, or wherever in the planta-tion the masters chose to gratify themselves. Yet Annie saw no mission to work either to ease the lot of such women or to see the war as a righteous one.

A cultural pattern of treatment toward the blacks was so much a part of Annie's upbringing that she did not question her parents' attitudes that reinforced in her acceptance of segregation and thus degradation.

Sarah Jane Kennedy (known always as Sallie) was born in 1841 in Meadville. Apparently the name chosen for her honored the memory of paternal grandmother, Jane Julia Ellicott Kennedy, and her great-grandmother, Sarah Ruston Kennedy. The latter was wife of Revolutionary War surgeon, Dr. Samuel Kennedy.

Sallie was opposite in personality from Annie and yet a complement to the quieter persona of the elder sister. Sallie plunged into life with easy charm and a vocal wit that marked her in a crowd. A tomboy among childhood playmates, she became a vivacious young woman among the society crowd, and she was never one to lack for an escort.

Sallie also worked as a mission volunteer—it was an expected role on the part of the young socialite—but she left behind the memory of social woes when she closed the mission door behind her. She went to church and enjoyed the range of worship and church social life, but she did not commit herself much. In her family, she was dependable when recruited for her share of family chores, but she did not go out of her way to be overly helpful. Her mother lamented in a letter written soon after Annie's departure for California that Sallie had gone off with a group of friends to play croquet, knowing that Catherine would be at home alone—and at a time when Catherine was suffering from depression.[14]

Because Sallie was the one who took the spotlight in social events and could carry off social repartee easily with a member of either sex, it was believed that the wealthy California congressman, John Bidwell, was interested romantically in her. And indeed, Sallie would fearlessly flirt and tease the General in company while she knew very well where his heart lay. After most of Washington sensed that John Bidwell was to marry a Kennedy daughter, Sallie delighted in leading curious acquaintances to believe that she was to be the bride.

Annie Kennedy (left), an unknown friend, and Sallie Kennedy, seated. This was probably in the early 1860s. Courtesy of California State Parks.

Yet Sallie and Annie were very close. Annie did not envy Sallie's ease with men, for Annie considered her own fate probably sealed as a spinster serving the Lord, or so she was fond of saying. She loved to chatter with her sister about the events of a party they had attended, comparing notes on the eligible males and the airs put on by aspiring socialites. And while Sallie could be a bit cruel, her sister was quick to defend, for she knew that much of Sallie's frivolous behavior was just "her way" of concealing a loving heart.

A baby girl, Helen, was born to the Kennedys and died in infancy. Her exact sequence in the family lineage is not clear.[15]

John Reynolds Kennedy was only four years old (born September 5, 1844) when the family moved to the Capital City. Both older and younger brothers were deeply loved by their sister Annie and for each soul she prayed as unceasingly as she prayed for their physical well-being, as if she made herself personally responsible for assisting them to salvation.

In 1864 Johnny, then about twenty, entered West Point, an appointee of President Lincoln. A military career was probably inspired by patriotic feelings for the Union cause at that time.

During his second year at the academy, Johnny caught a cold which lingered and took a physical toll in loss of weight and energy. His parents were alarmed, fearing that John might be the victim of tuberculosis, a common fate for young persons of both sexes in the nineteenth century.

The doctors thought Johnny's lungs were sound, but did not know another cause for his decline. He was at loose ends around home, and his sisters found him a tease and a nuisance. His mother was at her wit's end as to how to fill his time. Finally the doctors suggested a change of climate for Johnny—always a safe prescription—somewhere with cooler, less humid summers and warmer winters.

The congressman from California, General John Bidwell, who had been a frequent visitor at the Kennedys, in 1866, invited Johnny to go to Chico, to live in Bidwell's new home now almost completed on Rancho Chico, and take ranch employment. The outdoor life among the horses and cattle, as much as he felt up to, seemed to be the ideal for a frail young man. The offer was made independently of Bidwell's aspiration to marry Annie, but he would have been only too human to hope it might help his cause as a suitor. The invitation was eventually accepted.

In mid-November 1867, accompanied by a young black, Clayborn Jones, as valet and bodyguard, John Reynolds Kennedy sailed from New York and was in Chico for Thanksgiving. Jones, too, was assured by Bidwell of employment in Chico, once he was no longer needed by the semi-invalid young Kennedy. John Bidwell met them in San Francisco and had Johnny, as Bidwell always referred to him, well settled under the care of his house-keeper, niece Mary Reed, by winter.

All of the Kennedy children were caught up in the turmoil caused in the Capital City by the War between the States. It was hard to escape the many ramifications, including the change of status felt by black household help, though there is no hint that the Kennedys had difficulty. Once Catherine wrote to her daughter that she could not feel quite right having both colored and white servants dining together, but the Kennedys seem to have accepted some change in status in the black servants who "faith-fully" served their household in Washington for many years.

In the brief journal Annie kept in 1862 she described her mother discovering sick soldiers of Reno's company resting in the streets. Catherine had taken them medicine, bread, butter and coffee, meat, lemons and limes with Sallie and Annie helping. They were Pennsylvania men and grateful both for the food and the chance meeting with folks from home.[16]

Two letters that Annie saw fit to save dated back to the Civil War period, and speak of the poignant separation of friends—one of the North and the other of the South—who had pledged eternal friendship when Annie Kennedy and Mary Parker at-tended Madame Burr's school together. Some of this must be speculation on the author's part, but it is believed that Mary's father was probably a South Carolina representative to the U.S. Congress. The whirl of school life and Washington social life had swirled about both girls, but it allowed time for Annie to find in Mary an empathetic witness to Annie's recent conversion experience and then to become a convert under Annie's girlish coaching. How other to account for the label on letters concerning Mary Parker found in the Annie Bidwell correspondence in the California State Library, "death of young woman Annie had helped bring to the Lord."

There are two letters, undated except for month, and both from a young man, S. A. Ashe of Wilmington, South Carolina. One in May of the year tells of his own parents' and sister's deaths and of the want and poverty to which the people in the Confederate state had been reduced. He mentions that they have mail facilities only in the cities.

The second letter in July tells of Mary Parker's death. She was accidentally shot by a friend, Roger Cutlar, but she "had become my all-in-all in life." Ashe chides Annie for seeming to have forgotten that "you were fond friends in Mary Parker's youth. The demands of Society have been constant on your time ... rather than have permitted you to indulge in a sentimental existence. Still I know you once loved her sincerely."[17]

The great
romance

*D*uring the War between the States, in California no battlefields were necessary to resolve differences between sympathizers of the two factions. Governor Leland Stanford nevertheless set up home guard machinery.

In 1861, Stanford called upon Major John Bidwell, veteran of the Mexican War, to organize the northern part of the state for preparedness, assigning him the rank of brigadier general.

Bidwell had been active in California on the political scene as state government was being organized. In the fall of 1850, he had had the pleasant duty of bringing from Washington, D.C., President Millard Fillmore's signed notice confirming Congress' action to the California State Legislature. This body had already been elected in anticipation of admission into the Union as its thirty-first state, and as a free state—one not permitting the ownership of slaves.

General Bidwell found that the commission as general gave him greater status than perhaps was required by his duties. More of his attention was brought to bear on resolving Indian tensions than the War between the States.

He continued busily clearing land on Rancho Chico, the former William Dickey Grant from the Mexican era of California. Bidwell had purchased the rancho, plus additional acreage, with the gold he was able to take out of the Feather River in a fairly short period given to mining in 1848–50.[1]

Bidwell intended to make his ranch productive. The soil was very fertile, conducive to growing a wide variety of crops. Wheat was the big marketable item at first, and the world market eagerly devoured all the wheat that land could be cleared to grow in California.

Even before he realized much saleable produce from his new orchards, Bidwell came to grips with the prospect of problems in marketing from an isolated area far from seaports or a center of population. He concluded that his presence in Washington, D.C., as a member of the U.S. Congress might be a useful thing in helping determine where railroads and even new wagon roads would go.

Bidwell was easily elected a representative to Congress in the fall of 1864 to serve the sessions of 1865–66 and 1866–67. Congress at that time accomplished its business in a few winter months. Thus, early December 1865 found General John Bidwell ensconced in a District of Columbia boarding house. He probably had with him Raphael, an Indian lad he had taken under his care at a young age, teaching him English and using him as interpreter and valet.[2]

Bidwell was appointed to the House of Representative's Agricultural Committee at his request and eventually became its chairman. This was a powerful post during the era in which the U.S. economy was almost entirely in its agriculture.

Information on crop production had been gathered more or less systematically by the U.S. Census Bureau. Bidwell tapped the bureau information and in the process met its director, Joseph Calm Griffith Kennedy. The two men immediately developed a mutual respect. Kennedy's own farm, though now operated by another, gave him a background in farming over and above the statistical material at his disposal.

In time, Bidwell sought Kennedy's advice on how best to handle the former's suspicion that Isaac Newton, cabinet member for agriculture, was involved in some unscrupulous actions.

Personal information passed between the two men, they grew to respect each other, and Kennedy realized how the rather shy

Bidwell was isolated, without family and a network of friends. He invited the congressman to share the Kennedy pew at the Fifth Street Presbyterian Church where the family had taken their religious allegiance, as much due to Annie's commitment to Presbyterianism as anything else. He included Bidwell in invitations to social functions that the Kennedys hosted as part of their social season duties.

Not surprisingly, the "gay" season for Washington matrons and their children coincided with the busy congressional session. Here General Bidwell met many people in a social way whom he found interesting, such as Joseph Henry, secretary of the Smithsonian Institution. He renewed acquaintance with General William Tecumseh Sherman whom he had known in California during the Mexican War. He was to become better acquainted with General Ulysses S. Grant who as Captain Grant had commanded lonely Fort Humboldt near Eureka in 1854. Bidwell would certainly have been aware of Grant's presence at the fort and his reputation for drunkenness brought on by frustration and boredom. Of course, when John Bidwell met Grant again in Washington, the latter had gained the status of national hero by the forced surrender of General Robert E. Lee and the Confederacy.

If Annie Kennedy had taken small notice of Bidwell among the parties and receptions (even those in her own home from which she and Sallie sometimes tried to flee in boredom), he had taken notice of her. Short conversations as they left the Kennedy pew after church services were perfunctory at best, but they served to reinforce the very favorable impression this gentlewoman made on Bidwell. When he observed that she did not drink wine when it was served to others at the Kennedy table, he did not touch the glass of wine served to him. He looked for ways not to displease her, while at the same time knowing not exactly how to please her.

John Bidwell at about the time of his marriage to Annie Kennedy, 1868. Courtesy of California State Parks.

Bidwell did not return home to California following the end of the congressional term July 28, 1866, but instead sailed in August to Europe. He traveled to Ireland first where his diary suddenly comes to an end as he reached London.

Later Bidwell confessed to Joseph C. G. Kennedy that he became so overwhelmed with missing Annie after he left Washington that he could think of nothing else. After docking in New York on the homeward journey he went immediately to Washington on a Sunday morning and made a call on the Kennedys unannounced, as that household prepared to leave for church. He accompanied them to church, and from then through the rest of the year and after the Congress reconvened in December, Bidwell sought opportunities to visit the Kennedy family and to talk and walk with Annie, often escorting her home from church.[3]

His pent-up feelings were suddenly released one Sunday evening after church service as he was leaving Annie at her door. He begged her to talk with him a bit on the steps before going in, then burst forth with passionate confession of his sins and his despair at the prospect of being able to win her understanding and forgiveness. Quite an overwhelming moment for Annie, but one that did not give her displeasure!

As with most intimate experiences during the Victorian age with its narrow rules of propriety, neither Bidwell nor Annie ever alluded in writing to the exact nature of Bidwell's confessions. One revealing entry in her diary made nearly forty-four years later, the year of her husband's death, comes as close as she ever came to putting that moment in writing:

"The last Sabbath of the year 1867, My Beloved [her emphasis] confessed to me, with tears, his sense of sinfulness, as we stood on the doorstep of my home. The sermon by Dr. P. D. Gurley on the text 'Take Thy Pen & Write Quickly' had been used by God, & He had led me to pray it *might* be."[4]

Had John Bidwell known the great softening of Annie Kennedy's heart toward him that evening he need never have doubted that he held the key to her heart. The age old device had worked (and quite innocently on Bidwell's part) that a man who confesses his past sins and makes declaration that only the love of this sweet lady will save him from his worst self has thus made himself irresistible. Victorian literature is awash with such plots in such titles as *Elsie Dinsmore, Jane Eyre, St. Elmo*, and many more. This tried and true formula has no doubt worked from caveman days to the present. Annie's strong Presbyterian belief in confession, reform, and redemption helped reinforce her quite natural feminine vanity in being sought out as confidante to the confessor.

Two books have been published exclusively featuring the Bidwell's love letters from December 1866, to the eve of their marriage in April 1868.[5]

The letters, especially in the version most complete, *Dear General,* tell us something of the people they were and how each shared this information of themselves and their family values. They are not so much courting letters as letters written with the desire to sate their appetites for each other. Annie Bidwell's future seems to have taken a direction from which she did not swerve from that Sabbath evening on her parents' doorstep—though, of course, she did not let this be known until Bidwell had shown himself totally willing to be led into a new moral life.

What is uncertain is this: to what length did Bidwell go that winter evening when the dam burst and he released confidences detailing his sins? Did he then tell her of his liaisons with at least two Indian women and the children that had resulted? Could she have accepted that news and still felt the glow of affection toward him? Yes, in this biographer's opinion, she could do so and did.[6]

Bidwell's letter of December 31, 1866, following that evening is full of his relief at having shared his less-than-perfect past with her and having had no rebuff: "Strange that I have never found one to whom I could confess so much before. ... Promise to let no one see this letter. Burn it if necessary. I know I shall never find another to whom I can so tenderly confide in." [sic] And then for the first time Bidwell declared his love for her in that letter.[7]

In the letters that flowed between them from that date until Bidwell returned to Washington to claim Annie in February 1868, he wrote to her much of his early history. He described his family that had followed him to California, the sad death of his younger brother Thomas in Chico that year, and his separation by many miles and many years from his parents, now deceased.

Annie's letters to John also included much of family and friends. However, she concentrated on his redemption—what he must do to prove both to her and himself that he was reborn in Christ. This was required of her in the role that Bidwell had given her in pleading for her love. She was adamant that he be baptized a Presbyterian.

Lacking an opportunity for such affiliation in Chico, Bidwell joined a Methodist church on "probation." The tentative nature of his commitment to Methodism stemmed from Annie's wish that he become a Presbyterian and that she might come to Chico and help establish such a church.

Eighteen sixty-seven was a year of trial for John Bidwell. On the one hand, he desired more than anything else to marry Annie Kennedy, both because of his true infatuation for her person and for the increased social and political status he perceived such a marriage would give him.

On the other hand, he was a serious contender for California's governorship in the 1867 election, an office to which he had long aspired. But to win nomination from the Republican Party, to which he had shifted allegiance from the Democrats some years before, he would have to act in a way he thought to be dishonorable and totally foreign to the high moral plane Annie prescribed for him.

Political infighting during the nomination process led to desertion of the popular Bidwell by one faction of the party and he saw that in order to be acceptable to both factions in his party, he would have to make great concessions to men he considered wickedly unscrupulous and that it would cost him a small fortune to buy them off.

Bidwell was offered the nomination—was nominated by one of two warring Republican Conventions, which he did not deign to attend—and he finally wired his refusal after a painful struggle between his ambition for power and his ambition to win Annie.[8]

In October 1867, Annie wrote him of her great satisfaction with his steps toward redemption and gave John Bidwell permission to approach her parents on the subject of marriage. It was accepted Victorian custom that the woman's father (her legal support and protector) approve of such a planned proposal—no matter the maturity implied by her twenty-nine years. Bidwell immediately composed a letter to J. C. G. Kennedy, heavy with praise of Kennedy himself, "You were the very model of kind husband and indulgent father. ... Your house was the only place in Washington that had any attractions for me."[9]

Bidwell added, "Annie resembles you more than any other." He then asked Kennedy's permission to propose. Naturally this letter was shared with Annie by her father, and Annie's criticism to Bidwell was that he should have included her mother in his request!

Consulting the Kennedys, of course, laid open the opportunity for them to seem to bargain, one demand being that Annie should visit Washington as often and as long as they wished. That this might prove a hardship was easily passed over in the urgency of the moment and of course Bidwell agreed to such terms—one month out of every year, he suggested.

Catherine Kennedy fussed over the discrepancy in the ages of groom and bride, but could readily be made to agree that twenty years was not such an uncommon spread. She feared that perhaps John Bidwell's still ungreyed hair must be dyed! Annie, to her credit, answered and so if it is? "So long as he does not suddenly begin such a practice so as to look ridiculous before his friends as some persons we know have done."[10]

It is possible, though admittedly unlikely, that Joseph Kennedy was sufficiently observant to feel relief that his daughter might thus extricate herself from a mother-daughter dependency that had expanded over many years. Later Catherine's friends were to ask, "But how could you possibly let her go? She was so caring—so comforting." And Catherine asked herself, lamenting in her letters to Annie in California, how could she have given her consent? "But it appears I did so."[11]

The gossip in the capital had always been that General John Bidwell was a very wealthy man, and that he owned thousands of acres of rich California farmland acquired with California gold. To Joseph C. G. Kennedy this report must have brought satisfaction, and some envy. To his wife and children, who had often felt deprived by Kennedy's tightfistedness (whether imagined or not), the prospect of having unlimited money at one's disposal was very attractive, and increased the status of the Kennedys among their Washington peers. Annie, who had often chafed under the limits imposed on her ability to do good among the poor, took pleasure in the prospect of being wealthy. She was feminine enough to love the accouterments of wealth, including buying the newest fashionable wear.

41

All impediments to the engagement were, in reality, removed when Annie admitted to herself her love for this Western pioneer who had shown himself so amenable to her spiritual advice.

Still, one sensitive matter had to be cleared between them. Bidwell had assumed that Annie would welcome sharing her new home and household duties with its present occupant, his niece, Mary Bidwell Reed. Mary and her husband Harry Reed (an accountant for Bidwell) and their son had been living in the new home in Chico for some months.

Hearing that Bidwell had assumed that this arrangement would continue after her arrival as wife, less than three weeks before the wedding date, Annie wrote the prospective groom with fire behind her pen:

"That is an impossibility, for if you have promised your family a home with us I shall be hateful to them if I interfere, and if it is said that I refuse a portion of your large house to them, all Chico will scorn me as selfish. ... I want a home of my own, and I have vowed not even to stay in my father's house after marriage. I would not marry unless I have a home alone with my husband. ... I would not marry unless I can care for my home in my manner."[12]

Annie had surely known of Mary Reed's presence in the home—that she had been there to make Johnny comfortable upon his arrival in California. She had even read John Bidwell's words describing Mary as "lively, rolicksome, gleeful—very worldly," but also "a good, kind-hearted lady. ... Once we [I] used to think she was handsome." But she had overlooked the implications.[13]

John Bidwell rapidly backtracked from this delicate situation, admitting that he had had all the wrong notions about women's preference for steady feminine company. It is tempting to speculate how much this innocent failure of judgment on Bidwell's part laid the groundwork for a coldness that was to exist between Mary Reed and Annie Bidwell all of their lives. Nowhere is Mary's underlying animosity better reflected than in a book dictated years later by her granddaughter.[14]

Bidwell was so anxious to have his marriage an accomplished fact that he left California in January to claim his bride long before a date had been set by her parents for the wedding. His early appearance in Washington proved a problem to Catherine Kennedy, who wished to postpone the marriage and her daughter's departure as long as possible, and perhaps even to Annie, who grew more tense over the prospect by the day.

For weeks before the wedding, Annie was often reported to Bidwell as indisposed by headache and upset digestion. Her mother took care to explain to John Bidwell that her daughter was by no means an invalid, but Annie did have a delicate constitution that must be protected from stress as much as possible.

At last John Bidwell was successful in his plea to Annie to prevent the wedding and their departure being postponed farther. He must go home to California before his business was ruined. The spring planting season would be gone, as well as the lambing and calving season when livestock needed greatest oversight. He explained how mismanagement of Rancho Chico during his congressional service had already thrown him badly into debt.

"I am trying to come to the point gently, very gently, because I do not want to shock your delicate nerves. ... Promise me not to ask for [another] delay in departure."[15]

Reasons were found for Annie's fiancé to remove himself from underfoot as plans for the wedding proceeded, and he more or less wandered between Washington, Philadelphia and New York between February 8 and April 16. He made several attempts to visit with the Reverend Dr. Gurley, Annie's designated mentor, who on Bidwell's two calls at his Philadelphia retreat reported himself too ill to be seen. After an interview did take place, poor Bidwell was left to wander on feeling downhearted about his chances for salvation, though the kindly Dr. Gurley was hardly apt to wish to upset the marriage plans at that point. At first Dr.

Gurley planned to come to California with them to regain his health, but the truly ailing pastor backed away as the date came closer.

Rooms on shipboard for the trip back to the Pacific Coast were reserved, then postponed to allow for another Kennedy change of plans. Bidwell purchased furniture for the California house, new clothing, and had his wedding suit fitted in New York. By arrangement between the women, he met Annie's cousin in New York, one of her bride's maids, Fannie Reynolds, to help him in purchasing a trunk and other items needed for Annie's journey.

In Washington, Bidwell attended a few times at the impeachment proceedings against President Andrew Johnson in the U.S. Senate. With Annie and her sister Sallie he visited Susan Steward, the Afro-American lady's maid he was to engage to travel with Annie to California. He went to several sittings with a Mr. Ulke, the Washington artist who was painting his and Annie's portraits to commemorate the wedding.

Back in New York he filled hours riding streetcars—anything to fill the time.

Opportunities to be with Annie alone were rare. He took to writing her anything of importance and having the message hand delivered to her door.

Annie, too, was posing for Ulke's rendition of her in her pale blue wedding gown, Bidwell's gift of jewelry adorning her neck and shoulders. The long train of the gown compensates for such an unusual (for Annie) display of shoulders, one presumes, but also one may guess that these features of the gown left modest Annie a bit uncomfortable. For the wedding ceremony a full veil was added to the costume. Today the Ulke watercolor hangs in the Bidwells' bedroom at the Bidwell Mansion Historic State Park.

The wedding ceremony finally was performed on April 16, 1868, in the Kennedy home. It stormed hard all day as a row of carriages dropped guests at the door.

Fortunately, Dr. Gurley felt able to be in Washington to perform the ceremony. As it was a formal wedding, those who attended seem to be representative of that society in Washington with which the Kennedys liked to be identified: President Andrew Johnson, Generals Sherman and Grant, and many of the foreign diplomats with whom the Kennedys seemed to be in great favor, including their special friends, the Prussian ambassador Gerolt and his wife.

Few of the relatives from Pennsylvania or Maryland were in attendance, possibly because of the unpredictable traveling weather of spring. The guest list read a bit like that of a state reception, and the atmosphere was more like such a reception than of a family event.[16]

Bidwell had expressed himself as preferring a quiet wedding but Annie had written, "... that would never have done. It would seem like one of us being ashamed of the other! Our position in society has been a decided one, and when I marry it would not be proper to do so quietly."[17]

Beautifully decorated rooms, varied and delicious food, the prescribed amount of tears from the bride's mother, laughter and the giggling of the bridesmaids—an ordeal for both groom and bride in all likelihood, though apparently the exchange of vows was made before a much smaller group and the reception that followed was expanded to over one hundred guests.

A news item which reached the San Francisco *Weekly Examiner* nearly a month later, May 16, reported the wedding for California readers, noting that Annie's bridesmaids included sister Sallie, the two Misses Gerolt (daughters of the Prussian minister), the two daughters of Professor Henry of the Smithsonian Institute, cousin Fannie Reynolds of Meadville, Pennsylvania, and Miss Dixon, daughter of U.S. Senator Dixon of Connecticut.[18]

Annie seems to have had little correspondence with her wedding party in later life, leading one to suspect that Joseph and

Catherine largely chose the wedding party. The exception was with the Gerolts. Dorothea and Bertha had been schoolmates of Annie's and had gone with her to volunteer in Union hospitals in wartime.

In August 1869, while visiting in Washington, Annie wrote asking her husband's assistance in finding employment in California for the Greek professor that Dorothea Gerolt wished to marry—over her parents' opposition. This request baffled John Bidwell who knew nothing of employment available for a teacher of Greek.

"Even Englishmen cannot so adapt themselves to American ways as to be of any useful purpose to Americans—How then can a Greek?"[19]

The other Gerolt sister, Bertha, Annie noted in a much later diary entry, died in a Washington convent.

General John Bidwell had as groomsmen W. G. Sargent of Pennsylvania and a General Westar, again, one suspects, chosen by the Kennedys.

The newlyweds sailed from New York late the morning of April 24, the Kennedys and many friends waving from the pier. By midafternoon, Annie was suffering from severe seasickness as the steamer hit rough Atlantic water.

It may be said a romantic plot within a plot existed, for Susan Steward, the maid who ministered to the nauseated bride on her honeymoon journey, was on her way to join her lover, Clayborn Jones, the black valet who had accompanied John Kennedy to Chico six months earlier.

The honeymoon

*O*nce over her seasickness, the new Mrs. John Bidwell enjoyed the honeymoon cruise taking her to her unseen home. The Atlantic Ocean and Gulf of Mexico gave the passengers on the *Rising Star* excellent weather for deck strolls. The Pacific Ocean was not so kind. Excessive heat made both deck and stateroom unpleasant.[1]

On May 2, 1868, the ship docked at Aspinwall, Panama, and the Bidwells traveled by train across the Isthmus to board the S.S. *Sacramento,* following a brief visit with the U.S. Consul in Panama City. At Acapulco, Mexico, the couple again went ashore, to be met and welcomed by John Sutter, Jr., son of Bidwell's old 1840's employer at Sutter's fort on the American River. The younger Sutter was acting U.S. Consul in Mexico. A supper in the ship's captain's quarters entertained the Bidwell's on the eve of their disembarkation northward.

Annie first set foot in California on May 16, 1868. A most welcome sight, a touch of home, was there to greet her as Johnny Kennedy ran forward to give her a warm hug and brotherly kiss, reassuring her that for Johnny, at least, California's climate had worked wonders.

Nothing would do but that Annie should have a tour of famous San Francisco sites, and meet some of her husband's old cronies (perhaps "friends" is a more fitting word to associate with the staid Bidwell) who were waiting curiously to see the wife that bachelor Bidwell had found in the nation's capital. Then the trip up the Sacramento Valley was made by horse-drawn stage.

It was late afternoon of Monday, May 25, when the nervous,

yet exhilarated, couple knelt at the wide doorway to the mansion
and prayed that they have God's blessing on their married life.
On the fringes of the scene may well have been witnesses from
the Native American community a short distance west. Its bound-

Annie Ellicott Kennedy in the gown believed to have been worn by her at her marriage to John Bidwell on April 16, 1868. The watercolor by a Washington D.C. artist, Mr. Ulke, hangs in the Bidwell bedroom, a gift from a family member. Copy by
Lois McDonald. Courtesy of California State Parks.

aries touched the dooryard of the mansion though invisible behind thick creekside foliage and trees.

The privacy of the cruise, even Annie's illness which called for tenderness and special care from her husband, helped to both seal

Annie Kennedy Bidwell, April 1868, modeling the outfit in which she would travel from Washington to her new home in California. Courtesy of California State Parks.

and reveal their love. Annie sat upon her husband's lap, her head upon his breast, and confided her dreams and hopes. He in return talked of his aspiration to turn Rancho Chico into a veritable oasis of fruit-producing orchards and fields of grain. They savored many of what Annie was to refer to in her letters as "our special kisses."

As reality settled in, John expanded his reports to Annie to include his worries about property taxes coming due and his numerous debts on which interest must be paid. He explained that he would of necessity be away from home a great deal as he tended to financial affairs. Annie accepted this graciously, and set about establishing the domain of a good wife: a comfortable and welcoming household, run by efficient servants. She had a true challenge before her if she were to accomplish this.

She found that she must always be ready to greet and welcome callers. The first full day of their homecoming brought several couples to their door as well as America Bidwell, John's brother Thomas' widow. America was a sprightly young woman of twenty-eight or so, and she very much had the interest of her daughter Lily Bidwell in mind, knowing that John Bidwell, up to that time at least, had been dedicated to the welfare of his niece Lily.[2]

America's personality had the capacity to range between friendly or vindictive, or so it seemed to John Bidwell. Since he could not figure how to handle either aspect comfortably, he tended to avoid America when it was possible to do so—to do so politely, for snubbing was sure to backfire on him. Doubtless Annie had been told of her husband's discomfort and she was determined to be as tactful as possible with this new in-law.

There was also John's half brother Daniel Bidwell and his family to meet. Their home was a few miles to the north of the mansion on the Oregon Trail Road. The niece Mary Bidwell Reed, for whose position in John Bidwell's home Annie had felt competitive, had withdrawn with her husband and son to her father's house.

There began in Bidwell Mansion service a series of cooks and maidservants from San Francisco. They were hired on the recommendation of a friend of Bidwell's to whom he admitted he knew absolutely nothing about judging the merits of the young female Irish immigrants who eagerly took jobs to support their often-elderly parents.

Annie's black personal maid, Susan Steward, was well trained in domestic arts, and Annie assigned her to overseeing the Irish girls. This did not work well, for receiving orders from someone lower than they, as they perceived status, angered them.

A steady stream of correspondence between Annie Bidwell and her mother and sister in Washington bolstered Annie in making decisions about housekeeping problems. One of the first issues on which she appealed to Catherine for help was Hannah's and Kate's

Copy of a painting depicting the Bidwell grounds as they may have looked when Annie Bidwell arrived in 1868. The mansion was almost completed but the old adobe (left) still stood which neither Bidwell liked blocking the view. Another farm building also later razed is on the right. Courtesy of John Nopel.

protests that in laundering the servants' bed linens no provision had been made for separation of their sheets from those of Susan. They should not be expected to sleep on bedding shared with a Negro.

Annie was ambivalent, for Susan was by far the most valuable of the household help, but when Catherine strongly agreed that "discrimination in regards to bedding" was proper, Annie complied with the rule.[3]

Susan soon took the matter out of discussion, for she asked to be released from employment to marry Clayborn Jones. Annie was camping with Johnny in the mountains a few days during the heat of that first summer, 1868, when she received her husband's appeal for help in resolving a servants' quarrel resulting from Annie's directions that Susan "give the orders." She wrote John Bidwell at Chico, "Susan need not stay on my account … [if] she wants to go."[4]

Catherine and Sallie both wrote urging that Susan must be replaced with another maid at once—not dispensed with. Two servants (one the cook) were not adequate to care for such a large house.

Annie complained about the "uppityness" of the Irish girls on occasion, to which her mother wrote: "Why do you not put those inefficient servants in their place and get a more ordinary one which I am sure is needed for window washing etc.? I am sure General would agree—gentlemen are not expected to know unless told."[5]

John Bidwell felt far beyond his depth in handling the women servants. It was an area in which Annie had gained her expertise from watching her mother direct a household. John praised Annie extravagantly for her ability to handle the Irish girls. Over many years of relaying Annie's orders to the maids from Washington, Bidwell hardened himself to face their sometimes sullen Irish countenances.

Annie, on the other hand, felt no uneasiness in expressing her displeasure of a gardener or the carriage driver working about the grounds, if she felt he was slighting his work—or if she suspected his intentions as regards the female servants were not entirely pure.

Sallie and Catherine were still of the notion that General Bidwell was a wealthy man, and thus were shocked when Annie wrote of spending days helping to lay carpet. "You will ruin your pretty hands!" Annie felt constrained when talking of finances with her family, and learned to word her letters in ways not to suggest too strongly the frugality used in running her home at that time.

The county tax bill for Rancho Chico arrived in October 1868, for nearly $10,000 on an assessed value of half a million dollars. It sent John Bidwell into despair which he shared with his new wife. She wrote sympathetically to him from San Francisco, where, after a visit with him in November, she had remained to complete shopping for house refinements. She offered to economize by carpeting only the lower floor, but in effect canceled this economy by instructing that John must purchase nice silver as a gift for his niece Emroy "Emma" Bidwell, the second of brother Daniel's daughters, who was being married to Chico merchant Charles Van Duzen Hobart.

Annie tried to reassure her husband that his financial difficulties were mild compared to those of persons who had not property or methods of producing wealth. "Do not allow care to depress my dear husband. Think how many are oppressed by debt who have no land to meet it, no credit to support it, with a destitute and mortified family to support."[6]

In spite of these brave words, having to respond charily to requests for donations from charities at home did bother her. "People here think you are so rich, and all who come from California report and insist that you are—it embarrasses me so much for I know a great deal is expected of me [here]. ... [I am asked]

'Is it not nice to be rich, Annie, to give $30 and not feel it?' … I am much oppressed by your load of debt. I can't enjoy anything I buy. I must get a few dresses here as my silks are too warm."[7]

She did warn her family that Christmas presents from the Bidwells must be modest that first Christmas in California. Sallie urged her sister in turn not to worry. "We tried to tell you before you were married, when we heard that General Bidwell was so rich, that you would be exempted from expectations."[8]

The priority that Annie had set for her new life in Chico was that a Presbyterian church be organized, her new husband baptized in that church, and a building erected as soon as possible. There was delay while Bidwell took care of business matters in Marysville and Oroville (a seven day absence in June in which Annie teasingly wrote to him as "her run-away husband.")

Annie made her first trip to the county seat in Oroville with her husband in late June, meeting Judge Charles Fayette Lott. She took an immediate dislike to the judge. More than once Bidwell advised her that his fellow California pioneer Lott was powerful, and that he was believed to be honest, though his decisions as a judge sometimes were not in Bidwell's favor. Annie was never to muster more than polite feeling for Lott and his family.[9]

Annie never hesitated to express her dislike of persons among Bidwell's acquaintances whom she did not like. An elderly Judge McRae of San Francisco thoroughly "nettled" her by his desire to "take charge" of her when they were guests at the same hotel. He had paraded her up and down the Occidental Hotel dining room, introducing her as "Mrs. General Bidwell" to everyone. "How angry I was!"[10]

During mid-July, Bidwell gave in to one of the bilious attacks to which he was occasionally subject, though fortunately never during his trip east and back. Very possibly this was because Bidwell, a hearty eater to befit his active life, felt constrained among the dainty appetites of the Kennedys. If anything Annie was gratified to have an opportunity to wait on her new husband during the days he spent in bed during a few days of summer heat.

Although his experience during the 1867 gubernatorial nominations had seemed to sour him on politics, Bidwell still deemed it wise to attend the Republican Party Convention in Sacramento in August. In fact, Annie and especially her parents shared a desire that Bidwell might yet achieve his ambition to lead the state as governor. They had covered this secret ambition with assurances that the 1867 fiasco was of no particular significance, except as a matter in which he might take pride for his moral stance.

A group of Chicoans of Presbyterian background recruited by the Bidwells, and others with interest in affiliating, met on August 26 to organize a church with guidance from a visiting minister, Rev. St. Wells, sent from the Sacramento Presbytery. The new congregation moved ahead to hire its own leadership, and by October the qualities of clergymen to whom the call had been advertised were being weighed. These ministers were guests of the Bidwells while in Chico, setting a pattern of an open door to clergy that the Bidwells were never able or willing to alter.

On December 11, 1868, the Reverend A. Fairbairn was selected and he soon took up residence in Chico with wife and son Fred.

A frightening incident interrupted Annie's life in late August when she fell violently ill. Mary Reed, reputed to be an excellent practical nurse, was called in by Bidwell to care for Annie. Johnny Kennedy had been on the eve of departure for a visit home to Washington, but wired that he was delayed without giving a reason.

The source and nature of this illness is not clear to this day. When Johnny did leave nearly two weeks later he was instructed to minimize his sister's illness to their parents. Only a severe digestive upset. A wire from John Bidwell followed Johnny's, declaring to his anxious mother-in-law that Annie was again "quite well." He did not enlarge on her symptoms or diagnosis.

It was accepted that Annie's delicate constitution had been assaulted by some strange food eaten in California, and Catherine's letters for some time were peppered with advice on what not to eat, and how to treat stomach problems in the future. It was discussed with a Mrs. Ellicott, "who has a weak stomach too," and who recommended a flaxseed johnnycake be placed warm on the stomach. At best, one must expect three months to recover.

Catherine further urged Annie to come home to convalesce, and she had "discussed with Pa that he look for some opening in San Francisco" in order that Mother be close by.[11]

Victorian delicacy toward feminine matters being what they were, it is tempting to speculate that Annie and John wished to conceal the fact that she had suffered an abortive early pregnancy, a happening that would have been sure to greatly worry her parents who saw Chico as a frontier wilderness with inadequate medical care. For some months—even years—after this illness, mention was made in Sallie's private letters to Annie's periodic sessions of "nervousness" in relation to the "attack."

Annie's nerves were grated upon by unfamiliar silence punctuated by the unfamiliar sounds of Chico. The frogs on Chico Creek not far from the Bidwell's bedroom windows had a distressing effect on Annie's ability to sleep. John tried to "jolly" her into hearing the croaking as melody provided nightly by the frogs. She wrote to him bravely, "[I can] hear the melodious pipes of the frogs. I shall try to like their music for your sake and think it exquisite."[12]

The sounds from the Indian village adjoining the mansion grounds to the west were usually not unpleasant. Annie liked to hear the splashing and laughter of the boys as they dived into the creek from its banks bordering the rancheria.

She had quite a different reaction when in early September a death occurred in the Indian village. Many guests from outlying Indian communities in both Butte and Colusa counties joined the Mechoopdas in "horrible lamentations" twenty-four hours, nonstop, for two days. This was an unnerving experience, both because the noise of the wailing was unlike any human expressions of despair that Annie had known and also because she associated the ceremony with some pagan ritual that reminded her of the Indians' unsaved souls.[13]

John Bidwell tried to comfort his wife by reasoning and cajoling. The Native Americans were following customs as old and revered by them as any ritual that Annie found comforting in her religion. It was his belief that the whites should not interfere in these matters, quite the opposite from Annie's inclination. Her missionary spirit was at the fore, even though it had to be set aside at the time because the natives ran from her to hide, whenever she approached them, either from fear or awe.

Soon after her arrival in her new home, John had taken Annie to the rancheria,[14] expecting to delight her with a savage "suburb" so close to her own residence. She was wearing a white dress as they walked along the creek, suddenly appearing to a crowd of mostly women and children. Almost within the space of an eye's blink, the women and children disappeared into the windowless underground houses of the village.[15]

Because the presence of the Indian village so close to her home caused Annie to feel restricted in her freedom of movement around the grounds, in March 1869, Bidwell had some of his workmen, including the native help, take four days from usual farm duties and move the entire rancheria a mile away from the creek to along the north side of what is now Sacramento Avenue, east of where the railroad would eventually run.[16] Gradually the dirt covered underground huts were replaced with frame houses, in part because Annie encouraged that it should be so and the Bidwells assisted in the cost of these more acceptable homes, although the partially underground native huts were both warmer in winter and cooler in summer.

The story has been told by others, and may be partly or wholly true, that Nopanny, one of the native women who had worked inside the mansion before Annie's arrival, challenged Annie's authority to have the household keys shortly after the bride arrived. The story goes that Nopanny had said in effect, "I first wife, you second. I keep the keys."

It is difficult to believe that Annie would have tolerated such a situation, no matter how much she wanted to reach out in friendship to a group of people with whom she sensed ties that bound her husband and her to their welfare. Yet she and Nopanny did seem to reach an agreement over the custody of those keys that permitted the two women to be friends.[17]

The first autumn Annie lived in Chico passed with John gone at intervals, and until Johnny returned from Washington in December she spent many days quite alone. She made calls on women affiliated with the new church, planned work for the servants, and helped with suggestions for the new Presbyterian Sunday school that organized shortly before Christmas. Mary Reed and husband did visit Annie often. At that period, they tried to be friendly to the lonely bride, an attention which she seemed both to appreciate and to avoid.

Annie also helped in the organization of a Presbyterian Mite Society. A group of couples meeting for charitable work was active before she arrived, but Annie urged that their Presbyterian Church have a Mite Society of its own to which charity might be directed. (The "mite" is derived from the biblical parable of the widow's mite. Mark 12: 42–46)

The business journeys seemed inevitably to coincide with dates important in Annie's life. John was gone over Christmas to San Francisco, then home again only to leave New Year's Eve for business in Oroville. Annie wept in sadness and loneliness. Even Johnny had taken off to hunt ducks. While thus depressed she had frightening thoughts of dangers that seemed to lurk for her husband.

A rare rainbow following a winter rainstorm seemed to reverse her fears with new hope—a signal from a higher force that they were being watched over.[18]

It was not an easy time for the new bride, yet she tried not to complain unduly, for the financial troubles were very real. Bidwell's preoccupation with them was proof enough of that.

One comfort was the steady arrival of letters from Annie's family, especially her mother, and the hours spent in reply. These letters assured Annie that life went on much as before at the Kennedy home, combining Catherine's report of social life in Washington with questions and comments on what she envisioned Annie's married life to be like.

Catherine's chronic criticism of the behavior of her husband Joseph crept in, usually following the theme of his selfishness. "He arranged the lamp for his comfort and I know his letter to be of more importance than mine. I say nothing but scribble on hoping that you will be able to decipher."[19]

Sallie had gone to play croquet while Mother felt unwell and lonely. "Dear Annie, who always was better than anybody else, would have said, 'Mama would you not have me stay with you?'"[20]

Catherine was shocked that Annie should be doing hard work—laying carpets! "I have pictured you as the occupant of an elegant boudoir, surrounded by luxuries and enjoying the pastime of writing loved ones at home. But how different the reality."[21]

And of Johnny: "Lassoing six wild cattle!!" With his delicate health he should be planning a winter in Hawaii.

Annie had been delighted by the seeming improvement in her brother's health when she arrived in Chico. Johnny was up to and thoroughly relished the tasks that Bidwell had assigned him. He helped to fill orders from Bidwell's nursery, oversaw the picking of fruit for local sale, and was given the task of building a fruit house for storage. So enthusiastic was the young man that within two months of his arrival he had written to John Bidwell in Washington (whence John had gone to marry) with a plan Johnny envisioned for turning a big profit from the ranch![22]

During the summer months when the livestock was pastured in Big Meadows, Plumas County, Johnny camped with other ranch hands and helped with the stock. His skill acquired at lassoing made him a fairly valuable hand, though he was given to tiring easily even when at his best.

Johnny seemed intent on finding a mate now that he had found a man's work, and the first young lady in Chico with whom he showed signs of being smitten did not meet Annie's approval at all. When she left to visit Washington in mid-1869, she left orders to her husband to try to dissuade Johnny, always the little brother though now twenty-four, from spending so much time alone with that Miss Evans.

Catherine Kennedy's letters, often filled with details of dresses remodeled and new hats shopped for, in September 1868, tackled the subject of the name of the Bidwell's home, Rancho Chico.

"It almost wrenches my jaws to pronounce it. Where is your fertile brain and imagination that you cannot find a name for your home more pleasing? Your Pa seems to think it answers."[23]

Sallie's letters, and Catherine's also, shared one disquieting note about their elder brother. There was strong evidence of Joey's caddish behavior. His discharge had come through from the U.S. Army after his father determined to get him out of it, and he became a fixture again in the Kennedy household after Annie departed.

Although he was suspected of heavy drinking, Joey never drank at home. His chief sin had been in jilting his fiancée, a Reynolds cousin, Fannie Craighead, of whom the Kennedys were genuinely fond, having more or less grown up with her as children in Meadville.

Before Joey's discharge, Fannie spent much time in Washington where her grief at rarely getting a letter from her intended husband was bravely concealed and wept over by turn. As eight weeks would pass in unexplained silence, Fannie returned to Meadville before Joey's discharge, but only after she forced on him a choice of either breaking the engagement or making plans for the wedding which had been anticipated since before Joey received his commission in 1862.

The engagement was broken off finally by Fannie, and Joey as much as told his mother and sister that it was none of their business. Catherine wrote sorrowfully to Annie in many letters that Joey was proving to be the black sheep of the family.[24]

Joseph C. G. Kennedy, not reappointed as director of the Census, obstinately refused to struggle for a lesser position with the Census Bureau. "I know more about it than any one else, and devoted the prime of my life to the work, but why should I stoop?"[25] He was still struggling to establish a private business in which Joey might also be gainfully employed.

The winter of 1868–69 passed for Annie, and her first spring brought its special beauty to Chico. With the end of the muddy season came a spate of duties. An example would be the newly organized Presbyterian Mite Society plans for an "Old Folks Concert" to raise money with several performances. Tiers were erected in the Bidwell's dining room for this performance, there being no other home large enough in Chico.

Then Annie, with such other ladies of the church as Mrs. Joseph Wayland, Mrs. David Gage and Mrs. J. C. Mandeville, planned a Sunday school picnic for the children on May Day. The great moment came when homemade ice cream from the Bidwell kitchen was served, a special treat just coming into vogue through the invention of the ice cream freezer and a favorite with Annie, though John Bidwell disdained it.

In May Bidwell took Annie on her first trip to Cherokee, a thriving mining town on Table Mountain, to explore the caves. They stayed overnight at the Cherokee Hotel.

Paramount in the minds of the Bidwells was Annie's (and his) promise to her parents that she could visit back in Washington "one month a year." Every letter now arriving from Catherine reminded her of this promise. It had been nearly a year since Annie had left as a bride.

On May 25, John Bidwell went to San Francisco and while there met a Senator Williams who, with his wife, had just arrived from the East Coast on the first passenger train of the newly opened transcontinental railroad. They reported to Bidwell that the trip took only eight days and was reasonably comfortable and seemed danger free. That long-anticipated method of cross-country travel was chosen in preference to the trip by sea, and Bidwell bought the ticket that would start his wife on her sojourn far apart from him.

It seems rather strange that the protective Bidwell was willing to send his delicate wife on such an adventure alone, but she insisted that Mrs. Jewett of Marysville, wife of a merchant who had been a long time friend of Bidwell's from pioneer days, and who had booked for the same date to travel as far east as Chicago, would be sufficient moral support.[26]

On June 1, John Bidwell took Annie to Marysville, and early on June 2 kissed her goodbye for the arduous trip across country, a trip on which she would change trains several times and stop over at strange stations along the way. She booked each lap ahead as she did so, and got a berth on such few trains as provided them.

A look at
Rancho Chico

ajor John Bidwell, a veteran of the Mexican War, had arrived in California as a penniless adventurer well before the number of Americans among the population would have warranted an attempt to take over the fabled land. The golden "island in the pacific" had titillated imaginations of adventurous young (and old) men for perhaps hundreds of years.

Lacking funds—and a proper passport to enter a foreign nation—the 22-year-old Bidwell, along with other members of a party who had, in 1841, broken away from the Oregon Trail in what is now Idaho and headed straight for California, had looked for a way to earn meals and shelter. He found refuge with John Sutter, the Swiss adventurer and self-termed businessman who had gained a grant of land on the American River. Here Sutter was to provide a barrier from inland hostile Indians for the Mexican settlements governed from Monterey. Wheat that he proposed to grow could always find a market.

The early years of John Bidwell in California have been described elsewhere, as has his success at mining for gold in 1848 at a bar on the Feather River (Bidwell Bar). With money in hand, Bidwell purchased over 22,000 acres of one of the choicest areas for agricultural development in the state, the William Dickey Grant, Rancho del Arroyo Chico. [1]

Settling on Chico Creek's north bank by 1851, Bidwell had to contend with white squatters, Indian raids on his livestock and a shortage of labor. His log cabin, followed by an adobe two-story house and tavern on the Sacramento-Oregon Trail, provided adequate living space with rooms to let. A trading post, or store, augmented his income and brought travelers to the spare rooms and a bar in his adobe.

An ever fertile mind and ambition to match very soon suggested to Bidwell that if his envisioned fields and orchards were to have much significance, he must entice not only permanent settlers to the area but skilled workers and businessmen of all kinds, including bankers, whose ambitions would coincide with his own. The idea for a town materialized in 1860 when Bidwell was able to purchase a portion of the Farwell land grant on the south side of Chico Creek. In 1860 the town of Chico was laid out and lots put on sale.

Lots sold well, and Bidwell had wisely given away many lots for development of civic buildings and churches. His wheat sales, and those of farmers to whom he had leased land, brought in great sums of money. There was money enough for several years but it was hard, even for the prudent John Bidwell, to plan ahead closely for lean years.

The status of the town's founder was increased by his being appointed a brigadier general in the California Home Guards by Governor Leland Stanford as problems faced the state from possible uprisings among factions of settlers from Confederate states after their secession from the Union.

Bidwell had taken active roles in the formative years of state government. As one of the earliest Americans on the scene, he was known and generally respected from one end of the thirty-first state to the other.

John Bidwell was not a man to boast, and such behavior in other men made him uncomfortable. But he would have not been human had he not seen himself as a ranking resident of Butte County, and certainly as close to aristocracy as the town of Chico could claim. Having the money, and the dream, he decided to build for himself a grand house across Chico Creek from the burgeoning town. By this time he had put aside any thought of marriage or family; the home was to be for him and him alone.

Exactly when the name Bidwell Mansion came into use is not known. Possibly it was a suggestion of the architect, H. W. Cleaveland of San Francisco. Perhaps the residents of Chico began the usage, not entirely without spite. Whenever the name was adopted, to Annie Bidwell her home was the Bidwell Mansion from the beginning.

Bidwell relied on friends in San Francisco for advice in many matters dealing with domestic arrangements, and it was through one that H. W. Cleaveland's services had been hired. Cleaveland spent months in Chico, his first lodging outside the mouse-infested adobe being a small two-room structure erected behind the site chosen for the large house. The building still stands, though almost completely rebuilt by the Bidwells in the 1890s and readapted for use as state park offices.

The plan chosen for the grand residence was not a plan customized for Bidwell, though few, if any, other homes in Northern California resembled it exactly. The three-story structure—especially the third floor with its intended usage defined by a large dance floor and gaming rooms—could not have been conceived of by Bidwell as anything useful to him except that it was what was expected in any grand house of that time. The twenty-seven-room house was of Italianate style in architectural details.

The mansion turned out to be much more costly than Bidwell had imagined when he started the project. And his income depended on many factors beyond his control. The building's interior completion was indefinitely postponed in 1865 when Bidwell was elected to the Thirty-ninth Congress for 1866–67, and departed for Washington.

Home from his congressional term, Bidwell found that his ranch had been badly managed and he had suffered heavy financial losses. Nevertheless, with his heart set on marriage to Annie

Kennedy, he had the mansion brought near to completion for her coming. The finishing details and many furnishings had to be postponed. No doubt it was some comfort to him when he knew that he would have a wife's help in adding the finishing touches.

When Annie arrived at her new home in May 1868, the mansion, sitting some four hundred feet back from the dusty north-south trail, had between it and the road both the old adobe building and a wooden "farm house" which may have housed the original Bidwell store and post office. There were also a number of cottonwood trees that had already grown tall and served to either protect the privacy of the mansion or to obstruct the view, depending on one's way of thinking. There were other outbuildings that had been constructed in the 1850s, many now in need of paint and repair. Annie found the view rather ugly, although the house itself held all the requisites for a charming and comfortable home. She was assured by her husband that these blights to the view would be removed, and his diary notes the work progressing over some years.

More important to Annie was that her husband keep his promise to pull out all the many wine grapes that he had planted early on with an eye to their moneymaking potential. Even before Annie had given her consent to marry him, he had agreed to replace these vineyards, but the work was not finished until well after their marriage and Annie was on hand to urge the completion.

Annie's stubborn resolve to remove temptation to those who might fall victim to the terrible scourge of habitual drunkenness had gradually developed over the years since she joined the Presbyterian Church as a teenager. She had been accustomed to social drinking in her family and in society all of her life. Notes she had made in a little diary kept in the early 1860s refer to her having arranged to be home to accept a rather large shipment of wine from New York. Joseph and Catherine Kennedy followed the fashion of serving wine to guests as a matter of course. Kennedy, moreover, defended his conviction that the enjoyment of wine was a gift that had come down through the ages, from Christ's time and certainly from before. They must have had arguments about this over the years, though Annie was disinclined to disagree with her parents, whom she accorded authority over her life as part of God's will. The discussion continued into correspondence after Annie reached Chico, for Kennedy rightly assumed that she was the force behind Bidwell's destruction of good wine grapes. We have only his side of the exchange:

"I know there are those who do not coincide with this view, but I have reflected much on the matter and am fortified with concurring opinions of some of the wisest and best men, but am not disposed to advise others on the question. It is probable ... that drunkenness will prevail from the days of the patriarchs to the millennium, but that forms no good reason for depriving good people of an almost universally dispensed means of enjoyment."[2]

In May of 1869, in response to an offer from John Bidwell to ship grapes to Kennedy in Washington to do with what he wished, Kennedy responded that he thought shipping wine grapes to Washington was impractical. He added that "Temperance illustrates better than anything the true morals and refinement in which men have been educated, rather more I believe than abstinence."[3]

The beliefs of her father did not sway Annie Bidwell from her determination that wine grapes not be grown on Rancho Chico, and her husband never put into writing he left behind any doubts he had on the matter. It is curious that the story still persists in the Chico vicinity that John Bidwell did drink alcohol occasionally when out of the presence of his wife.[4]

Beyond her strict values as concerns production of alcohol for use as a beverage, Annie seems not to have had any input into John Bidwell's pursuit of many varieties of fruit and grain, from the United States and abroad. She learned to revel in joining his study of botany, learning and using with him the scientific names for both wild and domesticated plants. This was extended to sharing his love of the universe and the phenomena of the movement of the heavenly bodies.

As she developed her already keen and analytical eye, Annie came to deeply appreciate the natural beauty that Rancho Chico offered. She observed it from the lookout tower of the mansion, on walks along Chico Creek and drives or horseback rides along the many ranch roads. In all of California, probably Rancho Chico was the only place she ever felt truly at home.

Mr Sevain. Remember me to Miss Lyons, on whom, with her father, I hope you will call. Also please call on Mrs Densley, or Mrs Ormsby, if they are in town; it is only right you should, & you will oblige your wife.

My sheet is nearly full, so I will bid you a loving farewell, longing for your safe & speedy return to Y Your ever devoted

Wife, Annie

PS The Court plaster has receded from my arm. Vaccination does not seem to take, Hope you will not be injured by your trip to the contagious City. John sends his love. Adieu with a —

"Our Kiss" — from Your frow.

Depressed at her husband's absence on their first Christmas Eve, Annie none-the-less sent him by mail "our kiss," a special greeting often mentioned in her letters during the first year or so. Courtesy of California State Library.

The pangs
of separation, 1869

When Annie left on June 2, 1869, on the trip across the country to visit her parents, her excitement was tempered with ambivalence. Though she left behind a husband with whom she was beginning to establish a relaxed pattern of life, she was nonetheless eager to return to the nurturing home in which her parents had never failed to love and support her.

The journey itself was a challenge. The transcontinental train service had been initiated less than a month previously, five days after the driving of the golden spikes at Promontory Point on May 10. The travel route was hardly tested or predictable.

News of the difficulties encountered with construction, including difficult terrain, the unusually severe winter of 1868–69, and the logistics of bringing both supplies and food for the labor force had been followed closely by the Bidwells. Politics, which Bidwell was particularly sensitive to where railroad magnates' manipulation was concerned, had full play in decisions made in the construction as the competition between Union and Central Pacific Railroads came to a triumphant conclusion.

No sleeping cars were yet available for the Central Pacific's portion of the tracks, so Annie and Mrs. Mary Jewett, wife of Bidwell's friend in Marysville, who had facing seats, recessed the backs to make a bed the first night out. Annie wrote from Elko, Nevada, that she slept well enough—being short—but Mrs. Jewett had had a cramped night of it. On the second night, they had left the seats upright and filled in the space between with their luggage, spread the blankets they had brought, and slept as best they could.

Writing her second letter from farther away, Annie began to express the sadness that had begun to creep over her as distance separated her from John. She expressed worry that her husband was not getting his usual comforts, and that she had neglected those very duties while preparing for the journey. She reported that the Union Pacific tracks were much rougher than those of the Big Four—she could hardly hold a pen east of Promontory. She was held over while making connections in Omaha and could not get a room, having to wait hours in the depot for a connecting train.

Still, Annie's letter from Washington, D.C., after her arrival on May 11 sounded remarkably cheerful in spite of feeling unwashed and almost "too nervous" to write. "Tell Mrs. Gage the journey is easier than any of us expected."[1]

One incident on the trip was very disturbing to Annie, and cast a pall over the entire visit. One of her bags was stolen en route, including her trip diary, a gift from John, and all of her jewelry. Much speculation followed as to the thief, and not surprisingly persons at both ends of the country suspected the "colored" porter. Annie wrote that she feared the California label on her luggage "was my ruin!"[2]

The gentleman in San Francisco from whom John Bidwell had extracted a promise to look after the women and to escort them between trains had proved very lax. Henry Robinson had been little in evidence. This was not too much of a loss, presumably, for Annie was quite capable of attracting other men to assist her.

While Annie settled back into the arms of her family and her old room and the old friends eager to share her description of California, her husband wrote letters to her nearly every day, increasingly bereft.

From Marysville Bidwell had returned home after seeing Annie's train depart, by way of Oroville, where he had left a carriage in the stable. A careless stable hand had permitted the Bidwell horse Randy to founder from too much water while overheated, and John had to leave him in Oroville and go home in extreme heat with a rented horse. His first paragraphs to Annie described how oppressive the heat and mosquitos in Marysville had been. How sweet and cool their bedroom at the mansion was in comparison—albeit "having a strange vacancy about it."[3]

When in an amorous state of mind, Bidwell was apt to express it in rather bad verse. On June 3, 1869, his rhymes quoted the birds in their language of longing for her presence. "I am of not particular consequence without you," he writes, and he longs for the gift theologian Emmanuel Swedenborg claimed of being able to discern happenings at a great distance.[4]

Long before Annie reached Washington—before he had received her first letter—Bidwell moaned that he feared that the Kennedys must think him "hardhearted or neglectful, letting you go alone on such a dangerous journey. I believe you are equal to any occasion."[5]

Realizing that Annie would have arrived, his letter pictured her "so tired that your family will think I am not kind to you. Tell them I regret not accompanying you."[6]

His response to the first letters to arrive from Annie had showed a lack of tact that his wife must have struggled hard to understand and forgive. His comments were so pointed in mentioning important details she had omitted that she might well have had cause to be hurt. His demand to know of the money she had spent did bring a reply that testified to her feelings. She sent two pages listing every item, including those for which she had spent so little as five cents. Her total train fare, including sleeping cars when they were available, was $242.20. Apparently he got the message for he mentioned that she was overdoing it; he had simply been curious.[7] He apologized for not sending money. He had overdrawn his account.

Bidwell also wrote in a near diatribe that he could not and would not give more than $1,000 toward the new Presbyterian Church being built. He foresaw being stuck with the cost of it. Dr. Joseph Wayland, one of the better-off members, had provokingly said he would not subscribe, but he would give something.[8]

"You should come and keep the mite society in a glowing heat, and lead off the subscription papers. ..."[9]

"Help is scarce for harvest. I'm forced to pay the Indian boys $1.50 a day, but six of the order of aborigines are doing good service."[10]

He added to the attributes of their bedroom in the hot weather: "Our bedroom is comfortable." For the first two hours after [retiring at night] he slept almost nude with not a fly in the room to disturb until getting up time.

"I cannot bear the idea of you staying until fall."

"I must travel to the mountains or San Francisco to divert my mind."[11]

Waiting for the next letter to come from his wife, Bidwell's letters relaxed into accounts of his troubles with horses (the foundered one and another killed in an accident experienced by the driver of the Bidwell's carriage) and the servants. Kate's husband is "so annoying I can't stand him. If he hangs around much longer, Kate will have to leave. I tell them (the servant girls) not to bother me with things. Just serve good meals." The kitchen maid had a feud with the Chinese kitchen helper, coming to blows, and causing Bidwell to have to send to Mr. Jewett in Marysville to find and send another good "China boy." Kate had left in a huff, calling Hannah (Irish) "foreign trash." Bidwell was over his head and retreated to the opposite shore whenever possible.[12]

When he felt under less pressure he could write with amusement, describing the garden staff as made up of "John Henry, Capt., Edward, First Lt., two Chinamen 2nd and 3rd Lts., 6–12 aborigines of female persuasion with Wong and the adobe

Chinaman as skirmishers around the castle—Jones (African) spy!"[13]

Kate had come for her trunk and "loftily" departed for good.

A bit of news that Bidwell passed east was the arrival in Chico of General Cadwalder, chief engineer with the California and Oregon Railroad, exciting hopes that the railroad would go through Chico before the end of 1869. Annie wrote back beseeching Bidwell to use his influence to have the railroad pass to the east of the mansion. She reminded him that the route proposed on the west would pass through the grove where they had gone on drives together, where he had recited poetry to her—and they had exchanged kisses under the trees. That area should be preserved in memory of their love.[14]

Two weeks after Annie's departure, John Bidwell reported in a letter to her the rather curious call he had had from Mrs. Emma Wayland, who with her husband, Dr. Joseph F. Wayland, was a member of the Presbyterian flock in Chico. The often seriously earnest Mrs. Wayland reported a rumor going about (how large an audience this rumor had was not specified) that Annie Bidwell "never intends to return." Mrs. Wayland believed that to be true, and that "General Bidwell will follow her before long." Bidwell tried to reassure her that the rumor was groundless, but Mrs. Wayland said gloomily that though she hoped for his wife's return, it was very doubtful![15]

After his wife had been gone for three weeks, Bidwell began to count the time until her return. How was he to stand the five or six weeks longer before he might expect her home! No time had been set for her return, but since the promise was for a visit of one month, and allowing time for travel at ten days each way, it was likely that Bidwell looked ahead to early August for his wife to reappear.

Annie soon disabused her husband of such hopes. Her family was insisting that she stay until fall. The plan for Catherine Kennedy to accompany her daughter back to California for a long visit was meeting resistance. From a stance that she "could not possibly leave Pa," she gradually shifted to agreeing to the trip but needed much "more time" to prepare.

Though expressing worry about the debt Bidwell carried, and his report of poor flour sales and a $5,000 repair bill for the flourmill, Annie mentioned that she simply must buy some warm weather dresses to wear in Washington. And it would be so nice to carpet the lower and upper hallways and the north bedroom they planned to use for guests. And of course she had to replace the jewelry that had been stolen with the valise on the train—and to replace the bag itself. She had had to borrow some money from Papa.

She wanted her mother to have a good first impression of Rancho Chico. Could not the barns be whitewashed? And brown weeds cut and a fence added? And Hannah should preserve some peaches with extra sugar, the way Mamma likes them.

Annie wrote that her father was undertaking a suit of the railway for reimbursement for the loss of her valuables in the stolen valise. They feared that Bidwell would not follow through, "Papa is suing the train company as I feared you would not be willing to do so." Did Annie believe her husband weak in such matters—or only too busy?[16]

Bidwell used Annie's argument philosophizing over this worry about debt, stating that *he* should have more faith and rely on God's will: writing of the missing jewelry he begged her not to take the matter so to heart. "Let not your appreciation be so intense that the loss of any worldly thing will give you great distress."[17]

Annie wrote that the Kennedys had given a grand dinner party soon after she arrived home, and among the guests was General Sherman. He had great amusement telling funny stories about early California days and "teasing her" unmercifully. General Grant had laughed at her telling that John Bidwell thought Spanish girls were beautiful and had replied, "yes, but they grow to be as ugly as hogs when they grow old. I hope your wife will not grow as ugly as they, but not having been beautiful at eighteen, I may expect to escape."[18]

Annie was obviously feeling pulls from both family and husband. And perhaps it was irritation at Bidwell's ongoing pleas for her return that at times caused her to write snappishly.

He had written in response to a comment of hers about a fruit storage house: "'Your store,' you say. 'why not our store? Or is the store so rundown you don't want to be an owner?' I meant this just in jest!"[19]

She replied sharply: "I was thinking of Johnny's fruit house, and your disappointment on returning from San Francisco to find it so ugly, and your surprise that I had not interposed and had a more tasteful one built, and as I was thus rambling, it occurred to me that it was a little strange that you never consulted me about the farm house, and when I have mentioned that the foundation was begun last fall, and asked what kind of house it is to be got no response, for all I know is that one day I saw you and Mr. Broadwater looking over the plan for a long plain house and on my inquiring what it was you shut up the boards, replying, 'a plan for the new farmhouse.'

"How did it happen you never showed it to me, or talked the matter over with me? That was doubtless why I thought it was 'none of my business' what kind of fruit house was put up. I hope the farmhouse is progressing, however, so that the adobe can soon be removed and our grounds arranged, but of course I must be patient. ..."[20]

While back in her old family household, Annie became more aware of the problems with her elder brother Joey. She was gentle in remonstrating with him about his failure to attend church services and gratified when he did join the Kennedys on some Sabbath mornings. She wrote back to her husband that she wondered if God directed this visit home for her to be an instrument of good to Joey. She did not allow her hopes to rise too high, though her brother had attended a prayer meeting and Bible class and reacted favorably—something he had previously refused to do, even in boyhood.

The news that Fannie Craighead was engaged to Arthur Huydekoper, a member of a prominent Meadville family, pleased Annie and her parents but was tactfully omitted from conversations with Joey, who had been Fannie's fiancé for several years. Joey had explained to his sister Annie that he had agreed that his engagement to Fannie be broken for he had seen no way that he could support a wife and family. He had not mentioned the callous way with which he neglected to write to Fannie for weeks on end.

At last arrangements were made for Annie and her mother to leave Washington in mid-August, stopping by to see relatives in Baltimore and in Meadville. She wired her husband from stops along the way, including when they were delayed by washed-out tracks near Davenport, Iowa—and from Promontory, Utah, which they passed through on September 2.

Though Annie was upset and her mother disappointed that only Johnny met them on the stage at their arrival on September 4 at the junction outside Roseville, Annie refrained from expressing that feeling in her mother's presence.

She found later that John Bidwell had had to fire his ranch manager, a Mr. Collins, and sent word by Johnny that he was needed at home to give work orders. He did manage to get away to meet them in Oroville two days later.

In the first letter written to her husband after her return she put it in the record that "I was disappointed at my husband's failure to appear on the stage [to meet us]."[21]

It may have seemed to her in contradiction to his many written expressions of near despair at her long absence.

John and Annie Bidwell's first long separation had lasted over three months. By trip's end, Annie's weight had fallen to ninety-seven pounds from worry at the responsibility for her mother, who seemed to lack much idea of what might be involved in a long, cross-country journey by train.

Each had had a birthday during their separation. John had forgotten Annie's until the day itself, June 30, on which she turned thirty years of age. If Annie remembered Bidwell's fiftieth on August 4, she made no mention of it.

The contrast between the nature of their exchanged letters of 1869 and those of 1867 is noteworthy. Biblical references are rare in the 1869 letters. Over and above comments made about Rev. Fairbairn's sermons, his lack of facility at raising money, speculation from both Annie and her husband on what the planned Chico Presbyterian Church edifice might look like, and its greatest share of cost falling on a resentful John Bidwell, religion takes a much less prominent role. Their exchange of well-meaning barbs on the other's failure to see losses in perspective does manage to bring God in—to the defense of both!

Adrift between two ports

*C*atherine Kennedy's visit to Rancho Chico lasted fourteen months. During that time, according to his diary entries, John Bidwell was gone from home for at least one night on thirteen occasions, including two trips taken with Annie and her mother. One of these was a shopping trip to San Francisco, another an excursion by carriage and wagon to Big Trees, the spot in the western Sierra foothills where John Bidwell had experienced a lost and lonely night while separated from the party with which he had traveled from Missouri in 1841.

John Bidwell traveled with the two women on this nostalgic trip by stage. Annie was deeply impressed by the emotion he could not conceal when visiting the scene of a night he had there in the Calaveras Big Trees grove as a lost, hungry and fearful youth.[1]

On the nights that Bidwell was away from home, Annie usually wrote to him if she thought the letter would reach him before his return. Some of these letters reveal her sadness and feeling of near-estrangement from her husband's secret thoughts. When he was in San Francisco in November of 1869, she wrote asking for him to buy an astronomical globe. She had been taking her mother into the tower of the mansion on starry nights, repeating a favorite activity of her husband's.

She wrote: "It seemed to me you were not so distant from me when reading *Geography of Astronomy.*"[2]

"You know that I believe that I am more reliably attached to you than you are to me? I think that my affection would even survive bad treatment. Of course, I could not honor you as much if you were less kind, but I believe my desire to do you good, to see you happy, to love you, would survive any slight on your part, and somehow I do not believe you could love *me* if I did not conduct myself with perfect propriety, affection and self-denial. The judges of the Supreme Court of the U.S. hold their offices during 'good behavior,' if not they are deposed. 'During good behavior' passes like a shuttle through my mind. I hear it

Catherine Morrison Kennedy, Annie Bidwell's mother. Courtesy of California State Parks.

all day and it seems to deafen me to all sweet sounds: back and forth—'during good behavior.' I wish you could love me even when I vex, or unwittingly distress you, always love me, love me as I love you, love me as Jesus loves his erring people, regretting their imperfections, trying to make them better, but with a heart never chilled toward them."[3]

The presence of his mother-in-law in the household was both a distraction and an annoyance to Bidwell, though he was unfailingly polite, and when taking drives about the ranch for inspection purposes, he often invited Annie and Mrs. Kennedy to go with him. But it was difficult for them to recapture the intimacy shared when no visitor was in the mansion.

Catherine Kennedy's presence proved to be almost equally tiring on her daughter, perhaps more so, for Annie had no respite. Depression and lamentation, always a problem with Catherine, became severe and prolonged during the early months of 1870.

As John Bidwell left on trips from home, he could but pick up the atmosphere of sadness therein. He wrote to Annie of his wish that Catherine would not yield to her despondency and "recover her health from her nervousness—from the threatened loss of her reason … she cannot realize how her troubles are wearing upon you."[4]

There must have been many private conversations between husband and wife in which Bidwell bemoaned the length of his mother-in-law's visit, and in which she stoutly maintained that she had a duty as a daughter and a Christian to help her mother over difficult times.

Annie shared the dampening effect on her own spirits in private letters to Sallie, as she tried very hard to carry on with her duties as hostess and home manager. In spite of her efforts, February 1870 found Annie too nervous and ill to leave her room.

Sallie wrote: "I am sorry you are not well and if you would plainly tell Mamma I am sure she would not have the heart to worry you while you are not strong enough."[5]

In another letter the following month Sallie asked if Pa's letter to his wife had had any effect upon her behavior. If not, Sallie thought that Joseph Kennedy would travel to California and bring his wife home. That trip did not take place, of course, perhaps because of Joseph's reluctance to go into debt or take charity for the ticket, and (more likely) because Annie could not bear the idea of seeming to turn her mother out.

The Mite Society meetings were occasions in which Mrs. Kennedy could take part, and would often break out of her shell of despondency to chatter with the guests.

There was a nearly continuous string of other houseguests. These might be business associates of Annie's husband, visiting ministers and special guests—often H. W. Cleaveland, the mansion architect, who had become interested in investing in some projects in Butte County. If a noted dignitary was brought into town for community events, such as a speaker for the town's Fourth of July celebration, or an agricultural expert to address the farmers and townspeople at the Chico Agricultural Fair, it was usual for the Bidwells to extend an invitation. Rev. Fairbairn and his wife were regularly invited to Sunday dinner, leaving one to wonder whether others in the church felt this a prerogative of the Bidwells since they paid most of the church's bills.

Annie had servants to train and supervise, often under trying circumstances since the departing maids often gave no advance notice. During this period she broke in a new cook who had

Chico Presbyterian Church, built in 1871 and torn down in 1909. Courtesy of John Nopel collection.

arrived from San Francisco by steamer at the Chico Landing.

On August 31, 1870, Annie was overjoyed to realize at last the beginning of building on the Chico Presbyterian Church sanctuary. For her husband, it was more of a thorn. For over a year, John had shared with her his concerns about the church, by letter and after her return from Washington. A plan for the building had been discussed by the Mite Society more than once during her absence, and Bidwell had written to her that if built of wood, the edifice would cost over $7,500 and if brick, closer to $10,000. And he had seen no way that the building would become a reality if he did not contribute $5,000 of that.

Bidwell had earlier stated emphatically that he could contribute no more that $1,000, and if the building were to be started with only a portion of the cost pledged, he was certain to be stuck with paying for the balance. Annie gently coaxed her recalcitrant husband to do his duty in the sight of God and they would manage other expenses somehow. "Sometimes it seems our duty to abandon certain plans for improvement on the Rancho and give the means to God's church."[6]

When the wheat harvest was good, Bidwell was apt to be less critical of other church members. "Not a member of the church comes near, or seems to feel the slightest interest in what is going on. Perfectly willing I should buy the furnace, pay for it, put it in place, furnish the wood and then make the fire, provided it shall prove a success and make the room perfectly comfortable! But I do not intend to complain. You remember last year when we kept [my] men for nearly four weeks assisting to put up the walls of the church after everybody had begun to put in their grain. I was very impatient, as you know, but God blessed us with an abundant harvest. We lost nothing by spending our time and means in building His house."[7]

By the mere task of writing out his grievances, Bidwell had worked through his negative feelings, as often happened, Annie observed.

Annie and Mrs. Wayland, on two days in September 1870, went by carriage among church members and nonmembers alike to solicit funds and promises of help with a luncheon that would benefit the new church building. But this was only a drop in a leaky bucket. As was to become a pattern, John Bidwell personally had often to make the church solvent by paying off numbers of accumulated bills, meeting back installments of the pastor's salary, and standing good for building costs when funds dried up. Often, he fumed mightily about this to Annie. She seemed not to weary of reminding him of duty and God's will and seeing him come to accept her guidance in matters which concerned the church.

At last, arrangements were made for a November 15, 1870, departure of Annie's mother. Catherine Kennedy set out to return to Washington, both Bidwells accompanying her as far as Reno on the train. Then John Bidwell turned back toward home, and Annie went on as far as Salt Lake City, from which city all seats and sleeping accommodations had been arranged in advance for Catherine.

The impetus for her mother's decision to go home may have been in part from letters from Sallie and Joseph C. G. Kennedy telling of the anguish and sleepless nights they were going through caused by Joe's drinking. He was often late from home without explanation or apology. Sallie confided that her father had taken to locking the house doors at eleven o'clock, and she dreaded the outcome if Joey thus found himself barred. She stayed up those nights and waited to let the often intoxicated Joey in the door.[8]

The tug toward her old home in Washington, and particularly the feeling of duty toward her family there, haunted Annie Bidwell. The letters that came from her mother once safely back in Washington assumed the same pattern that had so long typified Catherine's up and down mental state. In January 1871, she wrote of suffering great distress of mind again, especially a great fear of the darkness. She *cannot* believe in Christ. The pastor there had told her, or so she reported, "If you cannot believe in Christ, who alone can help you, your case is hopeless." So she felt hypocritical if she took communion, and bereft of hope without.[9]

But in a paragraph or two, Catherine's letter might shift to details of a street bonnet she had redecorated with great success, and of a checker game with the two Josephs in which "Pa took so much time thinking between plays" that she and Joey nearly fell asleep.

Annie considered another trip home in the spring of '72, but the family member on the scene required her presence too. Johnny Kennedy shyly announced his intentions to marry Cora Wayland, daughter of the Dr. and Mrs. Wayland with whom the Bidwells held a rather uneasy relationship in the Presbyterian Church flock. John Bidwell termed the Wayland's ways as "odd." Still they were perfectly respectable, and Cora was a very sweet and considerate young woman, not yet eighteen but mature for her age.

John Reynolds Kennedy, twenty-six, and Cora E. P. Wayland were married very quietly by Rev. Fairbairn on January 12, 1871. The Kennedy newlyweds left for five days of honeymoon in San Francisco and then moved into a modest Chico house. Annie helped when asked, but she sensed that the Waylands were proud to an extreme and Cora's parents wished not to seem to be courting higher status in the community through the union. So the Bidwells kept their distance.

If Annie sometimes, too, seemed a bit lost in deciding how to settle a problem of social decorum, she still found her mother a guide in common sense matters. Annie wrote not long after Johnny had wed to confide to her mother that Cora called her "Mrs. Bidwell,"—so formal, yet was it proper, she inquired of Catherine, for so much younger a woman to call her Annie? Her mother without hesitation replied that if it was pleasant to herself, by all means ask Cora to call her Annie. Especially so, if that was what Johnny would like.[10]

Perhaps it was John Bidwell who came up with a proposal to cheer Annie, who was again finding herself at rather loose ends. An invitation, with offer to pay her fare west, was sent to Sallie Kennedy. Sallie accepted with joy, and the sisters were reunited on June 29 of that year 1871.

When Sallie wrote of being delayed on the eve of her planned departure because of their father's sudden panic at his being left to hold the Kennedy household together, Annie found her only refuge to indulge such disappointment behind the closed doors of her bedroom. She had cause to be weary. In May she had put up seven visiting pastors who came to attend the presbytery in Chico, as well as H. W. Cleaveland who tended to regard the Bidwells as his ready hosts whenever in town.

Cleaveland had been a friend of John Bidwell since the building of the mansion, but now he fell from favor. Bidwell had happened to walk into the parlor of a hotel where he stayed when in San Francisco, and "there sat Mrs. Reed, John's niece Mary, and HWC. I never saw greater apparent attachment."[11]

Annie never forgot this "dishonorable" behavior on Cleaveland's part, and what part of that lay in her general cool appraisal of Mary Reed is a question. Men, as a rule, were judged the sinful aggressors in such cases and the women helpless victims, but such improper behavior in a married woman was not apt to raise Annie's already rather cool opinion of her husband's niece.

Spring 1871 proved a very strenuous time with the arrival of a musician, Philip Phillips, and his wife and children for several days while Mr. Phillips prepared for and gave a benefit concert in the Chico (Bidwell's) Pavilion. The benefit was for all the Chico churches, but the entertaining, account keeping and much of the advertising had fallen to the Bidwells. Each church netted $8.75, which certainly allowed nothing for room and meals—that came as the largesse of the Bidwells! John noted in his diary that Annie took to her bed on May 24, "almost tired to death."

Annie Bidwell's younger brother, John Reynolds Kennedy, 1845–1877. He came to Chico in 1867, married Cora Wayland in 1871, and had two sons, both of whom grew up in Chico. This photograph was probably taken after his marriage. Courtesy of *Mansfield's 1918 History of Butte County.*

In the midst of the guests coming and going, one of the maids left and was replaced, with some delay, by a new girl from San Francisco. Catherine had foreseen two years earlier, with the wisdom she was capable of displaying in spite of frequent emotional suffering of her own, that the Bidwell's generous offer of their home to visitors on church matters might grow burdensome.

"So your home is to be headquarters for the ministers?" she had written. "The society will be very pleasurable and afford great pleasure. Still it could be a problem. My advice is not to do it as a rule. If you are sick or servants leave it could be extremely undesirable. It is not necessary to be so considerate."[12]

When Annie heard that her sister might not be coming after all, she wrote a despairing letter to her mother.

"My sweet delicate child," Catherine had written back, "who could have read them—letters that came to us—without fearing the result would be as it is—you are too busy entertaining, disappointed about Sallie."[13]

Her father relented at once when both wife and daughter attacked his position and Annie's collapse reached his ears.

Sallie was on the train only a week or two later. Bidwell timed a business meeting in San Francisco to end in Sacramento as Johnny and Annie took the newly recently completed train service from Chico so that the three together converged to greet Sallie as she stepped from the train.

Sallie, Annie and John Bidwell went by train to Tehama for the Fourth of July celebration that year, in part to share the wonder of the railway that now made Chico so accessible, both to the north and to the south. The vivacious Sallie went on many drives about the ranch with her hosts, often with Johnny and Cora along. Banter between Bidwell and Sallie had always come easily, and this visit proved no exception. Only Sallie Kennedy among the women acquaintances with whom Bidwell conversed had the ability to tease him without metaphorically curling him up like a disturbed pill bug.

"Good, bright Sister Sally," he wrote in a letter to Annie.[14]

The time flew rapidly as Sallie proved as easy to entertain by picking peaches as by an excursion with her sister to Calistoga to view the hot springs there. With John Bidwell in the party, Sallie went with her sister to Big Meadows and on a visit to spectacular Yosemite Valley.

Still Annie did not recover her usual level of energy. She missed church services several times, claiming that she felt unwell, a feeling she had not shaken even with Sallie's presence. She seemed to take little notice of the handsome spire going up on the almost finished Presbyterian Church. These periods of less than perfect health were reason for Sallie to indulge herself in waiting on her sister and sharing hours upstairs in the Bidwell's elegant bedroom. They chatted about many subjects and often, no doubt, shared concern over their parents and older brother, and perhaps about Annie's hopes and fears as well.

The sisters packed and departed together for Washington, D.C., on November 2. Annie seemed not to care that she would miss the December dedication of the new church which she had inspired by her wishes to reclaim her husband for God.

Cora was near the end of her uneventful pregnancy over which Mrs. Wayland hovered in maternal concern. A week after the sisters' departure, on November 9, 1871, Cora gave birth at home to a son whom she and Johnny named Guy Reynolds.[15] The sisters, Annie and Sallie, were still on their leisurely sight-seeing trip across country.

Far from seeming to resent Annie's absence, John Bidwell went about his business with greater ease of mind. He knew that Annie was freer in mind and spirit than when she had each day to face servants, guests, and Chicoans with an appearance of serenity and self-confidence it had not always been possible to feel. In spite of his "business-as-usual" attitude it seems probable that Bidwell was uneasy over Annie's losing her intense commitment to church and community at large, not to mention to her brother and her husband.

Annie was not to see her Chico home again for over six months. In her parents' Washington home that winter, Annie had not seemed to recover fully from the headaches and malaise. She tried to take her part in the "gay season" of January and February when society demanded entertaining or leaving one's calling card at every home that held an open house day. The whirl of Washington's political life went on day after day, often without Annie. Her mother noticed and commented that her old room served often as retreat.

At home, John Bidwell tried to leave the running of the mansion to the servants, but trouble seemed to stir up in the kitchen along with meal-getting and dusting. Hannah, the servant with the longest tenure, had come to Bidwell to say that Mary and Bessie, the two newest servants, were out late at night every time that Bidwell was out of town. Bessie's sister, who wanted a place on the mansion staff, kept feeding the other girls ideas of how best to persecute Hannah. "We must take a firm stand," wrote the beleaguered householder to his wife in an effort to build his own backbone before facing the squabblers, "and never let Hannah go. If she must leave, we must never take Bessie's sister in her place."

The mention of servant problems gave Bidwell an opportunity to write praises to his wife: "The fact is, Annie, you are the best hand I ever saw to manage servants—and the secret is this: You are so *kind, gentle,* firm and reasonable in everything that you make everybody love you."[16]

As if the mansion were a bed and breakfast for visiting dignitaries, guest rooms and dining table continued to be occupied by whomever the owner thought it proper to invite on their stopovers in Chico. The housework continued and the maids were needed. One of the houseguests was a traveling lecturer of some renown who used the nom de plume Grace Greenwood. She came to Chico to give an address at the Bidwells' invitation and while staying at the mansion in March 1872, she became too ill to travel. She was still in the mansion when Bidwell left for his trip east that month. The maids had rallied admirably as nurses as well as laundresses and fire builders. Bidwell learned their traits: Bessie was an early riser; Mary, industrious but "liked to listen—she could hear through walls!"[17]

On Christmas John had accepted an invitation to eat with his nephew Abram Bidwell and Abram's large family in their modest home. The year before, Abram had come to Chico to settle, and very shortly Bidwell hired him. He soon promoted Abram to general manager of the ranch operation.

Daniel Bidwell, the half-brother to whom John had "sold" a large acreage, was also at Christmas dinner at Abram's with his wife. It was a very sore point with John Bidwell that his brother had never paid him for the 700 acres that John had carved from the northern edge of his own holdings. They had finally worked out an agreement that the ranch Daniel Bidwell had "purchased," and on which he had built an elegant home, was to be considered "leased." There was little Annie could do but listen sympathetically when her husband complained about his relatives.

Was Chico again abuzz at the prolonged absence of Annie Bidwell? As time went by, undoubtedly tongues wagged and predictions were made about Annie's intentions. Bidwell may have suspected that he was being left out of the social life of the community; some evidence of its being so came to him in January when he learned of the upcoming double marriage of two of the most eligible young women in the area, the daughters of Bidwell's friend from the 1850s, Dr. William P. Tilden. Mollie and Belle Tilden were united in marriage to banker Charles Faulkner, newly established in town with a branch of the Rideout Bank, and *Butte County Record* publisher George Crosette. Both were acquaintances and business associates of Bidwell, and yet he had had to learn of the upcoming marriages through one of the church members![18]

Bidwell disliked weddings, and would probably not have gone if invited. Still, it was the idea of being passed over that caused him surprise. While no doubt it was satisfying in one way to lose the responsibility, Bidwell's failure to be re-elected to the Board of Church Trustees in January 1872 must have startled him.

The National Convention of Sunday Schools coming up in April in Indianapolis gave John Bidwell the necessary impetus to do something positive about his situation. Annie had said nothing to

Annie Bidwell in Washington, D.C., during a long visit "home." She was thin and shows some indication of long suffering from "nervousness" that began during her mother's visit to Chico in 1870. Courtesy of California State Parks.

him to bring doubt as to her love and loyalty, but something bestirred itself within him. He decided that he would go east and escort his wife home, putting Indianapolis on his itinerary. He went to San Francisco, was fitted for a new suit of clothes and massaged his financial contacts, coming up with a $2,500 loan for six months.[19]

On March 28, John Bidwell took the train from San Francisco for New York and traveled on to Washington, D.C., on April 4.

I "hastened to my wife at 6 a.m." he noted in his diary. The Kennedys planned a full social life for him, including a dinner party with Mr. and Mrs. George W. Gibbs and Mrs. Gibbs' mother Mrs. Kane. These longtime friends of the family were planning to establish a home in San Francisco. Bidwell renewed contacts with Prof. Henry of the Smithsonian Institute at dinner with the Kennedys. Bidwell and Annie called on President Ulysses Grant at the White House and Bidwell made an effort to see many congressmen whom he knew.

In the full flush of penitence, if such it was, Bidwell mentioned the possibility of taking Annie abroad in August, if they could possibly work it out. (It did not come to pass.)

Bidwell attended the Sunday school convention on a side trip from Washington to Indianapolis and Chicago in mid-April. Thereafter, John Bidwell dedicated his time to pleasing Annie by going with her where she wished. They went to Meadville and met many of the family dear to her heart. In Baltimore they visited Ellicott relatives of whom even the Kennedys were in some awe, though cousins Sallie and Maggie Ellicott were among Annie's closest girlhood friends and correspondents.[20]

Final departure from Washington was delayed until Annie completed a series of visits with Dr. Hill, the family dentist. Then on to New York, Maine and Massachusetts. They visited Kennedy family friends, the Lathers family. While at Cambridge the Bidwells toured Harvard College. They departed Boston on May 22 and wended their way home sightseeing through Montreal, Quebec and Detroit, Michigan. From Denver west the rail line encountered some delays from bad bridges, but in nearly every town of any size, Bidwell had contacts from his pioneer past. Even in so remote a city as Cheyenne, Wyoming, John and Annie had an invitation to a friend's home to wait out a delay.[21]

On June 6, they switched from the Central Pacific to the new Oregon & California line at the Roseville junction, bringing them back home to Chico at last in late afternoon that same day.

As Annie again resumed the duties as mistress of the mansion, Sallie wrote that in Washington after so many pleasant months together, "all [Kennedys] are affected with the most wretched blues." And Sallie was eager to get Annie's report on "what you think of Guy."[22]

And "Aunt Annie" did have some catching up to do with Johnny and his family too. As Cora had written to Annie in Washington, Johnny was thinner, pale and listless. The joy of his life was in playing with his seven-month-old son.

Gradually Annie began to build a circle of acquaintances in California with whom she felt relaxed. The Gibbs, who had moved to San Francisco from the East Coast, paid the Bidwells a visit, and their praise of Rancho Chico did much to raise its value in Annie's eyes. Augusta Gibbs's home became headquarters for many of Annie's visits to the city.

Franklin C. Lusk settled his practice in Chico in the early '70s. He was an attorney with a personal presence and reputation as to command respect. Bidwell soon advised the lawyer that he hoped to be a client of Lusk's thereafter on all legal matters. Lusk was a bachelor, but he soon built a large brick home on Second and Salem streets not far from the Bidwells and entertained lavishly from time to time. By joining his list of guests, the Bidwells rubbed elbows with prominent persons from all over the state, including Dr. and Mrs. Glenn from San Jacinto across the Sacramento River. When Lusk's mother came to Chico to live, Annie was enchanted by her, and her mother urged her to cultivate persons of Mrs. Mary Jane Lusk's refinement.

Johnny Kennedy and his little family left in December 1872, to spend the winter months in the Sandwich Islands (Hawaii).[23] The cold of even a California winter exacerbated his symptoms. His mother wishfully thought that John Bidwell might use his influence to get Johnny a position as U.S. Consul to the Islands. It was not seriously considered by either of the men as practical or possible.[24]

It was to John Bidwell's credit that he made no protest when being asked by Annie to finance John and Cora's second winter (1874–75) in a sunnier climate. "My heart overflows with gratitude when your kindness to Johnny is recalled. It was asking a great deal to ask of you that $2,000 when he left. Yet it was the price of his life, I felt, and in giving it to me I felt you gave me his life."[25]

The windy, wet spring of 1873 was followed in Chico by an unusually large population of rattlesnakes throughout the ranch. One barn so often produced a sighting that it was burned in June of the following year in order to rid the hay field of the snake population infesting the foundation.[26] The snakes were little more than a curiosity to Annie, of course, who rarely ventured out among the ranch fields except in a carriage and with her husband. However, Johnny had encountered a snake and killed it, thus adding to Catherine's list of dangers to worry about: wild Indians, wild cattle, and now wild serpents.

The Reverend Alex Fairbairn fell into disfavor with members of the Board of Trustees. The Bidwells noted a decline in the quality of his sermons. On one occasion, John Bidwell noted that the pastor had spoken extemporaneously, a practice frowned on as sloppy by Bidwell, who apparently never spoke extempore himself.

Fairbairn was sensitive to an undercurrent of dissatisfaction among the growing congregation and resigned from the church, to be replaced within a few months by the Reverend Dr. A. M. Stewart. Annie had never related to the Fairbairns or their adult son on more than the courteous level required. She had never felt like confiding in Rev. Fairbairn on matters of her personal faith. She had kept strictly to the expected woman's role of the day, teaching a Sunday school class and supporting the Mite Society. Even public prayer was not considered appropriate for women in the Chico church until many years later.

After Annie Bidwell's death, her friend Helen Sommer Gage related in an oral history interview that there was always a "stiff restraint" on Chico social occasions with the Bidwells. All the more surprising that on the fifth anniversary of their marriage,

April 16, 1873, a number of Chico couples gathered to surprise and honor them. The Bidwells seemed a bit taken aback by this event, and no records exist to identify the person who organized the party, only a scant mention in John's diary.[27] It was if a surprise party was a social event that Annie's repertoire of social skills did not cover, and she did not know whether to be pleased or embarrassed.

The event of the year that brought a true sparkle of happiness to Annie's eyes was the purchase in June 1873 of a camping tent and other necessities for living in the open. After a practice pitching of the tent, John and Annie, several out-of-town clerics, and their cook and driver set out for the Lassen Peak area. Annie rode horseback when she wished, a sidesaddle having been borrowed for her use. They camped first on Pine Creek thirty miles from Chico. On June 21 they were at Black Butte Lake where "ice froze in the water bucket," and members of the party climbed Cinder Cone. Trout fishing was at its best along Pine Creek, and they camped there again on the return to Chico a few days later. Their first camping run had proved a great success! Annie and John named the Pine Creek site "Camp Satisfaction."[28]

Another camping party set out on August 6, this time with Johnny and Cora. The campsite at Powellton became "Camp Repose." In Humbug Valley "Camp Brightness" was added to their itinerary. They traveled on through Camp Satisfaction to the Bumpass area near Lassen Peak itself, bringing them to "Camp Politeness," so called because of assistance that came from the Bunnell family's wayside inn nearby.

The chronic nature of Annie's attacks of nervous headache might suggest that she was subject to cyclical physical changes. There is only the trace of a suggestion that the trouble was connected to "female problems." Once a San Francisco doctor so thoroughly insulted and infuriated Annie by the suggestion that her problems were "female" in nature that no referral to a gynecologist was ever to be made again.[29]

There were days in which she disappeared from church happenings and daily household routines to the solitude of her
bedroom. Bidwell respected those times. He was one to take to
bed himself with any ailment, from a cold to a lame back. A small
single bed was put up in their bedroom to accommodate the
couple when illness indicated it would be more comfortable to
sleep apart, though for most of their married life they shared the
double bed in the master bedroom with windows facing the east
and south, bath and dressing room adjoining.

All of the spring of 1874 Annie suffered from a sore eye as well
as her "nervousness." A sore and lame leg was attributed to an
insect bite. She took to her bed during parts of March and missed
teaching her Sunday school girls class for several months. Still she
was able to attend services at church the Sabbath that her sister-
in-law Cora, now twenty-one, joined and took first communion.
On that same day, F. C. Lusk transferred his membership to the
Chico Presbyterian Church.

Catherine Kennedy was always alert to troubles on the Chico
front. John Kennedy had returned from his first winter in Hawaii
feeling stronger, but he had a cough that hung on and he was
basically unchanged in his symptom of low energy. And
Catherine had never seen her grandson, so her second visit to
Chico was arranged. On May 7, 1874, she arrived, escorted by a
Rev. Ames who was on his way to San Francisco. Catherine was
on hand to hear the Reverend Stewart's first sermon a week later
as Stewart took over as the second pastor to serve the Chico
church.[30]

On June 16, John Bidwell accompanied his wife to San
Francisco in search of medical treatment for Annie. They stayed
at the Occidental Hotel again, and Bidwell finally located the
highly recommended Dr. Sawyer and brought him to examine
Annie at the hotel. Sawyer applied a poultice, but recommended
that Annie stay for a week of further observation and treatment.
Bidwell returned to Chico and his mother-in-law went to help

97

Annie manage in the city. They were detained nearly three more weeks by relapses in both inflamed eye and swollen leg. It was on this occasion that one of Annie's physicians referred her to a gynecologist.

Annie was very pleased to have flowers from her husband delivered to her room for her birthday, June 30, but the joy from the flowers (she had expected that Bidwell would forget her birthday, as usual) was diluted by a stinging letter that came from the same source. John Bidwell apparently wrote whining like a spoiled child—a letter so offensive to Annie that she tore it up. Her reply, rather drenched in self-pity itself, was as follows:

"I apologize for my poor performance at letter writing, etc. during my illness. Lest I fall into error which had pained you, I will begin my letter with dates and acknowledgment of kind and interesting letters each day of my separation from you—excepting one day.

"Still I am guilty in your eyes of ingratitude and neglect and all I can do is ask pardon for the past and try to be more heedful of these things in the future. I have trusted so implicitly in your knowledge of me and in that affection which you have ever manifested that I have indulged perhaps in too much license. God grant I may not do so again, and if it did not seem too pitiful of me I would express the hope that you not carry out your suggestion that your letters cease. But I do not think that you intend to stop writing, nor do I believe that you *really* think I do not care for your writing. … Now dear General, confess that you were not considerate in feeling so hard on me. I don't believe that you intended sending Johnny down to find the state of my health."[31]

Perhaps John Bidwell's injured feelings were caused less by Annie's missing a day or two in writing than by the contents of one of the letters he did receive:

"Now, dear husband, I hope you will not be angry with me. Mamma, Papa and Sallie expect me to return with Mamma this fall to Washington. I hope for your approval and cheerful consent. ... I have a duty to my parents as well as to my husband and I thank God daily that they so seldom conflict."[32]

Though still lame from time to time after she got home, Annie did improve enough to join her husband in rides around the ranch—one time on muleback, a preference that John Bidwell was to follow most of the remainder of his life.

Catherine Kennedy's visit was broken by frequent overnight stays with Johnny and Cora. Catherine doted on Guy, now a toddler. She had not suffered a depressed period during her entire seven months' stay in California!

On November 4, 1874, the John Kennedy family took off again for a winter in Hawaii. On November 19, Annie departed for Washington with her mother just as Major A. M. Bailey arrived from San Francisco to take over as ranch manager, and Abram Bidwell was demoted to a position requiring less tact in handling of employees. At the same time, Bidwell hired George Stewart, son of the pastor, as a ranch accountant and assistant to Bailey.

Annie's absence was again to extend to over half a year. Left in charge, John Bidwell faced difficulty within his own household as Ann and Annette, the two housemaids at that time, had a quarrel ending in physical blows. He seems, in that instance, to have let them sort things out for themselves. The Bidwells had come to accept that their help imported from San Francisco might just as suddenly storm off again and needed constant handling with the proverbial kid gloves.

The maids broke into the camphor closet at the mansion and read the Bidwell's correspondence! They carried tales of the Bidwells' affairs around Chico! "It is too humiliating to have her [Annette] discussing our private affairs to a town audience. ..." wrote Annie. "Before you leave give Ann some advice that she must never repeat what we say or anyone on the Rancho says. Let her know it will come back to us!"[33]

1875—A year to seize the helm

o sooner had Annie reached Washington early in December 1874, than she suffered from the damp cold. She had a sore throat and though "I drew my shawl as much about my ears as possible, I think that this winter I ought to have some fur!

"I am a naughty and expensive creature this winter, but then I am *your* wife, and as your house and garden and all that belongs to you, must be in the best of order so far as modest propriety is concerned, so your wife has come under the same regime!!!— jesting aside, I do feel sorry that I must be such an expense this winter, but I will not spend anymore than is necessary for a respectable appearance in the circle where God has been pleased to place me, and to Him, morning and night, I look for guidance to know how to expend that which he has given to us. … It is my earnest wish to glorify him even through my clothing. To appear in modest, but not mean apparel, to have a humble heart and a thankful one under whatever clothing I may wear and also comport myself as a Christian."[1]

In another rebellious moment, Annie wrote to John that he should inform the Presbyterian Mite Society that she resigned her position as president![2]

A more serious event took place in the Chico church family during Annie's absence. The Reverend A. M. Stewart became ill during delivery of his sermon one February morning in 1875. By the following Sabbath he was dead—from an illness diagnosed as brain fever. As usual, John Bidwell was left to cope with the financial crisis faced by Mrs. Stewart. The pastors at Chico were chronically in arrears in salary received, and the Stewarts had no savings whatsoever. Bidwell paid for the doctor and the funeral expenses.[3]

Bidwell had written his wife in Washington that January announcing his decision to move his office out of the mansion to another building. He gave as reason the continual wear and tear on the carpets from the heavy and often dirty boots of the workmen, and though the ranch foremen knew to use the side entrance when coming to the office, other callers who might well be received elsewhere were coming to the front door.[4]

John Bidwell had agreed to go east to accompany Annie home as soon as he was assured of Major Bailey's ability to handle workmen, a trait Abram Bidwell seemed not to possess. Comfortable on this score, Bidwell set out by train on March 20 and met Annie and Sallie in New York City.

In fact, Bidwell was on a cloud of high spirits that stayed with him for over a month of constant visiting and receiving callers in their hotel. Annie was again in good health and spirits as they visited art galleries and scientific exhibitions, meeting old acquaintances and introduced to new. For two months or more before he left California, Bidwell had been observing his miller, a man named Foley, for continued instances of suspected embezzlement. Foley had been very clever. At last Bidwell was certain of his documentation and had gotten Lusk to open a case against Foley. When Foley's attorney successfully filed a demurrer in the local justice court, Bidwell openly blamed Lusk's casual approach in a letter detailing the matter to Annie. But, then, to Bidwell's amazement and delight, the county grand jury heard the case and indicted Foley for theft. With the trial date postponed until his return from the East, Bidwell took off to meet his wife in great elation. It was a feeling that lasted until their return home through Atlanta where they visited Ellicott cousins of Annie's, and west from Chicago.

Two weeks later, on May 15, Johnny, Cora and Guy Kennedy arrived home from Hawaii.

During the winter in Washington, Annie had returned to work occasionally in the mission where both she and Sallie had volunteered for some years. She assumed no great responsibility on that visit for she did not want to commit much time, but she observed the classes for the children and particularly the sewing room to which poor women could come for new fabrics and assistance in sewing. She noticed that the women preferred to sew new things for themselves and their children rather than accepting hand-me-downs that had been donated to the mission.

Although the Chico rancheria had been moved from close proximity to the mansion to the other side of the deer park several years before this, Annie had always been very aware of the presence of both women and children, the former often working as weed pullers for the gardener at the mansion. She had approached Indian women in a friendly manner several times. Most of them shrank away in timidity and awe and feigned that they could not understand. Probably they did know only a few words of English. Nopanny, the Indian woman who had met Annie at the mansion soon after the latter's arrival, and had stated her own position as "wife number one," retreated from further assertion on that matter but remained on friendly terms and offered to help.[5]

Annie had been shown examples of the clever handiwork of the Indian women by her husband—the baskets and the clothing fashioned from small animal skins and bits of brightly colored discarded clothing. She had the idea that the one common interest these two groups of women had—both in Washington and on the rancheria—was their pride in handiwork. She was determined to try one more time to find some common bond with the native women who lived so close to her but from whom she was separated by a deep chasm of pagan thought and custom.

During their relaxed days of travel, Annie informed her husband of her aspiration to win over the Indian women, and thus their children, to a school that she would teach. It was not an easy task convincing him, for Bidwell had strong ideas about the manner in which whites should relate to the Native Americans. He had told her that he believed that the Indians had a well-formed religious belief system, and that it worked for them. He was aware of the need to protect the natives from hostile whites. His experience with Indian problems, and with protecting his own rancheria Indians during the early 1860s, bears out that probably something more than self-interest motivated him.

The confessions that John Bidwell had made to Annie in the successful entrance to her mind and heart one winter night in 1866 were strong in her heart now. Curiosity—for it was curiosity as well as Christian motivation—about the existence of children begat by her husband was aroused in Annie as she viewed the dusky faces around the rancho. Whether she made mention of this now while pleading for permission to try to establish a school we cannot know. But she did play her hand well, and before the Bidwells set foot back in the mansion on May 11, 1875, she knew that a grand new project lay before her. By June 1 she had rallied a number of Presbyterian women to her cause, and on June 1 they met with her in a cottage formerly used for a farm office near the mansion to discuss an exciting missionary venture right there in Chico. On June 7, 1875, three women accompanied her to call on all the women in the rancheria and invite them to a school. They were Mrs. Hobart (the former Emroy Bidwell), Mrs. McMillan and Miss Mary Stewart.

The response was not very encouraging. The rancheria women were reluctant, some refusing to come to the door, and Nopanny gave the reason—that Pamaho's wife, the boy George Clements' mother, was very ill and not expected to live. Nevertheless, the school would be open the very next day Annie said to tell the women. Bright bolts of fabric were shown to the women who came to the door to listen to the Presbyterian ladies. They were told that they would have some of this fabric with which to learn how to sew garments for themselves.

Mary Stewart, the daughter of recently deceased Rev. Stewart, had been teaching school in another county when word came of her father's death. Now home for the summer, Miss Stewart accepted the position as head teacher of the school.

On June 8, the "staff" assembled: Mrs. McMillan, Miss Stewart, and Rev. and Mrs. Woods as well as Annie. But no pupils appeared! Annie and one of the other women drove to the rancheria at once and found that indeed Pamaho's wife had died and was being buried in the street between Indian homes.

The schoolroom was set up with tables and chairs in a rancho building provided by Bidwell, though exactly which one is not known. The women were given needles (highly prized), thread and scissors with which to fashion garments of their choice. From examples of garments Annie showed them, the women quickly learned to do fancy as well as plain stitching, keeping the teachers busy cutting out new garments. At times Annie preferred to be teaching the children.

The Indians at first were very respectful, but gradually the fear they had shown of Annie for nearly seven years disappeared. And in the process they learned words in English. More importantly, many of the women began to wish to learn more English and to want their children to learn. The first large class that assembled on June 15 continued weekly. As women dropped out, more emphasis was placed on the ABC teaching of the children. And as important (perhaps more so to Annie) the teachings of the Bible were the introduction to each session, illustrated with brightly colored books and posters.

During this exciting period a new pastor was installed at the Presbyterian Church. On June 8, 1875, the Reverend John Woods, still in his thirties, began his pastorate. Though he had been absent during the choice of Woods, Bidwell was pleased at the energy demonstrated by the pastor, and Woods endeared himself to Annie by showing great interest in the Indian school. Both he and Mrs. Woods supported Annie and the women's missionary project wholeheartedly.

One source of opposition to the school was Catherine Kennedy. She wrote to her daughter, "That school you have opened. My honest conviction is that you take a *wrong* and *dangerous* step. … Your feelings have got the better of your judgment and former intentions."[6]

Catherine may have been cautioning Annie merely on overusing her eyes, but the vehemence of her protest suggests otherwise. Catherine had not quite conquered her nervousness at possible treachery on the part of the Native Americans.

In spite of earlier resolve not to once again get entangled in state politics, John Bidwell gave in to requests that he run for governor that year as the nominee of a new Independent Party, formed in 1873 by farmers and anti monopolists. They had been greatly encouraged that year when their candidate, Newton Booth, won the gubernatorial election, but Booth wanted to run for the U.S. Senate. He ran for U.S. senator while still governor and was defeated, leaving the field open in two years for another Independent Party candidate for governor.

California farmers especially were feeling the sting of Central Pacific's railroad monopoly on shipping rates as well as other injustices in the tax structure which hit farmers especially hard. Bidwell joined the Chico Grange, Patrons of Husbandry, looking for natural allies, though he was soon disabused of the idea that his membership in a local Grange carried much influence and soon dropped active membership.

The anti-Chinese issue was gaining strength as fast as the Independents (or what also became known as the "Dolly Varden Party" after a popular multi-colored calico dress) lost support through splintering of the factions. A fourth party further split the field and Bidwell was to trail with less than half the votes garnered by William Irvin, the Democratic winner.[7]

That campaign for governor on which John Bidwell embarked in mid-July 1875, has been noted by political historians as perhaps the most abusive of Bidwell's life and character that he ever experienced, and worse than most on any scale measured.

Johnny Kennedy had been asked to accompany Bidwell[8] as he toured the major cities of the state (much against his mother's judgment), and it was doubtlessly painful to Johnny; however his suffering was nothing as to Annie's. She had chosen to stay in San Francisco where the daily papers attacked her husband as a foreigner, a Mexican citizen who gave up U.S. citizenship to gain free land holdings. He was contemptuously referred to a "Juan Bidwell" in one *Chronicle* editorial after another. More seriously, he was also accused of bribing a U.S. attorney general with $10,000 to assure immunity from federal interference in charges that he had illegally gained title to the Mexican grant awarded William Dickey in 1844. Deny the charges Bidwell did, but it was hard to fight the bribe charge. There was no evidence pro or con, but the damage was done by the mere suggestion of such a serious crime.

Annie tried not to upset her husband by writing to him of her personal anguish. His whole campaign was typified by remarkable personal calm, but he was the only serene person in the family. The Kennedys followed the campaign in the Western newspapers as well as through Annie. Catherine wrote indignantly when the suggestion was made that General got his land through fraud. "I would like to get hold of [that man] and give his nose a good twist. I nearly lost my dinner yesterday reading the long article in the San Francisco *Chronicle.* I was glad to hear through the General that you are in San Francisco and have the sympathy of congenial friends."[9]

As the campaign drew to a close, Catherine expressed again how she worried at Annie being called to suffer so. "I think political falsehoods cannot take from him the standing he has so long enjoyed in the opinion of all whose esteem is valuable. Annie, think how few could have gone through such an ordeal and come out of it morally triumphant. The strain that has been on you must be cast off as soon as possible as I fear you will surely suffer both bodily and mentally. ..."[10]

Annie took some comfort in describing a parallel she saw between Christ's sufferings and those inflicted on John Bidwell during his abortive campaign for governor.[11]

Once home in the mansion there were a number of other happenings to take Annie's mind off of the disastrous campaign. A little Chico girl had been orphaned, along with two older siblings. Sarah was cared for by the Bidwells in October while plans were made for the three orphans haphazardly by members of the community. Annie fell in love with Sarah and wished briefly to adopt her. It is not recorded what John Bidwell's reaction was to this wish, but Annie's mother responded, "You mentioned taking a little girl in your family and giving her a permanent home. Both Sallie and I were relieved that she was to be transferred to other hands. Mrs. Vincent [Washington acquaintance] said, 'O don't ever let her think of such a thing again for it never terminates well.' What she said on the matter is, I believe, the common experience."[12]

The following February, Annie was the organizational spirit behind forming a benevolent aid society to assist community families in distress, with women from several of Chico's churches participating.

In November a permanent houseguest arrived at the mansion from New York, a semi-invalid youth of twenty-one, William D. Stevenson, of Morristown, New Jersey. The Stevenson family was longtime friends of the Kennedys. An older son in the family was deeply religious and Annie had corresponded with him for many years though it "had always been my conviction that such correspondence is not advisable." She had hastened to give reasons and assure John Bidwell in one of her early letters to him that the spirituality she shared with Stevenson seemed to excuse any other impropriety. She enclosed to Bidwell one of the older brother's letters to her to illustrate the innocent nature of the correspondence![13]

In 1875 when the Bidwells were in Washington, the Stevenson family had asked them to consider giving their youngest son William the benefit of a change of climate. Now that the tubercular Stevenson was ensconced in the household where he often suffered from a general lack of energy and occasional severe nose bleeds, he volunteered to be of whatever assistance he could, and Annie immediately recruited him to assist in teaching the few older male Indian children who were still faithfully appearing once a week for lessons. Except, of course, when ranch work or attendance at powwows in other Indian villages took priority. The school was certainly flourishing, even though Annie had neglected it during her husband's political campaign. It was so much a success that even Annie's mother came around to giving approval.[14]

An event which rocked the members of the Chico Presbyterian Church occurred in November 1875. Mrs. Mickey, a young and not unattractive housewife and a church member arose at a Wednesday evening prayer meeting and accused the new pastor, the Reverend Woods, of improper behavior toward her. She exhibited to those present a ring, which she said Woods had given her in hopes that she might reciprocate in an "indecent" manner.[15]

The others at the prayer meeting reeled in shock at such a brash accusation, and the pastor vehemently denied any such impropriety. He had indeed sent Mrs. Mickey the ring but because he believed it to be one she had lost. To have her misconstrue his intention wounded him to the depths. Mrs. Mickey stuck to her story.

Annie wrote of all this to her mother, the latter having met Mrs. Mickey on her visit to Chico. Catherine responded, "Mrs. Mickey has disgraced herself by the course she has pursued. ... Mr. Woods lacked discretion which the state of public sentiment at this time in regard to ministerial improprieties ought to have taught him. I suppose he was embarrassed when he made his remarks at the prayer meeting. I am sure he must have felt mortified. ... I hope you will drop the subject from your mind for really you are too sensitive for your nature to dwell on such topics." Catherine then proceeded to remind Annie of things about Mrs. Mickey that did not reflect well on her character— things they had noticed during Catherine's last Chico visit. Mrs. Mickey had a tendency to gossip about others to the point of slander—in other words, Catherine saw only guilt in the accuser.[16]

John Bidwell entered in his diary his opinion, "I call Mrs. Mickey crazy."[17]

The public sentiment mentioned by Catherine, regarding the advantages ministers sometimes took of their female church members, referred to the notorious "sex" trial of New York City's Rev. Henry Ward Beecher, a trial which John Bidwell had attended during his visit to New York City in March of that year 1875.[18]

So the incident passed, and the Woods and their daughter Irene were guests at the Bidwell's Thanksgiving dinner with Mary and George Stewart, adult children of the late Reverend Stewart, and Major Bailey, the new ranch business manager. (Mrs. Stewart, with financial assistance from Bidwell, had moved in October to join family in Chicago.)

The closeness between the Bidwells and the Woods continued into 1876, with social contacts outnumbering the church-related ones. It was the first time that Annie had felt such harmony with a pastor of the Chico church. He was willing to preach to the Indians at the rancheria and to accompany Annie to the Indian dance performances within their roundhouse, which Bidwell had refused to do and to which Annie felt it improper to go without a male escort.[19]

The year 1875 ended with Annie and John attending a large and elegant New Years' Eve dinner party given by Franklin Lusk, Bidwell's attorney. This may not have been exactly crashing into the Chico social set at last, but it did give the Bidwells social status that seemed to elude them, and continued to do so much of their lives.

In 1992, Dr. Michele Shover explored in depth the position held by the Bidwells in Chico and concluded: "The Bidwells were not only on a different financial plane than the townspeople, but … they lived socially apart. They were surrounded by people, of course, but recognized none of them fully as peers. They entertained frequently and drew broadly. But Bidwell Mansion was neither Chico's living room, nor its community center. In addition, and on more personal terms, it was not an informal gathering place for an ongoing circle of close friends, the couple's counterpart in the community."[20]

John Bidwell, if left to his own decision-making in social matters, might have extended regrets to Lusk upon receiving the invitation in 1875. He did not much like Lusk as a person, often venting his feelings to Annie.

In July 1873, he had written: "I am in favor of cutting this man Lusk's acquaintance. If we continue to speak to him he will get too big for his breeches! Besides he is a tattler, if no worse. I do not care to be on intimate terms with such a busybody. He makes no discrimination between foes and friends for the reason that as soon as [he is] known, he has no friends."[21]

Conflicts

*J*ohn Bidwell was close-mouthed in revealing personal information about the Indians on the rancheria. He was reluctant to speak about any experiences he may have had with native peoples before Annie came to California. On at least one occasion she responded to a request from a stranger to Bidwell for his account of his memories of particular Indians he had known at Sutter's Fort. She had apologized for his failure to reply and explained that when he did not wish to speak on a subject, Bidwell refused to answer questions and turned away.[1]

Although Bidwell probably never regretted telling Annie what he had of his past, the incentive for confession had dried up!

It is possible that Annie was left to determine from her contacts in the Indian village which of the lighter-skinned residents were related by blood to her husband. Probably Bidwell had explained that when he came to the area before other whites arrived, he had become friends with the Maidu occupants of a particular valley village near Chico Creek. The men of the village had helped him clear land and plant his first orchards on land Bidwell had rented from the Edward Farwell Rancho south of Little Chico Creek; some natives had gone with him to assist him recover gold from the Feather River. Later in the 1860s when the Indians sought Bidwell's protection from hostile Indian fighters, Bidwell had been able to extend the villagers protection and a new site for their village on Rancho Chico land. Bidwell's contacts with the villagers was through their chief, and it is assumed that in exchange for protection, the chief had given an Indian girl, perhaps the chief's daughter, to Bidwell as "wife." There had evidently been two such liaisons prior to Nopanny, each of which produced a child.[2]

How Annie confirmed in her own mind that Amanda Lafonso, the young (perhaps not yet twenty), handsome and serene wife of the rancheria chief, Holai Lafonso, was John Bidwell's daughter is not known. Amanda knew some English—had had some schooling obviously. And Amanda quietly became an ally in the development of the school. She invited Annie and Annie's female houseguests at the time, with Chief Lafonso's permission, to the squaw dance in the rancheria, and later to the roundhouse dances, the ones attended with the Reverend and Mrs. Woods, only rarely open to white observers. John Bidwell had never witnessed these dances in all of his years of close association with the Indians, regarding the dances as a private ritual in which whites had no part.

When her husband was in San Francisco on business in February 1876, Annie wrote, "My school almost makes me weep for joy. I am so grateful that you consented to my having it."[3] She gloried in the clear sweet voices of the children, and listened while Amanda had explained how the small boys caught a mouse with bare hands—and customarily even birds were caught that way.

Annie tried to describe the dance she had witnessed in a letter to John, but decided "it is out of the question!" Warriors—a profusion of feather—wailing and a general howl of the bear dance—the artistry of the dance outfits.[4]

Amanda had referred to her as "Annie," in speaking to the other Indians, thinking it to be respectful. Annie had kindly said, "Call me Mrs. Bidwell, Amanda." Then George had pointed out the prominent characters of the dance, saying eagerly, "See, Mrs. Bidwell. ..."[5]

Had Annie suspected that the youth, George Clements, was her husband's son? When did she learn it?

In June of 1876 Annie entertained two artists from San Francisco for several weeks. She accompanied Mesdames Tichenor and Work about Rancho Chico and joined them in sketching picturesque spots. They had gone with her to witness the dances in the roundhouse on the rancheria. Soon after they had returned home, a house gift arrived for Annie from Mrs. Tichenor, a beautiful greyhound who soon earned himself the sobriquet of *Roamer*. He wandered away from the dooryard on several occasions within his first months but was always found, once as far away as Dump east of Chico. He never was broken of his independent spirit, and it was finally his downfall a few years later when the ranch shepherd at the Bidwells' outlying sheep operation shot and killed Roamer when he joined a band of unruly dogs attacking newborn lambs.

On July 20, 1876, Cora Kennedy gave birth to a second son whom she and Johnny named Joseph John. Again, Mrs. Wayland had taken over the feminine fussing that new mothers need and relish, so Annie stayed in the background. Johnny was unable to do any farm or other work outside now, and he was helpful to Cora around their house. Sometimes when the warmth of the summer overheated the Kennedy's little house, Johnny moved into the mansion until the weather changed. Painting around his home also disturbed his breathing. If Guy and little Joey were very sick and fretful, Johnny would accept an invitation from the Bidwells until both he and the children recovered. It was accepted now, sadly, but with resignation, that Johnny was never to get really well. His symptoms of shortness of breath, chronic cough and swollen limbs suggest that congestive heart failure was the basis for his lingering illness.

Eighteen seventy-six being the year of the U.S. Centennial celebration, the Bidwells took part in the September Chico program to observe the anniversary, then departed for the East where the "big" party was to take place in Philadelphia.

John left Annie in New York where she was met by her sister Sallie, and then he spent the next four weeks in Philadelphia, joined for a few days by Annie, her mother and sister. It was October 29 before Bidwell turned up at the recently leased Kennedy home on N Street in Washington, a smaller house more suited to the lessened social demands of Joseph C. G. Kennedy's new profession of financial adviser and real estate broker.

Bidwell arrived unannounced, taking a hack in the middle of the night from the Washington railway station. He had a tale to tell of coping with a drunken hack driver—so intoxicated that Bidwell had ordered him out of the driver's seat and taken the reins himself.[6]

Perhaps Bidwell regretted the weeks he had taken to visit and examine thoroughly all the fascinating exhibits at the Philadelphia Exposition. If so, he came to that realization as he arrived in Washington, and he soon announced that he must return home within the week to attend to ranch business. In a nervous frenzy, Bidwell purchased his return train tickets and took off, in his haste failing to kiss his mother-in-law goodbye, an omission she made much of to Annie. Bidwell heard of his grave error so many times from Annie that he eventually replied in some irritation, "Please give your mother twenty kisses for the one I lost."

Annie's first letter written after this short visit was agreeable enough. "My dear -John?—I must say adieu … to my good but naughty husband, whom, however, I forgive." The odd use in this sentence of "John?" was a reference to an attempt that Bidwell had been making over a period of some months to have his wife and in-laws stop the use of "General" as their common appellation for him. In truth, he had always considered the use of a military title in peacetime as an affectation. After the Civil War, many veterans of military service did continue to use in their names their rank as officers. Some were pleased and flattered thereby. Other sensed that it gave an advantage. John Bidwell had long before cautioned Annie to use his rank only when she needed to get attention of some railway employee or other petty official. He had gently been trying to break her of her affectionate use of "General" in speaking to or of him. One can almost imagine that he had most recently reminded her during the moments of irritation when he was trying to get away from Washington, *"And don't call me General!"* It was a habit that Annie and her parents never gave up entirely in spite of his protestation.[7]

Annie's letters that followed her husband back to Chico and greeted him that winter gave evidence that she had been brooding over a number of things. She began sending orders through the mail, and in an unmistakably whiney tone.

"Will you have Mr. Stevenson remain all winter? [He may have expected me to return with you.]

"I told him that if you made a good visit here, I would return with you, but if you made a shabby visit I would remain."[8] She had remained in Washington.

"I will try to be philosophical as yourself and shut my eyes to everything but the present duty … and be cheerful."[9]

"I often wonder if you ever pray for me and those I love."[10]

"Don't fail to be punctual at prayer meeting. So much depends on attention to these matters."[11]

"How I long for one of Mr. Woods' good sermons. The pastor here has such a monotonous voice. It is impossible to realize it is the same church through which I received so many blessings."

"My dearest—John? my precious husband. … I love to think of our happy table talks."[12]

She wrote a somewhat giddy letter reporting her and her parents' plan that John return to Washington in the spring to accompany her home.

He wrote back several times in as near anger to his wife as he permitted himself, listing the troubles he had at the ranch, capping it off with the account of how the Reverend John Woods had been witnessed, not by one but by three Chicoans, coming from a brothel in San Francisco![13]

To the first letter chiding her for assuming he could leave his responsibilities in Chico so easily, she wrote a contrite letter, admitting that it had been a foolish wish. "I beg over and over forgiveness for my unfortunate letter … [but] you have never spent over two weeks here at a time, since we were married eight and half years since. And a total of less than six weeks in Washington. … So I do not think you should think hard of me for wishing you were here. …"[14]

As to the account of the Reverend John Woods' by now irrefutable behavior: "The reference to Mr. Wood I struggled to disbelieve from the first. … I know how you scorn to challenge anyone who falsely accuses you. … And I know how despicable it is to believe rumors against people. I do not believe that Mr. Woods is a hypocrite. I believe he fell in an hour of temptation. I cannot believe his sermons were hypocritical."[15]

On hearing that Rev. Woods had resigned and left Chico without ever admitting himself guilty, Annie sadly accepted the truth of his fall, and expressed herself willing to forgive should he confess and repent, but she decided Woods should never preach again unless he did publicly repent.

The Chico church tried to keep the whole matter within the walls of the church; even Mrs. Mickey was willing to drop her demands for revenge in order to protect the church. It is more than likely that the matter did filter through the gossip channels of Chico in spite of the resolve of the Presbyterians. In fact, Bidwell was sure the whole town had heard the men who saw Woods leave the "vile resort" telling of it.

John Bidwell wrote over and over again to Annie in agitation over the matter. As chairman of the Trustees, he had had a visit from the Reverend Woods about his resignation, which was worded "I do not find this climate beneficial to my health." Bidwell had seen the couple and their daughter off on the train, and even paid up the $700 in back salary to Woods because of his high regard for Mrs. Woods and sympathy for her pain. She apparently believed none of the charges and was heartbroken. The report that Woods preached in Marysville two Sundays after his departure from Chico left Bidwell in near disbelief at Woods' apparent total lack of a sense of guilt.[16]

When John Bidwell got his dander up it was hard for him to cool down. Annie had written suggesting that John pick some wild grapes for jelly, and that it would be nice if he took little Guy Kennedy along for the ride.

"You ask me to take Guy with me to pick grapes!!!!! How could you be so out of tune! Or have so little appreciation for the situation here! Pick wild grapes! That would be like stopping to pick up an apple going over the falls at Niagara! ... I would like to have a few bunches myself, but do not expect to get a moment's time to pick them. Take Guy to pick wild grapes!"[17]

She wrote back of her worry that John was "so driven!"

He followed his letter of exasperation the next day by adding: "Well, perhaps I was a little cranky about the invitation to return to Washington so soon. ... And even now you seem to think I ought to spend more time in Washington. And I really fear you think I might if I would. And if you really think so, there is where you fail to appreciate the situation and feel the burden which I feel—and I feel it all for your sake—become wrecked and ruined—but staying away will do it and speedily. The debts grow amazingly and the means to meet them lag behind. ... You do not imagine how much I could have saved during my short absence [in Philadelphia and Washington]—not less than $5,000 I really believe. ... If you could see matters as they are you would persuade me ... to stay here with all earnestness at command."[18]

Annie: "[you say] my letter exceeds yours in the length of its criticisms! Well so it is! the scholar often outstrips the teacher!"[19]

He wrote: "Well, I hope we are just even—I have scolded back enough to balance accounts and now let us be friends. And even dearer than any other friends. I may get out of tune sometimes, but I try to get back as soon as I can."[20]

As Christmas, 1876, approached, Annie lamented again for the departed Woods, in part because Mrs. Woods would have handled the Christmas party and gifts for the children at the Indian school. There were plenty of other worries, but nothing seemed to impress on Annie that she should return home. William Stevenson was losing strength, but his family in New York decided that he should stay on at the Bidwell's, Dr. Wayland having implied there was no immediate danger.

Johnny Kennedy was finding simple demands of day-to-day life increasingly difficult, but Bidwell's interference there was out of the question with the Waylands' taking charge so determinedly.

Several years after Johnny's death an exchange between Mrs. Wayland and the Bidwells took place over an incident in which Cora's son Joey had run away, or been lost, and Annie sent the mansion houseman, Charlie Cunningham, to help look for him. Mrs. Wayland's response had been so violent that Annie was not to tell her husband about it for many years, fearing that he might say something to widen the rift, and it was hurtful to Cora.

"Mrs. Wayland had heaped abuse on him [Charlie] and told him to tell you and me never to cross her threshold again, for if she could not hire men to spy on her family, *General Bidwell* should not. ... Charlie was white with emotion when he returned from there. ... I'll never ask Charlie to go to Mrs. Wayland's again, or to do anything for Cora."[21]

Surprisingly, Annie did not seem to grasp the obvious signs that her husband was deep in conflict during the weeks that the Reverend Woods' scenario played itself out. The sins of Woods, out from under which he had crawled so smoothly, using his wife's feelings and the church's reputation as a shield, weighed on Bidwell. Had not he, John Bidwell, paid dearly for his own salvation? Did he not continue to pay by carrying the lion's share of the expenses involved with the Chico Presbyterian Church? He, Bidwell, had personally decided to go the high road in the contest for 1867 Republican gubernatorial nomination. He had resisted the temptation to win by promising high appointment to a vile individual. Had not this high standard of moral behavior during his pursuit of salvation (and, incidentally, Annie's consent to marry him) lost him his chance—probably forever—of being elected governor of California? His trust in his wife's judgment and in God's justice must sometimes have been tried.

In spite of his coaxing and the account of all the troubles in Chico, and more specifically at the mansion, Annie found it impossible to cut her visit in Washington. She wrote once that as sad as it was to see Johnny failing, still it might be God's purpose that they lose Johnny as a means to saving Papa and Joey.[22]

Strange reasoning, perhaps, but she believed that in some way Joe's salvation lay within her powers, and she hoped to use her younger brother's passing and the family he left behind as a wedge into Joe's better nature. She rarely fussed openly of her fears for her father's salvation, except to fret that poor Papa believes that living a good life is enough.

The Indian school had fallen completely apart with Mrs. Woods' leaving and William Stevenson's weakness overcoming him so that he scarcely left his room, and could certainly not be on his feet teaching. Bidwell wrote to her also that the Indians at the rancheria had started drinking; she was badly needed.[23]

None of his pleas moved her resolve. Nor could Brother Johnny's death, when it came a few minutes after the year 1877 opened. Terrible weather in the Eastern states, plus the dependence on Annie for comfort expressed by her parents, delayed the departure for home and her husband week after week in early 1877.

A house for
the dying

*J*ohn Bidwell wired his father-in-law of Johnny's death on New Year's Day within the hour of his passing. He then composed another telegram for the family in Washington, assuring them that all was being done that needed to be done, and that the decision to attend the services was entirely of their choice.[1]

Since embalming of human remains was not yet a practice, had any or all of the family decided to come, the body would have been preserved in ice. The first telegram he received after sending the news of Johnny's death indicated that at least two were coming from Washington for the services. A few hours later, when he received word that no one was coming after all because of extremely harsh weather along the route, Bidwell proceeded to choose Johnny's lot in the Chico Cemetery, which was still owned by Bidwell at that time. However, the Waylands preferred a lot that was owned by John Wayland, Cora's older brother. (John was later moved onto the Bidwell's own lot on Bidwell's orders after the elder Waylands' deaths.)

The funeral was arranged by Hallet and Loy, the Chico coffin suppliers, and by Bidwell and the pastor currently on trial to replace Rev. Woods at the Presbyterian Church, Rev. Agnew. Johnny was buried on January 3, 1877. John Bidwell noted in his diary that twenty-seven carriages were in the funeral train that gathered at the graveside. In the nineteenth century it was customary to judge the respect and liking held for a person in the community by the number of such carriages, and Bidwell was satisfied that Johnny was thought of highly and his family would be gratified. There were even Chinese joining the procession.

The correspondence between Annie and her husband in the month following her brother's death was tortured with her regrets and apology. If she had been there, she wrote, she would have seen that someone sat with Johnny every minute. Bidwell reported he had done that when asked, and he had been at the bedside when Johnny breathed his last. He reported faithfully to Annie the scene at the bedside, with the last words he heard from his brother-in-law: "I am so tired. I wish I could rest before I go."[2]

Annie expressed her gratitude to her husband for sitting with Cora and her family at the funeral in spite of his fear that Dr. Wayland would think he was intruding on their family. She had no idea that Cora would have expected the Kennedy family to come—during bad winter weather. There had been so many train accidents.[3]

Annie requested that the box used as vault for the coffin not be one of Hallet and Loy's prepared ones with their name stamped on the side. Alas, Johnny was buried before that request came and we can only hope that John Bidwell was as sensitive to such things as his wife. Annie requested that John stay at the gravesite until all the dirt was filled in and the grave smoothed. She could not bear to think of strangers roughly shoveling in the caked earth, another request made too late to have been met.

Her brother's death prompted Annie to write of how she wanted her own belongings distributed should she suddenly die. They were all amazed that Johnny had left no will. An unwitnessed one was eventually found.

At her request, John Bidwell sent all he had learned about the causes for Johnny's death. He had been low on energy for years, and increasingly had suffered, first from swollen limbs and then swelling of his face. As he grew sicker, the doctor prescribed an emetic, and Johnny had vomited for a long while, relieving his stomach of food that Bidwell announced had been in it in an undigested form for twelve days! The vomiting was followed by diarrhea which persisted up until his death.[4]

And still the general belief was that he had had tuberculosis. Doctors had always insisted that Johnny's lungs were clear. The belief in Johnny's lungs being tubercular—and of course not to be proved otherwise since no autopsy was performed—led to the denial of payment on his life insurance, even though Dr. Wayland insisted there had been no lung hemorrhage. He condescended to write to Catherine Kennedy and explain. It was all so puzzling to the Washington people, yet they scarcely felt justified to criticize having been too paralyzed to move when the news of Johnny's death came.

Annie's speculation was fueled by the misgivings of her Washington friends and family as to the quality of medical care in Chico. Why was there not a consultation of physicians, asked Annie? And a consultation now being called for in the case of the other invalid in Bidwell's care, young William Stevenson?

Annie had been told of a case "similar" to Johnny's in which the patient had been restored by body massages with bear grease, as well as being administered beef tea enemas. She expressed certainty that such might have saved her brother.[5]

Most particularly Annie's anxiety was made worse by how she had left the Indian school to fall apart. When she came home, all that would change! She would plan with the Indians themselves for their business affairs—would build a chapel—would provide for a teacher. Some of this anxiety came through in a request she made of her husband in late November 1876, after he wrote stating that the school had been disbanded due to lack of a teacher, and that the Indian men were rumored to be drinking on the rancheria.

She asked Bidwell to go to the rancheria and to read the Bible to the adult male Indians. Miss Jessie Lee, who had been teaching the younger children's classes in the school, was too timid to face the men. "It would benefit you more than you can conceive—obeying our blessed Savior," Annie pled.

"My conscience accuses me daily of my unfaithfulness to the poor Indians. ... We in the midst of luxury and every blessing have scarcely lifted a finger for these poor Indians." She reminded her husband that the Indian woman Nopanny who had kept house for Bidwell in the old adobe, and had learned English from him, had sent word through Annie that John Bidwell should go down "and read out of the big book." Nopanny had been converted by Annie, and had taken the charge placed upon Christians very seriously.

"Please do it, my dear husband. My heart is set on you doing it, for God commands you I believe." God had directed Nopanny to make the appeal, thought Annie.[6]

There was no rejoinder to this request, and Annie knew that at times, when pressed where the Indians were concerned, her husband could present a stone wall of silence which indicated she had gone too far in her supplications. He had allowed the school and supported her in it, but he was never to take a personal role in school or chapel services for the Indians.

How she wanted to come home! But her mother expressed terror at the thought of the journey in winter weather. (In the end it was Sallie who returned to Chico with Annie.) Still both her parents drew heavily on her for support during the time for grief. And Annie wrote that she could not bear to have her parents think that she held anyone on earth above them.

It was while they waited for spring and better weather that word came east from Rancho Chico that young Mr. Stevenson had also died.

In the short time that William Stevenson had lived in Chico, he had been an asset to the community. He had reached full manhood—had voted for the first time in Chico. He had accepted responsibility in the Indian school as long as he had strength—had been a popular friend with the young persons in the church, especially the younger men like George Stewart, Ben True, and Major Bailey, the ranch manager.

Bidwell had written Stevenson's brothers and parents repeatedly telling them that the young man was failing. Concerns of travel, both the expense of it and the presumed discomfort, had delayed them. His sister in Pennsylvania had written to Annie in Washington that it seemed to her the trip to heaven must be easier to contemplate than one to California! Too late! Too late!

Annie wrote: "To think of William's funeral from our house and I not there with you. None but God knows how I have endured in silence." Annie still struggled with parental authority. She was thirty-eight, yet wrote "I fear to disobey God who seems to direct me through my parents." "I never want to appear to my parents as caring for another more than for them, Dear General."[7]

One poignant sadness of Johnny's death was that two small sons, one only six months old, were left fatherless and in the care of Cora Kennedy, a widow but twenty-five years old.

It was the year in which the conflict between the local Chinese and the Caucasians who chose to protect them, and the virulent faction that sought to rid the state of Oriental labor, burst forth in some of its most heinous forms. In early March 1877, both Chinatowns in Chico were set on fire by arsonists. Bidwell was one identified by the anti-Chinese faction as an employer of Orientals. His soap factory (leased out) was burned, rebuilt and burned again. Only through great effort and the skill of the Chinese at fighting fires were most of their homes spared.

On March 16 several Chinese farm laborers were murdered on the Lemm Ranch east of Chico, to which law enforcement personnel, to their credit, gave immediate attention. With the help of detectives brought from the Bay Area, the suspected murderers were arrested and lodged in the jail in Oroville.

John Bidwell housed the detectives and was underwriter for the expense, not only because he employed Chinese and was thus a target himself, but also because he despised the cowardice and secrecy of the violent acts. One of Bidwell's barns went up in flames. He had a watch put on his house and grounds. Letters threatening him with retribution were received unsigned, except as from the "Committee."[8]

On April 10, 1877, Annie finally arrived home with her sister Sallie. Again, six months had passed with Annie appearing to allot her Washington family equal if not higher claim than her husband on her time. Bidwell must have been aware of the gossip this situation stimulated among the townspeople. He may have had this in mind when he wrote:

"I have often wondered if other people ever suspected how much I love you? Doubtless many have envied me ... [but] I have an idea that other people do not see you in the light that I do— that they see you as a sprightly interesting accomplished lady, but they do not know your firmness of principles ... what love you have for your relatives—brothers, sisters, parents. Till I became acquainted I never imagined that a being as faultless existed!"[9]

When going together on a camping trip in July 1877, the Bidwells and Sallie discovered Major Bailey, the ranch manager, seriously sick at Big Meadows where he had gone to check on livestock. A doctor was sent for from Chico and Bailey seemed to improve. Bidwell returned to Chico, never liking to be gone long during the crisis which had not abated between the town forces divided on the Chinese question.

Bailey died in the mountains, and was carried back to Chico on a ranch wagon. His coffin was placed (in ice) in the parlor at the mansion. Bailey's three brothers were contacted and eventually arrived and were housed at the mansion. Bailey's remains were interred in the Masonic section of the Chico Cemetery on August 5, 1877, later to be moved by the Bidwells to their own section held for "Bidwell friends."[10]

Less than a year later, in the summer of 1878, the Bidwell Mansion again had an intimate contact with death. A one-time ranch laborer and general ne'er-do-well named Cooley deserted his ailing wife and two small daughters. The three came to the attention of the Ladies Relief Society which Annie Bidwell and Mrs. Crew had organized. While Bidwell tried, unsuccessfully, to bring Cooley to any sense of responsibility for his family, Maria Louise Cooley and her daughters Helen and Lucy were brought to the Bidwell's.[11]

On the day of their arrival at the mansion, baby Helen died. Mrs. Cooley was bedridden for the less than three months she had still to live. During that period, Annie was happy that Mrs. Cooley experienced conversion and was baptized into the Presbyterian Church. In this Mrs. Cooley had support and frequent visitation from the women of the Presbyterian Church.

Maria Louise Cooley and Helen are buried together in the "friends" plot next to the graves of Major Bailey and William Stevenson.

The Women's Relief Society shared in care for Lucy for some months until the adoptive family of Maria Louise was located in Holyoke, Massachusetts, and the very much alive and lovable Lucy returned to them. Until this haven was found for Lucy, Annie for a while again considered adoption, then backed away from it. In February 1878, Annie went with Lucy to Sacramento to see her off on a train bound eastward.

Giving proof to the commitment that Bidwell had made not to desert his position supporting the legitimacy of the Chinese to live and work in California, in August of 1878 the Bidwells were asked to agree to the dying wish of Ah Mow, a Chinatown resident and one-time employee at the Bidwell Ranch. He had asked to die and be buried from the Bidwell Mansion! The mansion received him and permitted the burial services there. The request came from a Mrs. Geer, whose husband was a Bidwell Ranch employee, but, more importantly, Mrs. Geer was friend to the Chinese and confirmed that Ah Mow had been a Christian.[12]

The decision that Ah Mow be buried from the Bidwell home speaks volumes about the determination that John Bidwell had shown in 1878 when the bitter antagonism toward the Chinese of much of the town, including a number of his own ranch employees, had to be faced down. The act of permitting the body to be held in respect in his home was a symbolic gesture that Chicoans were not apt to forget.

The discharge of any employee openly espousing the "Caucasian Cause" was Bidwell's policy. If for no other reason, he could not have a segment of his men fomenting violence against others.

A happy camping trip

Before Sallie Kennedy's return to Washington in October 1877, she and some special guests were to be part of one of the more exciting camping ventures that the Bidwells were to experience.

Bidwell was always in correspondence with experts in the scientific fields that interested him. On this particular September adventure, three men whom Bidwell admired were in California. The Scottish John Muir, of course, was an adopted Californian. He had begun his life on the West Coast as a shepherd, but no work was lowly to Muir. He became well known for his work for the conservation of beautiful and rare natural resources. Muir believed that some natural wonders should belong to the people and reserved for enjoyment and education.

Now Muir and Bidwell had as guests the noted American botanist, Dr. Asa Gray of New York and Harvard University, Mrs. Gray, and Sir Joseph Dalton Hooker, the noted British botanist. Hooker had just completed a scientific trip to the Rocky Mountains when he accepted the invitation to go further westward to California.

In anticipation of a planned outing to both Mt. Shasta and Lassen Peak for this distinguished group, Bidwell devised a practical plan for transport of food, shelter and hay and the several horses needed. He booked passage for September 3 in a freight car from Chico to Redding for wagon, carryall and horses. With them, of course, went a stablehand to care for the outfit until the Bidwells and guests arrived two days later.[1]

Sallie Kennedy (left) spent the summer of 1877 with her sister and brother-in-law. She and the Bidwells found the warm weather tolerable wearing summer "whites." Courtesy of California State Parks.

On September 6, the party of six, plus servants, arrived at Sisson (now Mt. Shasta City). An attempt was made to scale Mt. Shasta by the party, escorted by Mr. Sisson. They had made it only halfway when the restriction of time brought a halt to the attempt. The Grays and Dr. Hooker returned to Redding and embarked for home.

The remaining members of the party went to the Lassen Peak area, first to the Cinder Cone near Black Butte Lake where the Bidwells had camped some years earlier. Muir was the only member of the party to climb to the top of Lassen. The weather was terrible—both rain and snow. They returned to Chico in late September.

Muir had the idea that he should sail down the Sacramento River in a primitive craft, so Bidwell had his workmen fashion such a boat from a hollowed tree. The craft was provisioned with fresh fruits and other edibles from the Bidwell's kitchen. The last the Bidwells and Sallie saw of Muir he was waving goodbye as he disappeared around a bend in the Sacramento River, his little flag fluttering bravely from the stern.[2]

John Muir and Annie Bidwell developed a strong friendship. It seemed based on Annie's response to John Muir's delicate interpretations of all of nature, including animals, and his lighthearted ability to express this in humor as well as lyrical, almost spiritual language. Bidwell himself, though he wrote extensively and clearly, was always a bit awkward and almost stilted in his choice of language to describe his own pleasure at the natural world. He must have been well aware of Annie's being drawn to Muir, and it is to Bidwell's credit that he seemed never to discourage her from correspondence with Muir or her meetings with him in San Francisco when she was visiting there. She urged her husband to do likewise—as he occasionally did.

In 1894, Annie wrote ecstatically to Muir, having received from him a lyrical description of the trip they had made to Shasta and Lassen some years earlier. The exact nature of the material is not stated, but it was definitely neither photographic or in pen or paint, since Annie wrote:

"Do you remember the night near Lassen when we slept under the firs and stars, with saddles for pillows and the heavens for a tent? And how you upbraided us for sleeping at all under such glorious trees and stars! How immense and brilliant the stars seemed. When these pictures rise before me they bring with them sweet odor of pines, with their wild music or solemn stillness, and the exhilarating emotions created by the great canons, dashing waters, mighty peaks, exquisite lakes, surprising by their beauty as well as by their existence. No pictures on canvas possess, for me this image, this magic power. I live the days over and over with all the pleasant rejoicing in more glorious visions, but I believe the beautiful, which has become a part of our being here, will ever remain with us, to add to our future enjoyment. For these too are the works of God, who is eternal!

"How I do thank you for this precious gift; not only for its intrinsic value—for it will carry me into the loved scenes again and lift me 'to the very skies of enjoyment.'

"General exclaimed, 'Oh Annie! What a *precious* gift. We must read it together.'"[3]

Annie's feelings were, of course, entirely innocent, growing from this friendship that had a spiritual quality given to it through Muir's special gift of interpreting nature. Perhaps it was due to Mrs. Muir's interpretation of the friendship that she never quite managed to accept for herself or her children the open invitation from the Bidwells to visit Rancho Chico.

Putting down
more roots
in California

*A*nnie accompanied her sister as far as Elko, Nevada, on the train when Sallie departed for home in October 1877, after the thrill of the summer's adventures at Shasta and Lassen. At John Bidwell's suggestion, a stopover was made at Lake Tahoe, and the women were thrilled by the beauty of the setting, and by the clearness of the deep blue water in particular.

The fact that it was nearly two years before she was again to see a member of the Washington, D.C., Kennedy family, gives an indication that Annie was beginning to feel more a settled part of the Chico life of her husband, and a determination to seriously focus her efforts on the mission work with the rancheria Indians. A large part of her satisfaction came from her developing friendships with other Chico women willing to assist her, although admittedly the ladies who volunteered were often rather short on durability. The new pastor at the Presbyterian Church, Rev. Ellis, did not stir the same warm feelings that a meeting of like minds with Rev. Woods had roused in Annie, but that chapter was put firmly behind the Bidwells and the church family at last.

The congregation had a difficult time after Woods' departure from the pulpit, finding no replacement that satisfied everyone. The Reverend Agnew, an Irishman with a heavy brogue, was a popular choice among many, particularly the less sophisticated members like Abram Bidwell. Franklin Lusk, the attorney, could not tolerate Agnew, "A laughing stock in the town!"

It was then that Lusk had irritatingly said to Bidwell, in effect, "Why don't you make the decision and be done with it? You know this congregation will go along with anyone you prefer."[1] But Bidwell had insisted on a democratic choice, and so it fell to the Reverend Ellis from Nebraska.

The church had its problems. During heavy winds and rains in the winter of 1877–78 the steeple blew off.

Ben True, the dauntless Chico constable who had stood up to rioters during the attacks on Chico's Chinatowns, was also a faithful member of the choir at Chico Presbyterian Church. He ran into a bit of trouble when he augmented the choir's delivery one Sunday with a trumpet solo. Watson Chalmers, a trustee about whom Bidwell (faithful to the caustic streak in his personality) complained privately to Annie, would say anything to hear the sound of his own voice on any topic at any time, spoke out vehemently against the sacrilege of using a brass instrument in church.

True had certainly showed his Christian spirit when, during the floods of January 1878, he had gone with Bidwell, George Stewart and Abram Bidwell to rescue the Chinese flooded out along the Sacramento River's edge.

Annie became better acquainted with the Carrolls, the Sacramento family who were longtime friends of John Bidwell. The Bidwells were often houseguests of the Carrolls. They stayed with them to attend the "brilliant" reception given by then Governor George Perkins in 1880. The Carrolls and their two daughters, Minnie and Leila, also visited in Chico and enjoyed the hospitality of the mansion. Mr. Carroll declared it the most handsome country estate in all of California. Minnie Carroll was to come under Annie's wing during ensuing years when the mansion was a haven for her and her children after her marriage to the prominent Bay Area businessman, Charles O. Alexander, often found her left alone to care for the children for weeks on end.

Annie Bidwell in a portrait taken before her hair turned gray in her thirties, as with most members of the Kennedy family. Courtesy of California State Parks.

The Gibbs family that had resettled in San Francisco from Washington (or rather seemed to maintain homes in both places) welcomed the Bidwells to stay when they went to the Bay City. Annie was rather annoyed with John in that he preferred the independence of staying at a hotel when on business in San Francisco, even (it seemed to her) begrudging the time to be social and call on the Gibbs when he was in the city. Augusta

Gibbs came to visit at Bidwell Mansion rather often, and occasionally with her husband who was deeply engaged in speculating on the production of new inventions.

Another easterner to settle out west from Baltimore to Black Point, was Annie's cousin Maggie Ellicott, now married to a Dr. Woodhull, who was attached to the U.S. Army at the San Francisco Presidio. Their home was at Black Point near the city. The Woodhulls came occasionally to Chico and provided ties between Annie's earlier life and her role as Mrs. John Bidwell. Some glimpse into Annie's continued lack of ease among Chico women came from a letter to John written during a visit with her cousin Maggie Ellicott Woodhull.

"I find there is a relish in our mutual society which I miss wherever I go [in Chico]."[2]

During her last extended six-month visit in Washington, Annie had written to her husband of the need to expand her mind. She took drawing lessons (not to be mentioned lest she find that she had no talent), and confided to John that she would return to take more French language lessons from Madame Burr while in Washington. John Bidwell wrote advising against more French. She already had as much skill as she would ever be likely to use—enough to "enable you to build on." He suggested that she ask her Papa to help her review her Latin, or study Spanish or German.[3]

This advice Annie cheerfully ignored, and it was a great delight to her to find a French teacher right in Chico—a Madame Trincano, who also gave music lessons. A weekly session in French was set up for the Bidwell library. Annie invited any other women in town who wished to join her in this cultural endeavor. A few did from time to time, often the younger single women in the church, but most dropped out or were irregular in attendance. Annie herself was not too faithful with the classes, but they were held off and on over several years.[4]

Annie's health seemed much better. Other than suffering from an occasional cold and sore throat, she managed to avoid the summer aches and chills of malaria, which was rampant among the ranch labor force. The carrier of malaria had not yet been traced to the mosquito. Bidwell himself tried to associate the disease in some way with the environment, and referred to it as found wherever masses of rotting vegetation are allowed to accumulate.

Inspired by their recent exposure to such botanical greats as Hooker and Gray, the Bidwells liked to go on botanizing jaunts of their own. In June of 1879 they took their new gardener, Mr. Proud, and explored the countryside of Dogtown and Nimshew for new plants to itemize. Another time they went along Clear Creek from Pence and up the streams of the Paradise Ridge. They camped in Helltown along Butte Creek near the cabin of a well-known folk poet, miner Pres Longley. Longley was so admiring of Mrs. Bidwell that he wrote an acrostic poem in her honor, which she thought so lightly of that it seems lost to posterity.[5]

Cora Wayland Kennedy had no hesitancy in accepting a helping hand from the Bidwells once the crisis of Johnny Kennedy's death was behind her and the Waylands permitted her to take over more of the direction of her own life. She was forced into this direction by the fact that Bidwell had been appointed to assist her in administering her husband's will.

John Kennedy's sons, Annie's nephews, left semi-orphaned at an early age, Joseph John and Guy Reynolds, ca. 1878. Courtesy of California State Parks.

Although the Kennedys owned a small home in Chico, Johnny had borrowed heavily upon it at Mr. Faulkner's bank, and Cora's signature firmly tied her to the commitment. Johnny had taken $10,000 insurance, and now the insurance company and their attorney, the seemingly disloyal Mr. Lusk, implied that Johnny had lied when getting the insurance. The insurance company claimed that Johnny's lungs had not been sound at all, and furthermore, Dr. Cheney, a fellow Presbyterian as well as physician, should have known that! It was with a sickening realization that Cora faced the need to work and support herself as soon as her children were old enough to be left in the care of others.[6]

Meanwhile she was heavily dependent. What little property Cora still owned after her debts were paid was watched carefully, for both Annie and John feared that Cora could easily be deceived by a dishonest buyer. For a short period, Cora showed signs of resentment typical of the elder Waylands at the Bidwell's managing of her affairs, and half inclined to blame them for the penury in which she found herself.

The children, Guy and Joey, were increasingly in evidence at the Bidwells over the years. The death of Dr. Wayland from pneumonia in 1880 added to the burden—they would not so have termed it—that fell to Annie and her husband. But the pleasure derived by the childless Bidwells appeared to be genuine, and John Bidwell discovered a capacity within himself to relate well to the little boys, even if it was to "spoil" them.

A visit from Annie's parents

As events were to evolve, Joseph C. G. Kennedy was to visit his daughter and son-in-law in Chico but one time, and that was in the fall of 1879. He had long refused to travel to California based on two given reasons: He would not accept the gift of the expenses involved in such a trip (though he did allow Annie to pay for both her mother's and her sister's travel expenses on several occasions), and he felt he could not be absent from his Washington office for an extended period. For the latter, his reasons were obvious. Though his son Joe was supposedly an associate in the Kennedy business of real estate and financial planning, Joey's dissolute ways made him totally unreliable. Even when sober, Joey seemed to carry a constant chip on his shoulder, suspecting that he was being taken advantage of.

Why Annie's father decided that he finally could get away in 1879 is not clear, but it had much to do with his having found a young man for his office who was much more reliable than his son Joe. Joseph M. Morrison from Crawford County, Pennsylvania, was a first cousin to the Kennedy children, a son of Catherine's brother Joseph.

Kennedy let Catherine precede him west by a month. This was a compromise, for she had vowed she would not make the trip to California again without him.

It was August 6, 1879, that Mr. Kennedy first set eyes on the ranch. He arrived just as the wheat harvest was beginning and was introduced to this delightful—to him—spectacle for his first time.[1]

While delighted to have his in-laws together in his home, Bidwell had to borrow money from a Chico bank to entertain, since farm income at that time of the year awaited the transfusion from sale of the wheat harvest.

Kennedy arrived at a time to witness a number of events. One was the violent act of which the anti-Chinese element was suspected. A barn with stored hay and much of a vineyard went up in flames on the ranch.

Guy Kennedy, now eight, received his first horseback ride as his grandfather watched, and was soon after to be presented with his own white pony by the Bidwells.

There were many fascinating things for the first-time visitor to see. Kennedy was driven to the Sacramento River landing in the cool early morning hours before breakfast, rode northward on a clear day to get a view of sparkling white Mt. Shasta, visited the hydraulic mine at Cherokee and lunched with a Spring Valley Mine official, Louis Glass.

The Kennedys visited the California State Fair and were guests with Annie and John at the Carroll's. They went with Annie as escort (it was too busy a time of year for Bidwell to be gone, he having had trouble finding a replacement for Major Bailey as manager) to San Francisco, Yosemite Valley, Madera, Big Trees Park and Los Angeles.

The Carrolls again opened their Sacramento home in October to the two couples who joined the enormous citywide reception and celebration held in Sacramento for the former U.S. president (as well as personal acquaintance of both the Kennedys and Bidwells), General Ulysses S. Grant. It was a glittering affair, and a suitable send-off for the Kennedys who boarded their train at Sacramento for Washington on October 25, 1879.

It was not an easy chore to host her parents, Annie found. The authoritarian nature of her father led to his constant changing of plans that Annie and her husband might have earlier devised as entertainment. A trip planned for a day might be vetoed entirely by Annie's father, who having been studying the local area from maps and conversations with Bidwell, declared he preferred to go elsewhere. He was less apt to try this when his son-in-law had prepared the itinerary, such as the tour made of Cherokee and its mines. With Annie J. C. G. Kennedy was constantly shifting directions.

The one practice her father had of greedily accepting railway passes gave her more anguish than any other perversity on his part. She wrote to her husband, who had not accompanied the other three on their travels to sites in Southern California, that knowing of John's strong dislike of the favoritism practiced by the railroad moguls when it served their purposes, and his personal aversion to accepting passes, Annie was led to almost any trick to buy tickets ahead before her father could be offered the free ones.[2]

Sallie's doomed love affair

For a married women, Annie was exceptionally close to her parents and siblings, perhaps especially to Sallie with whom she found more to share as the years passed. The easy relationship between Sallie and John Bidwell helped enormously in freeing Annie to continue to confide in Sallie as they had when younger, since Annie had vowed to hold nothing back from John.

Perhaps now the tie between sisters had grown even closer. One suspects that they exchanged many intimate feelings that both were reluctant to risk exposing to other family members, and as the family circle grew smaller, more of these intimacies were channeled to the other.

Annie's correspondence reveals large gaps where letters to and from Sallie certainly passed and were deemed too personal in nature to risk being read by later judges, these most likely being Annie's nephews.

Since none of Annie's letters to Sallie or her parents survive, it is to be assumed that the Kennedys were not the savers that Annie was, or that Annie had a much deeper conviction of the destiny that ruled her life with Bidwell, and that all might prove valuable to history.

Still, Annie did not save every letter from Sallie or from her parents. Into this category of lost letters is a vividly angry and vitriolic letter that Joseph C. G. Kennedy sent Annie early in 1880 after it became known to him that Sallie's hand in marriage was being requested of her father by Joseph M. Morrison.

Catherine and Joseph Kennedy discovered a few months after they returned to Washington from California that Sallie had fallen in love with the cousin Joseph Morrison whom Kennedy had hired to fill in at his office during their absence.[1]

Kennedy's immediate reaction was to accuse the couple of secretly carrying on a romance they knew to be wrong. For one thing, they were first cousins—that in itself was not illegal—but in addition, Morrison had been previously married and was divorced.

The Kennedys then professed that they had wondered at the pointed sermons Rev. Paxton had preached since their return from California—seemingly directed at the Kennedy pew—about the forbidden nature of marriage of divorced persons. Such marriages were said in almost all cases to be equal to adultery, and the never-married person of the union was most certainly adulterous as well. Somehow, the Kennedys learned that Sallie had been to talk with their pastor about her position in the church should she marry a divorced man.

Sallie was thirty-four, and for years had been a popular member of the Washington social set, with men and women both married and unmarried. Young people, including men, were in and out of the Kennedy home constantly, and Sallie had had many beaus. Her parents had speculated about her affections settling here or there for years, and now to learn that she had fallen in love with Joseph M. Morrison fell upon them like a black cloud of disgrace.

First, the father of the family assumed that Sallie had been seduced, if not physically, then emotionally, in her parents' own home in their absence. Morrison had taken advantage of the generosity shown him and the position of trust given to him in the Kennedy business.

The letter that Annie received from her father, a diatribe relating his accusations, was the first that Annie had heard of the love between her sister and cousin. She had heard mention of their cousin Joe Morrison many times, in allusions Sallie had made in letters sent in her parents' absence, and doubtless Catherine had chatted on about this Pennsylvania relative who had been hired by her husband while they were in Chico. Sallie told of occasions when she and Cousin Joseph and brother Joey had been in and out together at functions, and had dined together in the Kennedy home.

Kennedy's letter to Annie and Bidwell condemning the couple was as nothing to the letter Kennedy had written Joseph Morrison himself. He accused him of dishonorable intentions and behavior, of fortune-seeking, and of sneaking into Sallie's life when she was defenseless, her parents absent in California.

Poor Annie took to her bed with this news. As it happened, John Muir was visiting when the first angry letter from Annie's father arrived. Annie held herself together until Muir departed, then collapsed into bed on March 4 and did not leave her room again until March 28.[2]

Catherine Kennedy was equally distraught. She could not sleep or eat. At first she agreed with her husband's assessment and was angry at Sallie for her part in what seemed to have been deception.

Then the usually cool and inwardly guarded Sallie broke down and confessed to her mother that though neither had planned any such outcome, she and Joseph Morrison had realized, almost simultaneously, the strong love that had developed between them. They had talked seriously about the likelihood of this very response from Kennedy, had discussed putting aside their feelings, and after agreeing that it was impossible to deny their love, they decided to wait, first, until Joseph Morrison could reach a financial level adequate to support Sallie, and, second, until her parents could be convinced that his divorce was not a result of immoral behavior on his part, and that he left no trail of immoral behavior.

Sarah "Sallie" Kennedy, two years younger than her sister Annie and Annie's closest friend and confidante except for John Bidwell. Sallie was probably in her thirties and already turning quite gray. Courtesy of California State Parks.

Morrison's ex-wife had no grudge against him. (Kennedy at once had hired a detective to explore the culprit's background.) Often in those times, one or the other of an incompatible couple agreed to do the necessary "deserting," and this was probably the case with the Morrisons.

With such a show of emotion and appeal from Sallie, Catherine was quite soon won over to her daughter's side in the matter, and wrote Annie that in her opinion Kennedy should take Joseph Morrison into his firm as a partner and bless the union.

Young Morrison was well educated. He probably had attended Allegheny College in Meadville near where he grew up. He had been a teacher in Sagerstown, Pennsylvania.

On receiving Kennedy's blistering letter, Morrison wrote a strongly worded letter in reply to, as Catherine described it, the "really wicked and cruel" letter from the older man. Morrison declared there could be no estrangement of feelings between him and Sallie: "What kind of strange and unnatural sentiment would that be in a man who expects to marry your daughter?"

Catherine copied the two letters from Morrison to Kennedy word for word for Annie, in one of which Morrison accused Sallie's father of temporarily "dethroning his reason." He, Morrison, would gladly have his private character matched with Joseph C. G. Kennedy's any day, and it would not suffer in the comparison!

It had really rankled the young man that Kennedy had accused him of base fortune hunting. He stated that so far as he knew the only property that Kennedy had deeded his daughter Sallie was two "slave shanties," scarcely a prize for the fortune hunter.

Sallie got word back to Joseph Morrison that her father's feelings were not softened in any way. He had violently condemned them both, and told Sallie that if this marriage should occur he, Kennedy, could not go on living. And when he died, he did not want her, Sallie, anywhere near his body.

The unfortunate couple put aside any hopes of marriage. Sallie returned to the cheerful energetic demeanor that masked her feelings (so her mother reported), and Joseph M. Morrison faded from her visible life.

How Annie and John Bidwell reacted to this matter in their private conversations is not known, and of course, her letters on the subject did not survive. Only later, after Mr. Kennedy's death, did John suggest the marriage might now take place.[3]

Annie wrote back to John on her next trip to Washington in late 1880 that Cousin Morrison had been pointed out to her as he passed by on a sidewalk—too brief an encounter to form an opinion, but not so handsome as her mother had described, tall, wearing a straw hat, and looking rather preoccupied and grim.

John Bidwell's diary seldom included anything of so "private" a family matter. The freedom with which he expressed himself in letters to Annie suggests that he made no attempt to safeguard his diary, left in his bedroom all day, from prying eyes.

The rancheria school

*A*nnie had ecstatically told John Bidwell that she wept for joy that he had permitted her to proceed with plans for a school for the Indian women and children. Her twin ambition was to teach them to speak and write English, and that they should be converted to Christian ways and beliefs. Her second great joy was that the women in the main responded to her with friendliness, and with eagerness on the part of the younger wives. She often repeated that she felt it was from the opening she had accomplished with her sewing opportunities that the Indian women were willing to be her friends.[1]

With the commitment to the school in which both religion and literacy would be taught, she found that she had taken on herself a responsibility that often weighed on her conscience. She felt she sometimes neglected the Indians for her family duties, and in dividing her commitment to the Indians with that to her husband and her family in Washington there seemed never sufficient time to do justice to either.

Some details of the school's beginning have already been described in these pages, and Annie's achievements in introducing the younger Rancho Chico Indians into the mainstream have been summarized. But the tentative steps that led to the acceptance of the school as a part of an already well-defined pattern of Indian life on the rancheria have been skipped over.

Soon after her return home from Washington in May 1875, Annie had extended an invitation to the women in the Presbyterian Church to join her in opening a school for the Indians, and it appealed to those who could see the need. The first meeting to organize included only Mrs. Donahue and Mrs. McMillan, both wives of tradesmen; Mrs. Woods, the pastor's wife and Miss Stewart, daughter of the recently deceased pastor. They "organized" their approach, agreeing that Mrs. McMillan, who had had some experience, should be the teacher.

The following week Mrs. Hobart, Bidwell's niece and sister to Mary Reed, replaced Mrs. Donohue. The foursome now drove to the rancheria and with some trepidation sought out the Indian women in their homes to show samples of the fabric and patterns they were offering for making garments and to invite them and their children to what they termed an Industrial Mission School.

Only a few women were willing to leave their houses to speak to Annie or the others. Nopanny and Lizzie, two Indian women who had already learned to speak English passably, accompanied the four Presbyterian ladies and urged the timid Indian women and girls to come out. An invitation was relayed to the others to meet the following day in the vacated frame building near the mansion.

The rancheria women's attention seemed more taken with concern that one in their midst, Pamaho's wife, said to be George Clements' mother, was very ill. "Going to die."

With high but uncertain expectations, the following day at ten o'clock, three women were ready in the classroom (Emma had left the enterprise), joined by another pastor in town, the Reverend Rice and both Rev. and Mrs. Woods. But not one pupil!

Annie and Mrs. McMillan drove at once to the rancheria and found that George's mother had indeed died and the grave had been dug in the middle of the street between their homes and the burial rites just at an end.

The next school day, four Indian women did put in an appearance along with five children, among them Amanda and George. Both Amanda and George, who were approximately thirteen and ten years old, could read some already, it is noted in the record kept by Miss Stewart, who had been appointed secretary. It was not mentioned how or by whom they had been taught.

The school continued weekly. Each week the women and older girls, Amanda among them, went home with new garments that the "teachers" had cut from simple patterns to sew by hand with needles and thread distributed in class. The cutting out of these much sought items took too much of the allotted class time in Annie's thinking and detracted from the lessons, but that was where the interest largely lay.

On September 14, class was canceled when word came from the rancheria that all women and children were preparing for a Big Time, a traditional Maidu festival. George was reported as in Durham helping "clean" for the Big Time. In Annie Bidwell's notes, this event was connected to the burning, another traditional rite in remembrance of the dead, and many baskets were in preparation. Chief Winoka was being mourned at this time.

Attendance was poor as classes resumed. It was harvest time, and many of the boys had employment or tribal work to perform. When the reasons for the absence of half the student body was noted on October 5, the minutes reflect those excuses:

Emma's husband opposed her coming. Sesook "go to his sister's at Oroville." Lewis, "too lazy to come." Alissa and Samantha had "gone to Durham's." George "ain't want to come." Susy: "Can't learn. Don't want to come." Whether these are the words of the truants or of the reporter is not certain.

Attendance was reportedly poor on October 22 as many prepared to attend a great dance in Cottonwood. On October 26 no pupils showed up. They were too tired from the dancing!

On November 9, after weeks of poor attendance, school was canceled for the salmon season at Deer Creek.

In mid-November classes picked up again when William Stevenson, who had recently arrived from the East for health reasons, took over teaching the boys such subject matter as was deemed appropriate for males: arithmetic, geography, and writing.

The year ended with what was to become a tradition with Annie and the rancheria residents—whether students or otherwise—a feast to celebrate Christmas, with gifts for the children and special food for all in the rancheria.

The school struggled on during the winter months and on March 7, 1876, a record seventeen students, women and children, filled the classroom. The women demanded more and more sewing items, and Miss Jessie Lee, daughter of a Chico pharmacist, volunteered to help. She was to continue as a valuable asset to the school until she married in 1879.

Summer came on with extreme heat, and Stevenson had to take refuge in the mountains. The disgrace and fall from favor of the Reverend Woods had not yet surfaced. He was helpful, and preached at a service Annie arranged for the Indians in June.

No one was willing to take over the responsibility for keeping the ambitious enterprise going when the Bidwells departed for the Philadelphia Centennial Celebration in mid-September, and the school ceased to function. It remained closed for nearly a year. Even John Bidwell, who had been slow to approve the idea of the school, now wrote to Annie that by Christmas of 1876, the Indian men at the rancheria were drinking. He thought that if she would return soon to revive the good influence the weekly school had on the women, the men too would benefit.

It was a trying time for Annie. From Washington she wrote of her suffering conscience as regards the Indian children. She was coping from afar with the deaths of both her brother John and of William Stevenson. When she did arrive back in Chico, she had with her Sallie, and with the summer heat, many weeks were spent seeking respite in the mountains. There were Cora's financial matters to deal with and the traumatic death and funeral of the ranch foreman, Major Bailey.

Annie briefly held classes in June and July of 1877, with Miss Lee's help, to a small group of Indian children—not more than five or six. The school closed at the end of July until after Sallie's departure.

After the Christmas "feast" and gift giving that year, the school closed again. When it reopened, Annie resorted to paying teachers, most $5 a month, and school was extended to twice a week. Records are scanty, but as Annie's absence on her trips to Washington took her away at intervals, it was difficult to maintain momentum. At one time the school was closed for nearly two years.

Annie later credited the urging of Nopanny, the shadowy woman from John Bidwell's past, married now to Billy Preacher, with revitalizing the efforts to teach and convert the Indians of the rancheria. This was to include men and women alike, and in order to make the facilities more attractive and available, a new schoolroom and a nice chapel were constructed.

The chapel was dedicated on December 3, 1882. The all-out effort to complete school and church was assisted by John Bidwell, who noted in his diary both shopping for a stove for the schoolroom and putting seats in the chapel.[2] Both of these buildings were on outlying land north of the mansion and nearer the rancheria which had along its north side the Rancheria Lane, now Sacramento Avenue.

Reports published about Annie Bidwell have variously reported her having been "ordained" or "licensed" to preach and perform certain church rites for the Indians in their chapel. No such license has been found by this author, but in 1879 Annie Bidwell sought advice from a prominent Presbyterian pastor in San Francisco and was told that it was within the power of her own "session," the governing body of the Chico Presbyterian Church, to grant such authority.[3] The Chico Session probably granted her the desired authority in 1879.

However, she could not, and never did, perform marriages, this being a church rite that included the assumption of civil as well as religious authority.

As the school drew the attention of organized Indian philanthropies, it was named Indian Presbyterian Mission School. Annie began requiring her hired teachers to keep regular monthly reports to send to the Occidental Board of the Women's Foreign Missionary Society to whom she petitioned for assistance.

One of the teachers was Grace Stanley, a member of Annie's Sunday school class at the "downtown" church and still in her teens. Grace's father was an employee on the Rancho Chico. Grace's report for March–April 1885, lists twenty-three pupils. The names are an indication of time passing. Among the pupils is Maggie Lafonso, two-year-old daughter of Amanda, who was married to Holai Lafonso, chief of the rancheria Indians. Amanda still appeared in class occasionally, perhaps to assist, and always eager to have articles to sew.

The granddaughter of Grace Stanley heard related an occurrence in which the Indian women (and perhaps the men) were made irate over Grace's slapping of an unruly little boy. The Indian women were quick to express their reaction to the teachers, and word usually reached Annie if they had a complaint—unless she was in Washington. Apparently, Grace's action did not bring about her dismissal, but some parental feelings had to be soothed.[4]

One overwrought volunteer teacher quickly had enough. "Some teacher!" muttered the Indian women between themselves. "Ain't seen her but once."[5] It is suspected that a great number of goodhearted Presbyterian ladies shared the same fate, as well as members of Annie's Sunday school class who volunteered only if she was on hand to coax. Isabel Tilden Crosette obviously soon felt intimidated by the classroom of Indian women and children and found an excuse to avoid reporting for duty when she could. One day she dismissed the class early, causing Nopanny to write

to Annie Bidwell, "Funny new teacher. Ain't seen her again."
When Mrs. Crosette's name was mentioned in the school thereafter, the women all laughed.

It should be pointed out that the children in the rancheria
school were not given to feeling submissive or awed at the situation, once school became routine. They could be naughty, rude,
and needing of discipline. The mothers' presence in the school
had helped supply this control. As it came more and more to
resemble a standard classroom, teachers were challenged to rise to
many situations. Annie Bidwell attempted to follow the philosophy that Christian love and patient demonstration of behavior
models were the best teachers in this instance. No example has
been recorded of major problems, but approbation noted gives
some hint that all the students could not claim the praise given to
Lucy, a girl student who died. Annie wrote that "she [Lucy] was a
lady. Never guilty of a coarse act."[6]

By 1886, the Occidental Board of Women's Foreign Missions
was sufficiently impressed by Annie's reports to them that they
agreed to subsidize the school by paying the salary of a teacher.
Annie added to this by paying for special lessons: Mrs. Broyles for
music, for example. Annie Bidwell herself became increasingly
worn out and by 1887 had to leave the classroom entirely for
many months except for short visits.

The most enduring teacher to be paid through the mission
fund was Miss Ida Florence. Ida became a close friend of Annie's,
entrusted with the classroom and with helping in the chapel
services which Annie conducted Sunday mornings for many
years.

Annie Bidwell continued to attend the school's opening
exercises, given to religious teaching or worship, whenever she
could work it into her schedule. She was fond of the Indian
children, and the religious training had priority, if it came to a
decision in that matter.

153

When the mission fund could no longer pay for an instructor in about 1890, the Bidwells together petitioned the Chico Public School Trustees to admit Indian children as their personal wards. Heretofore, no native children had been educated in the public school system, except in special government boarding schools set up for Indians by the federal authorities. After her paid position in the school ended, Miss Florence served as a stenographer for John

Holai Lafonso, husband of Amanda from about 1882–1888, father of Maggie and Elmer Lafonso, and chief of the Mechoopda Tribe until his death in 1905. Courtesy of California State Parks.

Bidwell throughout the 1890s. At that time he was writing articles that had been requested of him telling of his days in California before statehood.

A number of the more advanced Indian youths, including George Clements, were entered into a school for Indians in Lake County in June 1884. An escort was sent for them from Middletown through arrangements made by Annie Bidwell. They remained until December 1886, though George had tired of the school, or worn out his welcome, and appeared back in the rancheria a year earlier.[7]

All was not well in the rancheria village in 1885. It was at a time when Annie Bidwell was working hard to revitalize the school and to interest the mission in financing more of the instruction. Drunkenness among the men had interfered with life there and with work for the ranch. There was a constant turnover in population which Bidwell sought to regulate. The intercourse back and forth with other tribelets in Oroville, Cottonwood,

Durham and Colusa County brought in people of whom Bidwell did not approve. They caused problems with drinking and gambling, and often were not willing to take steady employment on Rancho Chico.

Some strong gesture from the man whom all the Indians knew to hold power over their lives might ease problems in the school and increase the use of the chapel, both areas in which Annie Bidwell had deep commitment.

Thus it was that Bidwell prepared and read a proclamation on the rancheria grounds on June 21, 1885.[8]

The proclamation states:

1st.   Lafonso is chief, and is always to be respected and obeyed as such; and it is his duty to see that these rules be also respected and obeyed.

2nd. Billy Preacher is hereby made chief teacher in temperance and good behavior, and you are directed to pattern after him and to learn to be as good as he is.

3rd.   Luccayan was great and Good chief. He was Nopanny's father, and ought to be remembered by all and his memory respected because he was good.

4th.   This Rancheria is the home of these Indians, and of all Indians who may wish to come and live here, on condition: namely

   1st.   That they obey these rules.

   2nd. That they drink no whisky or other liquor.

   3rd.   That they obey Lafonso as Chief and pattern after Billy Preacher and be good like him.

   4th.   They must be temperate, industrious and good.

   5th.   That all Indians—men, women, and children—must unless in case of illness attend church every Sunday when there is church.

6th.   That parents must send their children to school when old enough, keep them clean, and teach them to be polite.

7th.   That these things are wrong, and therefore forbidden, namely, to swear; to quarrel; to steal; to fight; to hunt or fish on Sunday; and to play ball or other sporting games on Sunday.

5th.   All Indians who now live here or have their families here, and all Indians who may hereafter come to live here, are to have work when I have work for them to do, and they are to have full pay for all the work they may do or earn; but if they go away and work elsewhere, they lose the right to live here; for this place must not be a harbor for tramps or idle or otherwise not useful people.

6th.   All who do not know, or may forget these rules, or any of them, must ask Lafonso, or Billy Preacher, or ask Mrs. Bidwell, and have the rules read, until all shall know them from the least to the greatest.

Witness my hand this 21st day of June, A.D. 1885.

John Bidwell.

Developing new outlets for self expression

The most enduring of social groups, albeit one with a stated charitable purpose, was the Mite Society. Made up of both sexes, the loosely defined membership was of church couples and a few singles.

The "Mites" met at least monthly, and usually more often. The Bidwells were faithful in subscribing though not always in attendance at the evening get-togethers unless Annie was serving as president, as she did more than once. The Mites were also a social group whose meetings sometimes included entertainment. The hostess for the meeting provided refreshments, and to the gossip of the time was added a few prayers.

"Good" projects that might not be funded otherwise by the church budget included a new church carpet and supplies for the choir.

The Wednesday evening prayer meeting held a higher priority, and both Annie and John tried to be faithful in attendance when they were at home in Chico. Since more member participation was required at prayer meetings than at regular church services, they invariably gave John Bidwell an opportunity to observe, to listen to fellow church members, and often to react negatively, judging by acerbic comments in his diary or in letters to Annie. He tended to be intolerant of the foibles of his fellow church members and worked up a head of steam at many gatherings. Annie could and did soothe him during many an explosion on their way home from a church function.

A Miss Maud Blood opened an art studio in Chico in March 1881, and Annie Bidwell joined her class in landscape painting. On nice days a small group of women with easels, pencils and paint boxes in tow, were taken by the Bidwells' carryall to some part of the ranch to paint.[1]

The French classes taught by Madame Trincano continued to meet in the mansion, with usually no more than half a dozen girls and women. Most of them were not very serious and it is doubtful that they retained much of the little French to which they exposed themselves. It was, one presumes, the "in thing" to take French with Mrs. Bidwell.

There seem always to have been guests at the mansion, some requiring more entertaining than others. The noted photographer, Henry Weatherbee Henshaw, was a guest for a week or so at a time over the years 1890–1894. When in the area he photographed both natural scenes and the Indians of Rancho Chico.[2]

The botanist, Professor Asa Gray, with whom Bidwell corresponded and exchanged specimens, approached Bidwell about employing Gray's nephew. The young man seemed a reliable type and had expressed an interest in pursuing horticulture as a career. At John Bidwell's invitation, George Moses Gray came to Chico, first as a guest at the mansion and then as supervisor of Bidwell's orchards. He remained an employee for ten years before buying his own grape and almond ranch. He was a frequent dinner guest until his marriage, and always remained a good friend and fellow Presbyterian.[3]

Another botanist of national renown, C. C. Parry, discovered the Bidwell Ranch, and following his first visit in 1881 continued to find the mansion doors open to him and Mrs. Parry for well over a decade. Parry enlisted John Bidwell in finding plants that had not yet been classified, an assignment that was a joy to Bidwell. Annie was initiated into the fine points of identifying plants by species and subspecies.

Among female guests was Minnie Carroll, the teenage daughter of the Bidwell's Sacramento friends. This was a long-enduring friendship that later included Minnie's children, and for over a score of years helped fill any void that Annie might have experienced at her own childlessness.

The generous hospitality extended by the Bidwells was once tried severely by a young Mr. Richie, who came with a letter of introduction from a Washington acquaintance who had been the childhood friend in England of young Richie's father. The Bidwells were asked to let the young man look over Chico while exploring California as a place to find meaningful employment. Richie was welcomed on April 4, 1893. He soon learned to entertain himself, riding a Bidwell horse or even calling for a carriage for his own use. This might have continued indefinitely, one supposes, except Richie aroused the ire of the cook and waitress by leaving his place at the table vacant without advance notice to the cook. Worse, he showed up late for meals and expected the cook to warm up leftovers and serve him. After four months of increasingly rude behavior, even the hospitable Bidwells caught on that they were being used by someone who never offered his services in any capacity—nor did he even deign to attend Annie's morning prayers for family, guests and staff.

John Bidwell made a visit on the young Richie in his room and gave him until the end of a week to evacuate the mansion. Bidwell wrote letters to both Tom Alexander and Richie's father in England explaining, and he received apologies from the older men. But this Richie incident was a rare ripple in the smooth entertaining procedures worked out for the mansion by Annie.[4]

During 1887 when Annie was suffering from tuberculosis and convalescing in Auburn, the mansion staff had been reduced to one female and Peter, the houseboy. Another maidservant and groundsman had accompanied Annie to ensure her comfort. Bidwell had felt obligated to invite a visitor to Chico to dinner, a Mr. McDonald whom he did not know well but had promised a friend to entertain. As the evening wore on, Mr. McDonald settled only more comfortably into the best easy chair in the room. Bidwell was tired, suffering from a sore hip, and desirous of getting to his bedroom, one way or another, where he still had to write his daily letter to Annie. He called Florence Blake, the maid, and asked which room he should give Mr. McDonald.

Florence, who had already complained at having to be cook, scullerymaid and housecleaner, informed her employer that there was no other room made up.

"Well," said Bidwell. "You can make one up, can't you?"

"No, I cannot!" And the weary Florence stalked out.

The other dinner guest, a Chico resident, saw where the land lay and urged Mr. McDonald to spend the night at his residence. To Bidwell's relief, the unwelcome guest finally rolled his bulk out of the easy chair and departed.[5]

Relatives of both Annie's and John's often frequented the guest rooms. Cousin Maggie Ellicott Woodhull (and sometimes Dr. Woodhull) came from San Francisco. Both Guy and Joey Kennedy spent many meals and overnights in the mansion. If the weather was bad, Guy stayed with his aunt and uncle and was taken to public school by Bidwell's carriage driver. John Bidwell was quite relaxed with children, something he could not always achieve with adults in a social setting. He took to heart the requests of his Kennedy parents-in-law that he assume a father figure for the boys now that their father was dead.

After his visit to Chico in 1879, Joseph C. G. Kennedy had commended Bidwell for his loving indulgence of his nephews, though in a separate letter to Annie, her father had added that he worried about Guy's "lack of proper deference to his elders." "It is in the effects in later life that render discipline so important in youth."[6] Bidwell probably did not see it in his role to take Guy or Joey to the woodshed for a paddling, though he was inclined himself to criticize the boys' lack of consideration for their elders as the years went on. Guy had come home from boarding school while Annie was ill, and "he has not been in all day to ask about Aunt Annie! How strange."[7]

Perhaps it was with some thought of his need for adult counseling that Annie took Guy back to Washington with her for four months in early 1882. His grandfather might have his chance to instill respect for his elders in the ten-year-old boy.

Though the Bidwells were accustomed to lacking privacy for personal conversation at mealtime, it was not always without a feeling of sacrifice. Until the Chico Presbyterian Church acquired a parsonage, it was customary for the Bidwells to offer their home to a new pastor until he could find suitable lodging for his family. There were several short tenures in the pulpit in the early 1880s. Rev. Ellis was followed by a Rev. Warren. When Warren left in the fall of 1882, the Reverend Graham, his replacement, set up residence at the mansion while his family remained in Placerville, presumably to finish the children's school year. When Rev. Graham finally moved his family to Chico in May 1883, (the family as a whole having visited in Chico with the Bidwell Mansion as headquarters several times in the interim) John expressed to his diary his relief at losing the constant presence of Rev. Graham in his halls and at his table. While John Bidwell was not likely to be overawed by any of the Presbyterian pastors, he could be bored![8]

Visitors at the mansion did not require much additional physical work on the part of the hostess. When the domestic staff was steady she had only to give orders. But the relationships between cook, maids and household male servant were often tenuous, and subject to blowup at inopportune times. Over the years, the Bidwells had become accustomed to these occasional "wars in the kitchen" between servants—the tears—the accusations—the firings—the flouncing out of a disgruntled servant. Though he had at first hated the task, John learned to pass his wife's orders on to the female servants, and then leave quickly before being caught into justifying or explaining.

Bidwell's ability to manage the mansion staff without Annie's presence was well illustrated in September 1880. Bidwell received a request from his friend General Sherman, who was setting an itinerary for a cross-country tour by U.S. President Rutherford B. Hayes. Would he entertain the presidential party in Chico and expedite a tour of the Cherokee hydraulic mining operation?

It was during one of Annie's visits to Washington, but Bidwell agreed, and did the necessary shopping to complete furnishing of all the guest bedrooms. Some shopping was done in Chico with the housemaid Mary's help, and some purchases he made in San Francisco. Bidwell also arranged for some of Annie's friends, including Mrs. Carl "Willie" Sommer, to hostess for the one night the presidential party slept at the mansion.[9]

The occasion was formally structured with no time for conversation with the guests of honor. The presidential party of thirteen came by train from Marysville and were met by bands and an honor guard and school children on either side of the mansion driveway throwing bouquets. Chicoans gathered on the mansion lawn during the evening. Following dinner, President Hayes appeared on the porch which had been lighted with Chinese lanterns, and gave an address for those persons without invitations.

Then a receiving line formed in the hall, and as invited guests entered the front door they were introduced to the President and Mrs. Hayes by Franklin C. Lusk. Guests were passed on down the line until all had the opportunity to meet the visitors. John Bidwell apparently took a minor role in this pomp, and he had to make sure that teams and drivers were in readiness to take the entire party to Cherokee the next day where an exhibition of hydraulic mining technique had been prepared.[10]

A Women's Christian Temperance Union was organized in Chico in December 1883, by the prominent international WCTU organizer, Mrs. Mary Clement Leavitt.[11] Though Annie was to become the driving force in the WCTU movement, she was in the background for the organizing. It was probably arranged by Saline Woodman, wife of the Congregational minister.

The temperance movement, after years of little public response, received a transfusion of enthusiasm in a series of visiting temperance lecturers in 1884 and 1885. The Butte County Knights Templar lodges, a temperance movement of national scope in which both men and women were equal members, was particularly active in 1884.

When Annie Bidwell had established the Indian school and was able to direct her attention and energies to assisting in the temperance movement, she began to take more leadership roles. She started out in 1884 with organizing a number of WCTU branches in Butte County's smaller towns, Biggs and Gridley, and Red Bluff in Tehama County.[12]

The Pavilion, a large hall which Bidwell had constructed in Chico for public use, continued to provide the venue for temperance lecturers. The Band of Good Hope, a religiously oriented temperance group, had existed in Chico for many years. Along with the Mite Society and the Knights Templar, the Band of Good Hope invited both women and men lecturers for a special month of temperance recruitment in March 1884. The Bidwell Mansion was always available to house these visiting proselytizers, and both husband and wife were genuine in their support.

While Annie suffered pangs from her brother Joe's drinking problem, John Bidwell regularly faced the situation with drunkenness among the ranch employees, including the Indians if they were given alcohol. Employees who provided alcohol to one of the natives, even for purchase, were always discharged. Alcohol consumption not only caused fighting and loss of work. Even several murders on the ranch were laid to overuse of liquor. Examples of alcohol abuse were even closer to their personal lives, as Cora's older brother John Wayland caused family distress when in an alcoholic rage.

As Annie busied herself with recruiting new workers for temperance, she shared her activities by letter with her family back in the East. Joseph C. G. Kennedy's personal reaction to this is reflected in a letter to his daughter written in April 1884:

"I wish, my dear Annie, to mention in loving frankness that accounts of your travels in the cause of morals do not impress me as favorable as they perhaps would if you were not the center of a little principality affording a wide field for benevolent effort any man or woman should be expected to participate in. … All have not such opportunities surrounding as you have and enjoy. … Of course, I would not wish to curb your ambition to be a blessing to all, but in attempting too much may not some of your efforts be lost?"[13]

Her father suggested that giving kind advice to children and affectionate remonstrance with older persons might effect more good in the cause of temperance than can be gained by trying to eradicate alcohol through the force of legislation, or any course which seems to place guilt on certain persons—or is interpreted as hostile.

The record of Annie's lifetime work on behalf of total elimination of the sale of alcohol indicates how little power her father's opinion had on her on this particular issue, even though many times she had used as argument with John Bidwell that God required that she be dutiful to her parents. If God had given her the power implied by being the "center of a little principality," it was no more than her husband had promised her when he said that she would be the "Queen to preside at his Mansion."[14] And if of the mansion, why not also of Chico?

Family duty
to the fore

Though the pattern was set for visits to Washington at about two year intervals, the restful holiday implied by living as a guest in her parents' home was not always forthcoming. In spite of her mother's oft-heard reiteration that Annie had a frail constitution, the traveling she did across country, sometimes alone, at regular intervals on poorly heated or cooled trains, often with no meal service and with uncertain train connections in remote areas proved that she had a sturdy physique. It was emotional stress that made Annie ill, a fact that her husband came to know well during the thirty years of their marriage.

With her Indian school progressing, taught by teachers paid by the Presbyterian Home Missions (mainly Ida Florence), Annie turned her attention more freely back to family responsibilities.

Annie returned across country to Washington by train in September 1884, this time taking her nephew, Joey Kennedy, no doubt as her duty to bring grandparents and grandchild together. The Kennedys had only the two grandchildren, son John's boys Guy and Joey, and the grandparents lived some 3,000 miles from them, unable to give much practical assistance. Cora was in no financial situation to either travel with her children or offer her hospitality. She had begun to acquire training so that she could teach elementary school classes.

One senses that Grandfather Kennedy offered advice cautiously, perhaps more from fear of offending the Waylands than Annie and John. While no doubt a thoroughly normal little boy, Joey showed some signs of leniency in his rearing—as his grandfather had mentioned to Annie in an earlier letter! The eight-year-old Joey kept his aunt Annie on her toes, and did so until they reached Chico and home on February 28, 1885.

Annie had the extra responsibility of shepherding her mother as well as the little boy on passage from Washington to New Orleans. There the three travelers were joined by John Bidwell.

John had decided to visit the New Orleans Exposition of that year. In addition to the agricultural and farm machinery exhibits, which monopolized John Bidwell's interest as always, there were trips to take on Lake Pontchartrain and through the historic district of the Mississippi River city, much of it under rainy skies and coping with terrible mud underfoot.

During Mrs. Kennedy's 1885 visit in Chico, the pavilion which Bidwell had built for use as a meeting hall for Chicoans was converted into a storage building for sacks of threshed wheat. Bidwell had embarked on buying up the crops of local growers who would sell. Much of the wheat was being converted to flour in his new flourmill which had only recently been completed at great expense. The mill was much more mechanized than the one that had been burned six months earlier by a suspected arsonist during an anti-Chinese demonstration.

The challenge to Annie after the loss of the pavilion was to find meeting places for temperance and prohibitionist lecturers. Several of the larger Chico homes were used, including the Bidwell Mansion, of course.

Unusually torrential storms hit Chico and the Sacramento Valley in the fall of 1885. Heavy runoff weakened the supports of a wonderful new bridge across the Sacramento River which had been completed under contract by the Butte County Board of Supervisors less than three years before. Bidwell had made a major effort for the bridge, which would connect the wheat crops of Glenn County with his mill. The Bidwells had been in the first carriage to cross the completed bridge in September 1882, and their pictures had been taken with the other members of the group that successfully lobbied for the bridge. Now after the rains, the owners of heavy wagons, or even with large horses, were admonished not to try to cross it. This was a serious setback for trade between the communities on either side of the river.

Mrs. Kennedy, Annie's mother, was not in the best of health and often chose to stay at the mansion when Annie attended meetings, rode horseback about the ranch or helped at the Indian school. Mrs. Kennedy's problems were those associated with aging in females, that is prolapse of her uterus which affected her bladder and her ability to walk much in comfort. As the years went by, she consulted a number of doctors about this condition and was reassured that it was not a fatal symptom, but part of the aging process.[1]

Mrs. Kennedy left for home on October 22, 1885, in the company of San Francisco friends who accompanied her as far as Omaha.

Catherine had had a unique experience during her visit, one that impressed her greatly. Several Chinese leaders from the Chico Chinese community came to the mansion with a variety of beautiful gifts to present to Annie and her mother.[2]

As difficulties between factions grew in Chico, the presentation of such gifts to the Bidwells, considered as friends by the Chinese, accelerated. Apparently the Bidwells accepted them graciously but did not encourage or reciprocate in kind, nor were they necessary to insure that Bidwell did the right thing as he saw it.

The difficulties arising from Bidwell's hiring Chinese laborers on his ranch had been a common topic of conversation at the Bidwell table that year. Catherine wrote back to her daughter from Washington that she had considered the matter and decided that if the Chinese were truly grateful to the Bidwells for their support—as they appeared to be—they would just go home to China and take all the troubles with them![3]

Existence for Annie Bidwell was made much more pleasant by the resolve of her husband to take his financial situation beyond the uncertainty of living from the sale of one wheat crop to another. Perhaps he now concluded that he was never to have children to whom he might pass an agricultural empire. The things that he had promised Annie—such as trips abroad—had not materialized. Two reasons come to mind. Besides the constant shortage of cash, Bidwell did not much trust the men whom he had hired to supervise either the work force, the farming and fruit-growing, or wise expenditures for upkeep of the complicated and diverse businesses of mill, cannery, fruit drier, dairy, and plant nursery.

In the 1880s, Bidwell began to borrow money from San Francisco banks or savings unions at intervals in ever larger amounts, for instance $250,000 from the German Saving Bank in December 1884.[4] While the sale of grain, fruit, etc. might with luck be sufficient to pay off the loans, when it was not, Bidwell borrowed anew to pay off one loan and extend his credit on the ranch operation. An added plus was that his wife Annie received less nagging to observe constant frugality. The last of these loans, one with the Lick Trust of San Francisco and which mortgaged the ranch for a total of $350,000 was signed by the Bidwells as late as November 1899.[5]

The year of 1886 was filled with many comings and goings at the Bidwell Mansion. Some guests were, of course, WCTU organizers and lecturers. As that activity picked up in Butte County, Annie spread her interests to a broader arena. She attended the State WCTU Convention in Sacramento in May, and planned for Butte County's convention held in Chico.

As often happens, social life took on a tyranny of its own. In 1886, the Bidwells had invited a party of important friends from the political world to be guests at the mansion just prior to receiving word that Wesley and Laurinda Jay were planning to visit them at that exact time. Laurinda was the only full sister of

John Bidwell, two years his senior, and he had positive memories of their growing up years, perhaps among few such images from his childhood. Laurinda and her husband had managed the care of their parents, Abraham and Clarissa Bidwell, during years that John Bidwell was estranged, both by distance and through inclination.

It was necessary to ask Daniel Bidwell to host the Indiana visitors for most of this visit. This was, no doubt, a bit of an embarrassment, especially as relations between the John and Daniel Bidwell families were often under strain. John Bidwell had not known of his half brother Daniel's existence until long after he reached California, at which time he had invited Daniel to move his family from a stony New England farm. Half-siblings Laurinda and Daniel had almost certainly never met.

The Bidwells had so many guests that summer—Minnie Carroll, the young woman still mourning the death of her mother in Sacramento the previous December; Mrs. Gibbs and her mother, Mrs. Kane, the wealthy San Francisco friends who had moved west from Washington, D.C., and New York; Narcissa E. White and Mrs. Green with the WCTU movement—that no camping trip to the high country could be worked in. The Bidwells' only pleasure excursion was to Cherokee and to Table Mountain to look for rare plant species and be hosted by Louis Glass of the huge Spring Valley hydraulic mine.

Nor were the demands of instant missionary work to be neglected. Rumor came that someone at the Dairy Grove on the ranch was giving liquor to Indians. Annie enlisted the most available local woman to accompany her, a Mrs. Dixon, and took off for the dairy in great haste.

When a Chico Negro lad of ten years was jailed for a $10 pocket pick job on one of the rancheria Indians at the Chico agricultural fair, Annie visited him in jail to offer pious sympathy and soul-saving advice. Sinners were her favorite targets for sympathy.

The response to Bidwell's proclamation of June 1885 had produced results that satisfactorily filled the Indian chapel to overflowing on Sundays. Mr. Pickler, a local carpenter, was set to enlarging it.[6]

Annie Bidwell deserved a rest, but she packed her trunk and rallied her courage for a winter trip across the country. She boarded the train for Washington on December 15, 1886.

A murder

The year 1887 began on a triumphant note for John Bidwell, and it was almost certainly regarded so by his wife for they shared a commitment to quality education.

During 1885, a committee of Chicoans had met with Professor Reich of the San Jose Normal School to explore possible sites in Chico for a second state normal school which the legislature was considering. This committee had failed to come up with a unanimous recommendation, and since there was no certainty that the legislature would soon act, or would even decide on Chico among the communities competing for the school, the committee disbanded.

When John Bidwell received a telegram from the State Normal School Search Committee on March 4, 1887, a few weeks after joining Annie at the Kennedy's home in Washington, he was exhilarated beyond simple description. What site or sites on Rancho Chico would Bidwell consider donating for the school? The legislature needed to know at once.

Bidwell had joined Annie in Washington in mid-February, and then decided to take a steamer abroad from New York to the British Isles, a trip Annie declined to take. She could still recall her experience with seasickness on her first trip to California. The weather in late winter could be wretched. No thank you, she would stay and rest at her parents' home.

It was on the eve of his departure on this trip that Bidwell wired his answer to the search committee: "Take anything [from the ranch] but my dooryard."[1]

Joseph Calm Griffith Kennedy, Annie Bidwell's father. Courtesy of California State Parks.

He and Annie returned home promptly by the end of April, and by the twenty-eighth of the month he began surveying part of his cherry orchard along First Street south of Chico Creek for the normal school campus. In June he went to San Francisco and signed the deed releasing the land to the state of California.[2]

By chance the Bidwells were entertaining several of Annie's relatives (cousin Mary Cooper and her husband, and cousins Madge and Frankie Baldwin) when another fateful telegram arrived for the Bidwells, this time from Washington, D.C. It contained the news that Joseph C. G. Kennedy had been shot by an assassin on a D.C. street corner on the afternoon of July 12, 1887.[3] As soon as arrangements could be made, Annie departed for the East accompanied by cousin Madge Baldwin.

Bidwell's commitment to start immediate groundbreaking for the new normal school building was judged reason by both Annie and himself to excuse him from this family duty. It was Annie's third crossing of the continent in seven months, this time wretched with sorrow and worry as the journey that took her to her family seemed more tedious than ever before. It was a time for the necessary resolve not to give in to physical weakness, no matter how tired and heartsick she became.

Joseph C. G. Kennedy had left his Washington office on the afternoon of July 12, 1887, and stood waiting to board a streetcar when he was stabbed from behind and through the right abdomen. He fell at once, and was said to have given one cry, "murder!" The first to reach his side and pillow his head, until a physician emerged from the gathering crowd, was a Negro watchman from a nearby office building. The man who had stabbed Kennedy made no attempt to run, but amid cries of "Lynch him!" was said to have remarked in perfect composure, "Yes, I killed him, damn him."[4] Kennedy was seventy-five years old.

Ultimately, John Dailey, a laborer, who was convinced that Kennedy had cheated him in some earlier business transaction, was judged to be insane at his trial for the murder.[5]

Kennedy was eulogized in the newspapers of several Eastern cities, for his work with the U.S. Census Bureau. He was widely known from active political association with both Whig and Republican parties. Since leaving the census department, Kennedy had been involved in real estate and investments. The *Philadelphia Press* stated that Kennedy was "a small, gentle, soft-voiced, tenderhearted, lovable, somewhat fussy man ... who acquaintances would pick as least likely to fall by the hand of a man with a grievance."[6]

A telegram was delivered to Annie on the train east: "To the Conductor Pullman Train No. 2 or forward. Temporary burial made Saturday at 5 p.m. Ma bears up wonderfully."[7]

The summer heat made holding the remains until Annie's arrival against mortuary practice, even though the body had been embalmed because Sallie thought that Annie might wish to view her father before the remains were reburied in a new Kennedy family plot. Annie chose not to do so, having heard tales of unsatisfactory restoration of facial features in embalming.

Finding no help from their brother Joe with handling Mr. Kennedy's affairs, Annie and Sallie began to try to make order out of chaos. While Sallie went to the real estate office of her father to try to handle business that could not be deferred, Annie began to catalog and dispose of her father's huge personal library.

John Bidwell was sent a copy of Kennedy's will for his insights, he having administered a good many estates of friends over the years. He saw no particular problems but made this suggestion, "If Sally ever intends to marry Joseph Morrison, she ought to do so at once. ... Sallie needs help—just such help as a good husband would be." But, of course, the suggestion came too late. Morrison had married.[8]

Certainly the drunken brother Joe was no help. Annie wrote to John that she and Sallie wondered if they might help finance Joe's being placed in an asylum—probably a drying-out institution for alcoholics. John Bidwell replied, "We have no money to send him to an asylum. Plus he would never consent to go. ..."[9]

As Annie's Washington visit was extended time after time, her husband became impatient, though he always urged her to do what seemed right to her. Still he hoped she would not find it necessary to stay for the still unscheduled trial of Dailey. Annie wrote of having gone to visit the black man, a Mr. Mason, who had been first on the scene when her father was stabbed and had heard Kennedy's last words.

Annie felt that she should stay with her mother and that poor Sallie have a vacation before she broke down. Sallie thought that Annie should take her mother on the "vacation" in hopes that Catherine might recover some of her fading memory. Catherine refused to travel back to California with Annie. So the three women compromised by going together to Meadville to share the grief and stress with the extended Morrison and Reynolds (JCGK's half-siblings) family there.

On October 31, 1887, Annie arrived back home in Chico in the company of her cousin Clara Baldwin. If only she could now rest!

Her first letter from Sallie read, "You are now speeding toward Chicago. I shall miss you dreadfully—no one to relate disasters to, consult or anything else. My shoulders almost feel bent this morning."[10]

Sallie Kennedy takes the helm

*J*oseph C. G. Kennedy's will was brief, and its terms were later to be questioned and clarified by court order. He had named Sallie his executor, thus giving his final verdict on the worthlessness of his son Joseph. The basic clause of his will gave everything to his wife Catherine, and should she be deceased, to Sallie "should she remain unmarried." His son Joseph was to receive the old Ellicott property in Fountainville, Maryland, which Kennedy had inherited from his mother, if Joe occupied it. Annie was to inherit all in the event she was his only survivor. Special note was made that Annie was to have the gold medal presented to Kennedy by the king of Denmark and it should pass from her to Guy Kennedy. The medal had been presented to Kennedy for work he had done in organizing a system for recording social statistics in Denmark.[1]

There was no mention of any real estate (of which most of Kennedy's estate was composed) other than that at Fountainville, leaving Sallie with the impression that she was to convert real estate to cash in order to support Catherine. She spent many hours with Kennedy's attorney, and many more hours going through her father's papers at home and in his office. It would not be exactly true to say that Sallie disliked this. While worrisome, there was a certain pleasurable headiness achieved from becoming a woman of business.

Her letters to Annie following the latter's departure for home were peppered with updates from Washington. Catherine was ever more of a concern, prone to wander off "to pay a visit to a friend" if not watched. Sallie took her mother with her to

Kennedy's office when she worked there, only to be distracted by "ma walking up and down the office making it difficult to write as she wished to talk all the time."[2]

In spite of Annie's expressed anguish over the pain her sister and mother were undergoing, and her own trouble with dreams, Sallie seemed free of much distress over their father's absence. She wrote, "You left behind a *gorgeous* gown, and owing to circumstances, I wore it this week."[3]

Annie was advised not to be pained by her mother's doleful letters bemoaning the loss of her husband. "She's often quite merry when the letter is hardly in the mail."[4]

Sallie had been visited while working at her father's office by Joseph M. Morrison, the cousin whose ambition to marry Sallie had been precipitously shattered by the violent protests of Sallie's father some eight years earlier. Morrison stopped by to tell Sallie that he had since married, and cryptically said that he feared his wife was not the one Sallie would have selected for him. One is inclined to agree, Sallie having wanted to marry Joseph very much.

The reader will recall that John Bidwell had written to Annie in Washington following J. C. G. Kennedy's funeral that this would be the time for Sallie to marry Morrison—when she needed help, and her father was no longer on the scene to object.

"I hope soon to meet the new cousin [Joseph's wife Belle]," wrote Sallie later. "She lived at one of the principal hotels in New York and infer she or her father has money."[5]

A few days later Morrison brought this wife to the Kennedy office to introduce her, and later the couple was entertained for a day by Sallie and Catherine in their home. Sallie's comments on that office visit were snipped off the letter she sent telling of it to Annie.

The two, Sallie and Joseph Morrison, had been long since resigned to accepting that their romance was an experience gone, dead, and best forgotten.

Sallie, while considering the money at her disposal, expressed concern with Annie about Guy Kennedy's future. He was proving himself rebellious to both his mother Cora and the Bidwells, and some rather antisocial behavior on his part while attending boarding school in San Francisco had been reported to Sallie through her sister.

Sallie wanted to know more of Guy's character. "[Brother John's] boys seem to me almost like wards [of mine] because their interests are constantly involved in all that is done here [administering the estate of Joseph C. G. Kennedy]. I feel as if I was living in a generation that is past, one that is present, and one that is to come. In vain I look for my little quiet contented self of only five months ago."[6]

After his father's death, Joe Kennedy had made an effort to assist in straightening out the affairs of their father and continuing to make the business pay. Sallie praised her brother at first, and then suddenly events turned her against him: "As for [Brother] Joe, I think I will never mention his name again. He is coming to the office where I am working drunk."

There was some urgency to selling her father's real estate in Washington and his farm in Meadville as the business income came to a stop with Kennedy's murder except for a few outstanding accounts that Joe was discovered to be using for himself. "For nine months," Sallie wrote to her sister, "he has been spending all he makes in drinking, yet [he] tells us the servants that I am saving Father's money for my own benefit."[7] Sallie worried that her mother would have a hard time adjusting if it came to giving up their home. "Mother would find it very hard to be poor, although she is never extravagant."[8]

More and more Sallie was coming to find her emotional support in a social acquaintance, Thomson H. Alexander. He was a bachelor, divorced from his wife, his divorce occurring at about the same time as Joseph M. Morrison's. When Sallie's father had raged that the latter was not to be allowed in the Kennedy house,

Morrison had, in fact, made special mention of the double standard. Tom Alexander had always been a welcome guest in Washington social circles, including the Kennedy's.

Alexander was discreet, jovial, thoughtful, extremely tactful in company and a talented musician. Now his legal training was proving helpful to Sallie, and his ever-ready carriage at her door to run errands and/or take her mother for rides, and his willingness to patiently listen to Catherine's stories repeated over and over as if new, endeared him to Sallie without her quite realizing that her affections were being won over.

If Joseph C. G. Kennedy had been alive, who knows what he may have said? Alexander had not only been divorced, the charge of fortune seeking might well be applied to Alexander as it had to Joseph M. Morrison.

Sallie wrote in long letters to her sister that although from a once monied English family, the Alexanders had long since lost their wealth and neither Thomson's brother or sister in the area lived very sumptuously.[9] His ex-wife received alimony and sued him for increased support money at intervals for many years, even after his marriage to Sallie.

In March of 1888 Sallie accepted Alexander's proposal of marriage, only a few months earlier having declared to Annie, "I have no intention of marrying." Meaning to keep the engagement secret at least until the anniversary of her father's death, Sallie wrote Annie that her breath was taken away when she found that her mother had already delightedly informed almost everyone in their Washington circle of the engagement before Sallie and Tom had a chance to announce it.

"I am almost used up by congratulations," Sallie wrote to Annie, "from his family as well as my own. Last evening was the first we had been out since the newspaper notice—congratulations on all sides. My only annoyance is that people seem to think that I have been dissatisfied with my condition of single blessedness and have lost just so many years! A great mistake, for I would not have had it otherwise and feel my life was far from being thrown away."[10]

Her brother Joe continued the proverbial fly-in-the-ointment. He had not been told of Sallie's decision to marry, even by their mother, and did not know until he read the announcement in the newspaper. His response to visitors at the house was, paraphrased, that "it is good news. I am tired of supporting her." The outrageousness of this statement made Sallie "so angry I could almost have whipped him. And I can't keep mama from conversing with him."[11]

Sallie offered Joe that he move to the rundown Ellicott home on the Fountainville property and she would supply the money for materials to repair the buildings and fences, while holding off on transferring the deed to the property. This resistance on her part to formally deeding the property to him was a source of Joe's anger for the remainder of his life. Apparently Sallie was following both legal advice and that of friends, the reasoning being that without money, Joe Kennedy could not obtain alcohol.

Sallie and Thomson Alexander set the date for their marriage for October 19, 1888. The wedding invitations to the few friends invited were mailed. Sallie wrote that she was happy that Annie agreed that she should be married in white.[12]

The invitation addressed to John and Annie of the upcoming marriage was carried by ranch wagon from the mansion to the Aurora Mine buildings on Mosquito Creek north of Magalia where John Bidwell had prepared for Annie a health retreat in the foothills, a quieter and cooler spot than Chico. Annie had been diagnosed by Dr. Joseph Hirschfelder of San Francisco, less than a month earlier, as suffering from tuberculosis.[13]

Serious—but caught in time

When Annie arrived back in Chico in October 1887 from her father's funeral, having shared the grieving with her mother and sister (brother Joe had almost alienated even his sister Annie by his callous behavior) she could not separate her daily life from the grieving process. She had begun a diary again for 1888, and though like many earlier attempts, it was abandoned midyear, her entries indicate that her father's murder haunted her (she wrote to Sallie of bad dreams). Annie regretted not being physically present to share the nightmare "which still must be driving my mother and sister toward insanity."[1]

From afar, Annie projected on her mother and sister far more pain than they actually experienced. Sallie had certainly tried to assure her sister that all was under control and evidence of grieving little on display!

Catherine's growing dementia had altered her personality for the better. While their mother still had brief attacks of depression and lamenting for her husband, as Sallie wrote, "she can be as happy as a lark a few minutes later." One noticeable change for the better was that Catherine seemed to have forgotten her obsession with the constant displeasure from God at her inability to "really believe."

Annie's cure for her own woes was to plunge into the whirlwind of activities which her Chico commitments demanded. She was thwarted in this by a great weariness, punctuated by a persistent cough that would not be thrown off in spite of medications prescribed.[2]

Unlike her sister Sallie, Annie felt no exhilaration in day-to-day work on a problem at hand. On one of the blank pages at the end of her 1888 diary Annie listed her offices and duties for the year, but no date of when she put on paper the dreaded responsibilities:

President of Mite Society
President of Ladies Missionary Society
Vice Pres WCTU
Supt. Scientific Temperance Instruction WCTU
Spt. White Shield Dept, WCTU
            plus
Sabbath Services at Rancheria—weekly & daily
Member of Women's Relief Corps
Member of WCTU Free Reading Room
Cont. Member Youth Missionary Society
Cont. Member Chico Relief Society

Annie's health problem was exacerbated in March that year by the paint that was being used in complete redecoration of the downstairs rooms of the mansion. The fumes became almost unbearable. At dinner the evening that the parlor was painted, Annie developed a feeling that her chest had "closed completely." All at the table were crying from the heavy fumes.[3]

The dining table was usually a crowded one during all the early months of 1888. Houseguests included Dr. and Mrs. Parry, botanist friends. Two photographers had been given permission to record scenes from the ranch. Annie's Baldwin and Cooper cousins came for extended stays, and there were the usual special ranch employees given mansion lodging.

One worker who had a room and took meals in the mansion was M. T. Brown, who had been hired to survey the new Chico Vecino subdivision in 1887, as well as other projects around the ranch. Bidwell would have enjoyed the surveying himself, a trade learned in his youth, but he was getting to an age (sixty-nine) when surveying was hard on his back and legs. Recurring lumbago attacks made him fully aware of his limitations.

In addition to a houseful of guests, Lulu the maid was ill and in bed, and Annie felt obliged to rise often during the nights to give her medication. Moreover, there was illness all over town, including the scare from a case of smallpox. Annie was advised to have another vaccination from Dr. Stansbury, just in case her visits to the Indian village might bring her into contact with the dread disease.

Annie's throat became so sore from both the fumes and the cold air in the mansion coming in through necessarily open windows, that on March 24 she moved for ten days to Mrs. Wayland's home to sleep and rest. After Dr. Wayland's death, his widow had begun to accept as boarders persons needing light nursing care.[4]

Still Annie carried on, though she was too hoarse on occasion to perform her duties at the Indian school and chapel services and asked Miss Ida Florence to fill in for her.

John Bidwell was much involved with the construction of the new normal school building and decisions that had to be made about the selection of a brick supplier. Since state law forbade the use of bricks made by Chinese, though all of Chico's bricks had come from the Chinese brickyards for years, special brickmaking enterprises had to be set and the bricks tested. Bidwell was opposed to organized labor and swore to avoid the Knights of Labor or other groups espousing fair wages, even though it meant the normal school building was proceeding slowly.[5]

Bidwell was not only on the local board of trustees for the normal school but had been asked to serve on the Joint State Normal School Board, taking him as far as Los Angeles that spring for meetings. In addition he had accepted the presidency of the State Prohibition Conference. Both Bidwells joined in the happy laying of the cornerstone for the normal school building on July 4, conducted by the Masonic Order.[6]

While these matters were demanding Bidwell's attention, an accident had occurred in a storage room of the Bidwell cannery. A part of the building had collapsed bringing down shelves storing 40,000 cans and injuring a cannery worker badly.[7] All of this was distressing to Annie.

Finally, with the last of their houseguests gone, the Bidwells went to San Francisco on July 17, 1888, where John was scheduled to attend the convention of the California State Prohibition Party and accept the presidency of the state party.

On July 18, Annie kept an appointment made with a San Francisco eye, ear and nose specialist. Dr. Ferrer referred her on to a Dr. Joseph Hirschfelder for examination on the nineteenth. In consultation with both Bidwells on July 20, Dr. Hirschfelder reported on tests he had done and announced his diagnosis of Annie's symptoms as tuberculosis.

Bidwell entered in his diary that evening, "She has consumption! which amazed me! and overwhelmed me with sorrow!"[8]

A number of drugs were prescribed by Dr. Hirschfelder, including champagne. Annie tried to drink it at her husband's urging in spite of her moral stance on alcohol. She reported finding it like drinking vinegar.

The most important prescription was for complete rest in a much cooler climate than Chico offered in July and August. Bidwell rightly decided that to get complete rest, Annie must be moved from both the heat of the sun and the stress of her many, many commitments.

She gave in to his plans for her without protest. Annie Bidwell was as close to panic as her faith could permit. This change of affairs also pulled John away abruptly from concern about his own business concerns. He was willing to devote himself and all of his strength and resources to helping Annie get well.

Leaving Annie in San Francisco temporarily, Bidwell followed up on a lead of a guest home in Auburn which was at a somewhat higher altitude. Cousin Molly Cooper stayed with Annie in San

Francisco and made the move with her. Bidwell rented several rooms from a Mrs. Stevens in Auburn and made arrangements with a carpenter to add an open-air sleeping porch on two sides.[9]

Then, to Bidwell's great dismay, he had such a severe attack of what he first took to be recurring lumbago that he was forced to bed. Cora went in the carriage to the Auburn boarding house to get it ready, meeting Annie and her cousin Maggie Cooper arriving from San Francisco.

John Bidwell's extremely painful attack centered in one hip and he could scarcely dress himself. Dr. Stansbury prescribed liniment, first applied liberally to the hip and *ironed in*. This involved having Peter the houseboy apply a hot iron to the hip area though four layers of flannel.[10] Fortunately, the hip improved with this treatment and after a week, Bidwell was up and about.

Instead of improving at Mrs. Stevens', Annie grew worse and came home by carriage a week later to Bidwell's worried surprise. Her cough had grown worse and she was suffering from night sweats, a sign of weakness.

He set out alone at once to Magalia, known as a refuge for children and frail adults from the summer heat. It was a malaria free area and so generally believed to be more healthful. He talked with Magalia residents, including a Magalia miner, A. A. Perry. Following Perry's tip he went to the Aurora Mine near the confluence of Little Butte and Mosquito creeks. Mrs. Caroline Church, the widow of the former mine operator, still owned several buildings on the property and promptly offered one to Bidwell, giving him permission to outfit it to meet the needs of a semi-invalid. Annie was moved to the Church cabin on September 5.[11]

Not long after moving into the Aurora Mine cabin, Annie had been alarmed by new symptoms which sent John Bidwell to San Francisco to hurriedly consult with Dr. Hirschfelder. The physician recommended that Annie avoid the mountains and find another mild climate for the winter. So Annie was back at the mansion on September 29.

Following recommendations he had from friends, Bidwell went to the Ojai Valley, at that time very rural, and found a resort near Nordhoff specializing in lodging for semi-invalids. He reserved two cabins at the Glen Oaks Cottages resort where Annie was to live for almost six months.

Annie made the trip in stages: by train, and then from San Francisco by ocean steamer to Santa Barbara. The wife of Bidwell's surveyor, Mrs. Brown, accompanied her, as well as Annie's personal maid, Florence Blake. They were settled in by October 10.[12]

Until Annie felt her health restored sufficiently to return home late the following April, John Bidwell was traveling almost incessantly between Ojai, San Francisco and Chico. Dr. Hirschberger warned John that his own health would be impaired if he did not slow down.[13]

The greatest pleasure to come to Annie Bidwell during that winter in rural Southern California was a visit from the newly married Alexanders and Catherine Kennedy. Instead of a honeymoon to Vermont, they chose instead to visit Annie with her mother, and to reassure both Annie and themselves that all was well.[14]

Annie had met Mr. Alexander at the Kennedy home—probably not for the first time—on her trip east at the occasion of her father's death, but had no inkling—nor had they—that a romance would develop. Both the Bidwells found Thomson Alexander a pleasant and welcome addition to the family. He knew how to turn a conversation that was dragging, or suggest a new and clever version of some well-known card game. He loved to hunt, and the small game he found in the Nordhoff hills kept him happily occupied and away from the confinement of the small cabin that the Alexanders rented at Glen Oaks.

Convalescence put behind

When Annie Bidwell left the Ojai Valley near Nordhoff, she felt entirely restored in strength. Dr. Hirschfelder, in whose diagnosis and treatment the Bidwells had developed complete confidence, cautioned about tiring activity too soon, and had suggested that the summer heat in Chico should be avoided. Annie continued use of an inhalant containing asphaltum prescribed by the doctor, and took creosote and morrhual tablets. Whether Annie brought herself to continue the prescribed champagne is doubtful.

The staff at the mansion had been pared in Annie's absence to often only one woman and a male servant, the latter working both inside and in the gardens. The Bidwells continued to have houseguests, even in their absence. Dr. C. C. Parry, an avid collector of new plant species for categorization, had an open invitation and was free to come at will. Housing for traveling Prohibitionists was always provided, and meals prepared for them. Col. C. C. Royce, the man considering the job which John Bidwell now offered of overall manager and accountant for the ranch, had been told to make himself at home in the mansion while he acquainted himself with the ranch and the operation.

Royce decided to accept the position, and Mrs. Royce arrived on June 4 to look over the housing possibilities in Chico. Mrs. Royce had family in the East and was often gone from Chico, thus making a hotel suite the most logical place for them to live, especially as Col. Royce took many of his meals at the mansion. [1]

Annie's illness had been the clinching argument to Bidwell's decision to have a trustworthy person whom he would pay generously to take charge of all operations when Bidwell was not on hand. It was another indication (along with Bidwell's increasing willingness to borrow large sums of money) that he had decided that life was far too short—and Annie too precious—to tie himself to day-to-day money juggling and jousting with employees, tenants and marketing problems.

On May 11, 1889, Annie made her reappearance at a Sunday worship service in the Chico Presbyterian Church, the first in over a year. She attended her first Indian chapel service on June 30 but only as an observer.

Her husband was planning a pleasure trip for the two of them that she anticipated joyfully as hot summer weather approached. On July 2, the couple set out by train, making their way to Colorado Springs and from there to Manitou Springs, a popular resort not far from Pike's Peak. Here they happily explored the area on muleback, collecting specimens for Dr. Parry to add to his

John and Annie Bidwell with guide at Manitou Springs, Colorado, 1889. They have been collecting specimens for botanist Dr. C. C. Parry while vacationing away from the heat of the Sacramento Valley after Annie's bout with tuberculosis. Courtesy of California State Parks.

specimen collection. They took the tourists' excursion to the top of the peak.

From Colorado, the Bidwells returned westward by train to Portland, Oregon, turned north there to Vancouver, B.C., and then casually traveled by Canadian trains across the continent to Montreal, stopping a few days here and there. From Montreal they went south to New York and eventually arrived at the Alexander's home in Washington on August 2, 1889. Here John left his wife for her first visit since Sallie's marriage and returned home in order to be on hand—September 26—for the opening ceremonies as the very first class embarked on the teacher training offered by the new Chico Normal School.

While in Washington Annie visited her brother Joe on the Ellicott family farm at Fountainville in nearby Maryland. She praised the freshness of his homegrown vegetables at a dinner he prepared, and laughed with Sallie and their mother at the antics of Joe's trained mice. Having the farmhouse to repair and his gardens to keep had returned Joe, for the time, to sobriety and civility toward his sister Sallie. If all had been cordial on that occasion, it was a rare moment of sunlight peeping through storm clouds.

When Annie arrived back in Chico once more in mid-October, she could truthfully say that she felt as healthy as she had upon first arrival twenty-three years earlier.

Backwater as it may have seemed to some, Chico had its excitement in mere day-to-day events. For the Bidwells it included the deeding of land for a state forestry station and the opening of lot sales in Chico Vecino, Bidwell's "new town" as the subdivision had been described to the Alexanders. The details of this business were delegated to local realtors, Camper and Costar.

All mourned the fate in December of the free Sacramento Bridge so welcomed a few years earlier. The great floods of 1889 swept it away down river forever. Such events added zest to dinner conversations in dining rooms throughout Chico, and Bidwell's involvement in all such matters made the mansion or Bidwell's office the breaking point for much news.

Anticipating Annie's renewed efforts for the Indians, now that she had returned to health, Bidwell ordered the chapel again enlarged and repaired, and that year a Christmas feast with many gifts exchanged celebrated the return of the chapel's spiritual creator. Annie only gradually returned to weekly appearances but sometimes went by and gave little talks. By now, several of the Chico pastors were interested and volunteered to conduct services on some Sabbath days. This number did not include the Presbyterian pastor, the Reverend Graham, who had never publicly declared himself in favor of educating the Indians.

In 1889, Cora Kennedy went east for her first time, and took her sons. Her major purpose was to accompany Guy, now nearly seventeen, to Washington to live with the Alexanders and attend Emerson Institute, a high school level institution. Guy's short experience as a boarder at Trinity School in San Francisco had ended in a troublesome show of Guy's rebellious nature, perhaps what his grandfather had observed in 1879 as "lack of proper deference to his elders." John Bidwell made reference to Guy's learning problems in letter to Annie, described by the Berkeley school's headmaster as Guy's use of "jumbled, bungling expressions."[2]

Guy Kennedy attended Emerson during 1889 and into spring of 1890. Annie contributed regularly to his expenses, and Cora, now teaching elementary school in Chico, paid her share too. He missed considerable school with a very bad case of lagrippe, first thought to be typhoid fever, and did not graduate. Impatient, he insisted on returning to Chico in spite of Sallie's and his grandmother's pleas.

Continuing to protect her health to guard against recurrence of tuberculosis, Annie and John went camping in the high meadows again in July 1890, and followed that with a vacation trip through the Northwest. Both of the Bidwells suffered from severe seasickness on the ocean leg of their trip—San Francisco to Portland.

After recovering briefly in Portland they went on by train to Tacoma, Washington, and turned east to their next destination, Livingston, Montana. From Mammoth Springs, Montana, they traveled by carriage through the wonders of Yellowstone country.

Another meandering route by train brought them through Idaho (where they could get no hotel at Pocatello and sat up all night), then through Soda Springs, Idaho, and points along the Oregon California Trail from a much more comfortable perspective than when traveled by Bidwell with his party of pioneers forty-nine years earlier.

They reached home on September 30, as Bidwell once again felt the call of political ambition and prepared his talks for the campaign trail. He had been notified by the American Party Convention that he was to be their candidate for governor of California in the 1890 election in November. Knowing in advance that he had little chance of being elected on a ticket supporting Prohibition, he nonetheless decided to use the opportunity to spread the message as far as possible and enjoy the process from the perspective that he had little to lose.

Annie set out with him on his prescheduled speaking itinerary that went south to San Bernardino, west to San Diego and north through Los Angeles, Ventura, Santa Barbara, Tulare, Stockton and to Santa Cruz on the coast. Annie's stamina, however, gave out midway, and she returned home. Rested, she turned her efforts to helping organize a huge Prohibition rally to be held on election eve. Bidwell arrived home November 2, just in time to prepare for an enthusiastic hometown rally which overflowed the Chico Armory the following night.

Election day proved a fiasco for the American Party and its candidates. Money paying for votes, "sacks of it," according to Annie's diary, was being passed out at the backdoor of every saloon in town even after closing hours, on the night of the election. Later a newspaper article boldly charged that Gov. Stanford himself had put $75,000 into this effort amounting to simple bribery.

The Bidwells openly expressed only contentment as the votes were counted. Of course, the Republican candidate, Henry H. Markham, had won, but all along the campaign trail, Bidwell's dignified manner, his speaking style and his message, especially his message, had been applauded.

The enthusiasm in the wake of the election rallies generated a burst of activity from the small Suffrage for Women group in town and they began to circulate petitions supporting women's right to vote. Annie took a petition and dutifully pursued signers. As she began to seriously weary from it all, she wrote resigning her commission to the National Womens Christian Temperance Union. But all in all, the year 1890 had been one of positive experiences and with a more optimistic outlook for the ranch's fiscal recovery, for the Bidwells' health, and for their loved ones' futures.

Then the sensation of happiness turned to pain for Annie and brought on bitterness and deep depression. The unexpectedness of a personal attack on herself from a respected—and certainly unexpected—source added to the anguish from the blow. Who could have predicted it would come from the heart of her own beloved Presbyterian fellowship?

As Annie Bidwell recorded it in her diary, she had been driven to downtown Chico, probably for Christmas shopping, on a very cold December 15, 1890, when the impulse came over her to stop and chat with Rev. and Mrs. Graham. To her numbing surprise, the pastor launched an attack on her and her "political" activities with a fury of which she had not guessed him capable. A somewhat cold man, he was popular with the members of the church, and his tenure by 1890 of seven years in a church never before loyal to a pastor for more than two was evidence that he probably

felt he reflected the views of the majority of members in the
Chico Presbyterian Church.

John Bidwell had had his own heated words with Graham over
a subject close to both his and Annie's core beliefs, writing that he
had had a hot argument with Graham on Prohibition. "He has
nothing but derision for Prohibitionists."[3]

Annie did not record the specifics of the attack, but one
surmises that Graham struck out at the openness of her political
activities, and the unwomanly performance in so doing. Especially he must have cited God's will as the basis for his speaking so
harshly. As instructed in the Bible, a woman should be silent and
obedient except in matters concerning her household and her
children.

From the added note Annie wrote in her diary: "If I am what
he thinks me, with all my opportunities, what must he expect
those with less to be?" It must be inferred that Graham denigrated
the intelligence and reasoning ability of the female gender at
large.

Annie wrote in her diary on that fateful December day: "By
the grace of God I did not retaliate. Let me not forget his opinion
of me, that I may remain humble all my days." She went home
immediately and to bed, with "every bone in my body aching
violently."[4]

It was Annie's intent to share this episode with no one, except,
of course, her husband. John Bidwell was outraged, as briefly
stated in his own diary for that date: "Rev. Graham talked outra-
geously to my wife. He was simply furious." Thus began a cold
war between John Bidwell and the Reverend Graham that was to
last seven years.

When next the Reverend Graham met the couple, he was as
cool as if nothing more had transpired than the casual counseling
with any church member. Though Annie pled with her husband
that the waters not be further roiled, both Bidwells lessened their
attendance at church services. At times the memory of the epi-

sode made Annie truly weak, so she felt justified in giving illness as her excuse for missing a church service.

At times over those seven years, Bidwell refused to pay his pledge for the church's support, particularly further alienated by the coolness of Graham's reaction to Bidwell's campaign for the U.S. presidency on the Prohibition ticket in 1892. Bidwell believed from both that act, and from the nature of some of Graham's sermons, that the pastor did not support prohibition of alcohol sale and use at all. Temperance, yes. This was the same line of reasoning that J. C. G. Kennedy had made to his daughter, that the judicious use of wine is a pleasure to mankind and of no offense to the Lord. As a Presbyterian pastor whose purpose was to uplift the moral character of his flock, this was not to be tolerated from Graham with the deference one showed a parent!

It was by no means the first time that Bidwell had doubted Graham's commitment to Prohibition or even to temperance. He had written to Annie while she was convalescing at Auburn that the Reverend Graham's wife and children were visiting away from Chico during which time Graham was "boarding at Dooley's, a whiskey-beer place!" Bidwell had offered that Graham should eat with him at the mansion and gave him the times that meals were served. Graham had thought that it would not be as convenient as for him to continue at Dooleys.[5]

Annie's conscience would not permit her to stop financial support of the church, and she often scrimped in her household and personal budgets to pay the pledge, or at least part of it. She declared she would rather subsist on bread and water than neglect her duty. Even so, Annie was often seen with her husband in a pew of one of the other Protestant churches in Chico as the 1890s passed. In so doing, she acquired a broadening of her outlook that made her more receptive to religious creeds at some variance from her own, a process that had begun as she attended Episcopal services in San Francisco with Mrs. Gibbs, and Jewish services with Mrs. Hirschfelder.

Haunted by more family tragedy

*A*nnie's absence from the sermons of the Reverend Graham could be readily explained to friends by Annie's once again conducting the Sunday services at the rancheria chapel, an activity broadened to include a Wednesday prayer meeting for the Indians and the formation of a prohibition-support group which met regularly at the rancheria. As a part of the work with the natives, Henrietta Skelton, a Canadian reformer, became a regular houseguest at the mansion and a good friend who frequented the Bidwell's home for the rest of her life. Miss Skelton worked not only with the Native Americans but lectured to Chico audiences generally on the evils of alcohol.

The early 1890s brought a request from the *Century Magazine* and H. H. Bancroft, San Francisco historian and publisher, for the General to share his memories of early California. Fifty years had slipped away since the young John Bidwell had suffered the months-long trip from Missouri, much of it on foot. The state had now matured to an age where it could begin to look back, and to appreciate its own exciting heritage. Who better could describe the process than John Bidwell?

The *Century Magazine* published articles written by Bidwell, and his recollections were being recorded in several oral interviews, many of which were solicited by Bancroft. Annie helped in transcribing notes and in critiquing the drafts her husband prepared. This work gave her not only enjoyment, but a great pride in her husband. She laboriously copied faded notes of an early interview in which Bidwell described his full recollections of

California history through the Mexican War—much the same version as was to be preserved in print. She used blank pages of the 1866 diary in which General Bidwell had failed to finish out the year.[1]

Annie also expanded her own interests, many of which were made possible by the Chico Normal School's educational offerings. One such interest was voice training with Professor Warman, not for a singing voice, but for better public speaking. The teacher's theory on voice projection included physical exercises to strengthen throat muscles and improve posture. She was fascinated by a demonstration of the use of Indian clubs by the students in graceful drills that were body building and beautiful to watch.

Annie pursued her interest by an entertainment in the mansion, introducing the Normal instructors whom she admired to Chico persons she hoped to interest in further learning. She began a class in voice culture which Dr. Warman taught in the mansion. Like the French classes with which Annie tried to enrich the lives of the women of Chico, the voice culture classes gradually withered from lack of support.[2]

However pleasantly life proceeded for her, Annie still carried an underlying worry for her older brother Joe. She wrote often to him on his Fountainville farm, but lapses on his end of the correspondence grew more common and less acknowledged by him. Cora had luck in writing to Joe about the boys for a while. Then his answers to her also ceased.

The animosity which had grown between Sallie and Joe had progressed to pure hatred on Joe's end. He referred to her to Annie always as *Mrs. Alexander,* as if her marriage to the jovial Tom were added insult. No doubt on the advice of her lawyer Jones (and Thomson Alexander himself as a lawyer) Sallie limited the disbursement of their father's estate in Joe's direction. The loss of his personal pride in having to appeal to Sallie for money whenever it was needed to work on the rundown old Ellicott property in Maryland was humiliating beyond words.

Joe still drank heavily. How much was left for the sisters to speculate. He had no friends, his only companionship his ani-

Joseph Morrison Kennedy, Annie's older brother "Joey," in a photograph taken before he was commissioned in the Union Army, 1862. Courtesy of California State Parks.

mals, and when walking to the nearby railroad line he sometimes visited with the track maintenance crews—even having them for lunch. Though it provided one bit of social contact for Joe, the proximity of the railroad along the narrow stretch of land between his house and the Patapsco River marred the quiet of the farm. Noise and cinders flew at the trains' passing.

Joe walked to shop at the nearby village, sometimes along the tracks, and on one occasion his dog was killed by a train that seemed to loom suddenly upon them. Joe had a cow and chickens and a garden. He might have been content with such a life had he not been gnawed by the injustice of his situation.

Joe Kennedy wrote to his sister Annie, "From the manner in which I have been treated since my father's death my views about most Christianity has materially changed. I could to a considerable extent appreciate the results of the teachings of Christ, but I cannot now bring myself to feel that those who profess most to believe in such doctrines do so further than agrees with their desires to accomplish their own desires."[3]

He named several parcels of property sold by Sallie which his father had stated before witnesses were to be Joe's. "Taking and keeping another's property simply because you have it in your power and claiming to believe in God Almighty and a hereafter is a little too much. ... I did not prepare to spend my life working for someone else and the privilege of being my own cook. ... I like the place and prefer living here to being in the city but I cannot afford to be cheated out of what I feel is my own ... and moreover I will not be."[4]

Yet in spite of his declaration that he would get a job in town and rid himself of the control of "Mrs. Alexander," he did not seem able to rally his energy in that direction and fell further into despondency, and reliance on alcohol for consolation when he could afford it under Sallie's calculated plan to deprive him of money.

For one who threw herself on God's judgment, and prayed fervently that her brother Joe would yet be saved, Annie must have felt intense pain when a letter came from Sallie to say that Joe was missing. No one seemed to have any idea whether he had left his house by daylight or perhaps gone for a walk at night and stumbled down the bank into the river. As days went by, police as far away as Baltimore as well as railroad workers were drawn into the search.

Then on April 8, 1892, well over a week from the time Joe had been reported missing, the dreaded telegram from the Alexanders came to the mansion with news that Joe's body had been recovered from the Patapsco River.[5] Had he gone walking at night in a state of intoxication and slipped from the bank, or had his despair at his own weakness led him to deliberate self-destruction?

Annie departed at once for Washington, but her visit was brief. She remained to support her sister in the final disposition of Joseph Morrison Kennedy's remains next to his father in the Georgetown Cemetery, District of Columbia. Joe was fifty-two years old.

Annie was back with John by May 21. There had been little comfort for the sisters, only resignation to Joe's death. Early in 1893, Annie still wrote tortured letters to Sallie, who responded, "Try my precious Sister to feel that if Joe died in this way he may have been saved a worse death."[6]

It is impossible to know what happened to Joe Kennedy, either in his sad life or at its tragic end. To Annie it must have been but another example of the devil's evil power over mankind, with alcohol his tool.

While it is impossible to know, it is also impossible for the author to avoid speculating on this sad life from the perspective of the twenty-first century. Joseph Kennedy was born to greater privilege and with greater opportunity than was given the vast majority of his peers. Yet he had seemed to deliberately throw it all away and to estrange himself from his father, his sister and then from society in general.

When Joe Kennedy left for Civil War duty with the army commission his father had obtained for him in 1862 he was engaged to Fannie Craighead, a cousin from Meadville where they had grown up together as children. The first sign that Joe was not conforming to social expectations for an engaged man was the long lapses in Joe's letters to Fannie. She spent much of those war years with the Kennedy family in Washington, both families assuming that Joe would be married to her when the war ended as they had planned before he received his commission in the military. Gradually, Fannie's distress came to the attention of Sallie and Catherine, both of whom informed Annie. Catherine was horrified at her son's callous behavior toward the young woman.

"Joe's behavior gives me great solicitude. Poor Fannie fares no better [than for a long while]. She cannot stand the treatment. ... She writes to him two or three times a week and suffers in silence not wanting her parents to know—it has been eight weeks since she has heard from him."[7]

In time, the brokenhearted Fannie broke the engagement and went home to Meadville and her parents, William and Julia Reynolds Craighead. Annie pressed Joe for an explanation, and he wrote to her after his discharge that he thought Fannie would not be happy with him; she had wanted him to leave the army after the war's end, and he had no way to support her and a family unless he retained his colonel's commission in the peacetime army. And he thought the Craigheads did not approve of him, so it was better for Fannie that their romance ended this way.

Fannie was later to marry one of the prominent and wealthy Huidekoper family, which, with the Morrisons, Kennedys, and Reynolds had been major founders of Meadville and its institutions.

Joe developed no more romantic entanglements.

If Joe realized, while living in the male environment of army camps, that his sexual orientation was other than the norm, it would have been sufficient to distort his whole future. Back a civilian, he tried to work with his father, but Joseph C. G. Kennedy was not a man to work with Joe's mistakes in the business with sympathy or patience, and would have been even less so inclined at revelations by Joe of such intimate personal problems, had Joe ventured to find words to make them.

Joe did often seek counseling through pastors of the Presbyterian Church the Kennedy family attended, and these were times when his parents and siblings were optimistic that Joe might become a Christian, and for a true Christian this painfully evident problem of alcohol consumption would be solved. Joe seemed to build a relationship with a counseling pastor on at least two occasions, only to break off abruptly—as if he had desperately hoped to confide his problem to a sympathetic ear—only to give up as he sensed the frigid reaction of the pastor to a hint of homosexuality.

And so, we can speculate that Joe faced a life in which he saw only societal rejection or scorn and the certain disowning by his father if his secret escaped—and he was unable to carry that burden without his own personal escape through intoxication. Better to be scorned as a drunk than as a pervert.

Annie's chief reason for hasty return was worry about her husband. John Bidwell was not well. His health problems started early in the year and had led him to seek medical advice in San Francisco two weeks in February.[8]

John Bidwell's brave, if futile, campaign

*A*nnie had been reluctant to leave her husband to attend Joe's funeral while he still suffered from recurring bilious attacks. In November of the previous year, Bidwell had fainted while on the train between Chico and Sacramento. From November 11, 1891, for two weeks he and Annie had taken residence in a hotel in San Francisco while Dr. Hirschfelder tried a number of remedies.

In May, before Annie's return from her brother's funeral in Washington, Bidwell had returned alone to the Bay City for his second conference with Dr. Hirschfelder that year.

All political party conventions preliminary to the year's presidential race were underway, and though he was now firmly committed to supporting the aims of the Prohibition Party, Bidwell skipped the Prohibition Party Convention in Butte County held at Pentz. On May 13, he responded to feelers from the national level of the Prohibition Party about throwing his hat into the presidential race by writing to Mr. St. John, National Prohibition Party chairman, stating that he would decline the nomination for the presidential run if offered.

He met Annie at the Chico Depot on May 21 and as soon as she could repack they left for San Francisco, determined to stay under a trusted doctor's care until Bidwell was healed of his digestive malady. As events transpired, they were not to return to Chico until almost the eve of the November elections.

Settling into the Longworth Hotel, Bidwell was at first much preoccupied with his illness, especially recurring bouts of nausea and diarrhea. He was started on a milk diet, then cereals were added, and oysters. Dr. Hirschfelder came daily to the hotel to see him, and on rare occasions of his absence from the city, sent his medical associate.

The Prohibition Party National Convention was being held in Cincinnati, Ohio. Bidwell must have been feeling considerably better when the telegram came on June 23 from the convention asking whether he would refuse the nomination for president if he were not expected to actively campaign. After talking it over with Annie, and possibly with the doctor, Bidwell wired back: no, he would not refuse on those terms. On July 1 the wire came confirming his nomination.

The room adjoining their bedroom in the hotel was rented and Annie went out to rent a desk and a typewriter. She then assumed the triple role of nurse, stenographer and gopher. A flurry of letter writing kept both busy, first arranging matters with Col. Royce and other ranch employees so that Bidwell felt assured that the ranch operation would run smoothly, and then turning his attention to the brisk political correspondence.

Annie had been practicing on a typewriter at home and was not very good, judging from a diary report of having had to type an article three times to get it right. The Bidwells used the services of a typist-on-call and a printer for the long document he prepared that summer.

Bidwell was not much bothered by the press, until becoming infuriated at one July editorial in the San Francisco *Chronicle,* the paper which had carried the hateful accusations of Bidwell's questionable citizenship during the 1876 campaign for governor. The *Chronicle* now published a story accusing the Prohibitionist Bidwell of complete hypocrisy, charging that Bidwell until seven years ago was the largest brandy producer in the state with 500 acres of grapes grown for that purpose.

A denial of this fabrication was published by newspapers in the Eastern states and picked up by the Chico *Chronicle-Record* on July 16. Annie carefully preserved a copy of the clipping in her diary for 1893.

After a delegation from the National Prohibition Party visited on August 24 to inform Bidwell formally that he was a candidate for president of the United States, he and Annie turned to writing the platform on which he ran and including it in his "Letter of Acceptance" to be publicized. This was the only campaigning he would actually do.[1]

Bidwell's platform first appeared in *The Prohibitionist,* a national newspaper, where it attracted considerable response. Annie took many trips on foot to a printer to get copies reproduced of this document, rolled them in tubes—delivering the document suitable for displaying—and then mailed them to party members and others who requested. She had three printings—400 in all—to meet the demand.

Dr. Hirschfelder continued to watch his patient for symptoms, both good and bad, but by early fall Bidwell did feel quite returned to his normal self and was enjoying beefsteaks and other items from the regular hotel menu. He now accepted callers at the hotel and was wished well by many. He noted with pleasure a visit from his niece, Lilly Bidwell Collins, and her little daughter Alice, now living in Sacramento.

John Bidwell required no arm twisting by his wife, but she must have been extremely gratified that the platform given in Bidwell's Letter of Acceptance not only condemned the sale and use of alcoholic beverages but also advocated national suffrage for women. Other major points were Bidwell's endorsement of a federal income tax, advocacy for federal control of railroad and telegraph commerce, and the necessity to place a limit on immigration into the U.S. John and Annie's collaboration on the platform and the campaign, such as it was, stood as one of the Bidwells' proudest moments, one that reflected loving teamwork.

As John Bidwell's health showed more improvement, and Dr. Hirschfelder dropped his daily visits, in September Annie and John packed their trunks to go home to Chico expecting that Dr. Hirschfelder would dismiss him when returning to San Francisco from vacation. Instead the doctor forbade Bidwell to forsake the routine he was following.

The couple did not get back into the mansion until November 4, just three days before the election. Supporters in Chico filled the armory with a cheering crowd and friends had decorated the mansion with masses of foliage, flowers and banners. Knowing that hopes of winning the election were futile, nevertheless Prohibition Party members nationwide were united in agreement as to the choice of John Bidwell as their presidential candidate. As a result of the admiration, as often happens with popular figures, a number of infants around the country were christened with "Bidwell" in their name that year!

Returns from the Prohibition Party's national vote came in a few days later. Bidwell had polled over 350,000 votes—the largest presidential vote garnered by the "Drys" to that date.

As Bidwell improved that summer in San Francisco, Annie became increasingly busy with WCTU activities. Mary Clements Leavitt, Frances Willard's right hand, met several times with Annie and once with John to work on plans for the WCTU exhibit in the 1893 World's Fair to be in Chicago.

That year 1882 proved much too busy for Annie to keep a personal diary, or, any fragments she may have kept, she later destroyed. Her own health had been amazingly good, suggesting that an antidote for her blues was purposeful activity.

Aches, pains and pleasures of growing older

t fifty-three Annie Bidwell was far short of considering herself elderly, but she was keenly aware of her husband's increasing physical problems. Though still erect and with less gray than his wife, John, seventy-three, was often confined to his room with lumbago or neuralgia in the months following his return from Dr. Hirschfelder's care and the presidential election of 1892. He was not sorry to have an excuse to avoid the Reverend Graham's Sunday sermons. He and Annie now attended the Presbyterian Church with some regularity but preferred to go when a visiting pastor was in the pulpit. Routine decision-making for the ranch had now passed largely to Col. C. C. Royce and the individual foremen of the several farm operations. Having given in to the necessity of borrowing, even so far as finally to mortgage the ranch, money matters pressed less on Bidwell's mind.

Annie had acquired white locks, as had her sister Sallie, by the time she was fifty. Instead of the smooth sheen of swept back brown hair, her photographs now featured a face surrounded by dainty rolled curls, a softer look around her face than the pulled-back-in-a-bun look. She usually styled her own hair. After once going to a professional hair arranger in San Francisco, she irritatedly reported that she could do a better job herself.

Women were as sensitive to hair fashion then as to changes in clothing styles. Annie had never tried the fashionable hairdo in the 1870s which Bidwell had deplored in his niece, Mary Reed.

That coiffure was described by him as "simply horrible, all frizzled on top—her dark brown hair appears lighter like a poor old buffalo turns when he is shedding his matted coat of fur."[1]

Annie had arrived at a kind of permanent roundness. Though 126 pounds was lightweight enough when compared with the 230 or so pounds of her husband, spread over a four-feet-eight-inch frame that 126 pounds created extra padding around her middle. Annie disdained wearing heavy corsets unless absolutely necessary. The Bidwells took regular visits to the flourmill to weigh on the scales there, bathroom scales not yet being available. Sallie was rounder yet than her sister, but both women were attractive and neat and fashionable in their carefully put together toilettes.

For his part, after his semi-retirement from ranching, John Bidwell adopted a fashion made popular at the time by Mark Twain, an all white suit and vest for summer wear. It was hardly practical for the dusty Sacramento Valley, but the mansion kept a laundress and neither scrubbing nor ironing fell to Annie.

By the 1890s, the Irish house servants seem to have largely disappeared from the mansion staff. Florence Blake, an English native who served Annie as her personal maid for over fifteen years, was a good friend of Alice Beers, another loyal employee. With the problem of Irish bias toward blacks removed, Annie often hired as extra help the Negro Susan Jones, who as Susan Steward had come as Annie's personal maid from Washington after the Bidwells' marriage in 1868.

Poor Susan had problems with her husband Clayborn, and he in turn had severe problems with alcohol overuse. The Bidwells had tried to give employment to Clayborn Jones, but finally had to stop. Susan was called in for special tasks, and if the mansion was in need of a thorough cleaning, Susan could be counted on to be as efficient as ever, as well as grateful for the employment.[2]

The Bidwells were given no respite from entertaining in 1892 after arriving home from five months in San Francisco, and Annie noted that they had had houseguests of one kind or another at the mansion from November 4 to February 4.

Guy Kennedy, on long Christmas break from the University of California, was permitted to entertain many of his friends at the mansion. Other guest rooms were filled by several women on WCTU missions. A Mr. Mason, evangelist, was put up at the mansion as a matter of course. He was invited to hold revival services in Chico by a group of women from several Chico churches, calling themselves the Doers.

The Doers was actually a WCTU subcommittee, of which Annie was a part. They focused on organizing joint meetings among the Protestant churches to convert new members and to inspire backsliders into repentance. Mr. Mason was very popular and drew great crowds, but the Ministerial Union voted not to have him back. The ladies of the Doers ascribed this to jealousy and did invite him back in a splendid show of defiance.[3]

In spite of the Reverend Graham's well-known stance as to women's place in both church and civic affairs, when the Presbyterian Church members met in January 1883 to elect trustees for the year, a resolution was proposed to make women eligible to serve on the board. It was voted down, but Annie noted in her diary with elation that though many men abstained from voting, only seven women had felt intimidated into voting against it! Graham amazed Annie shortly after when, at a prayer meeting with both men and women present, she—Annie—had been asked to pray—a woman to pray publicly!

All activities in Chico seemed to focus on the campaign against alcohol, at least where the Bidwells were concerned. The plan for the Bidwells to attend the 1893 World's Fair in Chicago that year, coinciding with the National WCTU Convention in Chicago, had been planned for many months. Annie had taken the position of associate commissioner for the convention while in San Francisco during John's long convalescence the year before, but her reluctance to leave her husband caused her to resign the post early in 1893. She had generously also made a plan that the Alexanders should enjoy the exposition without the drag of Catherine Kennedy's care. Annie would go to Washington and stay with her mother while her sister and brother-in law, the Alexanders, visited the exposition.

All through the winter and spring months of 1883, Bidwell suffered recurring lumbago attacks that confined him to his bedroom. The most effective treatment was massage, and when he was suffering, Annie massaged his back and limbs at least every day. She applied olive oil, then alcohol, then rubbed in more oil and applied liniment. This was followed by a vigorous slapping of the aching areas.

In spite of the chronic nature of these attacks, the Bidwells were committed to going to the Chicago World's Fair. The couple left Chico on October 6, 1893. Almost the entire time they were gone from home—until December 20—they were subjected to weather that was cold, foggy and extremely wet.[4]

The World's Fair grounds were then south of the city of Chicago at Sixtieth Street of today. The site and midway were eventually to be taken over by the University of Chicago. Only a small attic room could be found when they arrived, and at an exorbitant $2.50 a day charge. Bidwell became thoroughly chilled and immediately took cold. This was the thirteenth of October, and since Annie's WCTU Convention was to be in Chicago, they moved to a more comfortable hotel downtown as Bidwell chose to pay the high carriage bills to travel by himself the few miles to the exposition buildings.

Even with skipping one day of the WCTU Convention to visit some exhibits which her husband said she must see, Annie had to slight the fair generally, in part because of a promise she had made her sister.

Annie left Chicago alone on September 21 for Washington, D.C. As she arrived to care for her mother, Sallie and Tom Alexander departed Washington for Chicago where five days remained for them to enjoy the World's Fair. The last day of the fair, Bidwell stayed in his hotel room. He had lost his cane twice and his glasses on another occasion (all had been retrieved) and his cold made him thoroughly miserable. Tom Alexander bought departure tickets for the three of them to Washington and assisted Bidwell to his train. (Bidwell took a different railroad line from the Alexanders in order to have the luxury of a berth.)

It was not an enjoyable trip even so for poor John Bidwell. Once he was in Washington, D.C., Annie took over the nursing duties, which Bidwell credited with "saving him" from far worse than the symptoms of a miserable cold. For a week he left his room at the Alexander's only to see a physician.

During the Bidwells' sojourn with the Alexanders they managed to attend two musical events. One was a black woman singer whose voice had earned her the appellation "Black Patti." In his general sour mood, John Bidwell noted that to him she was not a Patti but a failure. The train trip home to Chico, December 12–20, was characterized by snow and cold or rain and cold.

Fortunately, Annie had found time to work in the convention of the National Indian Association while in Washington, but she was too preoccupied trying to keep her husband comfortable, or caring for her mother, to make an entry in her 1883 diary after September.

To their amazement, back in Chico the Reverend Graham had asked Mrs. Henrietta Skelton, the WCTU lecturer, to preach for him on December 24! This unusual gesture from a man who believed that women had no business or talent for public speaking did nothing to soften John Bidwell's opinion of him. As the years of Graham's tenure in Chico passed, Bidwell was seen less and less often in the Presbyterian Church.

Recurring attacks of lumbago, neuralgia and severe respiratory congestion plagued much of the remaining years of John Bidwell's life. He found that his best form of exercise was on the back of his favorite mule, Linda, and the Bidwells often rode about the ranch on such animals. Annie adopted a bifurcated skirt to make the use of a regular saddle possible. She liked it, and her husband congratulated her for the good sense to put comfort and safety ahead of public opinion.

Return to
Dr. Hirschfelder

hrough the trip to Chicago and Washington in
1893, Annie suffered from "lameness of arm," a pain
and constriction in the shoulder that limited her use of
her right arm. Too busy with care of her husband through
his spring illness in 1894, and her own illness in April, she put off
seeing a trusted physician about the arm until a time coinciding
with her attendance at the Women's Congress in San Francisco.
She had sent letters withdrawing scheduled talks at both the
WCTU Congress and the midwinter Fair Missionary Congress
(on American Indians) in January. In February she had not felt
able to go to the Colusa-Glenn WCTU Convention, but
managed to work in an appearance at the Butte County
convention in March. She made time free to attend regular
"drills" of the Loyal Temperance League preparing for a stirring
presentation of temperance values by songs and marching,
choreographed for women and children.

It was not as if the Bidwell Mansion did not have a roster of
houseguests! On December 29, Minnie Carroll Alexander from
Oakland and her two small children came and stayed three
months. Her husband Charles Alexander was in and out as he
went on business trips throughout Northern California. The
Bidwells liked having the children, although Bidwell himself
might not appear from his bedroom for days on end. Maggie
Lafonso and Eamyo Conway were two of the older Indian children who were sent for to amuse the much younger Alexander
children.

When John Bidwell felt up to dressing and getting out of the house, he had ranch projects that were being done under his direction with a crew made up of mostly Indians. The network of roads about the ranch were being connected and improved. Among the regular workmen that spring of 1894 was George Clements, now with a wife Annie referred to in her diary as Clara.[1] George was also now a father and making a strong effort to support his wife and children.

Bidwell had attended the meeting of the combined Normal School Trustees in Los Angeles in early April 1894. During his absence and Annie's illness, Clayborn Jones had come to his sad end. Annie wrote of his passing to her husband. She had sent a carriage for Susan to ride in to the funeral of their former employee, for Susan and her family had been shattered by the way Jones had died from a gunshot wound delivered by his son while Jones was intoxicated and abusing Susan.

"So Claybourn [sic, spelling of the name varies in the Bidwell's usage] has gone to his sad account. It distressed me not to be able to have talked with him. You brought him here and I brought Susan and a sad fate is theirs. Could I have gone to him ... but Mrs. Carse [visiting evangelist who had volunteered to look after Annie in John's absence] so strongly objected to me going to him or his son that I yielded, feeling I was really too sick." It bothered her that Clayborn had wanted her to see his son before he should die.[2]

On April 26, Annie left for San Francisco by herself, forced at last to seek remedy for the pain in her arm and shoulder. She planned to attend sessions of the Women's Congress between medical appointments, but on some days after treatments on her shoulder were begun she was not up to it.

The Women's Congress was a general Federation of Women's Clubs formed in 1890 in New York to unite women in organizations promoting education, philanthropy, moral values, public welfare, civics and even fine arts. Both the WCTU and the various Indian associations were to hold meetings.

As ill fortune was to have it, Annie did not return home until August 15, over three months later. Extended medical treatment ended, as well as the congress, but the great railway strike of 1894 tied up the rail lines between the Bay Area and her home.

On May 5, 1894, Annie wrote to her husband John that she had seen Dr. Hirschfelder and had one treatment following which she had to go to bed to rest.

"I hope not to be so terribly frightened as I do when I go to a doctor. It is a terror, doubtless because of my nerves being un-strung, and my lack of strength; and my being alone to get home as best I can after treatment."[3]

The treatment given was evidently to "break shoulder liga-ments" that were "constricted." She got little enjoyment from the congress sessions either before or after daily treatments. Dr. Hirschfelder obligingly agreed to give a treatment after a late afternoon meeting.

"I went to Doctor's office after a meeting at 5 OC'. He broke the shoulder ligaments and Oh! Oh! But I did not scream until he put on the electricity and then *one scream!!!* He says a few more days to break it all up and then I will be well."[4]

"I despise myself for my cowardice—twisting my arm behind my back and then jerking it to break the sinew. I had to drop my head against doctor's shoulder and rest."[5] She compared her illness to his of two years earlier, which for him had been "worse than physical suffering."

Mrs. Royce went with Annie for her treatment one day and could not bear to stay in the room. Guy had accompanied her once too. "Have you brought Guy to defend you?" asked Dr. Hirschfelder playfully. "No, to defend *you*."[6]

Maggie Lafonso and Mary Keola [or Kea'a'la and sometimes Kelly] had been brought to San Francisco by Annie to show example articles of Indian handiwork, but the young women did not stay with her at her hotel. Annie wrote of sending the belt and flicker headband which belonged to Tonoka. Tonoka had made Annie promise that she would return the precious items to him in a few days, and the Indians took the precious items back to Chico. One of Haycey's bracelets brought admiring ahs. "The articles made more sensation at the Congress than anything else, it being the impression the 'Diggers!' cannot do anything worth seeing."[7]

Annie made two talks before groups at the congress, one about work being done with Indians in California and one on Prohibition. The Bidwells' old campaign nemesis, the San Francisco *Chronicle,* distorted the coverage of her talk about Indians. It was reported as a speech covering thirty years of work done on the Chico rancheria. Annie thought she had disguised that fact. It disturbed Annie because she knew that her husband never wanted publicity directed toward him in connection with Native Americans. He had hated the *Chronicle* since their acid and libelous treatment of him during his run for governor in 1876 and for president in 1892.

From our perspective, the treatments imposed on Annie for the cure of sore shoulder seem worse than the natural disorder left alone would have proven. She was never to be completely free of pain in her right arm, eventually losing almost all use of it. But when she reached home in 1894, she did feel much improved and ready to resume the constant meetings and perpetual guests.

John Bidwell's niece (Daniel's daughter), Emma Bidwell Hobart, now a widow, had suffered almost total loss of her belongings in a home fire. She and her foster daughter moved into the mansion. Rhoda Ferrall was a student at the normal school.

Annie also brought home with her from San Francisco the daughter of a woman's suffrage leader, Mrs. Hester Harland. Mabel Harland had questionable ability, and survived less than a semester's study after Annie had wangled her admission from the president of the normal school. This was but one example of the pressure that Annie, much more than her husband, brought to bear on the normal school for favors. The power that this little woman had to command the faculty and administration is remarkable.

Guy Kennedy, now a student in law studies at the University of California, asked that Eva Sampson, a young woman from Australia that he had met in the Bay Area, be invited by the Bidwells over the Christmas holidays.

As customary, the year ended at the rancheria with Christmas tree, feast and generous gift-giving.

William Morrison Alexander

The Daughters of the American Revolution was formed in Washington, D.C., in October 1890. Sallie Kennedy Alexander's interest was aroused, and she became actively involved immediately. She soon inspired Annie to apply for membership, both women using their great grandfather, Dr. Samuel Kennedy, as their qualifying participant in the American Revolution. Kennedy had been appointed by General Washington as "senior surgeon and physician to the general hospital of the Middle Department of the American Armed Forces." The hospital was said to have been built at Kennedy's own expense in Chester County, Pennsylvania.[1]

The letters that Dr. Samuel Kennedy had written to his wife during the war were inherited by Sallie, and the sisters pored over them and did more research on their ancestors.[2] Sallie listed a second qualifying ancestor, Major Andrew Ellicott, who had served in the Elk River Battalion of the Maryland Militia.

A cache of early Ellicott family letters, found among his effects after J. C. G. Kennedy's death, are probably now the property of the DAR, a gift from Sallie Alexander. A chair which was said to be a gift from Daniel Webster to J. C. G. Kennedy, and used by Webster in the "old Senate Chamber" in the Capitol, was also willed to the DAR by Annie Bidwell, who had inherited it from her father.

While reviewing copies of the applications made by Sallie and Annie for membership in the DAR, another application was found by the author at Bancroft Library. Annie had preserved an application to Children of the American Revolution made on behalf of William Morrison Alexander, age eight, adopted son of Thomson H. and Sallie K. Alexander. This copy of a document, like the other DAR application copies, is undated. Sallie is known to have been admitted to DAR membership during the first year after its creation (number 178), and in 1892 she was appointed one of several vice-presidents general.

This DAR application is the only record found among hundreds of family letters, diaries and other papers to indicate how it was that Willie Alexander came suddenly in historical documents to appear as a member of the family. Annie Bidwell's diary notations during her visit to Washington in 1895 give Willie the spotlight in the Alexander family. By then he was a child of at least four. From that time, Willie appears in Annie's diaries and correspondence as a favorite nephew and his activities as a member of Annie's family were lovingly noted.

The secrecy that surrounds the coming of Willie into the family might well have hidden the parentage of this child had Annie not tucked the DAR application away with others. There were no letters from Sallie to Annie saved for a period of years in the 1890s, and it is assumed that Annie deliberately chose to have them destroyed.

But the DAR application tells it all. Willie was the son of Joseph M. Morrison, the cousin whom Sallie had loved dearly but had given up any hope of marrying after Joseph C. G. Kennedy's 1880 tantrums when he discovered the romance. He never altered his view that Morrison had conducted a secret and dishonorable wooing of Sallie with fortune hunting in view!

Joseph M. Morrison married another woman in New York City where he went to find employment after leaving Washington. He brought his wife Belle to meet Sallie after Mr. Kennedy's death. Sallie wrote to Annie of this encounter which took place after Annie returned west from her father's funeral.

Willie's birth year is unknown—his birthday fell in February—and no hint has been found as to what befell his parents or how Sallie and Thomson Alexander came to know of the opportunity to adopt the surviving child.

It was no little challenge for Sallie, then fifty years old, to undertake the rearing of the toddler, and generous of her husband, Thomson Alexander, who might normally have felt jealousy toward this child of Sallie's former love.

Annie herself must have had mixed feelings, and she probably thought back to the year when she had written to her mother and sister during the first barren years of her marriage about her own desire to adopt an orphaned girl in Chico. The Kennedys had advised strongly against it, "for," as Catherine Kennedy had written, "these things almost never work out." By the 1890s Catherine's senility prevented her having opinions at all, and Sallie wisely sought none from her.

Annie was determined to assist her sister in any way possible to make the adoption work and Willie's life a happy and productive one. She first met the little boy in 1895, on her trip to Washington that year, her first visit since she had gone to relieve Sallie and Tom of Catherine's care while they attended the Chicago Fair in summer 1893.

Annie's first mention of Willie is on July 31 in her otherwise sketchy diary for 1895. She had given her new nephew ice cream "to his delight." And true to form, she had volunteered to care for the little boy and Catherine while the weary new parents took a vacation to Buena Vista Springs. Annie even volunteered the not very pleasant duty of taking Willie for his first dental appointments.[3]

Willie was a truly gifted child, his aunt decided; he had acted out for Catherine and Annie one of Annie's stories of Peter walking on water. Annie found that her mother delighted in the active little boy, joining in his play like another child might. Catherine's memory now lay with the past, with long poems she had memorized in elementary school repeated to her family with triumphant smiles and their applause.

Willie proved to be an apt student, both at piano to which his musical new father introduced him, and at assimilating the Bible stories that Annie read to him from her first day with him.

The 1895 trip to the East included a now rare visit to Meadville where her remaining aunts and uncles were becoming quite elderly but always expressed their delight at seeing her.

Eighteen ninety-five held other memorable moments for Annie Bidwell. The new rancheria chapel was dedicated. On April 1, the Chico *Enterprise* ran a story on the opening:

"The Indian chapel has been removed from General Bidwell's grounds into the Rancheria. The church has been repaired and greatly improved inside and out. An organ loft, a raised platform for the speaker, a vestibule and a bell tower add greatly. The chapel has been painted and whitewashed, a neat fence encloses the church and the yard has been planted in trees and shrubs.

"Yesterday morning the stars and stripes floated from the flag-staff, while just beneath the tower, for the first time, the new bell, purchased by the Indians, pealed forth a glad welcome, bidding the congregation 'Come into the house of the Lord.'[4]

"Services were opened by the Indians' patron saint, Mrs. Bidwell. The singing was led by the children and young men, Miss Ida Florence as usual presiding at the organ.

"Austin McLean gave a fine violin solo and later a vocal solo. Maggie Lafonso and William Conway each sang a solo in rich melodious voices. The Indian band was in fine time and their strains of music added zest and inspiration to the occasion."

This band was begun during the earliest days of Annie's work with the rancheria Indians. She had the enthusiastic cooperation of Mr. Neubarth, local insurance broker who was well known for his own band in Chico at that time. He cheerfully undertook to teach the Indians the basics of playing brass instruments. The Indians had an ear for music and quickly learned enough to perform in public, and they treasured the uniforms Annie ordered, giving the final touch! The band was helpful in presenting a positive image of the Native Americans and Annie tried to see that they played at any public occasion where band music was appropriate.

Over the years the members of the band changed, of course. The picture most often shown of the band dates to the 1890s. In 1908, when Annie bought new instruments and also both summer and winter uniforms, she listed the band members as William Conway, his son Isaiah Conway, Pablo Silvers, Rufus Pulisse, Birnie (most persons other than Annie spelled this *Burney*) Wilson, Luther Clements, Earnest Young, Walter Potts and Elmer Lafonso. Luther's father, George Clements, had been the drum player in the first band to be organized.[5]

The Bidwells felt that the Indians were sufficiently involved with the chapel that it would be safe now from vandalism on the rancheria grounds. The era was beginning in which Annie Bidwell used the chapel constantly as a living demonstration of her work and achievements. Visiting pastors and missionaries and numerous other curious persons were to be seen at chapel services, often followed by a tour led by Annie to the village itself, with inspection of the homes that Annie considered to offer the best demonstrations of good housekeeping.

The presence of the normal school was proving a blessing to the rancheria chapel. Several women faculty volunteered to assist with Sunday school classes and singing. Male students came to observe and use the experience as the basis for papers they wrote on Indian culture. Intrigued, they might volunteer to come back as teachers.

Annie and her entourage of students, missionaries and visitors seemed always to be welcomed by the Indians without hesitation, and if a number of the men of the village slipped out during these exhibitions of civilized living made possible by "their patron saint," she seemed impervious to their absence. John Bidwell did not participate in these events, either in the chapel or on the tours.

It is interesting to look at the choice of words chosen to

Indian brass band, 1908. Courtesy of California State Parks.

describe Annie: *patron saint.* While in that context, the words mean to protect and support, the Indians, especially the men, came to regard her as *patronizing,* a term implying condescension, if not outright ownership. The term was probably interpreted both ways over the years—and by different persons.

Guy Kennedy and Eva Sampson were engaged and planned to be married as soon as Guy's law practice was established in Chico. Eva had no family except one sister, Fannie. The Sampsons had come from Australia, and the parents were dead. It is not known whether they died in Australia or in the United States, but Evangeline seems to have spent most of her youth in Alameda on the bay.

Eva came again to the mansion early in December that year of 1895 and stayed three months with the Bidwells. Her marriage to Guy, a very quiet affair, took place the following October in Alameda. Only Annie from the Bidwell household attended and reported to her husband that it was a very high-toned service—no "obey" required of the bride! Annie reported to John that it had been an unusual affair in several ways. At the "wedding collation," Mrs. Smith, Eva's sister, had been asked to sit at the head of the table and Guy at the other end. When it fell to Guy to ask the blessing, "he did, but it was very trying to him."[6]

Nopanny–between two worlds

*I*n her writings about the Indian school and the chapel in 1905, Annie Bidwell told of Nopanny, student, supporter and beloved friend. She told of having Nopanny described as "beautifully formed, a young Martha, though dressed only in a short skirt of tule,"[1] by a lady who had been in Chico as early as 1855.

Annie's first encounter was with a fully clad Nopanny in 1868 not too many days after she arrived at the mansion as a bride. She was still a handsome woman of about Annie's own age. Held in Nopanny's hand was a large bunch of keys, mostly to the adobe house or perhaps Bidwell's farmhouse where he resided prior to the move into the mansion. Some of these keys Annie may have been seeking, though most would have been of little or no use to her. Annie no doubt assumed that Nopanny had come to deliver the keys, but if she held her hand out for them, she was startled by their immediate withdrawal. We can imagine Nopanny there, face and chin lifted in a kind of defiance which nevertheless carried with it a plea for understanding.

"No. No keys," Nopanny was reported by Annie to have said. "Me number one wife. You number two. I keep the keys."[2]

It was in Annie's eternal favor that she could face the woman with whom Bidwell had confessed a close relationship, not with anger and resentment but with understanding. The keys were to Nopanny a symbol she would retain in order that her earlier status be recognized. She might bow to the inevitable of the new world in which her Indian people now found themselves, but she would do so with recognition that she had played an important role in John Bidwell's life.

Nopanny was the daughter of Chief Luckyan, the tribal chief who signed the 1851 treaty between the valley tribes in the Bidwell Rancho area and the U.S. government. At that time, Nopanny would have been no more than eleven or twelve and scarcely considered a negotiable commodity between Luckyan and Bidwell when the latter played an active role in negotiations between the tribes and the U.S. Indian agent O. M. Wozencraft. (Bidwell is also a signer of the 1851 treaty.)

What might be implied by "wife" and through what rituals the couple may have made their relationship a binding one is not known, but it is believed that Nopanny kept house for Bidwell for at least a number of years, during which time someone taught her to speak, read and write rudimentary English. Her domestic skills were as exemplary as her behavior. In Bidwell's memoirs he writes of Nopanny's delicious grasshopper flour pancakes prepared for some of his visitors at the adobe.

Annie wrote that she always exhibited Nopanny's house to visitors to the Indian village for its example of neatness and cleanliness.

It is perhaps one of the foremost examples of a truly Christian spirit and the ability to relate, one woman to another, that Annie as a new bride recognized Nopanny's courage in facing a drastic change in her life, the ability to adapt to new situations, with which Annie herself struggled in 1868. Nopanny must be credited by her critics now, as Annie did then, with the strength to accept—with the grace that might be found in a woman of "royal blood"—what she could not change.

Stories about Nopanny's position in John Bidwell's life had been gossiped about among Chico women and repeated among their husbands from the day news was circulated of Bidwell's planned wedding to a Washington, D.C., socialite. Oh, they would let this new society creature know the facts of the life into which she had stepped, and the kind of man her husband was! But they underestimated the mettle of Annie, and could not have known that Bidwell had confessed all of this to Annie as he began his courtship.

Annie's reported reply to one of the vicious-tongued ladies can be understood. One version told is that she did not deny the facts of her husband's alliance, but stated, "Before I came into his life, he had no choice but to choose from what there was. And he always chose the best." Folklore, yes. But its reasonableness in the light of what little we know of Bidwell's life during the twenty-five years he lived in California prior to Annie's coming is strengthened by the references preserved in diaries and letters.

Nopanny was not the mother of Amanda Lafonso Wilson or of George Clements. Those women—the mothers of his children—are but shadows in John Bidwell's background. Amanda's mother was said to have been the daughter of an Oroville area tribal chief. Annie wrote of the death of George's mother at the rancheria in 1875, then the wife of Pamoho.

Nopanny's later husband was Billy Preacher, longtime Indian laborer on the ranch and one of the converts to Christianity, as was Nopanny herself. She had no children by Preacher.

As Annie Bidwell mentioned in her praising of Nopanny, the latter gave full support to both Indian school and chapel. She herself came to the school when it was opened, and she helped spread news of the offerings of fabric and thread to the rancheria women.

Nopanny continued to carry important messages from John Bidwell to the village residents. He relied on her help to find special workers for him or to undertake tasks herself that required great skill, such as winnowing a wheat sample that Bidwell planned to exhibit. She worked willingly with the yard and garden Indians, and at harvest, making few special demands, and when she had complaints, she did not hesitate to bring them to Bidwell or to Annie.

Nopanny was the fearless one who dared to scold Bidwell himself if she felt he did not keep his word to the tribal members, or if she thought his judgment unsound in his treatment of the Indians. Annie carefully saved a letter to her husband which Nopanny wrote to Bidwell in 1887:

Dear friend:

... Mr. Barham and Mr. King talk so rough to the boys. George Clements quit only 'count of Barham talking very rough to him. And now he is in your ranch working to do all he can for his wife and the child. Reason I state this before you is because I heard that you are going to drive George and his wife away. I don't think that is justice for you to do so. ... And I think George is right to go off wherever he can get work if your foreman don't like him. He cant not lay around and do nothing. He has got to work to support his wife and child.[3]

And there is another thing Mr. King didn't do while you was gone east. ... He didn't give us the wagon to haul wood. You know I asked you for it before you went east for King to give us a wagon, but he did not do so. And so this made me still sadder. ... Mr. Barham is very bad to the boys. He uses bad words to the boys. I dont like that at all. I think he must be drunk all the time.

You no Mr. Bidwell that we are dieing off very fast and you ought not to mention driving us from your place after we have been in this place so long. ...

Yours very truly

Mrs. Nopanny Preacher[4]

Nor did Nopanny limit her pricking of conscience to John Bidwell. During the beginning days of the Indian school when a religious service opened each day's class, Annie had told the Indian women that soon they—the Bidwells—would build a

225

church of worship for the Indians. Meanwhile she went back to Washington on a visit, her brother John's death absorbed her attention, and the school ceased to meet altogether. In fact, Bidwell had taken over the building loaned for use as a school for another purpose.

Nopanny indignantly remarked to Annie on her return to Chico in 1877: "pretty soon! pretty soon! All the time 'pretty soon!' and we never have it." But she had converted her own little living room into a place for worship and brought a dying man for whom she asked Annie to pray.[5]

Annie at once convinced her husband that they must build a chapel—that Nopanny was right.

It was Nopanny's request that John Bidwell himself should teach the men in the Indian village from the "big book." Annie relayed this suggestion, but it was in vain. John Bidwell held aloof from personal participation in any teaching in the rancheria school or leading chapel services.[6]

The Indian church on the Bidwell Rancheria. Courtesy of California State Parks.

When the enlarged and decorated chapel was moved and dedicated in 1895 on the rancheria grounds, the Bidwells sent a carriage for Nopanny who was too weak from fever at the time to walk to the chapel building from the Preacher's home. Annie commented in her diary how tenderly she had been helped from the carriage by her husband, Billy Preacher. Probably Nopanny was victim to chronic malaria with which many of the

Indians were afflicted and to which they lacked any natural immunity.

Nopanny did not limit herself to challenging only the white folk who seemed to pretend to be what they were not. She sometimes angered other Indians and they found intriguing means for revenge on her. "Old Tonoco," one of the older residents of the rancheria, and Nopanny got into a dispute which Tonoco said led Nopanny to strike him. He followed the example of the white community and swore out a charge against her for assaulting him with the Chico justice of peace, Harmon Bay. Judge Bay summoned Nopanny into court.

Annie was in Washington following the death of her father when Bidwell wrote to her of the matter. "She [Nopanny] talked to Justice Bay and was fined $6 which was of course an outrage!"[7]

The Bidwell diaries during the period in which he supervised the ranch operations are full of mentions of Nopanny acting as bridge between the rancheria and the mansion.

Nopanny did not limit her ambitions. She asked to be given the opportunity to learn and recite her catechism in the "downtown church." She was baptized there and made a communicant, the first one of her generation.[8]

John Bidwell did not let Nopanny's personal situation stray far from his mind, in spite of the wish to appear uninvolved. When she was ill, and Annie was not at home, he had flour sent to Nopanny's home. She was obviously an important person in his life, and to Annie's credit she recognized and accepted that.[9]

Annie never allowed the ailing rancheria residents to go hungry or without medical care when she was in Chico. It is believed that John Bidwell himself was alert to needs and sent assistance. Fortunately, John's cousin, Dr. Ella Gatchell, when she set up her practice in Chico, was always willing to attend a sick Indian. Annie ran a regular account with Dr. Gatchell for giving that care all the rest of her life, and called on other Chico physicians when need arose.

Although Dorothy Hill, in her *Indians of Chico Rancheria,* makes reference to Nopanny as Mrs. Bidwell's housekeeper, though she certainly filled this role for John Bidwell, there is no evidence that Nopanny was ever employed in the mansion in such a capacity, except possibly for very specialized tasks that recognized her expertise. She more often was asked to organize farm help among the rancheria Indians for some job Bidwell trusted to her.

Nopanny is believed to have lingered as a semi-invalid for many years, the exact date of her death not being noted, but a short letter from Nopannie [*sic*] to Annie in October 1909, would indicate that she was still able to function at that time.

She had written, "George Clements put me in to be a missionary and I would like you to tell me a few words to say."[10]

Annie was called to Nopanny's bedside during the last day of her life and found her in the process of dying, though to Annie she still appeared to be breathing. The experience made a deep impression, both on Annie and on Dr. Gatchell who had been summoned at the same time Annie was called.

Billy Preacher, Nopanny's husband, sobbed, "She's gone. I saw her go," and indeed, Nopanny's spirit had fled her body.[11]

It was another example of what Annie had witnessed in the Indians before—their uncanny ability to communicate with the spirit person.

"Susan B. Anthony kissed me"

The road to gaining suffrage for women in the United States was a very long one, perhaps one of the most drawn out of any revolution for greater rights within a democratic government, the democracy in this case having been reserved for its male members.[1] The date usually cited as the beginning of the suffrage movement is the assembly of a few Quaker women in Seneca Falls, New York, in July 1848. Elizabeth Cady Stanton, a brilliant woman who found marriage and constant childbirth left her stifled by a "mental hunger," invited three or four others to study women's situation and come up with an outline for possible reform legislation to be sponsored by men friendly to their cause.

Cady had married Henry Stanton, in part because of his abolitionist views. She found that whatever he might advocate for the Negro, he drew the line in offering the feminine sex, including the mysteries and powers of the ballot. Mrs. Stanton soon found her greatest ally in Susan B. Anthony, another Quaker, a spinster by that time at thirty-one, who had rejected "the draining trap" of marriage altogether. As a team, they started out on a campaign that was to be fraught with conflict. Other women joined the movement with different agendas, from those who were advocates of free love to practitioners of spiritualism.[2]

Annie Kennedy would have been aware of the movement, stirring up headlines and often ridicule among the Northeastern states. The more sensational fringes of the women's movement played a role in the highly publicized charges of inappropriate sex on the part of the Reverend Henry Ward Beecher. John Bidwell attended this trial for a day while in Brooklyn in 1875, the year in which his brief stay later in Washington so angered Annie.[3]

Apart from the sensational fringes that clustered like barnacles around the movement, the idea that women were as entitled as men to vote in a democracy must always have appealed to Annie. Her father may, no doubt, have had a more conservative view, but she found that her husband needed no coaxing. He had believed in giving women more equal status in society, including the privileges of education and the vote, long before he met the Kennedys.

Annie's preoccupation with religious fervor and the need to convert and save the sinner overrode her views on political issues, even though in the District of Columbia she was an observer of the political scene. The correct social role played by wives and other refined women in the Capitol City was naturally the role Catherine Kennedy stressed to her daughters, that is, proper protocol in making calls and maintaining a ladylike role during the "social season's" receptions and teas and reflecting well on one's husband.

Susan B. Anthony was less than a year younger than John Bidwell and she was to outlive him several years. Almost until her death she kept to a schedule of meeting with group after group all over the nation. She is probably the spokeswoman whose name is most identified with the suffrage for women movement, and her name is attached as an honor to the Nineteenth Amendment to the U.S. Constitution.

What year Annie Bidwell came to the attention of Miss Anthony is not known, but the two were probably in correspondence for some years before John Bidwell was to include women's suffrage as a part of his platform when he ran for the U.S. presidency in 1892.[4]

From the beginning of the movement for expansion of women's rights, several causes seemed closely related in the public mind. The beginning and expansion of the temperance movement came to be thought of as primarily another women's cause. Frances E. Willard certainly made no attempt to separate her objectives from those of Susan B. Anthony, and was identified as a suffragist also when she formed the first of the Women's Christian Temperance Unions. When the Women's National Congress came into being, and its meetings combined a wide number of causes popular with women, persons from many groups rubbed elbows. These included women's missionary work with Indians.

The real driver behind the suffrage movement in Chico was the wife of the Reverend James M. Woodman. The Woodmans came to Chico in 1863 and established a private elementary school, the school building doubling as the Chico Congregational Church for some years. Selena Woodman was the contact with the national movement, and it was she who recruited Annie to circulate petitions for women's suffrage in 1890. It was this activity of the several women in Mrs. Woodman's group prior to the elections of 1890 that had set off such a violent personal attack on Annie Bidwell by Rev. Graham, pastor of the Bidwell's own Presbyterian Church.[5]

Because of the exposure that Annie's name had in a number of causes, and no doubt because of her husband's public support for the cause of suffrage, Annie was invited in June 1895 by Mrs. Nellie Blinn of San Francisco to a tea she gave in honor of Miss Anthony, president of the National Women's Suffrage Association, and the Reverend Anna Howard Shaw, vice president.[6]

The tea was ably covered by the press, with a guest list and a description of table and house decorations (in deference to women who thought in such terms), as well as the statement that the two honored women had made "brilliant after-dinner speeches." A few men came in after lunch to pay their respects, including U.S. Senator George Perkins and John Bidwell.

Perhaps as a result of this introduction (though she probably had met Miss Anthony at an earlier time), Annie was asked to serve on the advisory council for the Women's Congress being held in San Francisco in May of the following year.

Whereas the press had been kind to Annie's remarks at the 1894 Congress, perhaps because her topic now was women's suffrage rather than the less-divisive Indian missions, the *Call* reporter "made a fool of her" in his write-up, wrote Annie to John. The *Examiner* also subjected her to ridicule. That negative experience nearly kept Annie from venturing out of her hotel room, even to attend a business meeting of the local suffrage forces. Miss Anthony had a stiffer upper lip and told Annie she must be there.[7]

A Mr. Powers, a Stanford professor, had somehow been given a slot on the congress agenda. His talk turned both Miss Anthony and the Reverend Shaw "livid," wrote Annie to her husband. Powers' open contempt for "old maid aunts" who worked to turn women from their proper role as wives and mothers made Annie shake with indignation. Somehow, she reported, Miss Anthony had marshaled her dignity to answer the professor with civility.[8]

"Bless you for not being such a tyrant that Prof. Powers claims man must be to fulfill his mission," wrote Annie to John.[9]

The shared emotions of that unpleasant day strengthened the tie of loyalty between the two women. Annie and Miss Anthony met at another suffrage function in October of that year when Annie had returned to the city to attend nephew Guy Kennedy's wedding. Annie was surprised then, almost beyond words, when "Mrs. Susan B. Anthony kissed me!"[10]

Correspondence between the two continued, even after Miss Anthony stepped down from the presidency of the national association when she turned eighty in 1900. Annie wrote in 1901 of her concern that the Indians in the rancheria village were being ignored in their request that they have a constable of their own to deal with misdemeanors—either involving Indians, or as some-times happened, troublemakers that came into the rancheria drunk or seeking trouble. She wrote that she herself was asking to be deputized as constable, a move which Miss Anthony praised highly.[11]

There is nothing found to suggest that this unusual step took place, nor would it have been feasible with Annie's frequent absences. For one thing, the Indians lacked U.S. citizenship and were therefore deemed ineligible for government services such as a constable to keep peace. Annie had little fear for her own safety on the rancheria—or more likely put such fears in the hand of God. Several instances are noted in her diary in which she stepped into situations involving drinking and gambling among the men on the rancheria and put a stop to them. One time she responded to a rumor that a brothel had been set up in the rancheria, but her hasty and spirited search turned up no evidence, for which she was grateful, having found George Clements to be one of the two men in the suspected building. She found no signs of prostitution practiced there.

It was not unusual for malicious whites, often those among the ranch day laborers, to manufacture such rumors, as Annie knew well.

The strength of the growing friendship with Miss Anthony was accentuated by many invitations to her to visit Annie in Chico. She was eighty-six when she finally came, no longer holding an official office in the suffragist movement but recognized everywhere as the heart and soul that had held it together, especially after Elizabeth Cady Stanton's death.

An extreme hot spell had made the West Coast valleys next to unendurable that July 1905, but by good fortune it had turned cooler and was very pleasant weather for Miss Anthony's visit. A ceremony had been scheduled, as it happened, of the presentation of a huge parcel of Rancho Chico for perpetual use as a parkland by the city of Chico—land along both sides of Chico Creek as far east as the Hooker Oak.

Annie had only recently returned from Washington with her nephew Willie Alexander. Coming by another route were Sallie and her husband Tom. The Alexanders arrived in Chico on July 13, the same day as Miss Anthony's train brought her and her companion, a nephew's wife, Mary Anthony, and a Mrs. Gross from the Chicago suffragist offices.

It was a delicious occasion for Annie Bidwell—more of the presentation ceremony in a later chapter—but in some ways the highlight of Miss Anthony's visit was her brief talk two days later to the Indians assembled in their chapel for Sabbath services. A glow within herself was all Annie could permit of the pride she felt as her two secret granddaughters, Maggie Lafonso and Lily Clements, shone brightly as soloist and piano accompanist.[12]

The letter thanking Annie for her hospitality to the Anthony party came in August 1905 from Rochester, N.Y., Miss Anthony's home. It was written by Susan's niece and commented on "your beautiful home," the graciousness of your sister and her husband, and the little chapel where your influence is such a help to the Indian community.

Susan B. Anthony commented also on the magnificent gift on Annie's part to the citizens of Chico, with its wise restrictions on alcohol on the grounds. For some reason, Mary Anthony added that her Aunt Susan sensed that Annie was vulnerable. "There comes to me one fear … that without the most scrupulous care and attention … a goodly part, if not all of that splendid heritage may slip from your grasp." She had seen "many excellent women lose everything by putting absolute trust on men. [Miss Anthony] is seventy-eight and has no ulterior object in view [in telling you this]."[13]

The old and the young

nnie's thoughts during the years of the 1890s were never far from two aging loved ones. On the East Coast, her mother, Catherine Kennedy, was in many ways a child again. She could no longer fill the Bidwell's letterbox with her chatty near-weekly missives as in the past. She was like a child in that her mind constantly returned to rote lessons from her school days. Her body, of course, showed the strains inflicted by nearly eighty years. Catherine was a mere three years older than her son-in-law John Bidwell, and like him was suffering the reminders of having lived past one's prime.[1]

Bidwell had no problems with his memory. He tended to dwell more on humorous and absurd items—often poetry—which he memorized from the daily newspapers and quoted at the dinner table to Annie's amusement as well as that of guests.[2] His problems were with chronic ailments that had begun in middle age as only occasional nuisances—biliousness, lumbago and neuralgia in back, muscles and joints.

Beginning with severe respiratory difficulties suffered while on the 1893 trip to the Chicago World's Fair and which continued later into their visit in Washington, Bidwell was subject to several bad colds a year, often with a cough that lingered and neuralgia or pleurisy in chest and upper back. In between these sieges which sometimes kept him in his bedroom for days or even weeks on end he preferred to be out on the ranch somewhere: clearing, burning, and planting.

When Annie received the telegram on February 9, 1897, that her mother was not expected to survive the latest attack of heart failure, she took off for Washington at once, but not before doing something never before considered necessary on all her many trips "home." She made arrangements for full-time care for her husband by someone with whom she could feel more confidence than the housemaids of the past.

For the two years that Bidwell's distant cousin, Dr. Ella Gatchell had been in Chico, she had shown great willingness to give her services in return for the welcoming hospitality the Bidwells showed her and for their help with getting her medical practice started. She and her teenage daughter Florence, who had since come from New England to join her, now moved into the mansion and took charge. This was in spite of the fact Ella Gatchell herself had lost her voice from laryngitis and the handicap lingered on, as Bidwell noted in his letters to Annie.

It was a "first," for Ella Gatchell, to be exposed to a lengthy observation of a household with many servants. In her early practice in Chico, the woman doctor's chief patients were children. In those days a female doctor was expected to move into the household to reside and serve as both doctor and nurse. The public had not yet quite accepted women as professionals on a par with male physicians.

Ella's letters to Annie in her absence were far fuller of intrigues among the maids than with reports on John. Details of an elopement between John, the houseboy, and Leona were worked in between assurances that Dr. Gatchell was taking good care of the lonely general.[3]

Annie made her return from her mother's funeral more quickly than on many trips. She was back in Chico within two months and brought with her guests who had never before visited California, her uncle William and aunt Julia Reynolds from Meadville. The house filled with other guests that spring and summer of 1897: Eva Kennedy's sister Fannie Smith and son Fred; young Arthur Hirschfelder, son of the doctor, and a cousin Sam Block; Artie French, daughter of the 1896 Prohibition Party presidential candidate, Henry French. All of these friends came from the Bay Area.

Henrietta Skelton, the Canadian missionary, was also made welcome, easily earning her way by work done in the Indian village. During this busy spring and summer, with the house bustling with many occupants, often days went by in which the man of the house made no appearance.

When the valley heat became too unbearable in August, many of the guests and their hosts and much of the household were moved to Big Meadows where life around their campfires at the old familiar camping spots seemed to do Bidwell no harm. He had a running sore on one leg that only the slightest bump or jab would reopen, requiring treatment of soaking and bandaging every day. In spite of his attempts to favor the leg, he seemed often to reinjure it. Still, that was no worse than he would have experienced at home, and Annie cared for him uncomplainingly.

Life experience has a stage in which the mature actor has the sudden realization that the generation behind is nipping at his heels, like an over aggressive puppy, partly in fun and often with a deep-seated need to establish a new balance in the relationship master and dependent.

Both Annie and her sister were experiencing this as the elderly ones in their households shifted into more dependent roles. Sallie Alexander was having a difficult time before her mother's death as she and her husband tried also to meet the needs of a small boy, not an easy task for the middle-aged, heretofore childless, persons. Sallie had found her lifestyle drastically altered as her mother plunged deeper into senility and her adopted son started asserting himself. "Willie (fourteen) was rude at luncheon which always tires me more than anything else," wrote Sallie.[4]

Of course, Sallie was not a stranger to challenges, having been faced with the unusual situation of being named over her brother as executrix for her father's will. She had come through that with flying colors, with no more than the deep and unforgiving hostility of her older brother who blamed her personally for his having been shut out from either the process or the proceeds of property sales. It pained Annie almost as much as Sallie—perhaps more— that their brother Joe had refused to speak to Sallie for months before his tragic death by drowning in 1892.

Now named executrix for her mother's will as well, Sallie had the unsettling experience of what seemed like a visit from the grave of her older brother. Catherine had willed all of her estate to her daughters, with the exception of some specially designated personal items for Cora, Guy, and Joey Kennedy.

Sallie wrote to Annie in guarded words that an attorney in the probate court had raised the question of Catherine Kennedy's mental condition and whether she had had the ability to make a responsible will. This suggested to Sallie that an anonymous (to her) someone had injected into the court proceedings doubt as to the will's legitimacy.[5]

How like our brother Joe, Sallie implied, to suggest that I manipulated our mother. But in this case, she added, the complaint must have come from "your side" of the country, and clearly the direction pointed toward Guy Kennedy, himself an attorney and capable of writing a letter to throw doubts into the settlement of Catherine's estate. Now, Sallie wrote to Annie, Cora had once puzzled her by asking that she, Cora, receive no large gifts from her or her mother. Now it seems that Cora had been uneasy over large money gifts passing between the sisters, and that Guy had on occasion let slip out in his mother's presence the suspicion that Sallie had been siphoning off estate money into Annie's bank account as well as her own. In no way had Cora wished to seem even an innocent part in this scheme, if scheme it actually was.

And why would Guy Kennedy have suspicions of his aunt Sallie? Annie knew that Guy had grown restive in the Alexander home when he was there to attend a prep school course in 1890. Guy never finished that school course and had insisted on returning home to California. Sallie was reminded of things that might have been said or sensed in the Alexander household leading up to Guy's precipitous departure.

Later Sallie wrote in 1893 when Guy was rumored to be quitting his Berkeley studies without any logical reason given, as had been the case when he had left Washington, "I am so much at loss to understand Guy's position ... an anomaly ... a stranger in his own land," wrote Sallie to Annie.[6]

Guy had certainly been aware of the household undercurrents during the Kennedy siblings' feud, and maybe—probably—heard firsthand from his uncle Joe, his side of the bitter dispute over the handling of Joseph C. G. Kennedy's estate. Guy also knew first-hand the obvious failing of his grandmother's mind—her introducing him to friends as her "nephew," the times she went missing from the Alexander home and had to be searched for in the neighborhood, her rambling little sermons on how Guy should be ever grateful to the ones who were giving him a chance to be educated in a fine Washington, D.C., school. Perhaps scarcely reasons to doubt her ability to make a will which truthfully reflected her wishes, but if not those reasons, Guy may have looked hard for other reasons to rationalize his grandmother's exclusion from her heirs Guy and Joey Kennedy, children of her deceased son Johnny.

The District of Columbia court decided finally to ignore the interjection of this question raised about Catherine's mental abilities, but the estate's settlement dragged on until at least 1901. Sallie's victory on this point left a residue of bitterness in the hearts of her nephews in California.

Although oblivious to much of the comings and going in the mansion during his episodes of illness, John Bidwell did not protest the presence of children in the house and when he could eat at the table, their presence made for much more lively conversation than when just the business-minded Col. Royce reported ranch problems and progress over dinner.

Guy Reynolds Kennedy, still studying, at the University of California. Courtesy of California State Parks.

During the later years of Bidwell's life, Maggie Lafonso was often at the dinner table with them, her brother Elmer, Eamyo Conway, and sometimes Mary Keola and Lily Clements.

When Bidwell's road crew was working, particularly when on the east and canyon side of the ranch, Annie often drove or walked to the noon campsite and prepared something hot for lunch. Usually this was eggs or something she could heat or fry over a wood fire, augmented by a salad or fruit prepared in the mansion kitchen.

Bidwell's outlying ranch work created the excuse for picnics on which she took several Indian children to play in the stream and eat ice cream carefully kept frozen in its container of ice and salt. There were picnics for other children, too. Members of their Presbyterian Sunday school classes, and occasionally a group of students and instructors from the normal school.

Bidwell had discovered a spot in Chico Creek far up into the canyon where a deep pool had formed among the rocks. This became the "swim place" noted in his diary, and during hot weather he liked to drive as close as possible to the little pool and bathe. He had a small raft fashioned for Annie to row out into the pool, and on rare occasions, she too would bathe.

She had devised how this might be done and yet maintain her modesty while camping when both Bidwells bathed in the hot springs near Mt. Lassen where they went on summer camping trips.

It was a pleasure to Annie that the Indian children enjoyed coming into the mansion and that her husband grew accustomed to their presence.

Then came the cataclysmic event which embroiled Annie in the lives of her husband's son George and his children and threatened to destroy every plan she had so carefully nurtured to deliver the Indians from their native ignorance while bringing the youth into closer relationship with the mansion residents.

It was a Sunday, February 12, 1899, that Annie had led the services in the rancheria chapel as usual, but left with a depressed feeling that the men present—and they were well represented that day—were restless for a reason she could not pick up. Perhaps it was expression of a misunderstanding or doubt as to Christian beliefs she had explained so many times.[7]

Elmer Lafonso, Maggie's younger brother, asked to walk home with Annie as younger boys often did to carry her books and charts. Elmer was invited to stay for Sunday dinner as usual, after which Annie excused herself to lie down and rest, still burdened by the feeling that she was failing somehow in her mission.

She had risen and was just about to go downstairs when Lily Clements, then about nine, met her at the door of her bedroom. Lily's words spilled over each other. Her father George was at home and had been drinking all day. Worse, he had made her brother, five-year old Luther "dead drunk" and Annie must come to the village right away.

Hastily Annie sought the assistance of Charlie Cunningham, the trusted house servant, and they drove a carriage at once to the village. Finding little Luther too drunk to walk, they picked him up bodily and brought him back to the mansion. On their way they saw George Clements weaving across the orchard in intoxication toward the mansion. Rufus Pulisse and Pablo Silvers were with him, apparently trying to dissuade the drunken man from whatever he was contemplating. Annie told Charlie to lay Luther on an upstairs bed and ran toward George and berated him for his terrible actions. He mumbled a denial of any wrongdoing and was then persuaded by the other Indians to return to the rancheria.

Once Annie had Luther in bed and sleeping from the effects of the alcohol, she drove to Guy Kennedy's office to ask him to have George Clements arrested. Guy was in his office on that Sunday but referred her to the district attorney, J. D. Sproul. Annie felt no pangs for breaking Sproul's Sabbath quiet to demand he make out a warrant for George's arrest.

Her diary for the day states, "I pour out my soul in gratitude that He calls me to His service in rescuing this little lamb."[8]

Bidwell's son George Clements, for such the other Mechoopdas knew him to be, had ever kept Annie at a distance,

Taken in a hop field near Wheatland, California, which employed many Indians during summer harvest. Thought to have been taken in the late 1890s, the picture includes George Clements, standing center in the rear, and seated, Jane (Clara?) Clements with children Luther and Lily. Courtesy of Dorothy Hill Collection, Meriam Library, CSUC.

to her disappointment, quite unlike Amanda. When enrolled in her Indian school, George often refused to attend class with no excuse other than "I aint want to come." He sometimes attended chapel services, but as often not. The seven letters he had written to her from the Middletown Indian School were saved by Annie, but they seem to be pitiful examples of form letters laid out by an instructor to be copied for practice.[9]

George had gone in 1884 with several other of the older rancheria children to an advanced level Indian school in Middletown, Lake County, in an arrangement made by Annie Bidwell when she felt that the more able students could not get adequate instruction beyond the village school. Bidwell noted in his diary that George had left the Lake County school in midterm and reappeared in the village with no apparent other reason than that he wanted to come home.[10]

Nopanny's letter to Bidwell in 1887 noted that George was by then married, with one child, and that though he tried to work and please the ranch foremen, they were harsh on him and used bad language. Nopanny had made an appeal to Bidwell to be more understanding and patient with the young man.

George had been in trouble with the law earlier over a domestic matter in 1895, probably for striking his wife Clara. When advised to do so by some of the Indians in the village, Clara had gone to John Bidwell and asked him to advise what she, or he, could do, about George's behavior.

Clara seemed a gentle person, and Annie noted that she kept a very tidy house. Annie had known that the couple were having trouble and had been to their house to pray with them a month earlier. Clara seemed clearly to be the injured party, and John Bidwell, for lack of any better idea, suggested that Clara have her husband arrested. Clara had done so.

What may have transpired then in Bidwell's mind is a mystery (perhaps it was at Annie's plea that he think more kindly of this son), but he went to Chico Justice of the Peace Robert Warren before whom George was to appear. After a discussion of the situation, George was let go with his promise to Judge Warren to alter his behavior to his wife to something less physically abusive.[11]

In spite of the promises George made to the judge, by 1899 Clara had left her husband, after calling again on Bidwell to inform him of her decision. He did not record the contents of this July interview. Clara fled the village leaving the children with George, probably as customary in the Maidu culture. There were two Clements children: Lily, nine; and Luther. Bessie, an older child in the household, may have been Clara's by an earlier marriage.

During the furor which Annie stirred up in her determination to have George Clements punished for this new infraction, John Bidwell tried to be as inconspicuous as possible. On weekdays he left the house at eight o'clock and took his road crew to a remote area on the ranch, getting home after five.

It was Monday, February 13, before Sproul actually had a warrant served on George, but Annie continued her pressure on the district attorney to get George before a judge as soon as possible. A date was set for Wednesday morning, by which time Annie had gone to see a lawyer with the purpose of obtaining guardianship of Luther.

When Annie showed up in the courtroom on Wednesday, she had with her Bessie, Lily and Luther as witnesses to their father's dastardly behavior. A bit late, and probably with some reluctance, Bidwell appeared and sat with his wife. George Clements appeared in court with an attorney, William Schooler of Chico, who relayed to the judge George's demand for a jury trial. This postponed the trial until the following Monday.

Meanwhile Clements made an effort to coax Luther to come home, waiting for him in front of the mansion. Luther resisted and told his father he did not wish to go home.

Annie was glorying in caring for "the dear little fellow," tenderly bathing him each evening and patching his garments or making new clothes for him. While Annie was praising God "that He did not let me flee from this distressing trial, but give the grace of the true shepherd," she might have pondered on George himself deserving some praise that *he* did not flee the trial, which might have been an understandable action considering the local prejudice against Indians he was apt to encounter in a jury trial.

After Sunday services at the rancheria chapel the day prior to the date set for the trial, George was again waiting outside for Luther, and led him home. That afternoon Annie's eye was caught by Luther's face peering 'round the corner of the mansion, "his little sad and angry face with tear-swollen eyes."

"My father would not let me come."[12]

At last the trial began, on Monday morning, February 20, with John Bidwell slipping into a seat next to Annie at ten o'clock as the proceedings were to begin. It was a courtroom crowded with both Indians and white persons, for news of the event had wide circulation on the Chico gossip exchange. Both Bessie and Lily were called to testify for the plaintiff's case, as well as Rufus Pulisse who seemed to have witnessed Luther's being given the alcoholic drink, though Clements' attorney also called Rufus as a defendant's witness. They were certainly making a poor case for George, Annie thought.

Then to her horror, "Willie" Schooler, who had often professed to her affection and admiration in the days he had been Annie's Sunday school pupil, rose and addressed the jury.

He "announced to the jury that this is a case of *persecution* on Mrs. Bidwell's part because she could not beat religion into George's head and could not otherwise punish him, therefore she used the law to punish him! This accusation was fairly screamed at the jury! How base. ..."[13]

The jury was split, ten for guilt and two for acquittal. George Clements was free.

Annie wrote "[I] Came home … and took [houseguests] Mrs. Stephens and children to see the Chinese parade … but my back! My head! My heart! How dark it all seems, yet for God's little one I would gladly die. Gave Luther a good bath & got him to bed. Thank God, I could go to bed myself resting in His infinite love, even in the weakness about me, for there is no path of light for me. I can but trust."[14]

Annie stayed in bed until one in the afternoon on Tuesday, then rose and wrote in her diary, "W. Schooler's crucifixion of me yesterday teaches me to willingly hear what Christ did for me, that I may suffer, & [sacrifice] my life for his little ones, & like our dear Lord, hold no ill-will for the crucifier. … Oh, Blessed Savior, forbid that my faith fail, & that Satan sift me not, as wheat."[15]

During the week while waiting for George's trial, Annie had been in contact with the Arents, directors at the Greenville Indian School, and had made arrangements for Luther's admission as a boarding scholar. To her surprise she heard from her rancheria source that Lily and Bessie wanted to go with Luther to Greenville. The task of preparing wardrobes for Lily and Luther took much of her time, though she tried to carry on all her usual activities with a calm face. Bessie had never warmed to Annie in the past, nor shown much response in school or Sunday school, but she may have been coaxed to go by the rancheria women who thought little Luther needed watching over. Five was a tender age to be sent off to a distant boarding school, especially alone.[16]

Money for stage tickets was provided—to Oroville and on to Quincy where the children would be met, lunches for three boxed up, and a trip made to the village to try to appease any doubters among the women who had up to this point shown Annie support. She showed a letter from the Arents, written to welcome the children and sending samples of the Indian school children's handiwork from Greenville. She shared these with Amanda, and brought herself to stop at George Clements' house and give the Arents' letter to him to read. He was reticent but very polite.

While Annie Bidwell had single-mindedly pursued her mission of the rescue of the Clements children, her husband had again demonstrated his reluctance to have any emotional involvement with the residents of the Indian rancheria. He gave Annie the support of his presence in the courtroom but said nothing. Guy Kennedy managed to be out of his office most of the week between George's arrest and the jury trial which had failed to convict him of child endangerment. Annie was fortunate that her Divine support had not deserted her.

But one must ask, what had transpired among the residents of the rancheria? Where did George get encouragement for his bold defense?

Looking back to the day of the drunkenness of Luther, a Sunday, it may be recalled that Annie had experienced a sinking feeling from observing the demeanor of the men in the chapel. Even then, the men's knowledge of the drinking in the village must have alerted them to trouble. Much discussion among the rancheria Indians must have followed the "kidnapping" of Luther by Annie. Anger at this intrusion on the village and on the rights of a parent may have swept over many of the men. Did Holai Lafonso, as chief-in-name of the Mechoopdas, try to caution them, to argue that the well-being of the village lay with subservience?

From the discussion with those men who were sympathetic to him, George Clements must have been inspired to fight the white man's idea of justice within the white man's system. How William Schooler was selected to represent him, and why Schooler was willing to challenge Annie Bidwell's integrity in a public trial is an unknown, but it is easy to think that the hands of many of the rancheria men went into their sparsely filled pockets to help George with the expense of that legal advice.

William Schooler was later to earn a name as a skilled defense attorney in Butte County, one time as partner to Guy Kennedy in the "famous" Slaughter rape case. Both Schooler and Kennedy were to specialize in criminal defense cases.[17]

As another footnote, Bessie was back at the rancheria within a week, somewhat to the surprise of Bidwell who noted it in his diary, but it lends credence to the idea that she had gone to help guard over the small boy Luther on his journey.[18]

George brought a new wife to the rancheria later that year of 1899. Annie determined to win Maud over and to work harder to bring George into a better relationship with the church.[19] Though she continued to write or contact the couple over the next year, George did not soften his stance toward her in spite of his unfailing politeness in her presence.

And so the young were challenging their elders. But who really came out the winners, either with Guy's involvement in questioning his grandmother's competency when she composed her will, or George Clements' bitter public accusation of Annie's need to conquer the souls of the villagers? Only time could tell that, but in neither situation had the wounds below the surface, opened by intense emotions, been healed.

Death comes to a pioneer

*I*n September 1897, the Chico Board of Trade approached John Bidwell about serving on a special commission to study much needed improvements on the Humboldt Road Wagon Road.[1] The existing road, a private venture of John Bidwell and several other capitalists, had been incorporated in the 1860s as a toll road over the Sierras and was first envisioned as serving the Idaho mines with supplies from Chico. The road for several reasons fell short of its original goal but did serve Butte, Plumas and Lassen counties quite well. It had been a public road for a number of years by 1897, but allowed by the counties to disintegrate to a degree that traders and pleasure travelers alike were often bogged down in winter and equally hindered in summer by rocks, holes and ruts in the crooked roads.

The prospect delighted Bidwell who needed a challenge to shake him out of the torpor in which bouts with lumbago and bad colds left him. He knew the route well. He had been involved in the 1860 surveys and he and Annie had traveled the road into the mountains through Forest Ranch, Butte Meadows and Jonesville on many camping trips. He knew its use for both travel between Chico and outlying areas such as Prattville and Greenville, and for driving livestock, including his own, to and from summer pasture.

Young Reuben Messinger had just been employed by Bidwell as coachman in 1897; Bidwell liked him very much, as did Annie. Driven in a light wagon by Messinger, Bidwell started out alone to first make notes on the road's worst sections and to explore for an easier grade ratio. The surveying aspect appealed to him—it was a skill he had learned as a boy and often turned to good use in his early days in California, as well as on Rancho Chico.

With additional men picked up at Fourteen Mile House and Forest Ranch, Bidwell worked all of November 1897, until the winter weather stopped the work. He slept some nights on bales of hay in the Lucas' barn at Fourteen Mile House when it seemed a waste of time to return to Chico overnight. This did no apparent damage to his back and limbs.

The board of supervisors, though presented with signed petitions from persons in Chico and others living along the road at a December meeting, tabled the request for funds necessary to do the work. Bidwell's report and its recommendations for future work was left in limbo.

John Bidwell during the last years of his life preferred to be driven, sometimes to outlying parts of the ranch and on road inspection trips into the mountains. His driver in this picture is Reuben Messinger. Courtesy of California State Parks.

In February 1898, a Good Roads Association was formed in
Chico, all members busily getting more petitions signed to
present to the supervisors. Bidwell amazed Annie by his seemingly
endless supply of energy and enthusiasm. The practice had begun
that Bidwell should never venture out on work in a remote area
alone; probably the doctor had strongly advised this precaution be
taken, considering Bidwell's history of sudden hip and back
seizures. It did not seem to dampen Bidwell's enthusiasm or hold
him back any to have the company of Annie, one or two of the
house servants, or occasionally Cora and Emma Crew.

The Board of Trade Roads Commission in July gave Bidwell
full authority to do what was needed, such as hiring a crew to
work with him and contracting out some sections. The surveying
he undertook himself. From June through most of September,
Annie joined him with the usual entourage of cook and housemaids, camping along the roadside. Only Bidwell's catching a
severe cold brought them back to the valley in early fall.

In spite of the disastrous events surrounding George Clements'
trial, or perhaps because of it, the couple was ready to return to
the Humboldt Road by summer '99. Even after a runaway team
threw Bidwell from a wagon on the ranch and put him in bed for
most of May, he would not be deterred from his determination to
see the job through.

By now the work had reached the east side of the summit,
leading down into Big Meadows. Here Bidwell hired ranchers
from the Italian ranch families who had settled along the east side
of the summit, the Fanianis and the Ruffas. In return for roadwork, the Chico work crew stopped work on the road to help the
ranchers with haying or other seasonal ranch tasks.

Annie loved that time. She did not have to neglect her pulpit
on Sundays for she set up a worship service in the camp, inviting
the ranchers' families. A fine dinner was served to all after she had
delivered her little sermon. The cook, we assume, had planned a

meal that permitted her to attend church, and the ranchers' wives contributed fresh meat and other dishes.

In many ways this was an idyllic time, one savored deeply by both John and Annie. She used the days to answer the many letters that came in steady stream from her associates in many organizations. She had her Bible study and sermons to prepare.

First and most important was looking after John. She sent letter updates to Sallie. Considered an important part of the work crew, she drove a gentle team hitched to the light wagon, with her pencil and tablet on the seat beside her. As the ground crew loaded the wagon with debris from the road she scribbled away, awaiting the signal to move.

The cheery voice of her husband would call, "Drive on, Precious," and she, answering, "Yes, Beloved," lay down her pencil and pad of paper to gently rap the horses' rumps with the reins.[2]

Annie loved rapturously the mountain summer thunderstorms that rattled over the camp and deposited quick, noisy showers on the roof of their snug tents.

A grand party was prepared on August 5 by a jubilant Lulu, the mansion cook, for Bidwell's eightieth birthday. The Fanianis, guests at Bidwell's invitation, contributed spring chicken which Lulu augmented with rice, potatoes, tomatoes, cream gravy, salads and fruit, topped off with a "good rice pudding" with cream from the Faniani's cow.

"To me he looks younger than I," wrote Annie in her diary of her octogenarian husband.[3]

Bidwell reinjured his arm on the job, and in spite of Annie's treatment and bandaging, it grew sore enough that Reuben was sent off for Dr. Stansbury one mid-summer day. Obligingly, the physician set out from Chico after dark that same day and arrived at the Bidwell camp at two in the morning. Bidwell was awakened and the doctor cleaned the open sore and rebandaged it, leaving instructions for an anxious Annie. After two hours of sleep in the bed the maids had vacated for his use, and a hearty breakfast, the doctor sped off by six to tend his Chico patients that day.[4]

In late November, weeks after the crew finished, Bidwell and Messinger returned to the mountains, driving the length of the route to check it over before he made a final report to the county supervisors. That trip caught the two men in a cold storm with driving rain, through which they traveled thirty-five miles in the open wagon.

"Astonishing!" wrote Annie in her diary, that her husband had no ill effects from such an ordeal.[5]

Although Annie had never cut her ties with the Chico Presbyterian Church as severely as had her husband, aspiring as she did to attend communion with Maggie Lafonso and to encourage other Indians to join the "downtown" church, both Bidwells were delighted when, after the Presbytery meetings of 1898, the Reverend Graham announced his resignation. The fourteen years he had occupied the pulpit, over three times longer than any of his predecessors, suggests that the Bidwells had fallen away from the once dominant role they played in the church. John Bidwell had not served on the board of trustees for years. The couple's attendance at one of the other Protestant churches in Chico became customary, and Annie, of course, had her Presbyterian services to conduct in the other Presbyterian church, as some referred to the Indian chapel.

Very probably John's financial aid to the Chico church returned to its former level with Graham's leaving. The membership, including the Bidwells, now came to listen to and evaluate the sermons of prospective applicants. The pastor finally selected was a young single man, the Reverend Willis G. White. As in days of yore, White spent his first two months as pastor as a guest in the mansion.

After the work along the Humboldt Road came to completion, John Bidwell returned to his earlier regular routine—up for early breakfast, out of the mansion by eight o'clock, and at work in some area of the ranch where roads needed smoothing or dead trees needed removal. One or more of the garden staff, and usually a crew of two or more Indians, worked with him and Annie made it a point to arrive bringing lunch whenever her schedule permitted, often with a friend or the houseguests of the moment.

During most of January's, February's and March's nice days, and now into April, John had accomplished clearing for a walnut orchard, and the planting of new trees from Bidwell's nursery had begun.

Then on a beautiful Monday morning, April 4, 1900, an hour or so after work began, Bidwell dropped the saw he had been using on a fallen tree and collapsed in pain. Annie and Dr. Gatchell were sent for and came immediately, as did Eva Kennedy, Emma Crew, and Florence Blake, Annie's maid.

The pain passed as he lay quietly, cushioned on coats with his head on a lap. He was moved to the mansion where he seemed to sleep, but in early afternoon his breathing stopped and death came very quietly.[6] The physician said it had been a heart attack.

For several days, Annie performed as if mechanized, planning the burial service and arranging for the opening of the grave. She had wired Sallie of the news at once after Bidwell's body was removed for burial preparation. The Alexanders wired back: they were coming. The date for her husband's funeral services was decided accordingly.

Many hands offered help, and some of these were pressed into writing the necessary wires and letters: to Bidwell's sister in Ohio, Annie's relatives in Meadville and Baltimore, his numerous friends in the field of botany, and the people with whom he had worked for decades in the Prohibition Party. There were hundreds of persons to notify, including their friends in San Francisco, Oakland and San Jose. But much of this was given to others to do, including Bidwell's longtime typist, Ida Florence Bohlander.

The word spread quickly to the Indian rancheria, and plans were made for the stunned residents there to take part in the burial service.

Especially tiring to Annie were the visits from sympathetic townspeople who came in to express sympathy and sorrow. After showing amazing strength and self-control for two days, Annie collapsed. Dr. Gatchell was very concerned because for some moments she could not find a pulse on the limp woman. She took dire measures. After putting Annie to bed in her room the doctor forbade anyone to enter except Mrs. Mary Reed who had nursed Annie in the past, and the servant who took meals and ran such errands as needed in and out of the room. Only one of these could at any time be in the room.[7]

On Annie's second day of lying almost motionless from exhaustion of body and mind, Minnie Alexander entered the room while no one watched and threw herself on the bed beside Annie, holding her close. She whispered, "Lean hard, beloved."

She repeated the same words from which she had received comfort less than six months earlier when her husband, Charles Alexander, had committed suicide. Following her husband's death in 1899, the grieving Minnie, her children and her mother-in-law had been invited to spend over a month with the Bidwells.

Annie later wrote of this experience, the prelude to a vision that was to give her peace, and she credited it for her will to recover:

Suddenly her friend passed out of the room again in a veil of silver, and she was alone, *but not to lean,* but to float. "I reached for pen and paper and wrote of my vision of a great storm. 'Lean Hard. Nay, verily, Lord, I can not "lean" but in the ocean of thy love, I *float* as the sea bird, with wings at rest, and I felt, and even thought, the sweet peace which comes from the sense of the power of Him— wonderful joy. God's coming to say, "Peace. be still".'"[8]

From that moment, Annie claimed to have felt her strength return to her limbs, and she was able to rise and join the household once more. No doubt Dr. Gatchell took care to see that people were not free to talk with Annie, except when asked for. Though this "vision" seems rather ordinary in the telling, to Annie it was a powerful sign that God would sustain her on her sea of despair.

When her sister Sallie arrived, she stayed with Annie during the nights, sleeping in the Bidwells' bed while Annie took the couch in their bedroom that her husband had often used for daytime napping.

The Alexanders arrived on the tenth of April and the funeral followed the next day. To accommodate the crowd assembled to pay their last respects (or, as always with some, to satisfy curiosity) the coffin was placed on the front portico of the mansion surrounded by members of the family. Rev. White and a few others made remarks. Community members gathered in the yard and garden. The newspaper reported that all the Indians who were physically able were gathered on the side portico behind Annie.

Sallie Alexander and Willie stayed with Annie until June 23. Tom Alexander left a month earlier. Sallie's presence helped Annie through the stressful emotions raised by the several eulogistic services held at both the normal school and the Chico Presbyterian Church.

The two women spent much time strolling around the grounds and sitting on the banks of Chico Creek. The cherry trees were glorious, always Annie's favorite trees to watch in their cycle of blossoming, ripening, and picking. The fruit of the several varieties was delicious, eaten directly from the tree.

Annie took Sallie up the Humboldt Road to show her the improvements in the public road that John Bidwell had finished so shortly before his death. They took tents and camped out briefly at two of the favorite Bidwell sites, including one Annie now decided to call "Robin's Nest" after a lovely remote spot the sisters had known in Pennsylvania.

Two months after her husband's death, Annie picked up her deceased husband's 1900 diary and read up to his last entry for April 3. For some reason, most probably a reaction of grief, she suffered a sense of having been shut out of John's life, by his death, of course, but also by the highly impersonal entries in the diary. This was Bidwell's style, and it hurt her that as he entered events in his day he had left out mention that she *had been there too.*

To his March 23 entry telling of a concert he had gone to in Armory Hall, she added "I and my husband at this concert." To his March 25 entry, to hear an address on "Christian Citizenship" she added "I with my husband. 800 present. Rev Mr. White sang a solo, enjoyed by my husband."

Where Bidwell had entered on March 28 his having gone to town hall to hear General W. S. Green, Annie wrote, "at about ten p.m. I went to Town Hall to return with my husband."

She then made an entry for April 4:

"On May 18, Friday, I *A.K.B.,* enter this solemn record, that at 2:30 P.M. my Beloved left us for his home with God, and so suddenly and so peacefully that we knew not that he was leaving us, nor the moment he went. A few moments after he had spoken in his usual tones we were conscious he had departed, though I was standing by his head, Eva had his right hand, and was seated by me. Emma was caressing his left hand. He had written his diary for Apr. 3rd; had written one and 2/3 pages of largest paper to Pioneer, had marked employees time in the household book: Had read about 4 A.M. to 6, and, was off to his work on Vallombrosa by '8 sharp.' On dismounting from wagon he said, 'I feel just like a boy!' Used the cross-cut saw; crowbar to remove bark, and in a little over an hour was prostrated from …" Annie did not finish the sentence.

The weeks of serenity with Sallie came to an end as they boarded the train for the East Coast. It was a blazingly hot summer, both to travel east and to endure after reaching the notoriously muggy District of Columbia climate. Annie's month-long stop in Meadville had provided some respite, but the short side trip Annie made alone to Ohio to see Bidwell's sister, Laurinda Jay, and other Bidwell relatives was tortuous as day after day of high temperature continued. It had been no better in Chicago where Annie spent two days at the Prohibition Party Convention and another at WCTU headquarters where she had first met Frances E. Willard. (That too had been during unhappy times, when Annie was returning from brother Joe's funeral in 1892.)

To please her Meadville hosts, Annie went to the New York Chatauqua with them for three days of cultural events.

Once in Washington and in her room in the Alexander's new home Annie collapsed, and the visiting physician ordered that she must never expose herself to the sun between ten a.m. and five p.m. until the near-tropical heat and humidity of summer passed.

Whether motivated by duty or real desire, in early winter Annie took herself from Washington to New York City to attend the WCTU National Convention on December 3, 1900. She sat on the platform as a member of the national board of directors. The week following, she spent in Philadelphia at the convention of the National Indian Association, basking in more attention and the sympathy expressed for a brave widow.[9]

Annie had been informed shortly after John Bidwell's death in a terse letter from Franklin C. Lusk, and in no uncertain terms, that the ranch on which she had lived for nearly thirty-two years was heavily in debt, and that if she did not begin at once to sell off the land to repay over $350,000 to the holders of the current mortgage, the Lick Trust certainly would foreclose and do it for her.[10]

The creation of subdivision maps for the ranchland west of the railroad began at once. Annie was gratified while in Washington to receive the deeds to sign as sales began to pour in—a total of some $60,000 before the end of the year 1900. The mortgage was entirely paid off through real estate sales by March 1904, as the rich ranchland was eagerly bought up.

John Bidwell had left two wills. One was in the event that he outlived Annie. The other foresaw that he would go first, and all of his estate was left to Annie. She made every effort, both before she died, and by the terms of her own will, to execute each of the bequests that he had made in the more detailed document written in case she died before him.

A rather disquieting two interviews took place a few weeks after John Bidwell's death, the first being with Lilly Bidwell Collins, John's niece, who came from Sacramento prepared to be invited as a houseguest. Lily had calculated that she should get about $40,000 inheritance from her uncle and told Annie that she would be grateful not to have to wait for it. She had had to borrow money to attend the funeral and to make this trip from Sacramento. Annie was caught wordless, finally stammering that she had no access to any of the estate of her late husband.[11] She gave Lily $20, to pay for her travel, from a small cash fund she had set aside from a gift from her mother several years earlier.

When America Fuller, Lily's mother, appeared on April 30 to add pressure to Lily's request, Annie refused altogether to see her, and told Sallie to refer all such requests to Col. Royce.[12]

The give and take of a successful marriage

rom a conversation overheard between two seasonal guides in the Bidwell Mansion State Historic Park:
"Do you think that the Bidwells were—well, do you think they had sex?"

"I wonder myself. And they didn't have any children. I've wondered about that."

The cramming up on Bidwell information expected of new guides includes no allusion to such delicate information. There is the matter of her deep religious belief, and his stern appearance in photographs, none of which show them looking at each other, or touching, let alone kissing! Even their wedding portrait was of them posed separately in different frames. The formidable accomplishments of the couple, together and separately, seem to have left little time for the carnal. And then there is the matter of all those separations. If modern couples hope to fulfill their marriage with a child, they keep at it![1]

Victorian propriety, the veneer of the "refined" class, ruled out the possibility of expression of sexual feelings publicly, or for that matter, any mention of those body parts and functions that might deal with intercourse or a woman's "trouble," the word used by John Bidwell to refer to pregnancy or any aspect of it.

Bidwell felt self-conscious about even using the adjective "our" with bedroom in his diary, leading numbers of guides to suppose he had a separate bedroom from Annie. Not so. In his letters to her it was "our bedroom," and other information popping up here and there in letters and Annie's diaries confirms this.

That the Victorian age also saw the sanctioning of "free love" as a lifestyle seems incongruous, but the fact is that the era witnessed some very explicit love affairs among rather prominent people. Queen Victoria herself was rumored to have had those carryings on with her stableman, Mr. Brown.

It was simply not talked about openly in polite society—or more precisely, not in mixed society or with the servants. So Annie Kennedy, who was very Victorian in her upbringing, and John Bidwell, who was not only a fast learner but of a naturally inhibited nature, were forced into very circumspect expressions of their intimate life together.

The separations that Annie had imposed on their marriage from the beginning inevitably meant that exchange of ideas and a revelation of feelings for months on end depended on their skill in choice of wording in letters they exchanged, many of which have been preserved. These letters clearly show that the couple was devoted to each other. John Bidwell found at last an intelligent and loyal mate to whom he could unburden himself in ways never before accessible to his proud nature. Annie had found material that she could mold into the person she had idealized as husband, not always without using her feminine wiles as well as her choice of words. Her logic was a feminine logic, and one that her husband appreciated as such.

Throughout their correspondence there are references to the importance Bidwell put on feminine refinement. Although he approved of women having the right to vote, he did not relish the idea of women taking active campaign roles where in the delivery of impassioned oratory their voices would become harsh and unpleasant. In so doing a woman would lose "one of her irresistable [sic] attractions to sway the most stubborn of the rougher sex."[2]

Mary Bidwell Reed, handsome daughter of John Bidwell's half-brother Daniel. She and Annie Bidwell were socially thrown together often but were not compatible. This hairdo worn by Mary Reed was described by John Bidwell as reminding him of the jagged hair of a molting buffalo. The frequent use of a hot curling iron caused ladies' hair to frizz and turn reddish brown after too many singeings. Courtesy of *Profile, Annie Bidwell.*

The late nineteenth century hairdo that Annie (and her husband) favored, was less damaging to the hair than the popular daily heat curling but it required time and the skillful hands of her personal maid to perfect the "sausage roll" style. Notice the WCTU "white ribbon," pledge of abstention. Courtesy of California State Parks.

When Annie sent him a new photograph she had had made in Washington following her father's death, he wrote that he liked it, *except* "there is in it a shade of sternness—or perhaps I should say firmness. If the latter, altogether lovely."[3] In her portraits made after John's death, that look of Annie's is unmistakably one of sternness.

Trust seems to be the key word to appreciating the relationship between John and Annie Bidwell. Complete trust between two human beings is rather rare, but he was so devoted that he was willing to continue the risk assumed with his confessions of past sin.

"Annie, you must always be my most confidential friend—
nothing in regards to my business must be kept from you, but
you must not disclose even a whisper to anyone."[4]

Annie, who had no dark secrets she feared exposing, still felt
reluctance to share doubts and fears with her parents, or even
with Sallie. "[I] should not write so sad a letter but am I not your
wife and to whom else on earth am I to talk to as my heart bids?"[5]

Annie's earliest letters to John after their marriage, and these
began soon because of his frequent business trips to Sacramento
and San Francisco, always ended with her enclosure of "one of
'our' kisses."

John, too, sent like tokens: His departure from home on their
first Christmas eve was followed by a letter from Annie almost
drenched in tears. He wrote of his remorse, especially as his
business purpose turned out badly, but sent "the sweetest kiss I
can give, Dear Annie."[6]

There was no dearth of written endearments in his letters, as
might be expected of newlyweds, that first year or two after
marriage:

"I can bear almost anything but your absence."[7]

"I plucked a white flower [en route to an outlying town],
perhaps a white mountain lily, emblem of purity—and what more
appropriate for my love."[8]

"Before we were married … how I almost went frantic for an
opportunity to share my esteem and ardent attachment for you
which had taken entire possession of my life."[9]

"Every woman I see makes me like you if possible more, for I
am reminded instantly of the contrast—which is glowing. The
most absent minded strangers could but observe the difference
between you and all other of your sex."[10]

"It seems like throwing just so much of life away to be absent
from you. I never see a man scarcely but I pity him because he has
not so grand a wife as I have."

"Nobody in this wide world is so precious as my wife—your name ought to be *love,* you're so loving."[11]

And these expressions of sincere endearment were to persist throughout thirty years of marriage. Even in his seventies as he wrote with pencil on rough paper to better control "a hand trembling severely," he spoke of feeling lost without his "precious, precious wife."[12]

And yet Bidwell could be maddeningly neglectful in the little things. She wrote, "I was not hurt by your hasty goodby, but you scarcely waited to give me a kiss. You were worried and annoyed at yourself to worry about little things."

At other times, she clearly *was* hurt, even though she still struggled to understand how her husband came to growl at her instead of kissing her good-bye as he deposited her at the train station for departure.[13]

On her return from her first long visit east, when she disembarked from the train at Junction—the nearest point to Chico on the transcontinental train line—no ecstatic husband was on hand to meet her! He had just discharged his foreman, he explained later, and so had sent Johnny Kennedy to deliver her to Chico. He was needed to stay on the ranch to direct the workers.

She was disappointed and let him know it, but all in all, Annie was remarkably accepting of the fact that her husband's close attention to ranch administration was done with the interests of both in mind.[14]

In spite of his fear that such remarks lay in the area of "poor taste," John described to her his lying in bed naked on hot nights with the windows open to the breeze. No doubt his elaborate apologies were intended to relay to Annie that on such nights he would have welcomed her presence.[15]

He could be a bit more explicit: "While I was in Dr. Harkness' [waiting] room, a man said that the juice of pomegranate afforded great wonders in the night."[16]

He had written of her loving artlessness which he so appreciated. Perhaps it was this artlessness that lay behind her reply from Washington some time later, "Oh, how I long for some of your pomegranate juice—more than any other fruit!"[17]

Her letters, too, were peppered with expression of her feelings of sadness at separation:

"How am I to endure the long separation from you which we have planned? All today I have felt as if I had a fever—restless—painful to stay many moments in one spot. No letter from you is probably the cause."

"Mama laughed at some foolish stupid remark I made to the wife of the Austrian Minister—she seemed to think my mind was frozen. Well, my ideas are all with one at Rancho Chico, and I *was* as stupid as an owl."[18]

He wrote in the same vein: "It is an uphill business to write and have no sweet letter after expecting one for two long days!"

Bidwell tried poetry (of a sort) to express his feelings from time to time. One sample should suffice:

I have thought of you all day as constantly as when we were
    first m- - - - - d. (his dashes)
My love is undiminished.
How fleet is a glance of the mind
When I think of my dear Annie
In a moment, I seem to be there
But questions, when will!? how can!?
Soon hurry me back to despair.[19]

They could quarrel by letter also, and perhaps more explicitly. "How sorry I am to have incurred your disapprobation [she wrote] in expressing the foolish wish that you would drop in on us [in Washington] in the spring. It was a foolish wish but I never professed to be always wise. Indeed I am more foolish than wise."[20]

In writing such, she chose to refute what John had written earlier: "I have been forced by a power I have no inclination or strength to resist, to believe that you are always right—that your judgment is mature—that your motives never err, and that you are indispensable to my happiness."[21]

She refused to be mollified: "I am sorry to have lowered myself in your eyes. You miss the spirit of my wish if you thought the object was to be with *me* and to have a *gay time*. Perhaps I should be happy without you. Many wives are happy without their husbands."[22]

By agreement, based on each other's confessed ambition to improve in all ways, correction of poor grammar and misspelling in letters took place:

He wrote: "Rooves? You meant roofs."[23]

She wrote: "Bottany? Is it not botany?"[24]

But he was sharper than she at catching misspelling. "You say mowes with a sickle. Is that the way you spell mows?" And "You spell lichen 'litchen'!"[25]

At another time, he wrote, "You are pretty good on hard names, but easy familiar ones you are apt to misspell!"[26]

She caught him in both misspelling and bafflement as to meaning: "It is a *muffler,* not a *muffer* that mama sent you for Christmas! You tie it loosely 'round your neck."[27]

Annie insisted that "I wish to have my faults corrected, just as you correct them, kindly, and with a compliment from you."[28]

After some fussing over the failure of the other in letter writing—he did not number his pages—she did not date her letters—they pledged to not repeat the mistakes in the future. Alas, reform failed, She wrote: "[after] your letter devoted *exclusively* to reproof for my failure to properly date letters, I felt so disappointed (not unmixed with unChristian emotions) that I felt like replying in a 4 page letter on the exclusive subject of your failure to carry out your plan of numbering your letters, and let you then appreciate my keen disappointment in yours at least. ..."[29]

She also complained, "I fear you do not read my letters carefully as you so often misunderstand them when the language is so very plain."[30]

These literary spats ended in forgiveness, of course, she to write "to my good but naughty husband, whom however, I forgive."[31]

And he: "Well I hope we are just even. I have scolded back enough to balance the accounts and now let us be friends and even dearer than any other friends. ... I get out of tune sometimes, but I try to get back as soon as I can!"[32]

From afar, Annie worried at the twelve and fourteen hour work days to which her husband sometimes subjected himself, followed by falling asleep over his letter to her.

"Do you intend to kill yourself in my absence? If you had warned me when I left that you intended to commit suicide I should be scarcely less surprised than I am at your really systematic method. God intended you to work during proper hours and to sleep on the same principal [*sic*] and to trust in him for the rest. ... You never worked so before and God forbids you working so now. It is the Devil tempting you to suicide."[33]

Over the years, she became more relaxed at her husband's report of long hours and the resulting weariness. "I am sorry you are so busy. Though I overwork myself, it is never on temporal things, which perish. For the souls of men, women and children I am glad to spend myself but not for that which 'perishes in the using.'

"Dr. says *you* [deliberately] overwork."[34]

Annie very often had directions to send back to the domestic staff at the mansion, and John eventually became fairly comfortable with entering the domain of cook and housemaids to deliver these orders, whether to check the winter clothing for moths or leave instructions for the cook to preserve a given number of jars of cherries. He confessed that he preferred to let the girls alone and unless their meals were poor or, as often happened, a violent quarrel erupted among the women or with the housemen and gardeners, he let them blunder along to hopefully leave him in peace.

"Spare me the menus. Just put good meals on the table."

His wife's orders to purchase items for her when he went to the city worried him enormously. He could manage gloves and stockings, even shoes, but was driven to seeking the advice of a male friend in picking a carpet pattern.

A request had come from a Mrs. Blake, a friend of Annie's who asked him as a favor to purchase a gift she wanted for Annie—a nice article for ladies' evening headwear for garden or party. He wrote in desperation to Annie: "What sort of thing is it? Vegetable or animal, or mixed? Did I ever see one? How long has it been in use? Is it a comb, a chignon, look like a bustle? Can I carry it in my valise? Send an express tomorrow."[35]

John Bidwell tried to follow his wife's well-intentioned directions regarding his clothing and manners. She wrote often on the subject of underwear advising him not to leave off his flannels too soon during the summer months, and to have Ellen sprinkle those garments before she ironed to prevent shrinkage.

"Isn't it time for you to have your hair cut? You look so much better with your hair properly short," Annie wrote.

"When are you coming back to cut my hair? I shall be shaggy as a wolf when you come home."[36]

"You might see Orphelia and have him cut your hair." Orphelia was Bidwell's favorite San Francisco hair and beard trimmer.

It was no good when Annie asked her husband to carry a message of congratulations, or report on a birth. Nothing embarrassed John Bidwell so much as thinking how to properly handle a new infant's arrival. When Annie asked him to pass on her congratulations to Mary, the housemaid, on the birth of her new baby, John replied that there was no way he could do it. "Never in this world could I think how to preface such a sentiment."[37]

When asked to report on her brother John's new son Guy, Bidwell reported driving by the Kennedy house and rattling a stick on the fence to get Johnny's attention so that the new father would come out to him. What if he were to see the mother in bed? What could he possibly say in such a situation?

Cora's sister Emma Wayland Davidson's new baby was shown him in spite of this squeamishness, and Annie asked for a description. He reported back to Annie, "Oh, it looks for all the world like a chipmunk," reverting as he was inclined to do to metaphors based on wildlife.

Annie felt free to criticize her husband's table manners, for he once wrote to her: "I have been very good and tidy about overdoing the egg business on the whisker exhibition—small mouthfuls is my motto, and do a more sure, if not so large, a business."[38]

Bidwell commented on his wife's love for the new French dessert, ice cream: "You wrote you took no ice cream at your party. *You* took no *ice cream* ! ! ! ! ! To me it would be pure punishment to swallow the frozen frothy stuff."[39]

Annie was critical of John's lack of social grooming: "I think the Gibbs [Annie's good San Francisco friends she had known in the East] believe your interest in them is not very great. I notice it in Mrs. Kane [Mrs. Gibbs' mother] particularly. Our friends are not too abundant."[40]

When John was expected in Washington to join her she wrote: "I am so anxious for you to do the right thing and treat my friends as you would like to be treated. I know it is a bore to visit according to city style, but it is also important that you should mix with strangers and cultivated persons. It wears off the edges. Not that *you* have any, but it would give me more ease if you would acquire more ease and pleasure in society."[41]

An amusing exchange of letters in June and July 1880, between Annie in Washington and John in Chico on the occasion
of John Sutter's death has been printed and reprinted and will not
be repeated in length here but it reveals how differently they
could view an occasion, and skirt on the edges of hurting each
other's feelings.

Before receiving her letter telling of visiting the Washington
hotel where Sutter died and of sadly viewing the body covered by
a sheet in the lobby, Bidwell had read of the death in a newspaper.
He wrote to her, "I hope you will attend his funeral if in the
district."[42]

Not only had she planned to attend the funeral, she had sent
flowers to the hotel and was so bursting with emotion and fear
that the newspaper coverage of Sutter's death would lack sufficient praise of the man, that she submitted her own written
statement to the Washington *Evening Star.* It was published, and
Bidwell read her unsigned article before her letter arrived telling
him of writing it. His response had been hardly flattering:

"[very] unsatisfactory story in the ... *Star.* ... does not state
who was with him or who administered to his wants in his last
illness. The article conveys he was neglected and someone felt in
defense to smooth the matter over with the article."

He later admitted that though he felt very sad at Sutter's
death, he had forgotten to fly the mansion flag at half-mast.

Annie was quite sentimental over the departure of the once
mighty Sutter, who had fallen from running his frontier empire to
an old age of poverty. She wrote John that she gave Sutter a
special place in her heart, crediting him with his having played a
major role in bringing them [John and Annie] together, a twist of
reasoning that John Bidwell may have had some trouble accepting
in the spirit intended.

John was in hot water enough when Annie reported back that
she had written the article in the *Star.*

"Hah! Hah!!" he answered. "So you wrote it? Well, you have had the benefit of my criticism."[43]

John Bidwell was never anything but praiseful and proud in the presentation of his wife to Chico society. The Chico ladies picked up at once on how he must view *them* in contrast. Mrs. Emma Wayland early declined Bidwell's request that she host the Mite Society meeting to be held at the mansion in Annie's absence: "To take *her* place I would have to be like Nicodemus—born again."[44]

Some aspects of living are too mundane to be found in diary entries and letters, but a casual remark here and there reveals such things as that on the few nights when the Bidwells had the dinner table or the house to themselves, they spent enjoyable hours simply chatting—or playing cards. That cards were acceptable to Annie seems to negate any thought that she was opposed to fun for fun's sake. During one of their first separations, when John had left Annie in a San Francisco hotel to shop after he went home to Chico, she wrote scolding him for having taken the cards home with him![45] Now she would have to buy another deck. Perhaps both played solitaire.

A favorite among old saws is that "the way to man's heart is through his stomach." Annie certainly saw it is as both a duty and a privilege to feed her husband well, giving the cook instructions to serve Bidwell two kinds of meat with each of his meals, and a full complement of vegetables and fruit.[46]

With the ranch gardens, fields, and orchards producing great quantities of delicious nuts, vegetables, berries, tree fruits, melons (the Generals' favorite being the casaba), eggs, milk and cream and freshly milled flour it took only a little imagination for each meal to resemble a culinary masterpiece if the cook was not lazy. When Annie was away, if John reported to Annie that the meals were getting less than satisfactory, Annie wrote directly to the kitchen staff and gave sharp orders to rectify matters.

Annie had fresh beef, lamb, mutton, squab, chicken and pork always available from which to choose for menus. Venison, too, seemed to be a staple.

The meals also featured salmon caught by the Indians during the run in Chico Creek. There were other fish caught in the Sacramento River by the Indians or the ranch hands.

Annie's nephews and, earlier, her brother Johnny, brought in geese and ducks from hunting expeditions. Even the quail, which Annie loved to see running about the creekbank and under the bushes around the mansion, were sacrificed as occasional delicacy for the family, though Annie forbad the Indians killing "the dear little creatures."

On special occasions, such as an anniversary dinner, the entertaining of special guests, or perhaps for entertaining members of the normal school faculty, Annie would develop a five or more course menu such as her mother served at a formal dinner in Washington.

Annie enjoyed writing into her diary what food she had served for events that she believed would leave a favorable impression of her abilities. These menus might be the simple but plentiful food served on the lawn at a reception for over one hundred college students, or a sit-down dinner for as many as 150 visiting dignitaries.

For an elegant dinner served to a special guest list in the mansion dining room, the menu would be similar to the following one served in February 1888 to the Lusks, (F. C., his mother and aunt), the Dr. Stansburys, Normal School Principal Edward T. Pierce and wife, Colonel Royce (manager of Rancho Chico), Cora Wayland Kennedy and several of the normal school faculty:

1. Raw oysters.
2. Veal soup.

3. Turkey and cranberry sauce, macaroni with cheese, mashed potatoes, spiced figs, olives.
4. Lamb and mint sauce, current jelly, rice fritters, kohl-rabi, sweet potatoes.
5. Quail and lettuce with mayonnaise sauce.
6. Ice cream and vanilla cakes.
7. Coffee.
8. Blanched almonds, shelled English walnuts.

Very French! Dining from six p.m. to eight-thirty.[47]

Annie's husband might have overeaten to the point of predictable biliousness by eight-thirty, but would have been as proud as a man can be of his accomplished wife. And the guests would have been less than genteel to have lamented afterwards on the absence of a table wine.

Ruby English described the serving of such a meal:

The waitress [clad in dainty uniform] sat in a chair behind a service screen in the dining room near the door to the serving pantry to which the cook or cook's maid would bring the food. Mrs. Bidwell rang a tiny bell to summon the waitress from behind the screen to remove the plates after each course. The plates would go into the sink in the serving pantry; utensils for the next course would be placed, by which time the hot [or cold] food would have been served on each plate and handed through to the waitress.[48]

Annie often sent word to the maids on proper demeanor through her letters to John. The waitress must have a clean apron and have smoothed her hair. Never, never reuse the same napkins for dinner as used at breakfast!

Annie gave orders as to which fruits and vegetables were to be canned or otherwise preserved. The kitchen staff had no spare time during the hottest months of the year as they toiled over peeling, boiling, sterilizing jars and sealing.

Annie at intervals took inventory of the food so preserved in the cellar, and in 1891 itemized: spiced currants, preserved red currants, spiced cherries, spiced gooseberries, spiced figs—all used as condiments and in pint jars. Preserved fruit included cherries, raspberries, green gage plums, peaches, and gooseberries— totaling in the hundreds of jars.

Jellies in glasses included plum and apricot; fruits preserved in tin containers were peaches and nectarines.

The Bidwells gloried in sending fresh fruit as far away as Washington and to friends in San Francisco. The temperature during travel had much to do with how palatable these gifts were on arrival.

John sent Annie fresh fruit when she was in San Francisco for medical treatment, or for one of her philanthropic duties.

Although it was one of Annie's most active periods of involvement with Prohibition efforts and with "her Indians," during John's last two summers on earth she accompanied him and a party of workmen (cook and servants too, of course) to camp along the points in the Humboldt Wagon Road that Bidwell had undertaken to regrade. Fresh food from the valley came up with freight wagons and purchases from local ranchers provided fresh chicken, milk and butter.

In learning to appreciate the ranch and wilderness as close as the highland meadows and mountains, Annie found that she was an outdoor person at heart. The love to explore the rancho together on foot, horseback or carriage led to many a "ramble" as Bidwell called them. Naming the ranch roads was a shared pleasure, especially as Annie got into the spirit of it. Two examples were Mazy Way and Winding Way. She yielded more of herself in learning to appreciate the ranch—though she did always love beauty in nature—than her husband was willing to try being a more social creature. To her credit she tried to show interest in replying to the farm matters of which he wrote. When he told of improvements in the dairy, she sympathized with the cows that now were to be subjected to headlocks and foot chains. "It will give our staid old cows in the east no ambition to move even to the sunnier climes of California."[49]

One difference of opinion between the Bidwells was resolved when John apparently convinced Annie to do things his way regarding pet animals. Love for such pets, especially for dogs, was second-nature to Annie, having been reared in a family that always had one dog, and often two. Catherine's letters to her daughter Annie seldom failed to mention the latest antics of a Tan or a Prince.

Sallie wrote asking Annie soon after her marriage about what pets they had, and she divined that Bidwell might not care for a new dog she had acquired—being of a small nervous breed. It seemed strange to Sallie that a household could really be a home without a pet. Annie's father wrote in a letter to the newlyweds that he could conceive of no greater happiness than to sit in a favorite chair with a good book and the head of a faithful dog in his lap.

The Bidwells' one experience with a dog proved rather tragic. When a Mrs. Tichenor of San Francisco, a houseguest at the mansion for several weeks in June 1876, sent Annie a young greyhound in appreciation, there was an understanding between Annie and John that it would be an outside animal, though it must have gone against any natural impulse on her part. Quite possibly Mrs. Tichenor had heard Annie telling how much she loved dogs and thus chose "Roamer" as a gift without consultation.

Roamer was the name given to the dog because soon after his arrival he ran away, and only after considerable search on the part of ranch hands was he recovered. Running away became a pattern with Roamer, and after Annie went to visit in Washington late that year, Bidwell had him chained. This disturbed Annie who thought the confinement would break Roamer's spirit and turn him against people. She wrote in each of a series of letters how Roamer should have a new draft- and-rain-free doghouse built at once. "Please have this attended to the first thing, for God has put the beasts at our mercy, and we ought to care for the helpless."[50]

It proved impossible to train Roamer to stay at home; Annie was gone so much that periods went by in which Roamer had little human attention, though Annie prodded her husband, "Did Roamer remember you when you got home? Was he glad to see you? … Please pay Roamer some attention![51] … I'm glad you took Roamer on a hare hunt."[52]

During the summer of 1882, Roamer ran off and joined a pack of other dogs running loose about the ranch. Word came to Bidwell that the ranch shepherd had shot and killed Roamer when the dogs were caught worrying the lambs.[53]

Annie was never to mention Roamer or express a wish for a pet again. She satisfied her urge for a creature as companion by keeping a caged canary. The mansion lacked so much as a cat to serve as mouser. When an inquiry was made by a townsperson if a kitten might be available for his child, Bidwell referred him to a haybarn far from the mansion.

John Bidwell is not known by this writer to have ever acted on impulse, and the rather rigid deliberation with which he pursued life, even after marriage, did not leave too much room for changing deep-seated habits. A review of his life confirms this trait. From the moment he first conceived of the notion of going to California, he planned the migration carefully. Once having reached a decision, he persevered, even after most of his recruited party backed out of the migration scheme in the spring of 1841.

Likewise, after his first exposure to the area in Northern California had led him to envision the Chico Creek area as a farmer's Eden, he did not falter from the pursuit and was waiting when the way opened for him to purchase Rancho Chico.

It might be posited that Bidwell's trek to explore the Feather River for gold was precipitous, hastily conceived after taking the first gold sample from Coloma to San Francisco for Sutter to confirm its nature. Hardly so. Had Bidwell been less self-disciplined or governed by the greed that motivated others, he would have failed to oblige his employer's orders and simply have taken off to the north.

Bidwell took the time to reason out that if one Sierra river yielded gold, then another might be expected to do likewise. It led him to his rich strike at what was to be called Bidwell's Bar on the Feather River.

Bidwell's search for a mate was doubtless tied to another long existing vision, one which he had about given up hope of achieving by the time he reached forty-five. She was to be a refined gentlewoman, educated enough to appreciate his own striving for intellectual excellence, and from a social background such as would enhance his own social status. And where in pioneer California was he to find such a woman?

Bidwell saw Annie Kennedy from afar not long after reaching Washington during his term as California congressman, in either late 1865 or early 1866. He was lucky enough to be introduced to her family and to her—and his later impressions reinforced his belief that she was indeed the model of the ideal woman.

The impulse that led him to act decisively came while he was alone on tour of Ireland in 1866 after the close of the congressional session. Annie Kennedy was what he wanted and he returned to Washington with the resolve to fight for her.

His sizing up of Annie proved to be uncannily accurate as to her ability to meet the need he had for both a loving confidante and a social beacon.

Like John Bidwell, Annie had supposedly given up the idea of marrying. Whether this was in part because of the shortage of marriageable men following the Civil War is not known. More likely it was because she, too, had built in her mind an image of who could fulfill her ideals. She may not have defined it as clearly as Bidwell's picture of feminine perfection, but she sensed that a mate must bring with him a mission on which her evangelistic spirit might hone itself.

What greater mission than to take a man who tearfully confessed his alienation from God and swore to follow her guidance until he found that grace to be found only by being in harmony with God's will? The added possibility of turning Bidwell's Mechoopda village into a Presbyterian model of Christian devotion and presenting it to God also must have come early to Annie in her dream of a marriage mission, especially as she apparently was unable to bear children. Add to this the other great mission of removing the scourge of alcoholic beverages from the earth—in which her husband was to support her completely—and one can see that from Annie's perspective as well as from John's this was a marriage made in heaven.

Both wanted social position and the wealth to make it possible as well. Bidwell had promised that she would be a "queen," and if the people of Chico refused to be her subjects, as they largely did, she still held court in the mansion and reigned therein.

And what of their love? Well, what is love? Can it be more than the reflection of oneself viewed in the accepting and loving eyes of another? However it is defined, Annie and John Bidwell lived with the certainty of it, and no greater proof can be required than that each was an equal within the sight of the other. The trust each had that this was so made their spats no more than the salt and pepper of a shared meal.

Annie served as a safety valve for her husband's often explosive negative responses to people with whom he had to associate and do business. Occasionally she was not on hand to bear the brunt of his wrath, and on one such occasion he became so enraged at Franklin Lusk, with whom, as a fellow trustee, he worked on the building and landscaping of the normal school, that Bidwell resigned his position as chairman of the grounds committee, and in the heat of anger even sent in his resignation to the State Joint Board of Normal School Trustees. He was coaxed back into finishing the landscaping, but he never forgave Lusk for having insulted Mr. Lyon, a planting expert that Bidwell had brought in from San Francisco.[54]

This loss of temper and the subsequent regret for his angry blowup would have been likely avoided if he had shared the matter first with Annie. He would have avoided the loss-of-face with Lusk that he suffered from the incident. Annie seemed to understand innately her role in keeping her husband on an even keel.

F. C. Lusk was ever a thorn in Bidwell's side. In 1887, when Bidwell stayed behind to help get the normal school built, he wrote to Annie in Washington of his frustration, "Lusk holds everything back in decisions on the Normal. I do not believe there will be any getting along with him unless he gets his own way in almost everything."[55]

A year later, when Bidwell wrote from his bed, confined with a crippling hip condition, and Annie was in the mountains for tuberculosis treatment, "Lusk made no effort to meet the distinguished General Morgan who had come all the way from Rhode Island [to consult on staffing the college]. An unmitigated shame!! Morgan can only conclude that he has been snubbed!"[56] Having Annie as his sounding board was very therapeutic, and she would gently remind him of his own evaluation of Lusk as a man with a very shrewd legal mind.

Having married late, both Bidwells were capable of enduring without hardship the separation of their physical persons for months on end. In fact, the correspondence of the courtship period held a great charm in and of itself without which there would be no tangible record of their love saved, to be savored and resavored.

During the many separations over the years, this great store of correspondence grew in the camphor closet, a wealth both of them valued highly. Both seemed to realize that the material in those letters might have a longer life in and of itself than existed in the prospect of rereading. The occasional caution to "burn this letter" seemed as much used to avoid exposing posterity to sloppy writing than to censor the contents.

The writing of the letters gave satisfaction in and of itself. Sallie slyly remarked when observing Annie writing to John that she interrupted Annie's "love making."[57] John's writing to Annie, often late at night, was a relaxing way to relive the events of each day, and a substitute for the physical aspects of love that became less important as the years went by.

Annie's addition of a huge concrete vault in what had been the laundry room behind the original mansion kitchen, and the use made of it, puzzled state employees when the state of California acquired the building. The vault evidently went in when the original kitchen was replaced. Bothered by the maids picking the lock to the camphor closet in the mansion at leisure during the Bidwell's long absences from the premises, Annie breathed much easier when she knew her private business papers and intimate materials were no more to be shared with the housemaids of Chico.

Depression

*I*n printed accounts of the period following John Bidwell's death, the statement has been made that Annie suffered near collapse after her husband's death, and for a while her life was in danger. This must be an exaggerated account of the brief loss of strength and will that came over Annie a few days after her husband's death while she waited for Sallie to arrive.

Otherwise, though Annie still complained of the loss of use of her right arm from time to time (a reoccurrence of the problem for which she had suffered many twistings of shoulder and "breakage of sinews" at the hand of Dr. Hirschfelder), and the days of "not feeling well—of pain in her head" that had taken Annie out of circulation a few days at a time ever since she reached adulthood, she showed remarkable stamina for a cosseted wealthy woman.

Annie had believed in the value of exercise for years. Her days had begun for years with a combination of prayers and a mild physical routine. As with most persons, prior to having an automobile at the door, Annie walked a great deal and rode horseback occasionally. In her diary she proudly reported that younger persons had said of her that, "She can outwalk us!"

Her attacks of illness seem to have more often been the result of emotional stress than of either bacteria or a failure of her physical system.

Her new status of widowhood brought with it, not surprisingly, some days of depression. She wrote to John Muir, the valued friend with whom she had an unusually warm rapport, that after her husband's death she walked "in perfect blackness, when not even a star seemed to shine to comfort."[1] It was a grieving made tolerable only by the many tasks that she had set before her.

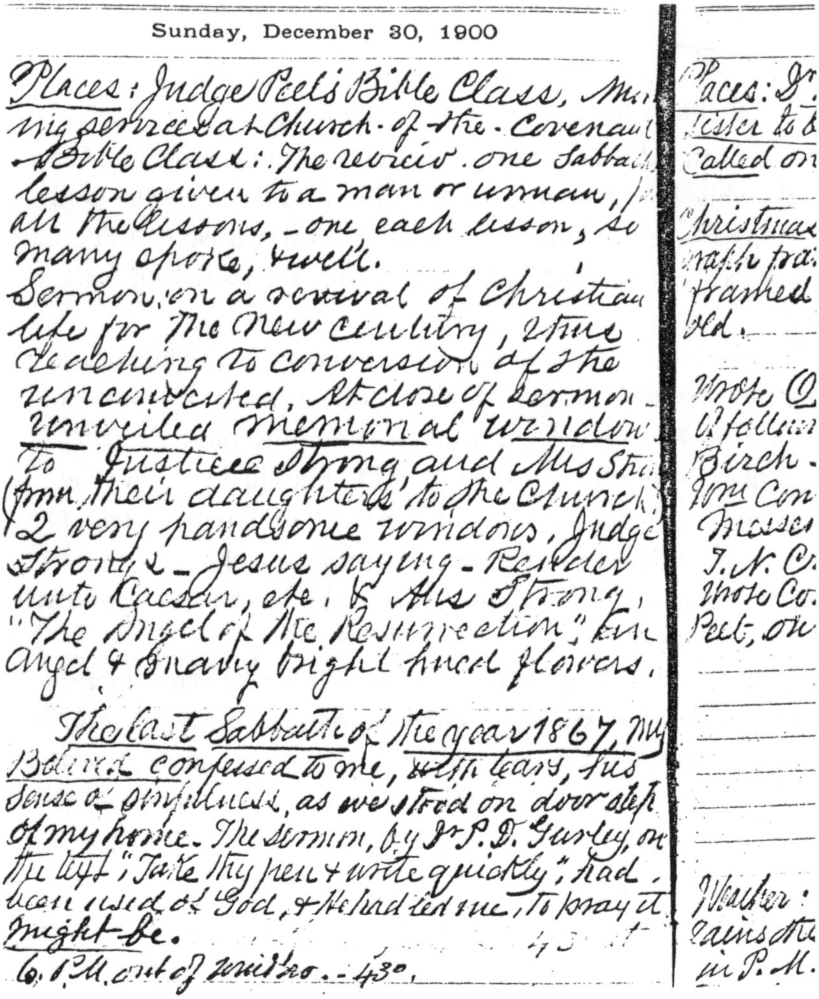

Sunday, December 30, 1900

[Handwritten diary entry, largely illegible. Readable fragments include:]

Places: Judge Peel's Bible Class, Morning service at Church of the Covenant. Bible Class: The review, one Sabbath lesson given to a man or woman, all the lessons, one each lesson, so many spoke, & well.

Sermon on a revival of Christian life for the New Century, true, leading to conversion of the unconverted. At close of sermon unveiled memorial window to Justice Strong and Mrs Strong (from their daughters) to the Church. 2 very handsome windows, Judge Strong & — Jesus saying — Render unto Caesar, etc. & Mrs Strong, "The Angel of the Resurrection" an angel & many bright hued flowers.

The last Sabbath of the year 1867, My Beloved confessed to me, with tears, his sense of sinfulness, as we stood on door step of my home. The sermon, by Dr P. D. Gurley on the text, "Take thy pen & write quickly", had been used of God, & He had led me, to pray it might be.
6. P.M. out of window — 43°.

[Right column fragments, largely illegible:]

Places: Dr ... ... called on ... Christmas ... ... thanked ... old ... wrote ... W follow ... Birch ... Mass ... J. N. C. photo Co. Peel, on ... Weather: rains ... in P.M.

From John and Annie's diary, 1900, the entry for December 30 which made mention of December 31, 1866 (Annie mistakenly remembers it as 1867). On the earlier date, Annie began seriously to consider marrying John Bidwell after his confessions of sin.

Once Annie began to write regularly in diaries, her noting that she had agreed to take on one more board membership, or to chair one more committee, leaves the reader with the impression that Annie Bidwell simply did not have the ability to say "No." These same diaries note many times when she had to renege on an agreement to speak at some meeting or other. But there are as many examples of apparent mentally whipping herself to follow through on an obligation.

The disappearances from Chico to visit her Washington, D.C., family had always given Annie a welcome break from duties, and it seems that she did not worry unduly about her Indian chapel services during these times. She allowed herself these trips just as she accepted the breaks the rancheria Indians took to attend their tribal functions or to work in valley harvesting.

Returning to a mansion with no John Bidwell in 1901 after a long recuperative visit in Washington must have been very hard for Annie. The fact that 1902 is a year in which she wrote no diary might mean this was a period of unhappy impressions on a near daily basis. A close study of Annie Bidwell's diaries over the years finds many examples of her unwillingness to enter unpleasant or negative events into her diary, though there are, of course, many such events that did get recorded.

The year 1901 was also a year for continuing Kennedy family conflict, and this very fact may have caused Annie to remove all traces of it from her correspondence, lest Guy, Joe or Willie later find in it confessions of anger or grief she did not want to share with these nephews.

In the summer of 1899, Annie on one occasion had taken a quick trip back to Chico, absenting herself from the Humboldt Road camp where John Bidwell was finishing up the realignment of the road. She had had forwarded to her a message from Attorney J. D. Sproul in F. C. Lusk's office that her signature was needed on a document from the District of Columbia concerning her mother's will.

The settlement of Catherine's will had dragged on, partially because of the doubt fed into the initial application for probate of the will. The question as to Catherine's mental competency to make a will had been raised. Also, much of the property Catherine inherited from Joseph C. G. Kennedy's estate had to be sold and converted to funds.

During her visit in Washington in 1901 after her husband's death, Annie attended two probate court hearings with Sallie, as well as an auditor's review of their mother's estate. Apparently at that time, final settlement was close at hand.

Then, seemingly out of the blue, in July 1901, a suit was filed in the Supreme Court of the District of Columbia—handled by McKinney and Flannery, a legal firm in the District of Columbia—on behalf of Guy R. Kennedy, Eva Kennedy, Joseph J. Kennedy and Cora W. Kennedy against Sarah J. Alexander and Annie E. Bidwell.[2]

The feeling of wrongdoing that Guy Kennedy had been nursing against his Aunt Sallie was now translated into a full-blown adversarial proceeding. The suit referred back to the terms of Joseph C. G. Kennedy's will, and to the supposed grievances of the legal heirs he passed over, the sons of John Reynolds Kennedy, deceased. The suit's complaint was that the testator Joseph Calm Griffith Kennedy had left large and valuable real estate holdings which, after the amount needed to support his widow for the remainder of her life (as his will had specified) should have been distributed to other legal heirs, his grandchildren, sons of Kennedy's deceased son, Johnny.

Some $6,000 of this could be traced, the suit claimed, in sums that Sallie paid to herself and to Annie Bidwell. They had been converting them to their own use during the lifetime of their mother, or so the suit claimed. Much of the money was difficult to trace, such as sale of extensive property holdings in Texas. The suit was brought to clarify these matters and to have justice rendered.

The inclusion of Cora in the suit as plaintiff suggests that she, too, thought her children had legal claim to money otherwise disposed of, some of it believed spent in the purchase of Sallie and Thomson Alexander's new Washington home.

The accusations included the illegality of Sallie's refusal to have deeded the Fountainville Ellicott property to her older brother Joseph, noting again that he had been assured of this by his father, verbally and in writing, though not by formal conveyance.

The suit demanded that Sarah Alexander give a full accounting of all properties from her father's and mother's estates and that a lien be placed upon them until this should be done and the claims of the grandchildren, under law, be settled.

This suit initiated by Guy Kennedy referred back to the clause in his grandfather's will that certain of his property should go to Sallie *so long as she shall remain unmarried.* (She had changed her status from unmarried to Mrs. Thomson Alexander before the estate was closed.)

In the suit of Sarah J. Alexander et al., v. Guy R. Kennedy, et al., Thomson Alexander served as defense counsel and developed the brief responding to the arguments made by the complainants.

Interestingly, Thomson Alexander seemed to feel at least partial sympathy with Guy, extending him friendly overtures over the years. Later, at some considerable effort on his part, T. H. Alexander, unsolicited, secured a license for Guy to present cases before the U.S. Supreme Court.

One matter was swiftly disposed of. On June 3, 1903, the court decided that the phrase "'so long as she shall remain unmarried' has no effect in law."[3]

Since this case and the necessary documents giving details of its disposition remain on file in the District of Columbia, as does Sarah J. Alexander's own will and its settlement, the way the suit's claims were finally put to rest has not been pursued here.

Thomson Alexander, who became Sallie's executor, some years later apparently made substantial payments to the grandchildren of J. C. G. Kennedy after her death, suggesting that the case had lingered long in the court with only bitter or bruised feelings to result from it. Much of Annie's initial anguish at this open rift among members of her beloved family was possibly recorded, to be later destroyed, in a 1901 diary.

In Annie's diaries over several years, entries indicate that she had at least twice tried to reason with Guy over the case—to explain to him his errors in misinterpreting Sallie's actions dealing with their father's properties. She had noted in her diary more than once that Guy "refused to understand."

Annie was probably the force that held the family in some semblance of unity over this time, at least so far as the public knew. No ripple of the problems seem to have disturbed or titillated the townspeople of Chico. For Annie's sake, Sallie and her husband maintained surface cordial relations with Johnny Kennedy's family. Tom continued to reach out to Guy, including writing a letter of condolence when the latter was soundly defeated for Butte County district attorney in 1906.

Whatever his thinking may have been as a family member not involved in this family dispute, standing to lose should the court decide in favor of Guy, John and Cora, was the Alexander's adopted son, William Morrison Alexander. There is no hint of resentment toward his "cousins" in Willie's childhood letters to Annie. Often he appended "love to cousin Joe."

By Annie's death, William Morrison Alexander had probably been told of the whole matter by his father. A wish to distance himself from Guy and Joseph is implied when he identified himself to a Sacramento *Bee* reporter as Mrs. Bidwell's cousin— which by birth he was—and not as a nephew, which his adoption by Sallie Kennedy and Thomson Alexander had made him by law.[4]

His decision not to settle in Chico, as Annie had hoped he and Gertrude might decide to do, may have rested in part on an uneasy relationship with the two Kennedy men.

$36,500.
  30,000.
300,000.
$366,500.   San Francisco, Cal., November 27 ,1899

      For value received, in Gold Coin of the United

States of America, I promise to pay in the gold coin afore-

said to "The California School of Mechanical Arts", a corpor-

ation duly incorporated under the laws of the State of Cal-

ifornia, or order, at the City and County of San Francisco,

State of California, One (1) year after date the principal

sum of Thirty-six Thousand Five Hundred (36,500) Dollars,

two (2) years after date the principal sum of Thirty Thousand

(30,000) Dollars , and three (3) years after date the prin-

cipal sum of Three Hundred Thousand (300,000) Dollars, and in-

terest on said principal sums from date hereof until paid, at

the rate of six and one-half per cent. (6-1/2%) per annum,

payable quarterly, in the gold coin aforesaid, on the 27th

days of February, May, August and November of each year. And

I further agree that, in case any installment of interest is

not punctually paid on the day when it falls due, according to

the terms hereof it shall then and thereupon be added to, and

become a part of, the principal, and shall bear interest from

the day when it falls due until paid, at the same rate as

said principal sums; also that upon, and at any time during

default in the payment of said interest, or of any installment

thereof, or of either of said principal sums, the entire un-

paid balance of said principal sums, and of all of them,

shall, at the option of the holder of this note, but not

otherwise, become due and payable; also that notice of the

exercise of such option is hereby expressly waived.

                  (1)

Both Annie and John Bidwell signed a note adding an additional $36,500 to the mortgage on Rancho Chico on November 27, 1899, less than four months before John Bidwell's death. The total lien held by The California School of Mechanical Arts against Annie's newly inherited property totaled $366,500. Courtesy of California State Library.

Widowhood—
a review

*A*nnie Bidwell lived eighteen years after her husband's passing. They were restless years. During her marriage, Annie had traveled from home many times, but always she was held by, and returned to, the strong magnet in her life that was her husband John. She had lost that anchor, and though her ownership of, and love for, the Rancho Chico still existed, the occupancy of the mansion and overseeing of the ranch as she thought John would have wanted now brought lessened pleasure.

The personal bond that strengthened her most of this time was with her sister Sallie Alexander. Her nephews held warm spots in her heart, but as they grew older they asserted their personalities in ways with which she could not always be comfortable. The love that they accepted and returned so freely as children now often seemed to carry with it demands on her purse, and the blame for their failures.

Though Annie probably refused to see how her relationship to the young Kennedys might hinder their professional advancement, when Guy was strongly defeated for Butte County district attorney by Lon Bond in 1906, he let his aunt know that much of the campaign ammunition against him was his association with "her" Prohibition cause. "Kennedy will close all the saloons!" read Lon Bond's flyers.[1]

The two most precious causes to which Annie Bidwell had pledged her support, both through both money and influence, were the drive to remove all alcoholic beverages from production in the nation, and to raise the Native Americans from pagan savagery to acceptance by society.

Annie believed that conversion to Christianity and education were the instruments by which Indians could assimilate into the mainstream. These two goals did not change. But the last years of her life drained from her the certainty of success with which she had begun her several tasks. Here too, she was to find her wealth as much a bane as a blessing.

Annie had given generously toward the education and support of both of her brother John's children, Guy and Joseph Kennedy. Neither were particularly good students, though once he set his mind to it, Guy achieved his law degree with fair grades. Joseph struggled in school and failed in the profession for which he finally trained, pharmacy.

The bridge over Chico Creek from the south side of the mansion grounds toward Chico. Date unknown. Courtesy of California State Parks.

There seemed to be no point at which they accepted responsibility for their own finances. Guy, at least once settled in law practice, earned his money from Annie through legal and real estate transactions for her, services for which, of course, she paid well.[2] As he also gained a reputation as an effective defense attorney and once he became less dependent on his aunt, he cast aside the obligation to embrace her causes. As a rising young attorney he took to having poker games in his basement, and they were liberally lubricated with alcohol.[3] If even a hint of this came to Annie, she was probably devastated, but as Guy succeeded as a defense attorney and earned appointment as Chico city attorney he learned that "being one of the fellows" worked better for him than being a Prohibitionist.

Guy had been largely supported by the Bidwells through all of his schooling, including Berkeley Law School. Joseph was helped through Berkeley High School and pharmacy school in San Francisco. He stuck to neither job as a pharmacist in San Francisco nor, when he tried again with the profession, in Tucson, Arizona.

Joey returned to work on the Bidwell Ranch where he took over the management of Annie's beef cattle at her suggestion, along with a small herd of his own, for which she promised him a retainer of $10 a month. This ten dollars seemed to become a perpetual income, even when there were no cattle. For years he was to write reminding her if she got behind in sending the stipend.

In 1906 Joseph Kennedy married a young teacher, Winifred Moon, a normal school graduate. The following year Annie paid all expenses for their baby's delivery and her layette; plus a Chinese houseboy to assist Winifred with her housework. Annie seemed resigned to the support of this family. Joe and Winifred named their daughter Annie Ellicott Kennedy, obviously as honor to her, and always to be a reminder to Annie of her duty to that family.

It must have given her uneasy thoughts when Joe wrote to her in ambitious terms while waiting for the 1902 suit filed in the District of Columbia to bring him wealth. In a 1910 letter he wrote his "dear little auntie" of planning to buy the office building at First and Broadway streets in Chico, John Bidwell's old office building. He would also like to own some of the Bidwell Ranch![4]

A mere two months after Sallie's death in 1912 Joe wrote of hoping soon to get $4,000 he expected from his aunt Sallie's estate. He was always in need of money; he owed Guy and Harry Crew money as well as Dr. Stansbury's bill. "And I would like to have my $10 per month [*from you*], it is now six months overdue."[5] Joseph was then over thirty-five years old.

Annie's accounts over many years show that Annie regularly paid Johnny and Winifred's telephone bill. In 1912, she loaned him $836 to buy an automobile.[6]

Guy's wife Eva was seemingly close to Annie, always available to help out. She seemed earnestly devoted to the work of the WCTU and the church. She was willing to assist at Indian chapel services if needed to play the organ. Annie enjoyed being generous in return, financing in part a 1902 trip back to Australia that Eva took with her sister, Fannie Smith Mathewson. Eva proved an agreeable traveling companion when she accompanied Annie to Honolulu in 1912.

Eva Kennedy was still secretary of the Annie K. Bidwell WCTU chapter when the building at Fifth and Esplanade was leased to the State Automobile Association. By then the Nineteenth (Prohibition) Amendment was in force, and the movement had lost its drive.

One of the first things Annie Bidwell took upon herself after the initial period of mourning for John was to find ways to remember him and to honor that memory. The enhancement of his burial area was one thing she enjoyed. She had the mansion groundsman build a bench with overhead trellis to shade her from the sun and make her visits to the site more restful as well as private—a place to read her Bible and pray. Sitting among plantings of flowers, with more fresh flowers brought almost daily during the warm seasons, she felt comfort beside the plain mountain boulder that was his only marker. He had wanted only the simple words "John Bidwell" chiseled into the stone. It seemed marker enough, in that it was John's request. She busied herself taking care of items specified in her husband's will: that larger or more impressive stones be erected for John Kennedy, Major Bailey and William Stevenson in the area at the south end of the Bidwell's extensive plot which he had set aside for "friends and family."

In later years, the Native Daughters of California presumed to cover the simple *John Bidwell* with a brass plaque. It might well have angered more than pleased Bidwell and accordingly would have saddened his widow.

Remembering a comment made by Mrs. Belle Royce in praise of John Bidwell's distinguished appearance when he was giving a talk at a local temperance rally, Annie decided to have a full-length portrait of him painted. She chose as artist the daughter of P. B. Reading, Bidwell's fellow Sacramento Valley pioneer. Alice Reading now lived with her widowed mother in Baltimore, working from a studio there.

The project was discussed during Annie's sojourn in Washington in 1901, preliminary choices of pose had been made from photographs, and Annie had gone over a number of tint selections with the artist for proper skin tones.[7]

In June 1903, Annie brought Alice back to Chico to stay with her, and the young artist devoted six months to completing the life-size painting which now hangs in the entrance hall of the Bidwell Mansion Historic State Park.

A good Kennedy family friend in Washington, Dr. Marcus Benjamin, who had spent much of his own early life in California, worked diligently to have Bidwell memorialized. With

Annie's help in furnishing information, he wrote John Bidwell's first "official" biography. In 1907 copies were printed for distribution to the many friends the couple had made in their scientific and political work.[8]

Dr. Benjamin also sought the support of U.S. Forestry Department employees, including Gifford Pinchot, chief of the Bureau of Forestry, with whom Annie had talked in Washington on several occasions. His suggestion was to name Lassen Peak and its surrounding volcanic marvels, already a proposed national park, as Bidwell National Park. Annie wrote to John Muir and requested that he write in support of the idea.

"General would be opposed to all this, and I am opposed to part of it, but the enthusiasm of others makes me seem to them disloyal to the General if I refuse to help them."[9]

At Benjamin's urging, Annie also enlisted John Muir to petition on behalf of having John Bidwell's statue selected as California's representative in the Statuary Hall of Fame, at that time still being developed within the original meeting hall of the House of Representatives. In 1905, Bidwell's name was entered in competition with that of Leland Stanford. Neither was chosen, though the California Society in Washington supported Bidwell in its lobbying efforts.

The project became politicized, not surprisingly, and so many statues were admitted that the building could no longer carry the weight. Today, each state has but one statue in the hall, California's being Junipero Serra. The second statue as approved by the state is of Thomas Starr King. It is in the Hall of Columns.

The urge
to build

An idea had been growing in Annie's mind since the summer after her husband died when she and Sallie had gone camping briefly in one of the favorite spots that the Bidwells had enjoyed together. Annie and Sallie had dubbed the site Robin's Nest since it reminded them of a favorite childhood haunt of that name.

As the sale of ranchland subdivisions proceeded very well, and Annie was assured that the lien on her property was cleared by sales from several subdivisions, she now had money to proceed with her plan to build a summer cottage at Robin's Nest on a half section of land that she still owned from her husband's Big Meadows holdings. This was a few miles from Prattville in a nicely forested area with several springs.

While visiting in San Francisco with Augusta Gibbs for nearly three months in 1902, Annie told her of the plan and extracted a promise that Augusta would be on hand for the groundbreaking. Augusta was ensconced in one of the carriages which, with supply wagons, made up the caravan leaving Bidwell Mansion on June 21, 1904. It was still very cool in the mountains, but the work crew needed all the summer months to build the exterior structure and to roof it against the deep snows of winter.

In the party with Annie and Augusta were a cook and a maid; two carpenters (one with his family); Reuben Messinger, the driver and general handyman for the ranch, and Reuben's wife and little girl Ruby. One of the Indian laborers, Hiram Hailah, brought his wife and they camped nearby with other Indians from the area who found employment on the project. During the summer, many of the Bidwell Rancheria Indians came to the site to work. A little tent community grew up around the project. In the Big Meadows area, not far away, Guy and Eva had their summer camp, and Joey had his cattle camp shared with one or more stock hands. Many Chico friends who spent their summer at the accommodations in Prattville came to inspect the new cottage.[1]

By 1904, the train from Diamond Match's huge mill provided passenger service on a daily basis between Stirling City and Barber, the Chico suburb where the factory had been built on the site of a trotting horse racetrack.

Reuben took Annie and Augusta to Stirling City to take the train to Chico in July for Augusta's return to her home in San Francisco. The rest of the crew, including Annie upon her return, stayed in the mountains until September 22. By that time the ten-room "cottage," as Annie referred to it, was basically finished.

A visit of six months in Washington followed. Then Susan B. Anthony's visit to the mansion delayed the work's beginning in summer 1905, but by late July Annie was back at Robin's Nest with a work crew. Special guests that year were Sallie, Tom and Willie Alexander. The Bidwell party traveled by wagons as usual, the larger one carrying supplies, tents and bedding, while the carryall provided seats for the party of campers.

That year, 1905, was vividly remembered for the automobile met on the Humboldt Road! Its occupants were the Hammonds, owners of Spreckels Meat Market in San Francisco. This noisy creature caused two runaways, and another near one when it passed the Bidwell party returning from the mountains. Their four-horse team ran up a steep bank in panic, and only luck kept the wagon from capsizing. Annie referred in her diary to the "outrageous conduct" on the road, supposedly of the car's driver who had not had the courtesy to stop and turn off the motor until horses passed.[2]

The following summer, 1906, was perhaps the jolliest of Robin's Nest seasons. Minnie, Harriett and Douglas Alexander from San Francisco were in the party as well as cook, housemaid, and carpenters, all arriving at the cottage on July 11. They were met by Joey Kennedy with Willie Alexander and Lily Clements. Willie, now sixteen, had come west on the train alone and had volunteered to precede the main party to open and clean the cottage with the help of Indians already in camp.

The workmen were putting finishing details on the interior and building furniture all summer, as well as constructing a barn and helping Reuben add a small cottage for his family.

Many other children were among the guests that filled the bedrooms of the cottage. Mrs. Harry Reed and children Marietta and Dan came from the Daniel Bidwell side of the family. Marietta was at an age to play school, and for several days she gathered a class of Indian children from the nearby Indian camp and instructed them solemnly in reading. Among the Indians camping in the meadows was Maggie Lafonso, who with Lily Clements handled the laundry and housekeeping chores for Robin's Nest.

Annie held a church service every Sunday for any and all persons who might be inveigled to come. It was a very happy summer, and ended abruptly when Annie brought Willie back from the mountains to Chico to depart with him for Washington and his return to school.

There was no laughter in Robin's Nest the summer of 1907; the building remained closed. In 1908, Annie and the Washington Alexanders spent a few weeks there, but in the two years following, the cottage had a lonely time of it.

By 1911, Annie was dickering with the Great Western Power Company over a fair price for her land and Robin's Nest. She made a journey to the cottage with Sallie and Tom for a few weeks in early summer, but she had made appointments in San

Francisco to explore offers of purchase for the remaining portion of Rancho Chico.

Annie had decided to part with all except a few orchards and the mansion grounds. Tom Alexander had agreed to assist her in the sale, and they left Sallie alone at the cottage with two servants as the last visitors before the cottage was closed.

The plans to dam Butt Creek and flood part of Big Meadows were making many changes in what had been Chico's vacationland. As

While building Robin's Nest, the Big Meadows vacation cottage, in 1904, Annie, guests and workcrew lived in tents. Courtesy of California State Parks.

events worked out, Robin's Nest was not sacrificed to the flooding necessary to create Lake Almanor, and Annie willed it to the Presbyterian Church as a retreat for Presbyterian ministers.

Her objective achieved in building a mountain vacation home, Annie's next building inspiration was to remodel part of the mansion itself. In 1907, Annie hired workmen to convert the small building behind the mansion (the original headquarters of architect W. H. Cleaveland in the 1860s) into a summer kitchen.

Then a new inspiration hit Annie, and she brought an architect from San Francisco to design the addition of an entirely new kitchen on the northwest corner of mansion's first floor. When giving a reason for this somewhat expensive undertaking, she stated that the kitchen girls and cook complained that they could hardly tolerate the heat in their bedrooms above the kitchen.[3]

It is tempting to look for more deep-seated reasons for Annie's undertaking these two building projects. She had enjoyed camping in a tent for over thirty years and to move the meal preparation into another building at that time seems to lack good reason.

The restlessness that dominated her life after John's death was certainly a factor in the decisions. The debts had been paid on the ranch and now money continued to pour in. And the urge to spend may well have been based on the same impulse that moved her to buy expensive furs in Washington during the winter of 1874 even as John Bidwell was making no bones about his financial woes. Her justification then had been, "I think that when God gave me my position in life, He expected me to dress [build?] accordingly."

There was another deep-seated need that seemed to drive Annie Bidwell during the years after her husband's death, and that was to see the people around her "happy." Her diary is filled with the accounts of days in which the children were "ecstatically happy," the young people meeting at her home left "singing and happy," and the elderly full-caste Indians at the rancheria greeting her and her gifts "with tears of happiness."

During the years that she shared her home with her friend Minnie Alexander's daughter Harriett, who attended Chico High School, it seemed that Annie did not really pay close attention to Harriett's comings and goings with her host of youthful friends. It was enough to observe that they were "very happy," and especially if she perceived their praise to be for her meals, her thoughtfulness, her goodness.

Annie Bidwell's diaries recorded all of her building activities described in this chapter. There is a whisper of her loneliness throughout these diaries. While in Washington the entries are filled with her recording of and comments on world events, as if she sadly missed the someone with whom she had shared opinions, if only by letter.

While Annie was gone from Chico she allowed the mansion to be used for approved meetings. She considered it necessary to always have a skeleton staff on hand, for the safety of the mansion if nothing else. One such use was for the Normal School Christian Men's Club reception, permission for which the young men had obtained by writing to her. Her diary includes a Chico newspaper's clipping with details of the mansion's elaborate decorations for this event, sent to her by the grateful students. At another time, the WCTU ladies met there to make rag rugs to sell as a benefit for the Annie K. Bidwell WCTU Temple. The newspaper writeup reached Annie and was carefully saved. She was gratified, one may be certain, by the inclusion of members of the Indian village in the work and to be entertained by Maggie Lafonso's singing.

The war to eliminate alcohol consumption

*D*uring the thirty-five years that Annie engaged as a warrior in the cause to suppress the use of alcohol, from 1883 when the WCTU was organized in Chico until her death, she may be said to have advanced from a private in the ranks to a general. Her promotions came from consistent hard work, but the advancement to top positions in the army were certainly based in large part by her willingness to keep financing the war generously, both in its local skirmishes and in the state and national battlefields.

If shear effort and devotion had been rewarded by similar recognition, surely Seline Marie Woodman, whose residence in Chico and enlistment in the cause preceded Annie's, would have led the list. She was the wife of the Reverend James M. Woodman, a Congregational minister who privately established the first school in Chico in 1863 on a block given by Bidwell for this purpose. Seline was the school's main teacher, having as many as eighty students by 1880 in what was known as the Woodman Academy.[1]

Seline never wavered in the day-to-day, year-to-year, battle in Butte County for both women's suffrage and for prohibition. She had started with regular temperance meetings held in her home or in the Woodman Academy some years before John Bidwell's marriage.

From her conversion to Christianity as a teenager, Annie shared in the ever-growing belief that alcoholic beverages caused great harm to society. She first witnessed the ravages on the families who sought help at the mission where she volunteered in Washington. True, she silently observed wine served with most dinnertime meals in the Kennedy household, if only to Joseph C. G. Kennedy, the head of the family. He had the final word over decisions of all kinds in his household as was customary in Victorian households.

Annie as a girl wrote in scattered diary notes that she was given the chore by her father to follow up on an order of wine that had not been delivered in timely fashion to the Kennedy home, and to pay for it when it arrived.[2] She indicated no distaste for the assignment, taking it as routine duty at that time of her life. She always abstained from drinking any wine herself, this being one of the first things John Bidwell took note of as he dined with the Kennedys. He wished to gain her favor, and also abstained from touching his wine glass. During the developing courtship of the couple, she could dictate her wishes, one being that Bidwell's wine grape production cease, and his sale of wine and whiskey at the Old Adobe Inn be stopped.

Needless to say, the alcoholic binges by which Joe Kennedy, the son, threw his household into despair and anger after his discharge from the army fed the flames of Annie's determination to fight the manufacture and sale and use of alcoholic beverage at any and every opportunity. Probably the one single largest factor in her crusade against alcohol was the major part it played in Joe's tragic life and death.

She found many other examples on which to build her case. Some were the tragic deaths of young men from "good" Chico families who died from fighting while intoxicated, or from the secret binge drinking that the Bidwells knew or suspected among the ranch employees. Annie's devotion to the Indians of the rancheria created in her a watchdog mentality, for when the native people were exposed to the high alcohol content of the cheap whiskey available to the laboring class, they were easily intoxicated, belligerent, and dangerous—especially to each other.

An annual event in Chico was the German picnic, organized for the local German families and featuring the music, food, and beer identified with that country. After denying the use of the Bidwell Picnic Grove, the Bidwells were not content, but tried to see that no other place was made available for this kind of enter-tainment. Driving to the Morehead Ranch after a rumor went round one year that Morehead's was to be the site of the picnic, John and Annie were curtly informed by Ardenia Morehead that they were too late. Yes, the picnic was to be on her ranch.

In May 1884, Bidwell wrote in his diary that he had dissuaded the Indian band from accepting an invitation to play at the German picnic, which he described as an occasion for "dancing, music, lager beer, a hideous carousal."[3] He noted with satisfaction the year that the picnic was rained out.

The forming of the Women's Christian Temperance Union brought the "sisters" together from all over the world. Frances E. Willard entered the movement when it was in its infancy in 1874. At that time she lived in Evanston, Illinois, where she had served as dean of women at Northwestern University. The WCTU was organized to launch a worldwide recruitment effort in 1883, the year the Chico chapter was formed.

Willard was the one among the WCTU creators who seemed most able to inspire paid recruiters sent out to touch the hearts and imaginations of women everywhere. Not only were women recruited to the cause, men were enlisted, and they too wore the "white ribbon" that identified those who took the pledge of abstinence. The WCTU soon broadened its platform from just the banishment of alcohol to include suffrage for women.

The committees which a WCTU branch charter specified as necessary to perform the work included: evangelism, law enforce-ment, scientific temperance, franchise, reading room, press, social purity, narcotics and organist. Several of these committee's instructive materials made a strong impression on Annie and influenced the way she spread her energies.[4]

During Selene Woodman's term as president of the Chico Frances E. Willard Branch of WCTU in 1897, Annie signed up to lead the Evangelism Committee. Certainly her work as pastor to the Bidwell Rancheria Indians fit into this committee's definition.[5]

The readings on the work for social purity also made a deep impression on Annie, for the committee dealt with how to clean home environments of sensual and suggestive materials for young minds. Since boys were considered more likely than girls to be sullied by worldliness, the responsibility felt by Aunt Annie for her three young male nephews made the matter very personal.

There are many mentions in Annie's diaries of making dolls and dolls' clothing specifically to give to little boys in her life, including the Indian boys. The literature stressed the need to develop the nurturing side of the male character as opposed to encouraging strictly male activities, such as hunting or playing soldier.

Another committee taken very seriously by Annie was that which advocated reading rooms where men and boys especially might find reading matter of wholesome and religious nature. To Annie the biggest gap in the social opportunities for boys and men was the time spent between work and home—time that many men spent in a saloon.

Such a WCTU reading room was established in the Indian village after Billy Simpson's murder. This sad tragedy took place but two months prior to John Bidwell's death when three of the single Indians who were working for him on his Vallombrosa clearing project became embroiled in a fight one night and Billy was killed. The other two Indians were convicted of murder (Annie attended the trial in Oroville to plead for leniency in judging) and sentenced to terms in San Quentin.[6]

Annie decided to convert Billy Simpson's house in the Indian village to a reading room, as an adjunct to the branch of the temperance organization which had been formed in the village soon after the chapel was opened.[7]

Annie maintained a correspondence with the two prisoners. One died in prison, but through her efforts, John Richards was paroled in 1909. Annie sent Richards money and new clothing in which to leave the prison, and guaranteed work upon his return to the ranch.[8]

After John Bidwell's death, as Chico Vecino grew in population, another WCTU was formed in the new community and named the Annie K. Bidwell Temple. The instigating force came from R. Foster Stone and Mrs. Stone, professional WCTU organizers who with Annie's help called an organizational meeting in 1904 at the Bidwell School on Nord Avenue. The new hall was built on a site at Esplanade and Fifth Avenue in 1905–06 in her honor and much of it at her expense, though the construction labor was donated by local men. Annie later had the "temple" dropped from the name as too ostentatious for her liking.[9]

The Chico Vecino hall had the rather dubious distinction of having its dedication ceremony disrupted by news of a catastrophic earthquake that had convulsed San Francisco the day before, April 18, 1906. The hall was never completed because philanthropic funds were drained off to assist the tragedy's victims, many of them well-known or related to Chico residents.[10]

Money was left in Annie Bidwell's will for completing the interior of the building as designed, but by the time her will was finally administered, Prohibition had been the law of the land and the hall had been converted to other uses.[11]

The conditions at Stirling City as the big Diamond Match mill opened limited the workmen's opportunities for recreation to the company bar and a whorehouse (a "dive" was Annie's name for it). The thought of this situation gave Annie Bidwell great anguish. She cringed at the knowledge that as a passenger on a train from Chico to Stirling City in 1904, a trip taken to try to recruit members for a Stirling City WCTU, she had of necessity sat in the same railway car with prostitutes.[12]

When Annie, with the help of a Rev. Hicks, attempted to form a temperance group in Stirling, she was rebuffed by the women who feared for their husband's jobs if they did so. Going to a Diamond official on the spot, she got permission to have a tent sent up from Chico at her expense. She herself supplied the tent with games and a variety of reading materials for the "honest, clean workmen." She was also later to donate money to build the "Little Brown Church" at Stirling City.[13]

Later as Annie complained repeatedly to any Diamond official whose ear she might get, the company officers in Chico thought it expeditious to appease her wrath. Promises were made by O. C. Barber, the president of the company. When in Chico, he paid a personal call at the mansion and promised that the "dive" would be closed.[14] Another official in the company, F. M. Clough,[15] had a beautiful polished table made as a gift to her, and she received a pass to travel on the Butte County Railroad to and from Stirling City at any time.

Annie also entered the evil town of Magalia where saloons were active (and according to Carrie Brydon, a local WCTU worker, one saloon had a sideline of prostitution).[16] A white ribbon campaign was carried to one of the saloons' doorsteps in May of 1899, followed by a religious service in Bader Hall nearby with a plea to "take the pledge."[17]

Miss Brydon had come to Magalia from the harsh winters of Canada because of a tubercular tendency. While living with a nephew there, she was horrified to witness not only his frequent trips to a saloon, but also that most of the men in town were dependent on alcohol. Over the years, Miss Brydon was a frequent houseguest at the mansion, and she was encouraged to continue as the scourge of the Magalia saloon crowd. She spearheaded the chartering of a Magalia WCTU and worked diligently to recruit male volunteers to build Magalia's own Little Brown Church. Their reluctance was evidenced in the many years it took to complete the building. Materials were largely financed by Annie Bidwell herself in the name of the Chico WCTU[18]

Annie Bidwell's major, and most expensive, foray into the creation of reading rooms, came with her experiment in downtown Chico. This is not to be confused with the public reading room which evolved into the Chico Public Library. Annie took part in this effort, but several other Chico women worked hard to accomplish this library, including Mrs. Helen Tilden (Dr. Thomas Tilden's widow), and Mrs. Thomas P. Hendricks.

In 1904, Annie approached the owner of a small Chico restaurant run by Hugh McEnery, a professed temperance man. She asked McEnery if she could bring reading materials for "decent working" men into the restaurant to have available for his customers to browse or read. He agreed to this, and gradually over the following months, Annie became more ambitious and asked McEnery to drop the serving of meals at his establishment entirely and to provide only temperance drinks and ice cream. They worked out a financial agreement that she would "bear all his loss" from giving up the food service.[19]

Annie then decided that a "boys game room" could be made from the restaurant kitchen and bought from McEnery his stove and boiler which Reuben hauled away for her. The cost of the appliances, plus the loss from food sales, began to mount up, but Anne stayed with her bargain month after month.

One particularly stormy interview with the reading room proprietor was held when word came to her that McEnery was selling tobacco as well as ice cream and temperance drinks. She challenged him on this during an evidently stormy session, and the tobacco sales were eliminated. But her session on the matter with the equally harried man sent her home to bed in nervous prostration.[20]

One of the charges put to each WCTU branch was to influence the press. Finding that neither the *Enterprise* nor the *Record* were willing to print every news release that she wanted, Annie initiated and stood costs of publishing a small weekly paper to be edited by a Mr. Rising and called *Fact and Figures*. Its main purpose was to spread the Prohibition movement's accomplishments in Butte County as well as relay news from the national headquarters. The subscriptions did not pay for all the cost, but Annie cheerfully bore the expense.[21]

Facts & Figures, always laughed at by the "Wet" element, suffered further ridicule in July 1908, when its editor was rescued from Chico Creek, bound as if an attempt had been made to drown him. Sensational publicity heralded this dastardly deed, but laughter followed when it was discovered that the editor of *Fact & Figures* had pulled this stunt himself in an effort to get publicity for the cause. The paper ceased publication soon after, with Annie making no note of the event in her diary.[22]

Nineteen hundred and four was a red-banner year for WCTU efforts on Annie's part. When the branches were urged to incorporate, Annie saw to it that Chico did so, enlisting the volunteer aid of Guy Kennedy. The day set for the meeting to complete the process, January 16, 1904, found Annie ill in bed with laryngitis. They met anyway, gathered around Annie's bed with Guy to both extract the information needed and to chair the meeting for his aunt.

The organizing board of directors elected Annie to be president and Eva Kennedy, secretary. Others on the board, almost all Presbyterians, were Mrs. Nikirk as treasurer, Mrs. Arnold (wife of the *Enterprise* editor at the time), Mrs. William Robbie (her husband ran the stone monument business and was Chico's mayor at the time of Annie's death), a Mrs. George Miller, Mrs. Fimple, Miss Mary Woodward, Mrs. Guill and Mrs. Helpenstine.[23]

In June 1909, the several Butte County WCTU organizations jointly voted to hire a man sent by the state Prohibition head-quarters to work within the county recruiting support for a drive to get the board of supervisors' support for an election to vote on closing the county's saloons.

For the year before Ira Surface's hiring, Annie had alone paid the salary of a twenty-eight-year-old man to work full-time on prohibition work. John Vaughn was from Scotland and had no family near, and Annie was quite fond of him. His work was cut short when he accidentally poisoned himself using a toxic sub-stance in an enema to heal hemorrhoids, whether on doctor's prescription or not is unknown.

Annie was deeply grieved and had Vaughn's funeral conducted from the mansion, the first such since her husband's death, and Vaughn's grave and stone marker were placed with other "friends" on the south edge of John Bidwell's special family section.[24]

Ira E. Surface was to be paid $100 by the month and expenses for his work. His salary was to come from pledges made by the local Drys. Annie kicked off the fund to cover his salary with a $110.61 advance, one month's salary and expenses.[25]

By July 1910, Mr. Surface reported that he had earned a total amount of salary and expenses of $1,574.88, of which $658.92 was still due him. The state Prohibition Party chairman, at that time James Woertendyke, attempted to collect funds from Butte County. The debt still stood nearly two years later when Woertendyke asked Annie if she personally would pay the debt if Mr. Surface agreed to accept less than full settlement. Mr. Surface was not willing and threatened to sue the Butte County WCTU. Annie was traveling in Europe most of the year 1910, and in 1912 was reeling emotionally from the sudden death of her sister Sallie. With the desperate appeal from the party chairman, she sent off $550 to meet the shortfall.

Only a portion of her money was ever forwarded to Mr. Surface for the state office itself was perpetually running short of funds. Surface was understandably outraged. There were so many beseeching hands out that even Annie lost patience at times, but this breach of contract with Ira Surface all parties wanted to keep out of the courts, and managed to do so.

Annie missed one of the most vitriolic local campaigns to close the Butte County saloons when she traveled in Europe during 1910's Butte County balloting, as provided for in the Wylie Local Option bill. The state legislature provided the machinery whereby communities could vote to close the saloons in just their own local precincts. Of all the Butte County elections, only Biggs and Oroville went dry. At a later referendum in 1915, Oroville voted to allow saloons back but limit the number to four.

The drive for universal prohibition of alcohol dominated much of the second half of the nineteenth century. It continued to gain steam, and finally was successful with the acceptance of the Eighteenth Amendment to the U.S. Constitution in 1919.

As often happens with popular causes, the Prohibition movement began to spin off a long list of related but specialized organizations. Among these were the Prohibition Alliances (a lodge-like organization), the Loyal Temperance Legion (a group of varied ages and sexes which practiced marching and singing at Prohibition gatherings) college girls' and women's WCTU, the Intercollegiate Prohibition Association, the Prohibition Train (to travel about the country with the message) to give a partial list. Each new organization formed in the interest of alcohol containment applied to Annie for funds. These, of course, were in addition to the liberal support she gave the Prohibition Party at each level, county, state and national—the political party on which platform her husband had run for U.S. president in 1892.

Many of these groups published a newspaper or journal, and Annie was supportive in that she subscribed to most for herself and her reading rooms and for those friends and relatives she thought might benefit. There were the *Vindicator,* the *Vanguard,* the *Patriotic Phalanx,* and the *National Inquirer,* as partial list.

Many more were designed and published for young people, and these, too, she bought for all the children in her life and for the reading rooms.

There grew to be a small army of men and women who traveled about the country lecturing on Prohibition topics "for a reasonable fee and lodging." Some of these were legitimate missionaries who sacrificed much to dedicate their lives to the good of others, such as Frances E. Willard herself, Susan B. Anthony, Mary Clements Leavitt, Henrietta Skelton, and Marie Brehm. The last named two stayed often at the Bidwell Mansion and had an open invitation to make it a stopping place either for work or relaxation. There were many men, too, in and out of the mansion guest room, such as J. W. Woertendyke and Quincy Lee Morrow, workers on the battle line for temperance.

Occasionally a charlatan crept into their midst, one of these being a Rev. R. A. M. Browne, who appeared from the East Coast in late 1913 and volunteered himself to Annie Bidwell to work throughout the state of California campaigning for a Prohibition amendment to the state constitution. Annie took him into the mansion, and Browne preached a few times at the Presbyterian Church at her suggestion. She then hired him to work under her direction at $150 a month and paid travel expenses. He wrote a song dedicated to her, "We Will Make California Dry."[26]

When the Reverend Browne was arrested on a morals charge, it was a difficult cross for her to bear, and one which her detractors made into reason to deride her.

The Sacramento Presbytery itself had begun to have suspicions about Rev. Browne's past, and after finding that the rumors that he had "deserted" a wife and three children in New Jersey were true, they suspended him from any Presbyterian pulpit in their jurisdiction. Browne disappeared from public view toward the end of 1914 but was discovered by an eager newsman to be living secretly with a married woman in San Francisco.

Mrs. Hendricks, the unfortunate woman, made a valiant, and public, attempt to tear herself away from Browne, and returned home to her husband, only to commit suicide two weeks later. She could not live with Browne, nor could she bear the thought of life with her husband, according to the ever scandal-hungry press.

Browne was arrested for adultery, possibly from a warrant sought by Mr. Hendricks. Browne's statements from jail seemed to reflect true repentance for the injury done. "I knew it was wrong, but a man cannot reconcile his love with his responsibilities always." Whether he apologized to Annie, and if Annie had the magnanimity to forgive him, we do not know.

Another opportunity to make jest of the mighty Mrs. Bidwell came in 1917, when the state teetered on the edge of achieving genuine reform. This time the case for temperance rested on legislation sponsored in the California Senate by Sen. W. F. Remington. The legislation was amended at least once to satisfy detractors, but the version which came close to passage provided that all saloons in California would be permanently closed, and alcohol could be served publicly only in eating establishments licensed to serve wine of restricted alcohol content with meals.[27]

Annie threw a bombshell into the midst of all the combined efforts of the Anti-Saloon League and the Prohibition state organizations supporting Remington's bill when she wrote to her assemblyman, C. H. Brown of Gridley, that she intended to vote against supporting the Remington bill. With great glee, the assemblyman showed her letter around among the members of the legislature in Sacramento.

"Well," he said (his words are paraphrased), "Now I have decided, that if the great Prohibitionist Mrs. Bidwell is against closing the saloons in California, so am I."

Prohibition workers from all over the state were embarrassed and alarmed. Surely Mrs. Bidwell did not understand the significance of passing such legislation.

Letters came to her from all levels of the state Prohibition Party, from Sarah Dorr, president of the California State WCTU, and from Senator Remington himself, who wrote that he was deeply concerned over her attitude, especially as his legislation, if made law, would put every saloon in California out of business. He begged her to recant and write another letter so stating.

Annie's dear friend and longtime ally in the Butte County WCTU, Mrs. Lilian Gray, wife of Oroville's hardware pioneer, Fred H. Gray, wrote, "Did you not vote to make Butte County dry? Is this not a chance to gain more temperate ground?" But Annie held firm to her stand, that only legislation providing for the *complete abolition* of alcohol—its manufacture and its use— would get her support. Remington's bill was narrowly defeated.

Temperate use of alcohol, or abolition of alcohol?

Annie had been exposed to arguments for the former from the beginning of her thinking on the subject. Her father, in wording very mild and with reasoning on the matter that he claimed had come to him through experience and from the words of the Bible and great philosophers, insisted that the judicious use of wine was given to mankind for their health and enjoyment.

The Reverend Graham, from whom the Bidwells were estranged through many of the years of his service in the pulpit of the Chico Presbyterian Church, had used the same arguments with John Bidwell soon after Graham came to Chico, and Graham never wavered, from the pulpit or otherwise, in spite of Bidwell's refusal to attend most sermons given by Graham after the latter's assault on Annie's prohibition work in 1890 and Graham's complete lack of support during Bidwell's run for U.S. president on the Prohibition Party ticket.

There were harsher judgments of Annie's stance to appear in print: A letter that Annie had written to the *Sacramento Union* in 1916 brought this response from a J. Cuiverez: "I am for prohibition strong but I can see where such damn fool reasoning is going to do us injury, and leave it to a woman to make an ass of herself

and injure the cause if she's given a chance to appear in print.
..."28

Annie Bidwell had the advantage of name recognition on both
coasts, and her frequent visits to Washington, D.C., made attending meetings of Prohibition organizations in New York and
Washington practical for her. Several times the Chicago stopover
on trips to and from coincided with conventions or board meetings being held near the national headquarters of WCTU.

When Annie did make an appearance, it was nearly always
rewarded with a place on the speakers' platform where she presented a diminutive but dignified—even regal—persona. Combine these elements—appearance, name recognition and generous
money support—and it explains much about her popularity in
the movement over and above that accorded the hundreds of
other hardworking women, as well as men, laboring in the Prohibition cause.

An interesting contrast to the life and work of Annie Bidwell
can be found in reading the story of Anna Morrison Reed.[29] John
Bidwell referred to her as a distant cousin of his wife's—something Annie never acknowledged in print.[30] Ten years younger
than Annie, Anna Morrison came from Iowa with her mother
and several siblings to Butte County as a young girl to join her
gold miner father Guy Morrison in Oregon City on Table Mountain. As the oldest child, when her father became disabled she
decided to support the family through her own efforts. She
turned to lecturing in small towns around the state, usually asking
only a voluntary collection collected at the end of her talk. She
was not unique in this effort at that period, but she did unusually
well. The nineteen-year-old girl spoke so eloquently of matters
concerning family life that her reputation preceded her as she
acquired a following, taking her to many towns, west to the
Pacific Ocean and north to the Oregon border.

Anna Morrison married John Reed of Ukiah, had five children, and after becoming a widow, once again was turned to

making a living. In addition to lecturing she began writing freelance for newspapers and was willing to work at selling advertising and collecting bills for one or two newspapers in Mendocino County. She had a winning, though forceful, personality and did well. She eventually became editor of *The Northern Crown,* a weekly, widely circulated throughout the state from Mendocino County.

Anna Reed's lectures and her writing won her an ever widening audience. In 1893, she was the first woman ever asked to give the annual address to the State Agricultural Society of California.

Mrs. Reed believed strongly in what she called "true temperance": She wanted to avoid destroying the livelihood of the hundreds who grew grapes and made wine in the state. "We see no reason to condemn honest transactions which grow from a legal business. ... Prohibition does not prohibit, but leads to crime and baser things, and has been a flat failure from the beginning of human life."

She was outspoken in her criticism of Annie Bidwell and such followers as the Reverend Browne. "Temperance and Prohibition are the topics that form the stock-in-trade of mercenary fanatics who without such topics would be bankrupt for a subject on which to harp for the dollars that support them."[31]

Time ran out in the lives of both women. Annie Bidwell's cause did win the battle for a national constitutional amendment, but as Anna Reed predicted, prohibition in the United States was to be declared a failure within a decade.

Rancho Chico:
The shrinking giant

On March 12, 1904, Franklin Lusk brought Annie the papers in which the Lick Trust certified the $350,000 lien as paid in full, and with it gave her clear title to the remaining portion of Rancho Chico. Thus freed from mortgage, Annie launched into a number of both sales and gifts of real estate.

The ownership of so much valuable land, and the realization that she was never again to be forced to wheedle a man for money, was an exhilarating experience. Thus 1904 was a turning point in her life. Her money gave her more control over the causes to which she was devoted, including the work of the state, Butte County and Chico WCTU branches.

Annie announced to Attorney Franklin Lusk, her legal advisor by dint of his having been the one chosen by her husband, that she planned to go on running the orchards and beef production on Rancho Chico as it had been for many years, with the help of foremen over the several operations and the overall management of Col. C. C. Royce.

In March 1904, Annie received another formal letter from Mr. Lusk laying out for her his professional opinion of her plans, the first having been in 1900 when he advised her to start selling land to avoid foreclosure. He nettled her a bit, which John Bidwell had long observed was Lusk's style. The attorney told Annie that she had no business trying to run the ranch, now reduced largely to fruit production, that it had always been a money-losing proposition and he did not think she was apt to improve on what John Bidwell, with much more know-how, had experienced.[1]

For mixed reasons, Annie put Lusk's advice aside. She loved the orchards, not just for any potential they held for profit, but because of their beauty, from the spring blossoming through the rich harvest seasons of cherries and peaches. She also considered the operation of the orchards, her husband's favorite of the ranch's crops, a kind of memorial to him. With Reuben Messinger as the foreman over the orchards, and Col. Royce running the drying, canning and marketing end of the fruit business, she now set herself up as the A. K. Bidwell Orchards Company. Of necessity, since she was committed in many ways to many people, almost all of the oversight fell to Messinger and Royce.

As Lusk predicted, and she herself more or less expected, the ranch continued to lose money. Sales continued of the subdivided ranchland, so there was always a cash inflow. In 1904, a flurry of land sales was initiated directly between Annie Bidwell, ranch owner, and buyers.

One major sale came as the new Chico High School District searched for a building site and decided that being next to the normal school would be advantageous. She sold for that purpose land to the west of the normal school along Chico Creek's south bank. Land sold included the high school parcel and the Rio Chico Subdivision further to the west between the high school and the railroad. She realized $18,000 from the sale. A Judge March was the middleman in the transaction; he agreed to sell the portion for the high school at the same price he paid Annie.

Lusk was aware of these deals Annie had made without his supervision, including the gift of a small lot, with a seventy-foot frontage on First Street between campus and high school site for a YMCA building. She relied on Lusk's office to handle the paperwork as they had for all the 1901–1904 sales arranged through Lusk's office to clear the debt on the ranch.

At the same time that Annie was making independent decisions on selling land, Lusk had sold land for another subdivision, with Annie's knowledge and approval, to a Mr. Styles of San

Francisco. Annie accosted Lusk, accusing him of having omitted the liquor clause in the Styles deed. He denied this. She proved him wrong, and Lusk had to make a special trip to San Francisco to correct it with Styles.[2]

In her diary Annie had difficulty concealing her resentment when, upon hearing of so many sales made without his office's prior approval, Mr. Lusk called on her at home and in his fashion lectured her on the dangers of a woman entering the world of commerce. She agreed to accept more guidance, but reluctantly.[3]

Annie directed Lusk to have the Rio Chico Subdivision surveyed before selling to Judge March. She personally appeared on the site during the process and followed the surveyor, stipulating exactly how the chief street (She named it Rio Chico Way) was to run—so that it would be "most pleasing" relative to the curving of the creek. She insisted that the homes were to face the creek, and when a fence built along the edge of the creek dissatisfied her, Annie insisted that it be torn down and altered.[4]

In 1904, Annie hoped to circumvent the law which banned land ownership by Indians based, in part, on their lack of U.S. citizenship. She wrote to California's U.S. senator, George C. Perkins, asking that he use his power to have land granted to worthy Indians.[5] He wrote back to her promptly, explaining that "Indians given land outright will be victims of those who would cheat them."[6]

Later, in her will, Annie was to leave selected Indians rancheria lots to be held in trust by the Presbyterian Church Board of Home Missions.[7]

By 1904, Annie was more closely observing the real estate dealers chosen by Lusk. For years she had let the sales proceed with no personal input, but when she decided to dabble in the process, woe unto the agent. B. Cussick had charge of sales in one Chico Vecino subdivision, but when the trustees and parents of the Bidwell School on Nord Avenue reported that Cussick had sold the lot adjacent to the school—one that she had promised

Annie Bidwell in 1905. Her husband had commented on his regret at seeing a trace of sternness creep into her photographs in the 1890s. In this photo chosen by her family for newspaper use at her death, Annie's sternness cannot be denied. Courtesy of California State Parks.

for a school playground— Annie demanded that Cussick locate the buyer and retract the agreement. Cussick sent word that she had never so informed him. She charged Cussick of "*a falsehood!*" in her diary entry.[8]

Annie set out for Cussick's office to accost him face to face. He was reported by staff to have gone for a haircut. She would wait. After two hours in his office during which there was no sign of Cussick, she left for home, enraged and certain that staying away from his office had been one more deceitful act on his part: "... his *3rd dishonest act.*"

It is probable that few of Chico's businessmen enjoyed the prospect of conversing with Mrs. Bidwell in one of her righteously indignant moods.

In March 1904, arrived the long-anticipated time when Annie could hand Dr. Joseph Hirschfelder $10,000, an arbitrary figure that John Bidwell and Hirschfelder had settled on as payment for professional services over many years, to both John and Annie. In his lifetime, Bidwell had offered the payment in the form of a deed to a fine portion of the ranch. Dr. Hirschfelder had adamantly refused, tearing up the papers John Bidwell had prepared transferring title to a real estate parcel. Now Annie was able to hand Dr. Hirschfelder a check for $10,000, and he did not refuse it.[9]

Over the years Dr. and Mrs. Hirschfelder became close personal friends of the Bidwells, entertained them in their San
Francisco home and were often guests at the Bidwell Mansion.
Annie had attended temple services with Mrs. Hirschfelder and
did considerable research on the way that wine is prepared for the
Jewish rites, a way that she seemed to find an acceptable use of
the grape. Arthur Hirschfelder, son of the doctor, often spent
weeks of summer holiday at the Bidwell Mansion with a cousin.
After Arthur graduated from medical school in Baltimore and
opened a practice back East, he and his wife still visited Annie at
the mansion, the last time within a few months of her death.

Friends they might have been, but Annie felt that she owed
this debt as a personal obligation, and in gratitude for the care
that Dr. Hirschfelder had given both her and her husband.

Annie had in her checking account the $8,000 remaining
from her sale after writing the check to Hirschfelder—to spend as
she wished. Most of the money was divided among her family
members (she sent Sallie $5,000), but she also ordered from Mr.
Neubarth a set of new brass band instruments for the Indian
rancheria band. A sum was set aside to pay for a piano for the
rancheria, and piano lessons for two of the Indian girls, Martha
and Lily. Maggie was to have voice lessons, and the Indian band,
new uniforms.[10]

The remaining section of cherry orchard south of Chico Creek
was deeded for normal school campus expansion in 1910, a parcel
that extended the campus to the creek.[11] Another parcel east of
the campus in 1907 was donated for a new Presbyterian church,
subsequently named the Bidwell Memorial Presbyterian Church.

Annie deeded to the state of California the land outside the
levee along the Sacramento River, ultimately to become the
Bidwell Sacramento River Park. For some time she was pestered
by the U.S. Department of Agriculture for the Hooker Oak Tract
to be used as a plant station. It was in February 1904 that they
reluctantly accepted her fourth refusal. That land surrounding the

Sir Joseph Hooker Oak was ultimately to go to the city as part of Bidwell Park.

In 1911, Annie deeded the city of Chico the land between the Presbyterian Church and the Esplanade for a children's playground.[12] The small irregular-shaped triangle between the playground and Front (First) Street, was donated to the Native Daughters of the Golden West, of which Annie had been made an honorary member.

The largest and most publicized of Annie Bidwell's land transactions was, of course, the gift of lands adjacent to both sides of Chico Creek from what was then the Cemetery Road to the far eastern ranch boundary, today's Bidwell Park. The first portion (called by the Bidwells, Vallombrosa) was deeded in 1905, the remaining more easterly portion in 1908.[13]

The ceremony for the acceptance of the gift took place as described earlier, on the lawn before the mansion on a warm July evening in 1905 during the first and only visit to the mansion by Susan B. Anthony. The Alexanders from Washington were also there. It was a perfect occasion for building Annie's ties with the townsfolk.

Annie had only recently arrived by train herself that summer of 1905 from a long hot journey with Willie Alexander. Willie had been sick along the way, necessitating a stopover in Portland, Oregon.

Now she told in her address to Chicoans how Col. Royce had stopped the town's plans of greeting her en masse at the train, and added, "I assure you beloved townspeople that I would never be too weary or fail to be uplifted by your expressions of love."[14]

She had prepared her remarks for the occasion with care. They included, in part: "From the first years of my residence on Rancho Chico a sadness has at times oppressed me as the thought has been borne in on me that someday the beloved Chico Creek would be destroyed by the diverting of its waters and the slaughter of its trees.

"More recently my prayer had been that these fears be laid aside and God who made the creek and blessed us with its custody, be trusted to preserve it when my power to do so shall have ceased. Then it was given me to see a way by which it might be preserved. ...

"It has not cost me a tear or heart-ache in the giving of it, but many a tear and sleepless night, and heart aching nigh-to-breaking, have I given, dear friends, and the best years of my life, in efforts for the betterment and happiness of this community: for the protection of your homes, in God's sight at least, far more precious than the gift of this park, precious as it is, and of which I believe you will prove yourselves worthy, teaching your children also, to hold it in sacred trust.

"... We have the great privilege and honor of having with us this evening one who has broken the alabaster box of her life and poured out its rich treasures to us—men, women and children— for all rise or fall with woman. She has opened the door of education to women; has broken bonds which have cruelly bound her and won ... our beloved Susan B. Anthony.

"I trust the day is near when women shall have a right, by ballot, to cooperate in its management as also in the management of all which concerns our race."[15]

It was a hot night, Miss Anthony was both aged and tired from long train travel, and her words to the assemblage were few.

In 1907, Annie opened two more subdivisions for sale of lots. That same year she drew up preliminary deeds leaving the mansion and its grounds (about twenty-four acres) to the Presbyterian College Board.[16]

With several orchards still retained in order that she might have jobs for the Indians and the pleasure of walking among "her" trees, in 1911 Annie sold the undivided remainder of Rancho Chico. It was particularly important to her that work be provided to any able-bodied male Indian on the rancheria, and her ranch accounts, at least through 1915, show a number of Indians on her payroll.

Annie did take one piece of Mr. Lusk's advice, that she consult her brother-in-law, Thomson Alexander. The men had met earlier, Tom having been requested by Annie to discuss some of the ranch subdivisions, and Lusk had been favorably impressed by him. Annie and Tom Alexander were in San Francisco working on the land sale in July of 1911, leaving Sallie, by her preference, at Robin's Nest for what was to be her last visit.

The sale of the remaining ranch acreage was to a Frank Paul, dealing through the J. P. Edwards and Montgomery Investment brokers of San Francisco. The commission alone to Edwards and Montgomery was $20,500.[17]

The nearly half a million dollars realized from the sale were added to her other investments, by this time worth at least $100,000. The interest alone would have provided Annie with ample income for the remainder of her life and leave a huge estate by Chico standards. She had great pleasure planning for its distribution in her remaining years, but it was no doubt depleted by the enthusiastic support Annie was to make to Prohibition causes during the last years of her life.

Annie named Guy Kennedy, not the law firm of Franklin Lusk, as her Chico representative for future dealings with the San Francisco brokers.[18]

While closing down most of the ranching operations, Annie sold her remaining cattle to her nephew, Guy Kennedy, in June of that year.[19] Part of her reason for holding on to the cattle was that their care had given employment to nephew Joseph Kennedy. Guy and his brother subsequently went into the cattle business as partners.

Loss of
two loved
grandchildren

hough she referred to Maggie Lafonso at the latter's death as *"Mine, mine* since she was five years old," and to Lily Clements as *"our* Lily," Annie Bidwell never compromised her husband's reputation by giving the slightest hint that these two young women were in all likelihood her husband's granddaughters.[1]

Her favoritism could not be proven; perhaps it was coincidence that these two seemingly received special treatment over the years, or it may have been simply because they stood out among the other village youth. There can be no question that Annie held the greatest of hopes for these two pupils of her Indian school. They were talented, intelligent, and of great importance to her, docile and receptive of her teachings in school and chapel.

Maggie's mother Amanda had grown up in the Bidwell Rancheria but how she came there is an unanswered question. Amanda's own mother was probably dead at an early age. Maggie's younger brother Elmer Lafonso, during his brief fling as an entertainer, was reported in a newspaper interview to be the son of an Indian princess and a chief of the Mechoopdas. This seems to tell part of the story correctly, and in her own account of her life, Amanda told that her mother was from the "Oroville Indians," and her father was a white man.[2]

In Indian fashion Amanda married Holai Lafonso, chief of the tribelet that lived on the rancheria, and if John Bidwell was her white father, as is believed, he had probably met her Indian mother through work with various local tribes in accomplishing,

with the United States Indian
agent O. M. Wozencraft, the
1851 treaty with the Maidu
tribes. Bidwell played a key
role in convincing the Maidu
to place themselves under the
jurisdiction and protection of
the United States.

Maggie Lafonso was born
to Amanda and Holai
Lafonso in early 1883 and
Elmer several years later.
Maggie was taken by
Amanda to Annie's Indian
school at age three and
learned rapidly. Both of the
Lafonso children were blessed
with beautiful voices; they
responded to instruction

Maggie Sowilleno Lafonso, Amanda's
daughter, at her marriage to Joseph
Charles Mitchell of Colusa County in
1907. Courtesy of Dorothy Hill Collection,
Meriam Library, CSUC.

rapidly, and by the time Maggie was five years old she was fluent
in English. Shy and polite, she was often summoned to the
mansion at an early age to sing for important guests of the
Bidwells, including such academicians as Dr. Shinn, head of the
Forestry School at the University in Berkeley, and numerous
visiting missionaries and pastors.

Perhaps none exemplified Annie's hopes more than Maggie
Alfonso. Maggie adored Mrs. Bidwell, a near-mutual feeling. To
please Annie, Maggie struggled to memorize the Presbyterian
catechism perfectly. For Annie, she regularly brought a flower to
chapel services to deliver with a shy, sweet smile. Her girlish voice
rang clear and true as she sang the hymns, smiling at Mrs. Bidwell
for approval.

Musical talent was not the only attribute in Maggie that
attracted Annie and others in Chico who came to know her. She

was even-tempered, a ready leader or follower, and she showed the same sweet serene nature characteristic of both Nopanny and Amanda. By the time she was thirteen, Maggie was always prepared with a solo hymn for the chapel services. So captivated was Annie by Maggie's natural grace that she had photographs made to send to her mother in Washington.

Maggie was one of only a few of the Indian children to be asked to dine with the Bidwells, not, of course when the Bidwells were entertaining formally, but among guests to whom Annie could display this lovely product of her training. At the same time this exposure was polishing Maggie's social skills.

John Bidwell was likewise impressed by what he saw as Maggie Lafonso's potential to rise above the lifestyle he had once assumed to be inevitable for Native Americans. Of the handful of Indians he mentioned in his will (the one made in the event he outlive Annie) Maggie was named to be recipient of a fund placed in trust for her continuing education.[3] The remaining Indians Bidwell named to receive such funds were faithful ranch hands, many of whom had worked for him from the earliest days of the ranch's establishment.

When Annie attended the Women's Congress in San Francisco in 1895 she took Maggie and Mary Kiala [Ke'a'ala] to accompany her and explain the intricate Indian basketry, feather and beadwork loaned for display by the artists of the Mechoopda village.[4]

Fearless in what she would attempt, Maggie wrote to Annie in Washington after John Bidwell's death that she was conducting the Sunday services in the chapel so that the others would not forget about the God of whom Annie taught. She was seventeen at that time.

When children were mansion houseguests, most often those of Minnie Alexander, Maggie came to play with them. She learned to take photographs with a simple camera to record for Annie events occurring during her absence, including the Indian war dances still being held when tribes gathered at the Mechoopda sweathouse.

Maggie was capable of organizing and shopping for the Christmas party for the Indians begun by Annie Bidwell when the school was started: gifts for everyone and special food that was termed a feast by the village residents. Annie noted that Maggie was able to give a party on a smaller budget than she, Annie, could do it.

Maggie was the leader in organizing twenty-four of the village Indians into a Prohibition Alliance in 1902, one of the many offshoots of the Prohibition movement. The lodge-like ritual of the alliance appealed to the Indians and to Maggie. Annie attended her first meeting of the alliance to listen with pleasure as Maggie sang and the Indian youths, Lily and Luther Clements, Martha, and the Nucholls children recited Prohibition poems and articles.

When in later years conventions were held in the state for the Indian Christian youth, both Maggie and her brother Elmer, among others from around the state, proved skilled in being interviewed by the press. They clearly itemized the goals of Indian youth, including the wish for removal of the cruel denial of citizenship with its exclusion from property and voting rights. Annie had doubtlessly coached them well for such occasions.

When Maggie had completed all of the schooling available through the Indian school and the public school in Chico, Annie arranged her admission to the normal school.

Maggie would pursue higher education in somewhat erratic fashion due to family demands. A situation arose which is somewhat difficult for us to understand because we do not know the cultural background for the divorce of Amanda and Holai Lafonso.

The situation seems to have been that Holai Lafonso and Amanda severed their marriage union about 1887 or 1888, whether at her request or by mutual wish is not known and cannot be understood without more knowledge of Maidu marriage and divorce customs. Amanda then married Santa Wilson, a village newcomer.

Amanda and Holai were still married in March 1887, when Nopanny wrote to Annie that Amanda had had a severe case of measles which kept Holai Lafonso from resting or sleeping. In April of that year, Amanda as Mrs. *Lafonso* wrote to Annie of the death of her baby. Possibly having measles during her pregnancy had been a factor in the death.

Nopanny in her letter of August 1887, to John Bidwell included a paragraph about a newcomer to the village, Santa Wilson, who wanted to build a home, and Nopanny wrote asking why he, Bidwell, had not tried to welcome this new and good ranch worker with living quarters in the village. Bidwell had understandably been cool to Wilson's settling in the village when he heard of the attachment between Amanda and the newcomer. Only two years earlier he had proclaimed Lafonso chief in the village. When he heard of the divorce of the chief and Amanda neither he nor Annie could have approved. Up to that point they had tried not to interfere with Indian customs that did not directly conflict with the Christian teachings that Annie was trying to instill.

In addition to being a very good ranch worker, Santa Wilson was to become a convert to Christianity and a devout supporter of the chapel. Annie accepted this new arrangement, as she often found it expedient to do when she did not understand Indian customs and was not yet ready to challenge them. At the time the parting of the ways for Amanda and Holai became known, Annie was in Washington.

In December of 1902, Maggie wrote to Annie Bidwell in Washington that she was holding Sabbath services regularly and that her father sent "love and remembrance." A few months later she wrote that "Mama has her new house built. The children

(Wilsons) have been vaccinated and are not very well. Birnie is going to school and doing well."

Amanda and Santa Wilson proceeded to have a large family, all of them eventually baptised by Annie in the Indian chapel. Birnie Wilson, as Annie spelled Burney, seems to have been the oldest Wilson. Sherman, Edward and Eva followed, possibly others. These children were accepted without problem as siblings by both Maggie and Elmer, who simply adjusted living arrangements in deference to their parents' wishes.

Santa Wilson was soon to become the chapel elder, as well as a communicant. The Reverend White at the 1909 Easter communion service at the Chico Presbyterian Church called Santa from the congregation and asked him to help serve![5] Later the Wilson's son Birnie aspired to enter ministerial training at Park College when he reached his late teens and sought Annie's help financially.

Rarely, but on occasion, Maggie would finish her letter to Annie by addressing her as "my mother." She and a few others did indicate that they gave Annie a special role that the term mother seemed to define to them. Maggie more often closed letters with "remember Maggie to be a faithful worker to her people," or a similar thought.

Elmer Lafonso finished at the Greenville Government Indian School in 1904. Attending the Presbytery meeting in Sacramento that year, Annie took Maggie and Elmer with her to sing for the assembled church leaders and pastors. She never tired of watching the faces of those who for the first time heard the sister and brother join in an anthem, their voices strikingly clear and expressive.

In 1902, Holai had fallen victim to the physical symptoms that came over the Indian people while still fairly youthful, almost invariably the prelude to death. Maggie took over care of her father, and because of his inability to work to support them, Maggie had to work at the farm jobs available either on the Bidwell Ranch or other farms when seasonal work was available.

Holai lingered in a weakening state through the years that Maggie had hoped to return to normal school classes. She did get away to attend the Young People's Christian Endeavor Conference in Capitola in April 1905, writing to Annie that she met nine other Indian youths there from Pasadena, and spotted afar the delegates from the Chico State Normal School, though none had spoken to her.

With her father unable to work, Maggie took harvest employment, working the summer of 1904 at "China Camp" in Vina so that her father could camp with her and enjoy the company of his friends from several tribes. When she worked at the Rancho Chico Fruit Camp, she could come to Sabbath chapel meetings, though it was a very long walk from the Bidwell packing operation to the village.

Thus was Maggie's life circumscribed by duty up until the sudden death of her father in October or November 1906. Annie

Packing fruit from a Bidwell orchard, possibly after Annie established her own company about 1904–1906. Mr. Lewis is said to be directing the process. Courtesy of California State Parks.

was again in Washington at that time, but Elmer wrote to her at once, as had Col. Royce, and Annie noted in her diary her sadness at the passing of "dear Lafonso,"[6] an Indian who had come to her and asked that she baptize him when he thought himself ready.

Maggie was then twenty-four years old. Perhaps she had regretted the loss of youthful years given to the care and support of her father, but that seems out of character for Maggie who seemed never to begrudge her decision, based as it was, no doubt, on Indian custom as well as her love for her father. She truly wanted to serve her people, which brought her into conflict between the ideals that Annie Bidwell had for Indian change and what Maggie saw was important to the residents of the village, particularly the older generation.

It is interesting to note the similarity of Maggie's expressed wish to serve her people with that of her brother Elmer. The latter wrote to Mrs. Bidwell until she died, whenever she was gone from the mansion for long. His chief purpose was to express his desire to gain more music education, but he added, "I must not forget my people."[7]

After her father, Chief Holai Lafonso, died, Maggie was able to convince the older Indians to give up the dance-sweathouse, and it was destroyed.[8] There were other sweathouses to which many of the Mechoopda men continued to go for their dance rituals. Maggie had a harder time trying to convince the rancheria Indians to give up the burnings, the annual ceremony at which the dead were honored by sending valuable items up in flames in memory of those recently departed.

In October 1907, Maggie wrote to Annie, "The burning is a question which is not settled yet." It had been discussed at church. "The young people are trying to banish all the old ways."

On November 1, 1907, Maggie wrote again to Annie that the people of the village had reluctantly voted to do away with the burnings, after one last rite. "Today is the date set for the burning. Baskets will be burned and American goods. I admit that many have lost a great deal by burning so many articles which they themselves needed but such times have passed away and now the older ones have given up the old ways."[9]

Annie's standing argument against the burning ceremony was that it wasted useable resources, among them exquisite works of basketry, bead and feather art which Annie knew well could be sold for money she thought the Indians could better use.

Joseph Mitchell, a young man from a tribelet near Colusa, Glenn County, and Maggie decided to marry in 1907 and Maggie with Mitchell in attendance called to ask Annie to conduct a Christian service. They hoped to marry the following day.

Annie hastily explained that they must have a license from the county if they planned to be married in the Presbyterian faith, and also that she had no authority to perform marriages, they being civil as well as religious in nature.

Maggie had anticipated the former, and the couple had been to Oroville already and procured a license. The Reverend White would be acceptable to them, they said, if Annie were there to give them her blessing at the service.

Maggie Sowillino Lafonso and Joseph Charles Mitchell were married in Maggie's mother Amanda's house with only family and a few close friends witnessing on December 21, 1907.

Then, in one of the "most glorious" Sunday services held by Annie Bidwell in the Indian chapel, the Sunday following Maggie's marriage, Annie with Rev. White's assistance baptized fifteen persons, four of them she noted to be "full cast" Indians, some of whom spoke little English. Maggie had faithfully explained to them the significance of the rite of baptism.

Among those baptized was Maggie's new husband Joseph Mitchell, several Wilsons (including Amanda herself) and two of the Conway family. After marriage, Maggie earnestly continued her work in support of her faith by starting a Sunday school among the Nord Indians. As her pregnancy made appearances more difficult, Elmer Lafonso took Maggie's place at leading the Indian chapel services when Annie could not be present.

Maggie's child was born in late summer, 1909, but Maggie never regained strength after delivering the child (dead at birth, or soon after) and began the sad decline that had been suffered by so many of the Mechoopdas. Annie visited Maggie many times during the fall, the latter described as sweet and patient propped up among the pillows in her bed.

Annie was attending a meeting elsewhere when she received word from Elmer that Maggie had died. She managed to return for the funeral on November 9. Annie, of course, had paid for all of the doctor's visits during Maggie's illness and for all costs of the funeral. Annie had long before begun providing caskets for each Indian burial if there was to be a Christian burial service, even adding the cost of the new embalming process that "modern" morticians had introduced.

In a despair that seemed to eat away all the reserves she had been able to muster over the years, Annie now felt she would have to give up her work in the chapel. She met with Elmer, Santa and Amanda and told them that she felt it best if they organized and conducted the church themselves as they were directed by God. For a while, at least, she could not go on.

Annie was not alone in the white community to react with sorrow: Maud Camper, a Presbyterian who had assisted in the Indian chapel from time to time, wrote her, "It was a great shock to know that Maggie's kindly useful presence is gone from us. I often in my mind see her standing beside me near the organ, earnestly listening, or with her long slender fingers—you know how I always talked about the beauty of her hands—touching chords or trying to bring out the harmony of the hymns she loved so well."[10]

The blow sustained by the loss of Maggie was the second to be inflicted on Annie by one of her dearest Indians. While Maggie's departure was not by her decision, the loss of Lily Clements came

George Clements with a step son, said to be Bud Bain. George lost an eye in an accident in 1907, perhaps accounting for the partial frown. The picture was taken after George left the Chico Indian village permanently, date unknown, but thought to be after 1910. Courtesy of Dorothy Hill Collection, Meriam Library. CSUC.

about from her deliberate actions. One could be said to be God's will, the other the work of the devil.

After George Clements' arrest for child abuse in 1899, Annie had obtained custody of George's children, Lily and Luther. In order to get the children away from George's influence altogether, she had them admitted to the Greenville Indian School in 1899. They had been in Greenville until graduating from elementary school except on a few occasions when Annie sent money for them to come on vacation to visit the rancheria.[11]

The children's mother, Clara, remarried to James Nucholls of another tribe, possibly Concow.[12] Annie seemed to accept without question the change in Clara's name to Jane or Jenny by the time the Nucholls came to live on the rancheria while he worked on Rancho Chico. Bidwell's foreman reported that Nucholls was an excellent worker in spite of being small of build. It was to the Nucholls home that Lily came in 1903 after graduating from the Greenville School. Luther still had more years to finish of his elementary schooling, as did the three sons of Jane and James Nucholls.

Annie was perplexed as to the next step for Lily. She consulted Dr. Edwin Paine, head of the Greenville government school, who suggested that Lily would make a fine nursery school teacher. He suggested that Annie start a kindergarten for the village children and put it under Lily's care. Lily had worked in this capacity while in Greenville, understood what was expected of a teacher and was good with children.[14]

Perhaps Annie had this in mind, but thought that Lily needed more training, when, during the early fall of 1903, she went to talk with Dr. Van Liew, president of the normal school. He gave permission for Lily to enter normal classes, as others did at that time, directly from elementary school and then to devote three years instead of two to complete the teachers' course.

The James Nucholls household added another child when a new baby, Myrtle, was born about the time that Lily arrived home from Greenville. Annie directed the building of another room onto the Nucholls' house for Lily's exclusive occupancy. She bought new furniture for the room and supplied Lily with curtains, sheets, towels, soap and ribbons for her hair, as well as new

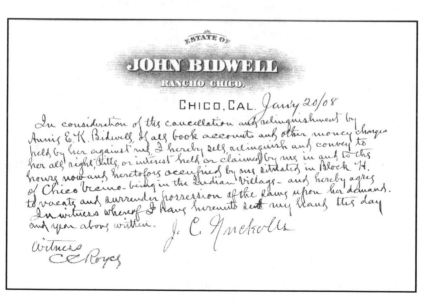

In January 1908, in her eagerness to have James Nucholls and Lily Clements gone from the village, Annie Bidwell released Nucholls from what he owed her in exchange for his home in the Indian village. It was a generous gesture for she wrote in her diary, "The house would be mine anyway," as indeed were both the land and buildings occupied by the Mechoopdas. Courtesy of California State Library.

underclothing and several new dresses made by Annie's dress-maker. One dress was purchased from Oser's, a Chico department store of high quality, so that Lily would make a nice appearance among the other college girls. Annie escorted Lily to the college and saw that she was placed in the proper courses. At that time, Lily was fourteen or fifteen.

Lily was also begun on piano lessons and a piano was rented for her and other Indian children to use in practice. At times, Lily came to the mansion and practiced on the Bidwell piano.

Lily was nearly the same age as Willie Alexander. The two got along well—both were musical and fun-loving—and from all signs, Lily would grow into a poised and well-taught young lady who could relate well to others in the world beyond the Indian government school or the rancheria. It must have concerned Annie that she was creating a creature capable of a role in the general society, yet doomed by the stigma of having been born Indian that could never be erased.

About the same time that Holai Lafonso died, so did Janey Nucholls. She died from no diagnosed malady and certainly at an early age. No doubt the death certificate gave a cause but the accuracy of these medical reasons is open to question—more so than even modern ones made without autopsy. Janey's passing left James Nucholls with tiny Myrtle to care for, as well as three older Nucholls boys who attended the Greenville school much of the year.

In January 1908, while Annie made a routine visit to the Indian village to inquire after the sick, Maggie Mitchell, not yet married two months, called Annie inside her home and told her distressing news. James Nucholls and Lily Clements had just announced that they had been married four months earlier in Oroville, and were living as husband and wife.

Amanda and another matron in the village whom Annie respected, Mary Asbill, anticipated that their benefactress would be upset at this turn of events. Probably none had visualized the anguish and anger with which Annie Bidwell reacted. Annie's diary is the best source for how deeply she was wounded.

On January 9, "We are crushed, and the village generally, at Nuckols' base conduct in misleading his wife's daughter, *our* Lily."

On the next day, Annie built up her courage to face the couple, but once inside their home she "felt ill and could not talk to them. Left their house and managed to get to Maggie's, where we planned …. My trust is in God only. My heart seems as if it would burst. My dear Lily, God's child in the wolf's jaws, & we helpless because she had been made willing to be, poor child. Hanging is too good for her 'father.' He is the Devil incarnate."

A heavy schedule of WCTU and Anti-Saloon League meetings helped Annie to put the matter in the back of her mind at intervals, but she was determined to take action. She composed a letter to James Nucholls ordering him to leave the Indian village at once and forever. While this letter was being reviewed by Dr. Gatchell, Col. Royce and Guy Kennedy, she called on members of the chapel congregation to see how they would react to the banishment, and the Conways, Silvers and Franks added their approval to that of the Asbills, Mitchells and Wilsons.

Annie's letter brought a prompt reply from Nucholls, who seems to have been an intelligent person with a fair amount of education. He had been active in the chapel and especially so in the Prohibition Alliance, Annie having praised his intelligent reading of the scriptures in her diary. (His rendition was ranked better than that of some she heard in the Chico "downtown" church.)

Nucholls agreed to leave willingly, asking forgiveness for himself and Lily. Annie wrote back that there could be no forgiveness without their true repentance. Thus Lily Clements, like her father George, walked out of Annie Bidwell's life forever.

Nucholls wrote Annie another letter but was referred to Col. Royce for further communication. Nucholls wrote that he knew he owed Mrs. Bidwell money and offered to pay by giving her his house in the village. Her answer through the colonel was simple. She would cancel the debt, but adding, "the house *is mine* anyway."

Up to this time, Annie had tried to be tolerant of the Maidu customs, logically assuming that Christian practices would eventually replace them. The dance house had gone, the burnings been discontinued, and now, Annie decided, she would permit no more relationships such as was just discovered to be the case with Jesse Slack, a twenty-one-year-old rancheria resident. About the time that Nucholl's evil had come to light, it was pointed out that Jesse had recently brought to live with him a new "wife," the thirty-two-year-old previously-married Susan Gilbert. Annie called on Slack and issued the sentence of banishment.

In the startled Jesse's case he was given one chance to redeem himself and the next day found him on the train, railroad fare paid by Annie, and with three dollars to get a marriage license for himself and Susan.

For an interval between the defection of Lily Clements and James Nucholls and the death of Maggie, the Indian village had seemed to reach a new peak in pursuing "white" civilization— surely surpassing even the fondest dreams of Annie Bidwell when she started to work with the village Indians.

For several months, Annie was forced to give up her work at the chapel and among the village residents. During a period from October 1908, through February 1909, she was very ill. Her symptoms specifically involved her throat and vocal chords and a general physical collapse.[15]

Early in 1908, Annie had been ill with what Dr. Gatchell termed a case of mumps, a recurrence of the disease which Annie had in childhood.

In the fall of 1908, cramps, nausea and diarrhea set in, too intrusively to continue any of her activities. Annie did not feel well for two weeks, but the schedule of events related to her prohibition work soon found her at meetings, often when she should have been in bed. It seemed a pattern with her—this frenzy of activity that was apt to culminate in sudden collapse.

At last Annie decided on her own to stop all medications prescribed by doctors, even those by Dr. Gatchell. These popular drugs of the time included cocaine, arsenic and iron, from a modern viewpoint drugs sufficient to overwhelm any human system. Annie determined to "deluge her body" with fluids and to wash out the accumulation of poisons.[16]

At first, the fluids-only treatment appeared to be working a cure. But on October 15, Annie succumbed to an illness so severe that it was over three months before she was able to leave her bedroom or her fresh-air bed on the upper veranda outside its windows.

Dr. Gatchell strictly forbade visitors or any contact with newspapers or material thought to be dangerously overexciting. Annie's mention in her diary of herpes suggests that she may have suffered from shingles.[17]

Massage and "electricity" made up the primary prescribed treatment. Often Annie was unable to sleep unless massaged during the night. Cora Wayland Kennedy, though teaching daytimes in one of the Chico schools, stayed with Annie at the mansion and cared for her at night and on weekends, with Eva Kennedy filling in by turn.

Annie's throat swelling was combined with a near complete loss of hearing. Her weak right arm became numb and it was necessary for others to write for her.

The Indian chapel continued to meet regularly, first with Maggie leading the services, and when her pregnancy was far advanced, Elmer Lafonso taking over. The villagers kept themselves informed of Annie's illness, and when she was able to venture out again, on one of her first short walks she happened to meet the Indian William Conway. His behavior was very gratifying to Annie as she recorded in her diary:

"[William] came to me, his face beaming in smiles, & eyes moist with tears: seized my hand in both of his & pressed it to his breast, whispering 'I am so glad! So glad! Our prayers were surely answered. I prayed every day & would lie awake at night thinking of you, and would get up from bed & fall on my face and pray.' And this an *Indian!* I have never seen gratitude & affection so strongly displayed, with such dignity, his form erect, yet expressing in manner such tenderness. To my knees I went on entering my room, & thanked God for my dear people—my Indians!"[18]

At Easter, Rev. White of the Chico Presbyterian Church invited Santa Wilson, an elder at the chapel, to help in serving the "downtown" communicants.[19] Annie's pride in this was only increased when Rev. White took Santa with him to the annual Presbytery meeting in Sacramento where Santa presented the list Annie had prepared for him of all baptisms and communicants in the chapel since its beginning. In time most of the village Indians active in the chapel were to become communicants in the "downtown" Chico church.

In May, the three WCTU branches in town held an institute at the Indian chapel, after which dinner was served to the women. Presiding was the WCTU state president, Sara Dorr. Elmer sang a solo; the Indian brass band played.

A year
of travel

During the nine years following her husband John's death, Annie had gone at frequent intervals to visit in Washington with her sister Sallie Alexander, Sallie's husband Thomson (or Tom), and their son William. The first trip had been a few months following John's funeral when she had gone back to Washington with the Alexanders because she could not face her great loss alone. [1]

Late the following year, 1901, Annie had returned to Washington on sudden notice to help Sallie care for her very sick little boy Willie, as he was fondly called. Taking on motherhood in her fifties had not been easy for Sallie, and she was grateful and generous in sharing motherly duties and the pleasure they gave to Annie.

Annie's time while in Washington was devoted almost entirely to soothing the feverish child and, as he recovered, to reading to him and playing bed games so that Willie stayed immobilized as the physician ordered. She developed a closer emotional bond with Willie than ever with Guy or Joey Kennedy, in part because the jealousy of the Waylands was always in her mind.

As the next eight years passed, each year saw either the Alexanders at the mansion, with summer weeks spent at Robin's Nest, or Annie at the Alexander's home in Washington. As Willie grew older, he came alone to visit his aunt. In 1911 the Alexanders came to Chico without their adopted son, to be joined in a few weeks by William and his bride, the former Gertrude Bruner of Washington.

Willie remained very close to his aunt, once writing in 1903 after a summer's solo stay, "I suppose it is getting cool in Chico or rather at my other home as I have a home at both ends of the continent and a mother in each."[2]

Annie had always been reluctant to travel by water after her first experience with seasickness on her honeymoon. She nevertheless agreed to go with Sallie and Tom and a party of East Coast friends to Europe in the summer of 1910. Annie decided to take as a companion her young friend, Harriett Alexander.[3]

Digressing here, it is important to bring Annie's long friendship with Harriett Alexander up to date. Minnie Carroll, Harriett's mother, as a member of the prominent Carroll family that John Bidwell had known before his marriage to Annie, had often been welcomed as a houseguest by the Bidwells both before and after Minnie's marriage.

After Minnie's marriage to Charles O. Alexander, a prominent Alameda County businessman and politician of the Bay Area, Minnie made long stays in Chico at the mansion, first with baby Harriett and then with Douglas after he was born. Alexander, while pleasant enough, rarely lingered for more than a day or so in Chico on the weeks-long holidays that Minnie spent with the Bidwells.

Charles O. Alexander committed suicide a few months before John Bidwell's death. At that time he was in the process of being censured for the disappearance of funds at the Oakland Post Office of which he was assistant postmaster. U.S. Senator Perkins was reputedly at work in Washington to have the matter covered up when Alexander gave in to his despair at his seeming disgrace and drowned himself in San Francisco Bay.[4]

The two widowed women, Minnie and Annie, were drawn closer together by shared loss. They visited often both in Chico and in San Francisco as the two Alexander children were growing up. During one summer, 1905, Minnie and both children were guests at Robin's Nest. Harriett was sent alone to Chico several times to spend all or parts of the summers as she grew older.

Minnie became more and more discontented in widowhood, and often depressed. She began living months at a time abroad and farming her children out, so to speak. Harriett most often ended up in Chico with Annie, sometimes with her pet dog in tow. The dog was made welcome by pet-loving Annie. For reasons unknown, Minnie's son Douglas, who had been very close to Annie for most of his childhood, now became disenchanted with the Mansion and Rancho Chico and chose to go elsewhere.

As Minnie lingered abroad, Annie offered that Harriett should live with her during the school year 1908 and attend the new Chico High School while Douglas attended a boys' boarding school.

Harriett Alexander was of a sunny, loving personality. She liked to go with Annie to the Indian chapel and to help her by teaching the younger children at Sunday school. Annie made the mansion open to Harriett for entertaining her friends, and the young people that visited as a result seemed to provide great pleasure to Annie, both in the planning and the entertaining. Among the young men was Irvin Clough, related to the family of F. M. Clough who represented the huge Diamond Match operation during its establishment in Stirling City and the Barber mill adjacent to Chico.

As Harriet finished the school year in 1908, she was

Annie Ellicott Kennedy Bidwell, about 1910. Courtesy of California State Parks.

unusually listless and tired, so that Minnie took her to Dr. Hirschfelder upon her return home for the summer. He found alarming symptoms and placed Harriett in a private sanitarium for treatment. It was over a time when Annie herself had succumbed to several illnesses, so when summer 1909 arrived, and with it a "wildly happy" Harriett restored to health and back at the mansion, Annie was grateful.

During the summer months that year many of Harriett's old high school friends were in and out of the mansion. The era of the automobile had arrived, and Harriett and her cousin Gladys Brigham, who had come with her from the Bay Area for the summer, were often taken for auto rides and on outings of which Annie had no part, certainly by her own preference.

It could be said that Annie lacked much imagination when it came to the looks that passed between a young man and young lady, or any other of the symptoms of rapture that accompany first love. When Harriett returned home, Annie had a vague notion that something was afoot. She had received communication from Minnie that indicated her displeasure with Harriett—and by extension, with her. Annie wrote to Gladys for clarification. On September 2, 1909, Gladys wrote back the details of the story:[5]

On return to the Bay Area, the girls had been met at the ferry by Douglas. "Aunt Minnie was in bed and really looked so badly that we didn't talk much, but next morning Harriett told of her fondness for Irvin [Clough]." She had not been diplomatic, but "said in a very blunt manner 'Mother, I am engaged to Irvin.' You can imagine the scene that followed. Aunt Minnie wants Harriett to give up Irvin for the next two years—having absolutely no communication. If at that time they still care for one another she will give consent."

Irvin Clough had been a friend of Harriett's all through high school. During the summer of 1909, their friendship had grown to love, and Minnie was inclined to think that Annie had been blind to improprieties she should have noticed. Gladys in defense of both Harriett and Annie wrote, "Now you know how little Harriett and Irvin were alone and they seldom went out but they simply insisted on my accompanying them. ... It would seem a shame that our glorious visit with you be followed by so much trouble."

After praying over the matter, Annie offered a solution, though one that was still rather hard for the young lovers to contemplate. Harriett was invited to join the upcoming tour to Europe with Annie and the Washington party. After the tour ended and Annie and the Thomson Alexanders returned to the states, Harriett stayed on in Paris for the second year of her forced separation. She became "companion" to a San Franciscan living abroad, Mrs. Spreckels, whom they knew but met again in Paris while on tour.

The trip abroad was a triumph for Annie. While the rest of the party were confined with seasickness during the usual days required to acquire "sea legs," Annie walked the deck from the first day, letting the wind blow on her face, glorying in the action of the waves, and crowing about it in her diary.

From February 2, when they set sail, until July, when the Alexanders departed for home and left Annie in England for a medical examination by throat specialists, the party visited first Egypt, then Constantinople, Greece, Italy, France and finally England.

Annie managed to include attending a Worldwide Christian Endeavor Convention in Glasgow during her stay, as the guest of a Scottish WCTU member, and meetings with several other similarly involved women she subsequently invited to visit her at the mansion and with whom she corresponded the rest of her life.

The physicians with whom Annie consulted used X-ray to explore her throat, mouth, eyes and nose. She had been made to close her lips over an X-ray bulb as they hovered over her, covered with a black cloth.

"No cancer, absolutely. Nor tuberculosis bacilli. ..." The thickened spot in the lung would subside with perfect rest, sunshine, open-air life and avoidance of drafts. The vocal chords had been partially paralyzed by pressure from the lung spot. Rest was an absolute necessity but the prognosis looked encouraging.

Annie returned to the United States in the early fall of 1910, but she delayed her return to California for nearly two months, touring New York State's vacation sites with the Alexanders.

It was almost as if Annie wished to avoid taking up the schedule of activities in Chico: the normal school with its student receptions and lectures; the Prohibitionists and their constant drain on her time and money; the Indians, from whom she had made her emotional break, if not her financial one. But she had promised to be home for the dedication of the new Bidwell Memorial Church on First Street on November 20, and she arrived just in time to receive the grateful acclaim to which all could agree she was entitled after her exceedingly generous financial contribution to the new church.

Aware of her impending arrival, some person or persons in Chico organized a reception for her at the depot—reported in both local papers as totaling over 1,000 people. The Indian band among other bands played as she was assisted into "a carriage and drawn to her home by the school children of the city"!

After Christmas passed that year, Annie left the mansion again for two months in San Francisco. She summoned Elmer Lafonso to join her in the city to have his singing abilities judged by a renowned voice teacher. Annie also arranged to have Elmer asked to sing at a San Francisco Presbyterian church, as always impressing his audience with his beautiful voice and his sincerity of manner.

Annie was guest of honor at the exclusive California Club, at Augusta Gibbs' arranging. Her appearance there was described in the following newspaper account:

"Mrs. Bidwell has been a good angel to the Indians in Northern California ever since coming to the state in the late fifties, and since the death of General Bidwell [she] has been pastor to the Indians thereabouts, who fairly worship the ground she walks on. Many of them work at the big ranch, and here they have always been kindly led from absolute primitiveness to gradually adopt the ways of civilization.

"No greater antithesis could be imagined than the gracious, dainty little silver haired woman … and the vicissitudes she underwent, living among the naked Indians and gradually taming them by loving kindness and patience, until today no story of the aborigines of California would be complete that omitted to relate the part played by General and Mrs. Bidwell in the early days.

"Mrs. John Bidwell … is in town as the guest of friends … looking sweetly picturesque, with her masses of snowy white hair, her rose-pink complexion. …"[6]

Although Harriett Alexander had been cut off from communication with Irvin Clough by terms set by her mother, Annie had kept in touch with Irvin by letter and also in person. No doubt this conduit helped to keep Harriett's spirits up as she waited out the two years. When Annie met Minnie in New York for lunch during her stay in late 1910, they apparently had a frosty interview, with no sign of Minnie's relenting on her terms for accepting Irvin as a son-in-law. As the end of the exile period drew to a close in 1911, Annie sent Harriett $400 for the ocean voyage and train fares back to the waiting Clough and marriage.[7]

The Washington Alexanders visited Annie during the summer and fall of 1911, both on holiday and for Thomson Alexander's help in arranging the sale of what remained of Rancho del Arroyo Chico.

Good-bye
to Sallie

nnie's diaries cease abruptly at the end of 1911. Several factors were involved. One was surely the loss of feeling in her right arm and hand and the difficulty of writing legibly. There may have been diaries after 1911 that she destroyed rather than have that material open to family members, or even those she envisioned seeking it out in research libraries. Certainly she did destroy much during the last year or two of her life, and perhaps some that slipped by she would have included in this censorship had she remembered its location in the great mass of correspondence that by that time had accumulated. Or it may simply have been, as Annie wrote in her letter to Col. Armstrong, "... so many incidents of distressing nature ... that I could not write anyone. ..." Keeping a daily diary would have been like rubbing salt in an open wound.

Letters of condolence at Sallie's death that Annie saved are in the most part from her young Indian friends, such as Elmer Lafonso and Birnie Wilson. By happenstance, a copy of a letter that Annie wrote in November 1914, probably the copy prepared for her secretary to type or recopy, was saved, and it tells best the events surrounding the loss of her sister. It was in reply to a letter she had received almost a year before from one of the party that had traveled with her through Europe.

"My sister's death was so sudden and sad that it was impossible for me to write about it. Sad in that I was ignorant of her illness until too late to reach her alive. There were so many incidents of a distressing nature connected with my sister's illness that I could not write to anyone at that time, and to this date.

"She was not satisfied with her physician and requested him to have a 'consultation' to which he replied that when he thought a consultation necessary he would have one, which he had not until Mr. Alexander had telegraphed me of his alarm at her condition. My sister's physician and the one called in consultation did not consider my sister's condition critical until she was passing away! She wrote me that she was not ill, simply tired, her letter reaching me after the telegram a few hours.

"I left for Washington on the first train for the East, but arrived about four hours before the funeral. She expressed such a longing to see me, and receive a letter from me, while Mr. Alexander had a letter and a telegram in his pocket from me, which he in his distraction forgot to report until two hours after my arrival.

"Mr. Alexander was quite ill from grief and we took him, with a nurse, to Atlantic City. It was all so sad and still is."[1]

The Chico *Record* fills in with some details. Annie had just given a large farewell reception for the Royces at the mansion when news of Sallie's imminent death came. The telegram telling of the death on January 16, 1912, was delivered to her on a train as she headed east. From "relatives in Chico" the *Record* was told that Sallie was known to be suffering from heart trouble, but ptomaine poisoning was believed the killer.[2]

Sallie's death left Annie with only her devotion to the cause of Prohibition to cling to. In 1914 she was asked to join the Executive Board of the California Prohibition Party and gladly accepted. Annie described her activities in the Armstrong letter quoted above:

"I have traveled several thousand miles, and had not only charge of my especial district but have attended … meetings in Los Angeles many times. To my friends my power of endurance has been inexplicable, as also to me, except on the grounds that

God had work for me to do, and fitted me to do it. I had many persons working under my instruction, for which my many years of cooperation with my husband in prohibition work, prepared me to undertake. … I enjoyed the work."[3]

It was during this year that the arrest of one of her paid lieutenants, Rev. R. A. M. Browne, caused Annie embarrassment not mentioned in the letter quoted above.[4]

Annie increasingly lost the use of her voice. The London doctors had told her that this was probably from nerve damage. The final campaign for women's suffrage in California in 1913 was largely won without her active presence, though she wrote a letter to the Chico papers giving her strong support. It was a temperate letter:

"Voting is a more effective way for women to express themelves than haranguing public officials to obey the law. We do not expect enfranchisement will convert California into a Garden of Eden, but women hope to do much better work removed from under the heel of men."

She added that raising the "terrors of jury duty"—some persons having suggested that it would be too much for a woman to be confined and expected to hold her own against men's better judgment in such matters—holds no more basis in truth than the once expounded argument that women were not strong enough to be nurses.[5]

And what of
the rancheria?

*I*n about 1912, at Annie Bidwell's request, Amanda
Wilson drew up a list of the Indian residents living in
the rancheria at that time. They totaled forty-eight,
including fifteen children, nine couples, two widows and
thirteen single men. This does not mean that this number were
constant residents, or that the population did not fluctuate as
work took both men and women away for months on end,
during harvest seasons especially. But there were permanent
homes provided for this population.[1]

At that time, Amanda also put into writing her knowledge of
Indian customs, most of which Annie copied largely unedited
into her own written accounts on Indians and used in her talks
before various groups.[2]

Santa Wilson and his sons, William Conway and his sons, and
old, old timers such as Billy Preacher, Rufus Pulisse (Pulicy) and
Pablo Silvers always had steady employment offered them in
Annie's shrinking ranch enterprises. Annie's personal business
records, kept while she and Reuben operated the Bidwell Orchard
Company, show a half dozen or so of the older Indians on her
payroll, and quite a few occasions on which she had loaned
money to members of the village.[3] Large loans to Elmer Lafonso
are noted, but also their repayment in good time through the
sewing services of Genevieve, Elmer's wife, and Elmer's own work
as a carpenter at the mansion.[4]

Some of the most promising young Indian men, in Annie's
eyes, were away at school. Annie had arranged for several to be
admitted in Park College in Missouri, a small Presbyterian insti-

Amanda Lafonso Wilson at the door of the Indian village church about 1940. At that time she was regarded as "chief" of the Mechoopda Tribe, having had the trust of Annie Bidwell bestowed on her after the death of her first husband Holai Lafonso. Courtesy of Dorothy Hill Collection, Meriam Library, CSUC.

Elmer Lafonso, son of Amanda and Chief Holai Lafonso, date unknown. Like many Native Americans, Elmer had a beautiful tenor voice and was encouraged by Annie Bidwell to develop this gift. He sang "Saved by Grace," at her funeral. Courtesy of Dorothy Hill Collection, Meriam Library, CSUC.

tution she supported. Luther Clements was the first to go to Park College, from where he wrote of having lost all contact with his father George.

These young men were quite faithful in their letters to Annie, perhaps driven by a constant shortage of funds to meet costs of medical and dental care, or tuition for additional study. Birnie Wilson, in particular, wrote in April 1912, for help in his aspiration to get more training at the Haskell Institute when he decided that he wanted to pursue a career as minister to the Indian people.

Elmer Lafonso wanted desperately to pursue more vocal training. Without doubt, he saw his talent, much admired by society at large, to be the key to his rising from the stigma of an Indian rancheria. This was in spite of his love of his people, who he vowed never to forget.

He wrote to Annie in the fall of 1910 that he had been doing a lot of singing in the new Big church—"I sang a solo part in the anthem last Sunday at church and as I sang I prayed that we mite [*sic*] all look to Jesus. ... [I sang] also at Normal and the ones who heard me over at Normal stated in the papers that if I had training I would make a mark in the musical world."[5]

He later wrote, "There is a man here [at Normal] who is a tenor teacher. I have taken a few lessons from him, but on account of the building I have to do, I cannot take the lessons too. Two lessons a week at one dollar a lesson and I get $1.50 a day, $9.00 a week and pay $5.00 to my mother for board and washing. But I am thankful to God that I am in health that I can work. ... I ask if you can make some arrangements to help me."[6]

In 1911, the vocal teacher in San Francisco to whom Annie took him had also told him that with training in New York he might aspire to a career in opera, but Elmer had to put any such dreams from his mind.

Following his exposure in San Francisco that year, Elmer was hired to sing a few performances with a company that was billed as a vaudeville troupe, though Elmer wrote to Annie in some dismay, to claim that it was not such a tawdry group as to be termed vaudeville.

A story following one of his performances appeared in the San Francisco *Call* and featured Elmer's picture and a headline "Aborigine Singer Has Quiver Filled" with many "Red Men" melodies. It was obvious that the focus of the reporter was on the "full-blooded Indian," and not at all on Elmer's potential for the classical entertainment world.

"He owes his vocal training largely to the beneficence of Mrs. Bidwell of Chico," the article went on, "and it was in that little town that he was educated and weaned from whatever of Indian modes and manners he might have acquired from his father." Elmer was obviously embarrassed at the questions the reporter was pursuing, and he dodged questions probing for details of the supposed savagery of his people by simply stating that his father "had forgotten everything in the past save that he was a chief with few survivors. ..."[7]

After Elmer married in 1912 or '13 he settled into life at the rancheria with his wife Genevieve. They had two daughters, Donna Mae and Genevieve, as remembered by Annie Bidwell in her will.

Genevieve was an excellent seamstress as well as general housekeeper. Both of these talents found use at the mansion. Elmer worked as a carpenter in Chico when he could, in building his own rancheria home and with such carpentry jobs as presented themselves at the mansion. Genevieve was one of the four maids who served Annie Bidwell in her last year, and along with Amanda she was trusted by Annie to use good judgment in distributing among the rancheria women Annie's clothing and personal belongings that remained at the mansion after other terms of Annie's will had been met.

In 1912, Annie wrote to the Presbyterian Board of Home Missions asking if Elmer might find work where he would have the oversight of the California Indian Association in which Annie was an officer. For a while Elmer was in Oregon, perhaps on such an assignment.

Luther Clements was sent to Park College through Annie's efforts. The last letter she saved from Luther was written in April 1915, from the Haskell Institute in Kansas, the boarding school for more advanced studies, in part supported by federal funds. Luther reluctantly asked for help with dental work. He reported that most of his letters to his father [George Clements] were returned to him, and he didn't know where his father was much of the time. "I play football and baseball, weigh 175, and am wonderfully strong physically." He wrote also of teaching religion to other Indians at a nearby reservation.[8]

Luther enlisted in the U.S. Army when war was declared on Germany in 1917. Neither Luther nor Birnie were to see Mrs. Bidwell again. Elmer, married and living on the rancheria, was one of Annie's pallbearers and sang a solo at her funeral. He was a close friend of Annie, and a sincere one, as surviving letters written to her show.

In her will Annie Bidwell left small bequests to most of the surviving residents of the rancheria with the hope that they would be able to fend for themselves thereafter. Some funds were left in trust with Amanda Wilson for a few elderly persons who still spoke no English.

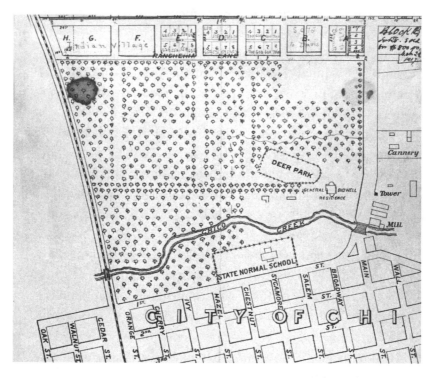

Map of the grounds surrounding the Bidwell Mansion, including the Indian village north of what is Sacramento Avenue today. Courtesy of California State Parks.

It was intended by Annie that the Indians should, if and when possible, get title to their lots in the rancheria land. Because at the time of her death the Indians as noncitizens could not own property, Annie left the twenty-six-acre rancheria in trust for the Indians to the Board of Home Missions of the Presbyterian Church, which in turn transferred the land to the U.S. Department of Interior's Bureau of Indian Affairs.

In 1959, legislation was passed by the U.S. Congress providing that Indians who had formal or informal assignment of land should have formal deeds transferred to them.[9] In April 1955, the Mechoopda tribal members with claim to land had met and formed, first a committee, and later, in 1962, a nonprofit corporation. The Bidwell Band Association, Inc., was declared open to membership for all persons living on March 1, 1958, whose names appeared as beneficiaries on Mrs. Bidwell's will, plus all children born to said beneficiaries.[10]

Sherman E. Wilson, who was still living in a rancheria lot at the time, was named chairman of the organizing committee which included his daughter Thelma as secretary. Luther Clements, Isaiah Conway, Juanita Simpson and Genevieve Aranda made up the balance of the board of directors of the association.[11]

By 1965, when the remaining occupied lots, plus money from sales of unoccupied lots, was finally distributed, it was ascertained that forty-six members of the Mechoopda Association were eligible for shares.[12]

The Indian chapel, a Chico landmark on West Sacramento Avenue, in July 1961 was totally destroyed by flames believed to have spread from a grass fire.[13] The chapel had been declared community property by the Mechoopda Association, as had the cemetery.

There were still Indian families living in homes along Sacramento Avenue into the 1950s, including Sherman Wilson. The chapel continued to stand, but at the time it burned in 1961 it had been long boarded up with no one to conduct services there. Some Mechoopda Association meetings may have been held there.

As the years pass, members of the tribe have been buried one by one in the Mechoopda cemetery on Sacramento Avenue not far east of the railroad tracks. The young people have drifted away from Chico, but many have indicated their desire to return to be buried. The cemetery remains a sacred spot for the Indians whose heritage lies within the locked fence placed by the association in recent years.

Although Annie Bidwell was credited, and indeed credited herself with converting "her Indians" to the point that they gave up their dances, their burnings and most of their tribal practices, the fact is that altering the surface of one generation's mores does not remove a culture. Even while Annie lived, the Indians visited the dance houses in other areas.[14] They traveled elsewhere to join in burnings. In later years at least one person who had been a child in the Chico Indian village told of witnessing the holding of Indian burial rites over the graves of their departed after Mrs. Bidwell had left the cemetery—even in the burial of Maggie Lafonso Mitchell.[15]

Now that two or more generations have passed, the descendants of the Mechoopda choose from the beliefs of both cultures depending on their individual needs.

It has been claimed that the residents of the Indian village called Annie Bidwell "our Little White Mother." Research into the Bidwells' records give no credence to the general use of the term. True, the young men and women who were forced to depend on Annie for many favors, including money, respectfully used the term "mother" occasionally. But so did Willie Alexander, Annie's nephew who wrote of having a mother on each coast, referring to Annie and Sallie.

The old women in the village who learned but a few words of English and were said by Annie to have wept with joy when she returned from a lengthy absence, may have grasped the term "white mother" as one of respect and dependence. She housed them, fed them and in illness sent medical aid for them. There is every reason to think that they were as genuinely fond of her as anyone in a subservient position is likely to be.

This is a point to insert some possibly subjective remarks concerning Annie Bidwell's long ministry with the Chico Indians, especially when looked at in the perspective of her seeming disinterest, while growing up in Washington, to the fate of the black slaves and former slaves. One reason for her interest is probably that with the Mechoopda tribelet she had a "captive population" of sufficiently small size that she could target the whole village as *her mission,* with reasonable assurance that her husband's control over the Indians would maintain the stability of the rancheria's population. The other reason lay in her deep personal need to touch the lives of Bidwell's children and grand-children and to have them love her even though that affection between them must always be shrouded by her husband's secret.

Over her lifetime experience living at the mansion and inter-acting with both the Indian rancheria and the community of Chico at large, the truer bonds of friendship and pleasure, each with the other, seem clearly to be those Annie forged with mem-bers of the Mechoopda tribe.

Allies in
the cause
of education

*P*hoebe Apperson was born within three years of
Annie Bidwell; she became a teacher, but her
active teaching ceased when she married the wealthy
George F. Hearst. Phoebe Apperson came from humble
beginnings, was not particularly well-educated, and drove herself
into a life of philanthropy in part to fill the time on her hands
resulting from her husband's preoccupation with making money
over making an investment in home life. He acquired so much
wealth in publishing that he apparently scarcely noticed the good
causes to which his wife put much of it.[1]

Phoebe Hearst devoted much of her life to philanthropic
work, endowing a number of charitable causes, many being
similar to the causes that Annie Bidwell embraced. Education at
one level or another became the beneficiary of most of Mrs.
Hearst's charity, from endowments to large universities in support
of everything from mining education to architecture, and to
kindergartens for the urban poor. She organized working girls'
clubs. She endowed libraries. All told she had an amazingly long
list of interests and the deep pockets of her husband from which
to draw.

The two women could not have escaped knowing of the other.
The Hearsts owned, among large real estate holdings in Califor-
nia, a large ranch in Butte County south of Oroville. Neither
Hearst spent much time at that ranch, and Phoebe may have
never even visited it. Probably Phoebe Hearst first met Annie
Bidwell while attending a Women's Congress.

Chicoans were not alone, of course, in their awe of the Hearsts and Mr. Hearst's great wealth. Evidence of the latter was visible nearby in the luxurious mansion built on the Hearst Ranch in Butte County by owners who rarely deigned to visit it. Helen Gage in her essay, "Mrs. Bidwell as Her Friends Knew Her," called Phoebe Hearst "a close friend" of Mrs. Bidwell, but there is little other evidence to support this.[2]

Annie had proved her own sincere interest in good education throughout her married life, quite beside the Indian school. After the normal school was begun in Chico, both Bidwells made it a point to attend and encourage college functions. They entertained students in the mansion often, and permitted various student clubs to hold functions there.[3]

Each normal school graduating class was entertained at a

The Bidwell parlor with dining room beyond and group of ladies. Annie liked to decorate the inside of the house lavishly with plants and flowers. The flag drapes were a permanent part of the decor. Courtesy of California State Parks.

garden reception whenever Annie was in Chico, and she made it a goal to be at home in both January and June for the graduating class ceremonies, at least until after her husband's death. Her diary over several years details the number of guests at her garden receptions in June, usually a hundred or more. In June 1907, she entertained in the mansion itself, and limited the guest list to forty-two, seated at two tables in the dining room. That year she reached the peak of her college entertaining, as she followed the graduates' dinner in a few weeks with a party for 145 Normal alumni, fed at tables set up on the north, east and south sides of the veranda.[4]

After months of absence from Chico—most of 1910 and early 1911—Annie planned on her return to hold her June reception for the graduates and faculty, no doubt thinking it was expected

A group of Indian children in the Mechoopda village, probably about 1906. Myrtle Nucholls is believed to have left the village with her father after he married Lily Clements and was banished in 1908.

of her. Only forty-four sent acceptances. That was the last year in which she put forth the effort to be a part of the social life of the student body and faculty.

None were more interested than the Bidwells in the visiting lectures and entertainments that were brought to campus. One year the Bidwells housed the male chorus from the University of California at the mansion, then managed to make a statement in the midst of the concert by rising abruptly from their seats and walking out in the middle of a choral number which happened to be a drinking song. Almost certainly it would have been Annie who initiated that move, and John followed her, for it is doubtful that John Bidwell would have relished making a scene, especially over so trivial a matter. To Annie, students could never be exposed too often to high standards of behavior, and especially among their mentors which Annie conceived herself and John to be.

The normal school president came to the mansion soon after and apologized extravagantly to the Bidwells as he tried to explain why it had not occurred to him to censor the students' program selections in advance.

The Annual Teachers' Institutes for Butte County Schools were designed as on-the-job training, and teachers usually took two or three days from each school year to attend. So also did the Bidwells attend whenever possible, both to enjoy interesting lectures on travel and science and to see and evaluate how teachers were being prepared.[5]

The Bidwells held memberships in the California Teachers Association. Annie tried to find time to visit several public school classrooms in Chico every year, letting her interest be known in the work done by good teachers.

Annie was a generous donor to the Congregational Church's Mission Branch when it maintained a short-lived school in Paradise known as the Sierra Polytechnic Institute. She was a guest at its dedication and later at the institute's "Paradise Chatauqua," where she was invited to be a speaker.

On her first visit to the rather bare-bones institute building on College Hill in Paradise, she wrote in her diary, "They have cut down *all* the trees. Oh! Oh!" but to her audience she had commented favorably on the knot holes in the wooden walls that admitted cold air but also bore evidence to commitment to education over luxury.

Annie's concern about conservation of the forests and the prevention of needless cutting of trees anywhere was extended into a campaign in which she petitioned the Butte County Board of Supervisors to have laws passed curbing the cutting of roadside trees within county rights-of-way—trees that provided shade and beauty to travelers. She described an experience that triggered this action in a talk given to the normal school student body:

"In the summer of 1903, in passing over the Chico and Humboldt Road on my way to Big Meadows, I saw a sight which appalled me, the entire denudation of timber off a section of land through which the road passes, not a tree being left in the double track roadbed nor anywhere near it to shelter man or beast from the fierce rays of the mountain sun. … Later in the season when returning homeward over the same road I witnessed still greater devastation of the giant fir and cedar trees bordering and within the road beds."[6]

While visiting in Washington Annie asked, and received, from Gifford Pinchot, U.S. director of forestry, a mini-library of all the department's publications on conservation and preservation, and she made a gift of them to Chico Normal School Library. Annie had attended the National Forest Congress, and repeated in a talk before the normal school the lecture in which was said, "Nations have always recuperated from wars, but none from the destruction of their forests."[7]

For some years Annie sponsored an annual writing contest on conservation at the normal school and awarded a prize to the winner.[8]

It could have been no surprise that Phoebe Apperson Hearst, then living in Pleasanton near San Francisco, invited Annie Bidwell to serve as a member of the Women's Board of the Panama-Pacific International Exposition held in San Francisco in August and September of 1915.

When Annie spent weeks or months in San Francisco, as she did during the last few years of her life, she often stayed at the Hotel Ramona. In 1915, however, she had a suite at the Marguerite Apartments and no doubt had a maid and possibly a secretary. Annie may also have been a guest at the Hearst home for part of her long stay, though the association seems not to have been based on personal friendship but on Mrs. Hearst's search for women of high commitment to service for women.

Among written comments on Mrs. Bidwell's life appears the story that Mrs. Hearst did not think Annie had sufficient wardrobe, coming from the rural town of Chico, and so helped her arrange for more gowns.[9] Preserved correspondence between the women consists of only one brief letter from Mrs. Hearst asking Annie for a sample swatch of the fabric used in an elegant blue brocade gown that Annie had a dressmaker fashion some months earlier. Probably Mrs. Hearst had in mind coordinating this color with the furniture in the area where Mrs. Bidwell would serve as a hostess in the Women's Pavilion on some days.[10] So indeed the women had discussed wardrobe.

By this time, 1915, communication by telephone was becoming common, as was the use of the motorcar. Though Annie's voice was not always to be depended on for talking through the telephone, a maid or secretary was always on hand to relay messages for her. Annie's voice actually seemed to carry through the phone wires better than on occasions in which she had to raise her volume to address an audience. The telephone may well be the culprit for the lack of correspondence from this period.

Two revealing items appeared in the Chico *Enterprise*. One on August 21, 1915, obviously came after the paper got news that

Mrs. Bidwell had sent from San Francisco for her maid, probably Ruby Dailey, who later claimed to have accompanied her employer during the World's Exposition stay in San Francisco.[11]

"Mrs. Bidwell is very ill in San Francisco and left Chico several weeks ago for a change of climate as her health has been failing. ... She suffers from neuritis ... has sent for her personal maid," according to the *Enterprise* story.

When Annie read this newspaper item in the Chico paper that she had delivered to her in San Francisco, she became indignant and fired off a letter to the *Enterprise* editor. It was printed by him in a news story of August 24, 1915, as follows:

"Mrs. Bidwell writes to the *Enterprise* to say that she has had nothing but a cold and had been treated by Dr. Hirschfelder. She is not in San Francisco for ill health but to attend duties as a member of the Women's Board of the Exposition. 'I promised the president [Mrs. Hearst] to be in San Francisco August and September for that purpose.

"'I am attending the Indian Conference, having been 40 years Western Vice President of the National Indian Association which hosted the National Conference.

"'Also I am honorary Vice President of the Committee of 100 of the American Association for the Advancement of Science and have promised to attend its August meeting. I am also a member of the reception committee and must attend the Public Reception.

"'I attended the funeral of Emily Hopkins, President of the Women's Federated Clubs of California.'"

Mrs. Bidwell's actions always made news in Chico until her death and continued to do so over the years as Chicoans followed the settlement of her estate.

Exit

*P*hysical problems for which Annie Bidwell had sought specialists' care over the years continued to cripple her. The right arm and shoulder that had undergone such painful manipulation by Dr. Hirschfelder in 1894 were, by 1915, almost useless to her. Her voice did not regain full volume (perhaps she had not enough of the rest recommended by the London specialists), and often she could not speak above a whisper and a hoarse whisper at that. She was fortunate to have a large house staff and a secretary at her hire.

The servant situation at the mansion had changed significantly since the early days when Irish maids were hired from San Francisco and seemed always coming and going. Florence Blake, who served Annie as personal maid for over fifteen years prior to her own marriage and came back as a married woman during the last year or two of Annie's life, was English born and Protestant in religion. The Roman Catholicism of the Irish girls had sometimes resulted in split loyalties between church and employer.[1]

Florence could be trusted to respect her employer's privacy. After John Bidwell's death and the death of the wife of William Proud, a Bidwell head gardener, Florence married Proud in 1905. She named her one son William John Proud.

After Sallie's funeral in 1912, Annie stayed on in Washington for some months, and when she returned to Chico Will and Gertrude Alexander came with her. For nearly a year they lived at the mansion, giving Annie hopes that they might decide to settle in Chico. While she was away in Southern California working on a Prohibition election campaign, Gertrude was entrusted to oversee the operation of the mansion staff.

In 1913, Gertrude Alexander suffered a severe illness and Annie paid for her medical care and then a trip to Santa Barbara for the couple so that Gertrude might convalesce. The young Alexanders then returned to Washington, D.C., leaving Annie to nurture the hope that they might return if Will could not find a successful profession in the East.

The normal school provided a source for Annie to recruit secretarial help for herself, often by personal request, as with Annie Bidwell's plea to Annie Meriam in 1903 soon after the latter came to Chico as the bride of Professor Morrison E. Meriam. During her first year in Chico Mrs. Meriam often devoted several hours weekly in taking dictation and writing letters for Mrs. Bidwell. Mrs. Meriam was not alone in her willingness to give of her time. Annie felt free to recruit the single women on the normal school faculty, not only as secretaries but also to assist with the Indian church or school, or in WCTU work with the female students.

By 1916, Annie was hiring secretarial help, the volume of her mail and other writing taking considerable time each day.

In both 1917 and early 1918, Annie had residence part-time at the Ramona Hotel in San Francisco. By then work on her will absorbed much of her attention and she had decided to take the delicate and private discussions about disposal of her wealth to a San Francisco firm, while Guy Kennedy was retained to give the day-to-day legal advice she needed in Chico.

Annie Bidwell obviously gave serious thought to how she would distribute the estate inherited from her husband. It was a few weeks only before her death when the last codicil to her will was signed in San Francisco.[2]

Her first aim was to follow John Bidwell's wishes as expressed in his own will—the one written to apply should he outlive her—so the bequests to every living descendant of his father Abraham

Bidwell were included in hers. Some of his other stated wishes were easily accomplished. As soon as money was available after his death she had moved several coffins from their original burial site to the lot Bidwell had reserved when he sold the cemetery.

Mrs. Maria Cooley and infant daughter are believed to be the first burials in a section created in 1878 by John Bidwell for the "Bidwell family and friends," to which Bailey, Stevenson and John Kennedy were now moved, Bailey from the Masonic Section and Kennedy from a Wayland lot. On Annie's

Joseph John Kennedy, Annie's nephew, unsuccessful pharmacist, later a successful cattle rancher. He married Winifred Moon. Annie Ellicott Kennedy, named in Annie's honor, was their only child. Courtesy of California State Parks.

orders, more elaborate stones were placed on the new grave sites of John Kennedy, Major A. M. Bailey, and William Stevenson.[3]

Annie authorized and paid for a number of other burials in the "friends" section. These included the reinterment of an aged black woman, who died at age ninety-nine in May 1900. "Aunt Eliza" Ragan was said to have been a former slave in Tennessee. She got to Chico somehow and scrimped out a living as a seamstress. Annie had been introduced to Eliza by John Bidwell, and she found Aunt Eliza's faith very inspiring. Both Bidwells kept a protective eye on Eliza, but Annie was in Washington when Eliza died and had no part in arranging that first funeral.

After John Bidwell's death another generous whim led Annie to have an infant from a near-destitute family living in Stirling City buried in the friends' lot. While volunteering for Women's

Christian Missionary society work in the Chico Infirmary in 1906, Annie had visited a meningitis-stricken child, eleven-month-old Evelyn Dorthy Wiggs. The mother was newly from San Francisco and apparently alone in making decisions for her daughter's burial.

Annie is said to have comforted Mrs. Wiggs with the promise that she, Annie, would bury the little girl "next to the General." The story later was expanded to being told around Chico that Mrs. Wiggs, when she found that her baby was buried far from the Bidwell grave and among strangers, was very unhappy with the arrangement.

In 1908, the young Scotsman, John Vaughn, whom Annie had hired to work in the cause of Prohibition and had been accidentally poisoned, was buried among the "friends."

In August 1917, the Presbyterian Church minister then on his third year in Chico, Orlando Elton Hart, was buried in the friends area. Rev. Hart had been vacationing that summer at Robin's Nest, which Annie had designated as a retreat for Presbyterian ministers. Hart became ill and made the tortuous trip home by train on a circuitous route through Susanville, Reno, and Sacramento to Chico before his death from pneumonia at the new Enloe Hospital.

Annie also promised that Rev. Hart's family should have burial rights near him.

Guy Reynolds Kennedy, Annie's nephew, 1930, Chico defense attorney and Chico city attorney for a number of years. He married Eva Sampson—had no children. Courtesy of California State Parks.

Thus burials of Hart kinfolk have continued over the years, some nine or ten of them, the last being in 1997.

A large portion of Bidwell land is still unoccupied between the group of graves listed above and those of John and Annie. Cora Wayland Kennedy, buried in 1932, is the only family addition to this area, next to her husband John Reynolds Kennedy.[4]

Guy and Joseph Kennedy, Annie's nephews, chose to ignore the Bidwell burial area. Instead they had a large Kennedy vault built for themselves and their wives at considerable distance away.[5] Some might say they demonstrated the Wayland streak of resistance to the Bidwell influence. Others believe that Annie banished Guy from the area reserved near herself and John Bidwell's graves when it became known to her that Guy drank. If indeed she learned this of her nephew, and it was common knowledge by her death, it must have been a hard cross for her to bear.

Whatever John Bidwell may have planned for this section, it is still largely vacant in 2004 and seems destined to remain so. Asked about this, a person employed currently by the Chico Cemetery shrugs and suggests that no one else ever measured up to Annie's standards, including members of the Thomas, Daniel and Abram Bidwell families.

John Bidwell's will directed that all his property, other than the cemetery plot, be sold and his debts paid. The beneficiaries that he named were added to those named in Annie's final will and codicil.

Had Annie preferred to leave the ranch to a relative or relatives—quite conceivably to one or more of her nephews—the terms of her husband's will seemed to forbid that. It very probably would have not been her decision even if left up to her. There simply was no living relative who showed the predisposition or the drive to take on management of the huge, remarkably productive, but money-losing operation, that in his lifetime John Bidwell had created of over 22,000 acres of virgin land.

369

The "remainder of the estate"—that converted to cash in Annie's lifetime—was quite large. The sales of the numerous Bidwell-initiated subdivisions brought in money that paid all debts. When the bulk of the remainder was sold in one piece in 1911, Annie added nearly half a million dollars to the already sizeable amount she had accumulated over the years. The San Francisco Union Trust Company had been selected as repository and as executors of her estate. She was a wealthy woman for that time, and even with the many causes she supported and the people she had helped in her lifetime with loans and gifts, she knew that it would be her privilege to make a few large, or (as she chose) many quite sizeable, bequests. Much of her time during her last years was spent thinking and praying about these gifts, and the sense of power that it gave her must have been satisfying as family and friends faded away.

As she grew older and became wealthy, Annie showed a disturbing tendency toward self-centeredness. Her diary is sprinkled with comments like, "I gave that." "That was a gift from *me*." This suggests that contemplation of the wealth at her disposal *did* make a change in her personality.

Without a calculator at hand, how did she know when her tens of bequests totaled or surpassed her total estate? She must have charted and figured, and finally, realizing the unlikelihood of achieving perfect balance, directed which bequests were to be reduced in size if there should be not enough money. And there were many of those, including the namesakes of Bidwell and the Mechoopda Indians.

The administrators had troubles when it came close to the end of distributions, and combined with the problems of selling some of the mansion grounds, and the buyers' obtaining clear titles, final settlement was delayed for years. The restrictive wording in the deeds—for all time as concerns alcohol manufacture and sale—were restrictions that title companies refused be held responsible for.

It was 1934 before Annie Bidwell's estate was put to rest. Court action that year successfully removed the reversionary clause from the land titles. This had been Annie's stipulation in her will that if at a *future* date some of the former Rancho Chico land was found to be used for alcohol production or sale, that land would automatically revert to Cora Kennedy!

Cora had died in 1932. In fact, both Eva and Guy had passed away before closure. The matter was resolved by the purchase of all reversionary rights by a title company in San Francisco for $1,500 through extraordinary legal action.[6]

Annie Bidwell's will was divided into several sections. There were the bequests to the many organizations she had supported, the foremost one being $5,000 to the Mary Jewett Fund of the Women's Auxiliary of the Society of California Pioneers. Mary Jewett of Marysville, wife of a friend of John Bidwell's from early times, will be remembered as having accompanied Annie on her first transcontinental train trip in 1869, but she was also instrumental in forming the auxiliary.

The California and the National Indian Associations received $4,000 and $3,000 respectively.

If one may place significance in comparing the generosity of one donation over another, it would seem that Prohibition causes took favor over the Indian cause. The former received sums totaling $16,000, plus an additional $16,000 spread among several WCTUs. Of course, trying to total the amount donated to the cause of Prohibition is futile, for Annie had steadily poured money into many manifestations of the movement over at least fourteen years prior to her death.

The Presbyterian Church, local and national, plus its many levels of missionary and educational work, was endowed with $18,000. The gift of the mansion and grounds was in addition to these sums, with title automatically passing the day of Annie's death.

The stipulation that living descendants of John Bidwell's father receive bequests in amounts proportioned by the degree of relationship called for search and research in the years that followed Annie's death. Even so, one descendant of one of John's half-brothers had not been located by 1934, and the estate was settled without knowing that this Bidwell had years earlier been murdered by his wife in the state of Washington, and the imprisoned widow had never known of a search.

Bequests ranged from $5,000 to less than $30 among the Bidwell heirs in the final settlement. Dr. Gatchell was, of course, remembered generously.

Annie's relatives fared well, with each nephew and his wife receiving $10,000. (Gertrude Alexander, the exception, inherited only $5,000.) With her special education funds added, a total of $14,500 was put in trust for her grandniece and namesake, Annie Ellicott Kennedy. Many other cousins from both the Reynolds and Ellicott families were remembered with small gifts.

Nor did Annie forget the Indians individually, with thirty-two listed for bequests from $1,000 down to $200.[7]

Former servants and gardeners were remembered including two Chinese gardeners. Most generously endowed of the ranch employees were Reuben Messinger, Florence Blake Proud and Fred Petersen (long-term gardener) at $3,000 each.

An interesting omission is Elmer Lafonso, but Annie probably had given him his full bequest prior to her death. Harriett Alexander Clough is also missing from the legatees; Annie may well have felt that Harriett received an inheritance in the amount Annie spent over the two years that she had helped Harriett live abroad while meeting her mother's harsh terms of consent to Harriet's marrying Irvin Clough.

Annie left $2,000 for the Reverend W. G. White, and to his son John Bidwell White, $1,000. There were a dozen or so persons whose claim on Annie was that their parents honored John Bidwell by adding Bidwell as a middle name; most of these had grown to middle age by the time their legacies were paid them, and most reduced from the original amount stipulated as estate funds petered out.

Several pages of her will codicil were taken by Annie's listing of furnishings and special family treasures she had at her disposal. She tried to distribute these fairly without doubt, and with an eye to special interests and tastes of her relatives. Of course provision had to be made for those items that would have escaped Annie's memory. To Cora went all of these, as well as Annie's clothing. Cora was given the discretion to give away anything she saw fit. Amanda Wilson and Genevieve Lafonso took similar roles in the Indian village—to hand out to others the assorted bed or kitchen linens that remained after all else was cleared away.

The mansion's fate had been decided in March 1914, when Annie deeded the mansion and surrounding grounds to the College Board of the Presbyterian Church Education Trust for a coeducational school to be established there after her death. She retained a deed of life estate, allowing her to reside there so long as she lived. Annie had also deeded Robin's Nest to the church for a Presbyterian retreat, with deeds to all the nearby lots presented earlier to her nephews and their wives for summer homes or camping sites.[8]

Not a part of her story, but of interest to those who know and love the mansion today: through a series of transfers within the church by the Trustees of the Presbyterian Church of America, by 1921 the mansion was placed on the open market where the president of the normal school (by then Chico State Teachers College), Charles M. Osenbaugh, put into motion steps that led to its purchase by the state of California.[9]

It is necessary now to back up to that period of months, if not years, that preceded Annie's death but were marked by her decreasing stamina and loss of interest in the old causes. For this period, we can but present a kaleidoscopic view that relies on an assortment of memories, none of which were recorded at the time

and grew faint and possibly distorted by the passing of years.
Ruby Dailey English was not always very accurate in recording
events when they occurred and the passage of time between
Ruby's leaving Annie's employ at Annie's death in 1918 and the
1964 taking of the oral interview tended to cloud her memory.

Mrs. English told that she had accompanied Mrs. Bidwell to
San Francisco and served as her personal maid during the four
weeks devoted to attending the San Francisco World's Fair, no
doubt correct, and that she often handled secretarial duties for her
employer. Ruby could play the piano, which her employer enjoyed. Ruby had kept all the household accounts, a fact resented
by Florence Blake Proud when the longtime former servant came
from San Francisco to help out, or so Ruby recalled, and Mrs.
Proud especially resented that Ruby occupied the upstairs
servant's apartment and bath with its own little porch.[10]

Ruby's taped recollections told of one of Mrs. Phoebe Hearst's
rich relatives from the East visiting with wife and three children.
This was an error, for almost certainly these visitors were Dr. and
Mrs. Arthur Hirschfelder. He had been a frequent guest from his
boyhood days.

Annie must have enjoyed the music of children's laughter in
the house, perhaps thinking of them as "wild with joy," as she had
often described Harriett and Douglas Alexander in her diary on
their arrivals to visit at the mansion.

Ruby told that even in her last years Annie Bidwell thought
nothing of entertaining fourteen or fifteen at dinner, but what
groups these may have been we do not know.

There seem to have been children playing in and around the
mansion as long as Annie was alive. She had built for her namesake an elaborate playhouse on the grounds where little Annie
Kennedy brought friends to play, and often children ran into the
house and up the stairs to the toilet, or into the kitchen for
cookies. "Happy as larks," Annie would be thinking.

Don Mathewson, nephew of Guy Kennedy's wife Eva, spent hours at play in and around the mansion. He told his children when he was an elderly man of having slid down the banisters in the mansion as a boy, no doubt until some chiding maid chased him and his friends into the yard to play. Annie Bidwell had a soft spot in her heart for Don; his mother is believed to have been killed in the 1906 San Francisco earthquake for she is never mentioned after that date in Annie's diaries, and Donald was often in residence with the Kennedys and a guest at the mansion.

Annie's perception of joy in the children may have been twisted by her own wish to see it thus. The author was told not long ago by one of Don Mathewson's daughters that he expressed reluctance to talk about this period of his life, which he recollected as one of unhappiness.

Every morning at nine o'clock, without fail, every person in the mansion, guests, servants and children, was expected to appear in the library for Bible reading and prayers.

Guy Kennedy, by now firmly established as a respected defense attorney, and at the time of Annie's death, Chico city attorney, came to the mansion at regular intervals to take care of his aunt Annie's financial accounts and counsel in any legal matters. Theirs was not an entirely smooth relationship, and reports of hearing quarrels and voices of both raised during their evening work sessions sifted out into the community through the staff—in spite of lectures given each new household employee when hired, that what went on within the walls of the mansion was private. Guy was one of few who dared to disagree with Annie to the point of argument, some of which antagonism may have originated much earlier over Kennedy estate challenges. If Annie suspected that Guy refused to be a "white-ribbon" wearer, she must surely have reproached him regularly.

An elderly man once approached the author after a Prime Timers' meeting in which the influence of the Bidwells had been discussed.[11] He was obviously still able to feel resentment when he recalled a childhood experience: Mrs. Bidwell had caught him stealing cherries over the orchard fence. He said that this little white-haired woman had shrieked at him and shook her fist, "Would you take the food out of the mouth of an old lady?" This memory is possibly distorted and magnified over time, since Annie had very little ability to speak above a whisper during her last years.

The memoirs of Elsie Bidwell Baumgarner of a visit from Greenville to her cousins living in the Daniel Bidwell home in Chico relate Elsie's nervousness at being invited to tea by Aunt Annie about 1915. Her cousins warned her that one slip of manners would be met by humiliating correction from this formidable hostess. Elsie was happy to write that "everything went well and Aunt Annie was very nice."

Later memories dictated by another of these cousins were not so kind. Annie Bidwell was pictured as fiercely jealous of her husband's niece, Mary Bidwell Reed, the very young woman with whom Annie had refused to share her household when she came to Chico as a bride. Annie was remembered by Mary Reed's granddaughter as one who thwarted Reed's wishes whenever she could—family hearsay, of course, but reflecting the iciness that existed between John Bidwell and his brother Daniel's family.

A Chico native who was born the year after Mrs. Bidwell's death heard many things spoken of her while he was growing up. "Don't get me wrong," he wrote. "She did much good, but to Chicoans she seemed domineering and arrogant."[12]

Annie showed a deep-seated need to control the use of her gifts. An example of this might be her action in an event that took place late in the year 1905, a few months after she had deeded the major western portion of "Vallombrosa" as a park to the City of Chico.

In December 1905, it was reported to her that maple trees planted around the edges of the town park (given by John Bidwell in his lifetime and today termed the City Plaza) were being cut down on order from the city trustees to make room for orange trees.

Annie sent word to Mayor Clark by both Reuben Messinger and Mrs. Belle Royce that "if these trees were removed I would not give Chico another acre of ground." Later Annie went personally to the city, and the reason given by a shaken Chico city trustee for the removal was that the maples were so deformed as to be unfit for a park.[13]

At once Annie enlisted Dr. Van Liew, normal school president, to ask the faculty to protest the maples' removal. Professor Morrison E. Meriam undertook to circulate a petition for her among the faculty for that purpose. Belle Royce took another petition to interested town citizens. Annie's diary reported "an immense number of signatures" but fails to tell who won on the issue, or what compromise was reached.[14]

Annie Meriam, wife of the normal school teacher and father of Ted Meriam (himself a beloved icon of the city of Chico and the university at the time of his death in August 2001), when recording life in Chico in her diary after she came here in 1903, seemed to reflect the fact that many people connected with the normal school felt a restriction forced on them by the long-standing habit of the school's administrators to quickly acquiesce to any request made of them by the Bidwells.[15]

Of course, John Bidwell's prominence in the state, his membership on the Joint State Normal School Trustee Board, and his having donated land for the campus set the stage for a relationship of patron and benefactor.

One incident illustrating Annie's interference with the usual channels of justice occurred in June 1906, when Annie heard that Col. Royce had signed a warrant for theft of cherries against a normal student named Smyth after the Bidwell watchman caught him across the fence dividing the campus from the Bidwell's cherry trees. Two young women students came in tears to the mansion and asked that Annie intervene, for Smyth had only taken the cherries because they asked him to, adding that they thought the cherries were on the normal grounds. Annie knew that was untrue, for the line was very clear.[16] However, she comforted the crying girls and promised to get the young man off. When she appealed to the dean of men, Professor Adams, he refused to dismiss the charge. Annie then went to the Normal president, Dr. Van Liew, and asked for a conference with all the persons concerned. Here she managed to extract Dr. Van Liew's reluctant agreement, in order that her "promise to the girls might be kept." By this time the charge had been filed in the justice court by Prof. Adams who refused to withdraw it!

The scene moved next day to Judge Faulkner's court, where Adams demanded that Smyth *prove* that he had thought the cherries were on the campus. This proof was not forthcoming, of course, but Annie pled Smyth's cause and the matter ended with Smyth receiving a harsh lecture from Judge Faulkner and a dismissal of the charges.[17]

The author has observed college administrations for nearly sixty years, and it seems certain that much of Annie's interest in the normal campus and faculty members was seen as an intrusion and rankled with the normal school's presidents, as well as some of the faculty.[18]

Annie Meriam gave no reason when entering her decision in her diary, but when the news of Annie Bidwell's death came in March 1918, and elaborate plans were drawn up for the school children to be dismissed and lined up along the cemetery route to throw flowers, Mrs. Meriam told her son Theodore that he would not go to school that day.

Three-fourths of a century later, Ted Meriam wondered aloud, "I never understood why my mother wouldn't let me go to Mrs. Bidwell's funeral," the grievance still showing in his voice. The holiday nature of the event was by no means lost on the children.

Annie Lund Meriam was an intelligent woman, a former mathematics teacher in a private school in the East, an independent woman long before she met and married fellow teacher Morrison E. Meriam. In Chico she joined the WCTU, became fairly active in the women's suffrage movement and after women's suffrage in California was legalized in 1913, became a voter and accepted appointments offered her on town committees to study issues pertaining to parks and land use planning.

Mrs. Meriam certainly listened to what went on around her, and the couple must have discussed community issues and been aware of a community split on at least one of the Bidwells' causes. Without frequenting saloons, she knew the depth of feeling of owners of such businesses as they witnessed over the years Mrs. Bidwell working with all her influence and wealth to put them out of business. The customers of these bars felt similarly threatened at the thought of losing a form of relaxation and social life provided by the bars. Certainly the German community, whose picnics were such an object of scorn by the Bidwells, would have had few warm memories of the couple.

The Meriams had no special church affiliation when they arrived as newlyweds in Chico. After discussion they decided that the Presbyterian Church was probably a politically sound choice to make. As members of at first the original and then the new church built on First Street, they witnessed both the public adulation of the Bidwells and heard the soft-spoken snidery behind Mrs. Bidwell's back.

Morrison Meriam was a distant cousin of John Bidwell, a fact he never revealed during his tenure at the normal school because he did not want any special notice taken of him on that account.

What could be more hypocritical, the Meriams must have thought, than to send one's children—who doubtless had heard denigration of the Bidwells around the dining table at home, whether children of saloon owner or jealous housewife—to throw flowers in the path of Mrs. Bidwell's coffin as it made its way to the final resting place?

The causes of death given for Annie's demise on March 9, 1918, varied from "cerebral paralysis" to "old age." The attack began with a severe headache, according to Ruby Dailey, during which Mrs. Bidwell had complained that "My head feels like it's full of piles of grass." Dr. Gatchell came at once and brought in other physicians to consult, but nothing could be done.

Annie was ill ten days, seemed to rally and was allowed to sit up, then suffered paralysis and passed into a coma from which she never awakened. During the days before her death, the three nephews, their wives, and Cora Kennedy gathered in the mansion to await the end. Even Thomson Alexander, Annie's brother-in-law, came from Washington, D.C., with his new wife.[19]

According to newspaper report all of these were at Annie's bedside when death came, though Ruby Dailey recollected only that she and two nurses were there. If one is to believe the Sacramento *Bee* of March 11, also beside the bed was "'Mandy Wilson,' a protégé of the deceased from the Indian village who loved her mistress passionately."

Ruby reported that Mrs. Bidwell was buried in her beautiful blue dress, probably the expensive silk brocade that she had worn at the San Francisco World's Fair in 1915.[20]

The Reverend W. G. White, who as a young single man had conducted the burial service for John Bidwell, returned to Chico to repeat that final rite for Annie on March 12. The Presbyterian Church choir sang several numbers. Elmer Lafonso, obviously shaking with emotion, sang "Saved by Grace." Eight of the village Indians carried the casket from the mansion to the cemetery, though all the male Indians of the village were designated pall bearers and stood on the veranda as a group during the funeral services where Rev. White exhorted them to remember their benefactor's teachings. An estimated 2,000 persons crowded the mansion and into the yard; 2,400 school children scattered flowers as the funeral procession passed to the cemetery.

Today the name of Annie Kennedy Bidwell is scarcely recognized beyond Butte County, though of course her papers, as those of her husband, are ranked high as a source of details for nineteenth century research in both the California State Library's California collection and in the The Bancroft Library on the University of California, Berkeley, campus.

In the major reform movements to which she devoted herself, Annie Bidwell was basically a follower, not a leader, with the exception of her devoted work with the natives of the Mechoopda Indian village within Rancho Chico. She was not as visionary as her husband, but she valued knowledge and recognized the importance of mental exercise through all of one's life for healthy and alert outlook. Her understanding of life around her was through a somewhat tunnel vision that never permitted her to be sidetracked from the pursuit of her own rigid goals.

Annie's life story is both dramatic and romantic, and on the whole a happy one in spite of the tragic deaths of her older brother and father. She never faltered from the course she felt that her God had set for her, whether handling relationships within the Kennedy family or keeping secret those personal relationships of her husband prior to his confession and repentance made to her alone.

Annie Meriam's diary, written after reflection on the occasion of Annie Bidwell's death concluded, "Mrs. Bidwell really was quite a remarkable woman." Few will argue with that conclusion. Annie's decision to leave the comforts of Washington, D.C., for the reputed wilderness of California was in itself a mark of courage, and it took grit to live in a community for forty years that never really made her feel at home.

Most will agree that Annie Kennedy Bidwell left Chico a richer community and its history more interesting through the happenstance of her residence here. Surely none can doubt that she made John Bidwell a far happier man than had she not come into his life.

Bidwell Mansion, Chico, California. Courtesy of California State Parks.

Chapter notes abbreviations

AKB .... Annie Kennedy Bidwell
BCHS .... Butte County Historical Society
CMK .... Catherine Morrison Kennedy
CSL .... California State Library
CSUC .... California State University, Chico
DAR .... Daughters of the American Revolution
JB .... John Bidwell
JCGK .... Joseph Calm Griffith Kennedy
Sallie K .... Sallie Kennedy
SK .... Sallie Kennedy
SKA .... Sallie Kennedy Alexander
UOP .... University of the Pacific
WCTU .... Women's Christian Temperance Union

Notes

Glimmerings from childhood, pp. 13–18

[1] Letter, AKB on a Chicago-bound train to JB in Chico, 9-6-1895. AKB Collection, California State Library.

[2] Letter, AKB in Chico to JB in Oroville, 12-22-1868. Annie Bidwell papers, CSUC Meriam Library, Special Collections.

[3] Letter, AKB in Chico to JB in Marysville, 12-24-1868, AKB papers, CSUC Meriam Library, Special Collections.

[4] Letter, AKB in Chico to JB in San Francisco, 12-28-1868, AKB Collection, CSL.

[5] Letter, John Kennedy in Meadville to Annie Kennedy in Washington, early 1868, AKB Collection, The Bancroft Library.

[6] Letter, AK in Meadville to Sallie Ellicott in Baltimore, 6-30-1856, CSUC Meriam Library, Special Collections.

[7] Letter, AK to Sallie Ellicott, 10-5-1855, CSUC Meriam Library, Special Collections.

[8] Letter, J. C. G. Kennedy in Washington to John Reynolds in Meadville, Bidwell Mansion State Historic Park Archives, date illegible.

Introducing a family, pp. 19–33

[1] These were Dr. Samuel Kennedy, Major Andrew Ellicott and Lt. William McMillan. Information included in applications for DAR membership and Ellicott family history, Annie K. Bidwell papers, The Bancroft Library.

[2] Crawford County History, (founding of Meadville) California State Library, Sutro Library Branch, San Francisco.

[3] JCGK in Washington to AKB in Chico, Dec. 1879. AKB Collection, The Bancroft Library.

[4] Letter, AK in Washington to JB in Chico, 4-8-67. *Dear General.*

[5] JCGK newspaper obituaries and eulogies, AKB Collection, The Bancroft Library.

[6] Catherine Kennedy in Meadville to Annie Kennedy in Washington, 11-2-1862. AB Collection, CSL.

[7] Letter, Catherine Kennedy in Washington to AKB in Chico, 5-17-68, AKB Collection, CSL.

[8] Letter, Sallie K in Meadville to AK in Washington, 11-25-1860, AKB Collection, The Bancroft Library.

[9] AKB Collection in The Bancroft Library has many letters written by her father's friends in support of son Joe's commission.

[10] Letter, CMK in Washington to AKB in Chico, 5-27-1872, AKB Collection, CSL.

[11] AKB diary entry, 4-2-1902.

Notes

[12] Journal, AK, Civil War period. AKB Collection, The Bancroft Library.

[13] Ibid., AKB Collection, The Bancroft Library.

[14] Letter, Catherine Morrison Kennedy in Washington to AKB in Chico, 5-28-1868, shortly after Annie was married. AKB Collection, CSL.

[15] Letter AKB in Washington to JB in Chico, February 1877 after Johnny's death. AKB Collection, CSL.

[16] Annie Kennedy's wartime journal in AKB Collection, The Bancroft Library.

[17] Letter, S. A. Ashe, Wilmington, S.C., to "Miss Annie" in Washington, year unknown, AKB Collection, CSL.

The great romance, pp. 34–46

[1] McDonald, L., "Years of Decision," *Ripples Along Chico Creek,* 1992.

[2] Raphael was told about in an interview Annie reported having with William J. Conway in 1913 on his memories of the Bidwells. The interview is among AKB's papers at CSUC, Meriam Library, Special Collections.

[3] Letter, JB in Washington to AKB in Washington, 12-31-1866. *Dear General.*

[4] Diary entry 12-31-1900, made in John Bidwell's unfinished diary of that year by Annie Bidwell after his death.

[5] Hoopes, Chad L., *What Makes a Man,* 1973; Linda Rawlings, Ed., also *Dear General,* 1993, publication of the California State Department of Parks and Recreation.

[6] This theory will be further discussed.

[7] Letter, JB to AK, 12-31-1866. *Dear General.*

[8] *Ibid,* letter, JB to AK, 6-18-1867. A more complete description of the politics of the 1867 election can be read in chapter 5, "A Career in California Politics." Michael Gillis and Michael Magliari, *John Bidwell and California,* 2003.

[9] Letter, JB in Chico to JCG Kennedy in Washington, 10-15-1867. Archives, Bidwell Mansion State Historic Park.

[10] Letter, AK in Washington to JB in Chico, 10-07-1867. *Dear General.*

[11] Letter, Catherine M. Kennedy in Washington to AKB in Chico, 8-17-1868, Annie Bidwell Collection, CSL.

[12] Letter, AK in Washington to JB in Washington, 3-8-1868. *Dear General.*

[13] Letter, JB in Chico to AK in Washington, 3-5-1867. *Dear General.*

[14] Margaret Ramsland, *The Other Bidwells,* 1972. CSUC Meriam Library, Special Collections.

[15] Letter, JB in Washingon to AK in Washington, 3-27-1868. *Dear General.*

[16] List of wedding guests, AKB Collection. The Bancroft Library.

[17] Letter, AK in Washington to JB in Chico, 12-29-1867. *Dear General.*

[18] San Francisco *Weekly Examiner,* 6-16-1868, reprinted from N.Y. *Examiner,* Richard Schillens Collection of Historical Materials for Chico, Redwood City Public Library, copied for Paradise Genealogical Library by Carllene Marek.

[19] Letter, JB in Chico to AKB in Washington, 8-20-1869. AKB Collection, Calif. State Library.

The honeymoon, pp. 47–63

[1] During the voyage John Bidwell kept two journals (both printed in his published diaries) in which he made daily entries. One account he had promised to send the Kennedy

family in Washington as soon as they disembarked at San Francisco. That copy is a bit more detailed, especially with remarks about Annie's courage in overcoming her seasickness.

[2] Bidwell continued to provide for Lily, sending her to Mills Seminary in Oakland in 1877. He had also paid for his brother Daniel's daughter Emroy's education at a boarding school in Oakland some years prior to his meeting Annie Kennedy. Letter from Lily Bidwell in Oakland to JB in Chico, 2-6-1877, AKB Collection, CSL.

[3] Letter, CMK in Washington to AKB in Chico, "as to discrimination in regards to bedding of the servants, we think alike." AKB Collection, Calif. State Library.

[4] Letter, AKB in Big Meadows to JB in Chico, July 1868. AKB Collection, State Library. Susan and Clayborn were married shortly after and they lived at the mansion for some months, both employed by the Bidwells.

[5] Letter, CMK in Washington to AKB in Chico, 7-21-1868. As above.

[6] Letter, AKB in San Francisco to JB in Chico, 12-22-1868, AKB Collection, Calif. State Library, as above.

[7] Letter, AKB in Washington to JB in Chico, 6-28-1869. AKB Collection, Calif. State Library, as above.

[8] Letter, Sallie K in Washington to AKB in Chico, 12-25-1868. AKB Collection, Calif. State Library, as above.

[9] Letter, JB in Marysville to AKB in Chico, 3-30-1870. AKB Collection, Calif. State Library, as above.

[10] Letter, AKB in San Francisco to JB in Chico, 11-20-1868. CSUC Meriam Library, Special Collections.

[11] Letters, CMK in Washington to AKB in Chico, 9-15-1868, 9-28-1868, 10-8-1868, 10-16-1868, see above.

[12] Letter, AKB in Chico to JB in San Francisco, 4-5-1869. AKB papers, CSUC Meriam Library, Special Collections.

[13] "Mechoopda Indians," AKB MSS, The Bancroft Library, published Bidwell Mansion Association, 1980; JB Diary, September 12-13, 1868.

[14] Rancheria is a Mexican/Spanish term for a small settlement of Indians. It is used interchangeably with "Indian village" in this book.

[15] Ibid.

[16] JB diary, March 1869.

[17] This story has come through in several versions. The one written to me by Craig D. Bates, curator of ethnology at Yosemite Nat'l Park and a student of the Mechoopda Tribe, was told to him by Henry Azbill: "Annie Bidwell also told Henry that when she arrived in Chico at the Bidwell Mansion for the first time, Nupani was introduced to her as the housekeeper. Nupani kept a large ring of keys of the mansion, and one day Mrs. Bidwell approached her, saying that she had been at the mansion for some time now and wasn't it time that she had the keys. Nupani drew herself up and, pointing at her chest said, 'Me Mrs. Bidwell number one, you (pointing at Annie) Mrs. Bidwell number two, I keep the keys.' And Nupani kept the keys until she died." This will be discussed in the chapter "Nopanny—Between Two Worlds."

Prof. Hector Lee's Folklore Collection at CSUC Special Collections (1947) includes Ben Hudsmith's statement that a story had circulated in Chico that John Bidwell had had a Mahala.

[18] Letter, AKB in Chico to JB in Oroville, CSUC Meriam Library, AKB papers, Special Collections.

[19] Letter, CMK in Washington to AKB in Chico, 7-26-1868. AKB Collection, Calif. State Library.

[20] Letter, CMK to AKB, 6-23-68, AKB Collection, State Library as above.

[21] Ibid.

[22] Letter, Johnny Kennedy in Chico to JB in Washington, December, 1-6-1868. AKB Collection, The Bancroft Library.

[23] Letter, CMK in Washington to AKB in Chico, 9-28-1868, AKB Collection, Calif. State Library, Calif. Room.

[24] Ibid.

[25] Letter, Joseph C. G. Kennedy in Washington to AKB in Chico, 5-4-1869, Bidwell Mansion State Historic Park Archives.

A look at Rancho Chico, pp. 63–69

[1] For more detailed account of Bidwell's agricultural beginnings and accomplishments, see Gillis and Magliari's *John Bidwell and California*, chapter 4.

[2] Letter, J. C. G. Kennedy in Washington to AKB in Chico, 5-4-1869, Bidwell Mansion State Historic Park Archives.

[3] Ibid.

[4] The author has heard the statement about Bidwell's behavior among male friends made by a Durham, California, resident giving a tour of the Durham house, former home of W. W. Durham, Bidwell's contemporary. Also overheard in conversation with Chico Cemetery staff.

The pangs of separation, 1869, pp. 70–78

[1] (Mrs. Sybil Gage, described by John Bidwell as "handsome and accomplished," was a Butte County resident who matched the social and educational achievements of his wife. She was even able to make John Bidwell feel at ease when she threatened to come and care for him if he got sick in Annie's absence! She was the New Hampshire-reared wife of David Gage, superintendent of the huge hydraulic mining operation at Cherokee.) Note: "Gage" the almost illegible name in Annie's letter *may* be "Gates" but no Gates has been identified.

[2] Letter, AKB in Washington to JB in Chico, 6-14-1869. AKB Collection, Calif. State Libary.

[3] Letter, JB in Chico to AKB in Washington, 6-22-1869. Ibid.

[4] Letter, JB in Chico to AKB en route to Washington, 6-4-1869, 6-8-1869. Ibid.

[5] Letter, JB in Chico to AKB in Washington. Ibid.

[6] Letter, JB in Chico to AKB nearing Washington, 6-8-1869. Ibid.

[7] Letter, JB in Chico to AKB in Washington, 6-24-1869. Ibid.

[8] Letter, JB in Chico to AKB in Washington, 6-29-1869. Ibid.

[9] Letter, JB in Chico to AKB in Washington, 7-2-1869. Ibid.

[10] Letter, JB in Chico to AKB in Washington, 6-23-1879. Ibid.

[11] Letter, JB in Chico to AKB in Washington, 6-25-1869. Ibid.

[12] All through June and much of July 1869, Bidwell's letters detail servant problems.

[13] Letter, JB in Chico to AKB in Washington, 6-19-1869. Ibid.

[14] Letter, AKB in Washington to JB in Chico, 7-5-1869. Ibid.
[15] Letter, JB in Chico to AKB in Washington, 6-18-1869. Ibid.
[16] Letter, AKB in Washington to JB in Chico, 6-16-1869. Ibid.
[17] Letter, JB in Chico to AKB in Washington, 6-19-1869. Ibid.
[18] Letter, AKB in Washington to JB in Chico, 7-2-1869. Ibid.
[19] Letter, JB in Chico to AKB in Washington, 7-2-1869. Ibid.
[20] Letter, AKB in Washington to JB in Chico, 7-26, 1869. Ibid.
[21] Letter, AKB in Chico to JB in San Francisco, 10-9-1869. Ibid.

Adrift between two ports, pp. 79–99

[1] This incident was related in a letter from John Bidwell to their friend, naturalist John Muir, 4-20-1896. A little note added to her husband's missive by Annie described her seeing tears in her husband's eyes on this emotional occasion. John Muir Collection, Holt-Atherton Library, University of the Pacific. Annie's letter missed cataloging in Muir's collection. The sharp eyes of Mike Gillis or Mike Magliari spotted it while researching for *John Bidwell and California,* 2003.

[2] Letter, AKB in Chico to JB in San Francisco, 11-25-1869. AKB Collection, CSL.

[3] Ibid. The *Geography of Astronomy* is now among rare books "carried by pioneers" in the California State Library.

[4] Letter, JB in Marysville to AKB in Chico, 2-2-1870, CSL.

[5] Letter, Sallie Kennedy in Washington to AKB in Chico, 5-15-1870, AKB Collection, CSL.

[6] Letter, AKB in Washington to JB in Chico, 7-9-1869, AKB Collection, CSL.

[7] Letter, JB in Chico to AKB in Washington, 11-8-1871. AKB Collection, CSL.

[8] Letter, Sallie Kennedy in Washington to AKB in Chico, 9-26-1870. AKB Collection, CSL.

[9] Letter, CMK in Washington to AKB in Chico, 1-11-1871. AKB Collection, CSL.

[10] Letter, CMK in Washington to AKB in Chico, 3-24-1871. Ibid.

[11] Letter, JB in Chico to AKB in Washington, 8-5-1871. Ibid.

[12] Letter, CMK in Washington to AKB in Chico, 8-17-1868. Ibid.

[13] Letter, CMK in Washington to AKB in Chico, 6-26-1871. Ibid.

[14] Letter, JB in San Francisco to AKB in Chico, during Sallie's visit in August 1871. AKB Collection, CSL.

[15] JB Diary, 11-10-1871.

[16] Letter, JB in Chico to AKB in Washington, 3-16-1872. AKB Collection, CSL.

[17] Letter, JB in Chico to AKB in Washington, 3-25-1872. AKB Collection, CSL.

[18] Letter, JB in Chico to AKB in Washington, 3-3-1872. Ibid.

[19] JB diary, 3-15-1872.

[20] Ibid., 4-4-1872.

[21] Ibid., 6-1-1872.

[22] Letter, Sallie Kennedy in Washington to AKB in Chico, 5-23-1872, AKB Collection, CSL.

[23] JB diary, 12-2-1872.

[24] Letter, CMK in Washington to JB in Chico, 3-8-1873. AKB Collection, CSL.

[25] Letter, AKB to JB, 2-1-1875. AKB Collection, ibid.

[26] JB diary entries, 6-4-1873, 7-13-1873, barn burned 6-15-1874.

[27] JB diary, 4-16-1873.

[28] JB diary, 6-17-1873, 8-5/18-1873.

[29] Letter, AKB in San Francisco to AB in Chico, 8-2-1875, AKB Collection, CSL.

[30] JB diary, 5-20-1874.

[31] Letter, AKB from San Francisco to JB in Chico, 7-1-1874, AKB Collection, CSL.

[32] Letter, AKB in San Francisco to JB in Chico, 6-29-1874. Ibid.

[33] Letter, AKB in Washington to JB in Chico, 3-14-1875. Ibid.

1875—A year to seize the helm, pp. 100–110

[1] Letter, AKB in Washington to JB in Chico, 12-1-1874. AKB Collection, CSL.

[2] Letter, AKB in Washington to JB in Chico, 12-8-1874. Ibid.

[3] JB diary, March 7, 1875.

[4] Letter, JB in Chico to AKB in Washington, 1-17-1875. AKB Collection, CSL.

[5] The papers pertaining to the Indian school saved by AKB are filed together in the AKB Collection, Calif. State Library, boxes 31 and 32.

[6] Letter, CMK in Washington to AKB in Chico, 6-27-1875, AKB Collection, CSL.

[7] The recommended source is chapter 4, "A Career in California Politics," Gillis & Magliari, *John Bidwell and California,* 2003.

[8] Letter, CMK in Washington to AKB in Chico, 6-15-1875, AKB Collection, CSL.

[9] Letter, CMK in Washington to AKB in Chico, 7-22-1875. Ibid.

[10] Letter, CMK in Washington to AKB in Chico, 9-16-1875. Ibid.

[11] Letter, AKB in San Francisco to JB in Visalia, 7-29-1875. Ibid.

[12] Letter, CMK in Washington to AKB in Chico, 12-5-1875. Ibid.

[13] Letter, AK in Washington to JB in Chico, 6-4-1867, *Dear General,* p. 70-72.

[14] Letter, CMK in Washington to AKB in Chico, 3-19-1876. AKB Collection, CSL.

[15] Letter, CMK in Washington to AKB in Chico, 12-22-1875. Ibid.

[16] Ibid.

[17] JB diary, 11-18-1875; 12-1-1875.

[18] JB diary, 3-30-1875.

[19] Letter, AKB in Chico to AB in San Francisco, 2-1-1876, 2-4-1876. AKB Collection, CSL.

[20] Dr. Michele Shover, "John Bidwell: A Reconsideration," in *Ripples Along Chico Creek,* Butte County Branch of the National League of American Pen Women, 1992.

[21] Letter, JB in Chico to AKB in Washington, 12-3-1876. Earlier comment on Lusk, JB to AKB, 7-6-1873. AKB Collection, CSL.

Conflicts, pp. 111–119

[1] Letter, AKB in Chico to a Mr. Johnson in reply to a letter written to JB, 5-15-1891. AKB Collection, Calif. State Library, Calif. History Room.

[2] Letter to author from Craig D. Bates, Curator of Ethnography, Yosemite National Park, 11-3-1998. Bates has made a special research project of the Mechoopda Tribe. "As to other children which Bidwell had by two different Indian women [other than Nupani] the two whom I know about are Amanda Wilson and George Clements. The descendants of these people, some of whom still live in the Chico area, regard the fact of Bidwell being the father of their ancestor as common knowledge … so commonly known that it was the basis for extended family relationships within the native community."

[3] Letter, AKB in Chico to JB in San Francisco, 2-4-1876. AKB Collection, CSL.

[4] Letter, AKB in Chico to JB in San Francisco, 2-7-1876.

[5] Ibid.

[6] JB diary, Oct. 29, 1876.

[7] Very early in marriage Annie found that being called *husband* irritated Bidwell. Only later did he protest the overuse of *General.*

[8] Letter, AKB in Washington to JB in Chico, 11-13-1876. AKB Collection, CSL.

[9] Letter, AKB in Washington to JB in Chico, 11-4-1876, 11-13-1876.

[10] Ibid.

[11] Ibid.

[12] Letter, AKB in Washington to JB in Chico, 11-16-1876, AKB Collection, CSL.

[13] Letters, JB in Chico to AKB in Washington, detailing the church's agony over the Rev. Woods' disgrace: 11-12-1876, 11-14-1876, 11-22-1876, 11-26-1876, 11-27-1876, 11-30-1876. AKB Collection, CSL.

[14] Letter, AKB in Washington to JB in Chico, 11-24-1876, AKB Collection, CSL.

[15] Letter, AKB in Washington to JB in Chico, 11-25-1876. AKB Collection, ibid.

[16] Letter, JB in Chico to AKB in Washington, 12-12-1876. AKB Collection, ibid.

[17] Letter, JB in Chico to AKB in Washington, 12-1-1876. AKB Collection, ibid.

[18] Letter JB in Chico to AKB in Washington, 12-2-1876, AKB Collection, ibid.

[19] Letter, AKB in Washington to JB in Chico, 11-24-1876, AKB Collection, ibid.

[20] Letter, JB in Chico to AKB in Washington, 12-2-1876, AKB Collection, ibid.

[21] Letter, AKB in Washington to JB in Chico, 8-11-1895, AKB Collection, ibid.

[22] Letter, AKB in Chico to JB in Oroville, 11-18-1873. AKB Collection, ibid.

[23] Letter, JB in Chico to AKB in Washington, 12-27-1876. AKB Collection, ibid.

A House for the dying, pp. 120–127

[1] JB Diary, 1-1-1877 ff.

[2] Letter, JB in Chico to AKB in Washington, January 1877. AKB collection, CSL.

[3] Letter, AKB in Washington to JB in Chico, 1-18-1877. Ibid.

[4] Letter, JB in Chico to AKB in Washington, 1-27-1877. Ibid.

[5] Letter, AKB in Washington to JB in Chico, 2-7-1877. Ibid.

[6] Letter, AKB in Washington to JB in Chico, 11-24-1876. Ibid.

[7] Letter, AKB in Washington to JB in Chico, 1-28-1877. Ibid.

[8] Gillis & Magliari, *John Bidwell and California*, chapter 7 "Bidwell and the California Chinese," pp. 318-324.

[9] Letter, JB in Chico to AKB in Washington, 3-7-1875. AKB Collection, Calif. State Library.

[10] When John Bidwell sold the cemetery he reserved a large piece of land with the express objective of making it available for friends and family.

[11] JB diary, June 7–June 28 ff, 1878. August 8–14, 1878.

[12] JB diary, Aug. 27-Sept. 1, 1878.

A happy camping trip, pp. 128–131

[1] JB diary, 9-3-1877 to 10-8-1877.

[2] Letter, John Muir to the Bidwells and Sallie Alexander, 11-10-1877. With permission of the Holt-Atherton Special Collections, University of the Pacific. The letter has been reprinted several times including in the Oakland *Tribune*.

[3] Letter, AKB to John Muir, 1-24-1894. Used by permission of the Holt-Atherton Special Collections, UOP.

Putting down more roots in California1, pp. 132–137

[1] Letter, JB in Chico to AKB in Washington, 1-24-1877. AKB Collection, CSL.

[2] Letter, AKB in San Francisco to JB in Chico, AKB Collection, ibid.

[3] Letter, JB in Chico to AKB in Washington, 11-25-1876. AKB Collection, ibid.

[4] The JB diary makes reference to Madame Trincano's French classes in the Mansion library over a period of years. The other participants varied but from time to time included Cora Kennedy, Callie Jones, Mrs. Earll and her daughter. It would seem that no one learned much French through these hit-or-miss classes, few of which were attended consecutively by the purported students other than Annie.

[5] JB diary, 6-4-1879. Longley scholar, John Rudderow of Chico, has been searching for this missing poem.

[6] Letters, AKB to JB. 2-16-1877 from Washington; 6-3-1878 from San Francisco; 6-5-1878 from San Francisco. AKB Collection, CSL.

A visit from Annie's parents, pp. 132–137

[1] JB diary, August 6 through October 6, 1879.

[2] Letters, AKB, traveling through the state, to JB in Chico, September 1879. AKB Collection, Calif. State Library.

Sallie's doomed love affair, pp. 141–146

[1] Letters from CMK in Washington to AKB in Chico for the month of March 1880, which include the text of Morrison's letters to J. C. G. Kennedy, as well as details of events as Annie's mother suffered an emotional roller-coaster from role of horrified parent to sympathetic mother. AKB Collection, California State Library, California Room.

[2] JB diary, March 4–March 28, 1880.

[3] Letter, JB in Chico to AKB in Washington, 8-7-1887. AKB Collection, CSL.

The rancheria school, pp. 147–156

[1] The preserved papers describing the beginnings of the Indian school at the rancheria on Rancho Chico have been catalogued together in the AKB Collection at the California State Library, California Room, in box 31 of the collection.

[2] JB diary 11-3-1882. Other entries around that date indicate John Bidwell's active part in building and furnishing the buildings though he did not participate in services or classroom.

[3] Annie's letter to JB dated 12-16-1878 from San Francisco quotes her informant "No printed rules exist. The trustees may direct as circumstances suggest."

[4] As told to Sara Stanley Baz, granddaughter of Grace Stanley, by her family, and repeated to the author.

[5] From notes kept by Annie on the Indian school, 6-13-1880. AKB Collection, Calif. State Library.

[6] Ibid.

[7] Noted in JB's diary, December 1885, that George Clements had returned from Middletown.

[8] The text of this proclamation appears in JB's diary, 6-21-1885.

Developing new outlets for self expression, pp. 157–164

[1] Annie had not yet begun to systematically keep a diary, but JB by this date was entering names of all overnight guests at the mansion as well as most of the daytime visitors. Annie's activities that required use of a carriage and ranch employee's time were usually noted.

[2] JB's diary. Also Ira H. Latour's *Silver Shadows,* 1993. Also William A. Jones, "A Naturalist's Vision: The Photographs of Henry Wetherbee Henshaw," Butte County Historical Society *Diggin's,* vol. 30, no. 2, 1986.

[3] JB diary, Oct. 1879–Dec. 1880; George Moses Gray, His Reminiscences of the Life of General Bidwell, 1999.

[4] JB diary.

[5] Letter, JB in Chico to AKB in Auburn, 9-15-1887. AKB Collection, CSL.

[6] Letter, J. C. G. Kennedy in Washington to AKB in Chico, 12-18-1879. AKB Collection, The Bancroft Library.

[7] Letter, JB in Chico to AKB in Auburn, AKB Collection, CSL.

[8] JB diary, 5-9-1883.

[9] JB diary, 8-26-1883, 9-23/24-1883.

[10] Weekly *Butte Record,* 10-2-1880.

[11] JB diary, Dec. 8-10, 1883. Leavitt was a guest at the mansion.

[12] These WCTU organizing trips were noted in JB's diary, early 1884.

[13] Letter, J. C. G. Kennedy in Washington to AKB in Chico, 4-3-1884. AKB Collection, The Bancroft Library.

[14] Letter, JB in Washington to AKB in Washington, 12-31-1866. *Dear General.*

Family duty to the fore, pp. 165–170

[1] Letter, CMK in Washington to AKB in Chico, 11-14-1885. Such personal matters were never mentioned in mixed company. Catherine wrote after visiting a New York specialist.

[2] JB diary, 10-1-1885.

[3] Letter, CMK in Washington to AKB in Chico, 3-1886. AKB Collection, Calif. State Library, California Room.

[4] JB diary of 1884 mentions several trips to borrow small sums in San Francisco to meet this or that obligation. Then on Dec. 27 he received the $235,000 loan from the German Savings Bank.

[5] Letter, JB in Chico to AKB in San Francisco, 11-25-1899. AKB Collection, CSL.

[6] Again, JB's diary is the major source for details of the Bidwells' life in this period, including the fate of the Sacramento River Bridge.

A murder, pp. 171–174

[1] Joseph F. McGie, *History of Butte County,* vol. 1, p. 43.

[2] JB noted the essential facts in his diary. Other sources include W. H. Hutchinson, *When Chico Stole the College,* 1983, Butte Savings and Loan Association; W. H.

Hutchinson, Clarence McIntosh, Pam Herman Bush, *A Precious Sense of Place: the Early Years of Chico State,* 1991, Friends of the Meriam Library, CSUC.

[3] JB diary, 7-13-1887. Obituaries and eulogies of J. C. G. Kennedy in the AKB Collection, The Bancroft Library.

[4] Philadephia *Press*, July 13, 1887. Newspaper clipping in AKB Collection, The Bancroft Library.

[5] AKB diary the first year in which one of her diaries has been preserved. The trial was in the month of January and there are several references to it in Annie's diary.

[6] Philadelphia *Press,* July 14, 1887. AKB Collection, The Bancroft Library.

[7] Telegram, Sallie Kennedy in Washington to AKB en route, 7-18-1887. AKB Collection, California State Library, Calif. Room.

[8] See chapter "Sallie Kennedy Takes the Helm."

[9] Letter, JB in Chico to AKB in Washington, 9-11-1887. AKB Collection, CSL.

[10] Letter, Sallie Kennedy in Washington to reach AKB in Chico, 10-25-1887. Ibid.

Sallie Kennedy takes the helm, pp. 175–179

[1] The terms of J. C. G. Kennedy's will are given in the AKB Collection, The Bancroft Library.

[2] Letter, Sallie Kennedy in Washington to AKB in Chico, 11-21-1887, AKB Collection, Calif. State Library, Calif. Room.

[3] Letter, SK in Washington to AKB in Chico, 11-11-1887, ibid.

[4] Letter, SK to AKB, 11-25-1887, ibid.

[5] Letter, SK to AKB, 11-21-1887, ibid.

[6] Letter, SK to AKB, 11-4-1887, ibid.

[7] Letter, SK to AKB, 5-5-1888, ibid.

[8] Letter, SK to AKB, 11-30-1887, ibid.

[9] Letter, SK to AKB, 5-25-1888, ibid.

[10] Letter, SK to AKB, 5-5-1888, ibid.

[11] Letter, SK to AKB, 5-5-1888, ibid.

[12] Letter, SK to AKB, 5-31-1888, ibid.

[13] The Aurora (or Church) Mine 2–3 miles north of Magalia on Little Butte Creek was very productive over many years and with several owners, later named the Princess. Mrs. Caroline Church, the resident at the time Annie resided there, was probably a widow continuing to operate the mine with hired miners.

Serious—but caught in time, pp. 180–185

[1] AKB diary, 6-30-1888, Annie's prayer to God to save her mother and sister from insanity.

[2] AKB diary entries indicating illness: 1-29-1888, kept home from meeting by illness; 2-1-1888, Cora and Joey accompany her to a doctor.

[3] AKB diary, 3-16-1888.

[4] JB diary, 3-24-1888 and 3-31-1888.

[5] Letter, JB in Chico to AKB in Auburn, 8-17-1888. AKB Collection, CSL.

[6] JB diary, 7-4-1888.

[7] JB diary, 6-2-1888.

[8] JB diary, 7-20-1888.

[9] Rooms were for Mollie Cooper, Cora Kennedy, a personal maid from the mansion and Charley Cunningham, the Bidwell's carriage driver who assisted Annie with horseback and carriage rides. Fresh air was prescribed to improve her appetite.

[10] Letter, JB in Chico to AKB in Auburn, 7-30-1888. AKB Collection, CSL.

[11] JB diary , 8-31, 9-5, 9-13, 1888.

[12] JB diary, 10-10-1888.

[13] JB diary, 12-3-1888.

[14] JB diary. The Alexander party remained in Ojai from October 28, 1887 to December 7, 1888.

Convalescence put behind, pp. 186–193

[1] Although Annie kept a diary intermittently throughout 1889 and 1890, JB's diaries are the best source for tracing the activities of the couple.

[2] Letter, JB in Chico to AKB in San Francisco, 8-2-1894. AKB collection, CSL.

[3] Letter, JB in San Francisco to AKB in Chico, 12-6-1886. John Bidwell Collection, CSL.

[4] AKB diary, December 15, 1890.

[5] Letter, JB in Chico to AKB in Auburn, 8-17-1888. AKB Collection, CSL.

Haunted by more family tragedy, pp. 194–200

[1] It will be remembered that in 1866, John Bidwell took a trip to the British Isles but became so lonesome for a sight of Annie that he could think of nothing else but getting back to the Kennedy household. His diary held no attraction for him if its pages were devoid of sightings of Miss Kennedy—thus the blank pages. The account copied by Annie has been recorded in published CD-ROM.

[2] The voice culture phase ended with Annie's departure for Washington when Joe died. She kept no diary for 1892.

[3] Letter, JMK in Fountainville to AKB in Chico, 11-21-1889, AKB Collection, The Bancroft Library.

[4] Ibid.

[5] JB diary 4-8-1892.

[6] Letter, Sallie Alexander in Washington to AKB in Chico, 1-29-1893, AKB Collection, California State Library.

[7] Letter, CK in Washington to AKB in Chico, 9-17-1868, AKB Collection, Calif. State Library, Calif. Room.

[8] Bidwell had a severe attack of "biliousness" in January 1892, spent February 1–16 in San Francisco being treated with various medications by Dr. Hirschfelder.

John Bidwell's brave, if futile, campaign, pp. 201–204

[1] JB's diary gives a good day-to-day account of the efforts to treat Bidwell's stomach problems and the teamwork done on the campaign from a hotel room. Gillis and Magliari's chapter on Bidwell and Politics copies most of the Speech of Acceptance with the platform's highlights.

Aches, pains and pleasures of growing older, pp. 205–210

[1] Letter, JB in San Francisco to AKB in Chico, 8-5-1871, AKB Collection, Calif. State Library.

[2] Both of the Joneses, Susan and Clayborn, died in the mid 1890s. While drinking, Jones was often abusive of his wife and children and during one drinking episode his son warned him off, then shot him, a wound which proved fatal. Susan lived a few years longer. The events are described in letters to JB by AKB, he being absent from Chico at the time.

[3] AKB diary.

[4] Both of the Bidwells kept a diary during this trip and they serve as the basis for the facts used here.

Return to Dr. Hirschfelder, pp. 211–215

[1] In a letter of Oct. 24, 2001, Craig D. Bates, curator of ethnology at Yosemite National Park and a historian of the Mechoopdas, wrote to the author "I do not have a record of George Clements marrying someone named Clara. I wonder if Clara is another name for Jessie Holmes? I do have a record of James Nucholls marrying a Jessie Holmes and wonder if Jessie, Jennie and Clara are the same person?"

[2] Letter, AKB in Chico to JB in Los Angeles, 4-9-1894. AKB Collection, Calif. State Library.

[3] Letter, AKB in San Francisco to JB in Chico, 5-5-1894. Ibid.

[4] Letter. AKB in San Francisco to JB in Chico, 4-26-1894. Ibid.

[5] Letter, AKB in San Francisco to JB in Chico, 4-28-1894. Ibid.

[6] Letter, AKB in San Francisco to JB in Chico, 5-6-1894. Ibid.

[7] Letter, AKB in San Francisco to JB in Chico, 5-6-1894. Ibid.

William Morrison Alexander, pp. 216–221

[1] AKB Collection, The Bancroft Library.

[2] These letters are believed to be in the DAR archives.

[3] AKB diary, July–August, 1895.

[4] The flying of the U.S. flag on the Indian chapel strikes the author as a touch quite out of keeping with the sacred nature of the building, the Constitutional division of church and state, and the fact that Indians were not granted citizenship in the United States until 1924, well into the twentieth century. Annie had once stated that the Indians identified the U.S. flag as a sign that God watched over them.

[5] Both John Neubarth, a Chico cigar manufacturer, and his son August, an insurance broker, were band musicians. The latter was well known for his Chico Band. Both men may have assisted with teaching the Mechoopdas.

[6] Letter, AKB in San Francisco to JB in Chico, 10-5-1896. AKB Collection, Calif. State Library.

Nopanny—between two worlds, pp. 222–228

[1] Annie E. Bidwell, from notes in a box (32) labeled Indian paper in AKB Collection, California State Library. In these notes Annie says that Nopanny was the daughter of Chief Luckyan. In a talk given in 1906 on the Mechoopda Indians, she says Chief Yummarine. John Bidwell wrote Luccayan in his 1885 Proclamation, JB diary June 21, 1885. This is but one illustration of the difficulty that English-speaking people had with mastering the Indian names and their apparent interchanging use of names.

[2] In a letter to the author of Nov. 3, 1998, Craig D. Bates, curator of ethnology, Yosemite National Park, wrote: "Henry Azbill told me that he had heard that Bidwell had had a son by Nupani, but that the child died as an infant, or perhaps at birth. ... Azbill also told me that around 1917 when he worked for Mrs. Bidwell, assisting her in putting her papers in order, he came across a letter to Mrs. Bidwell advising her that Mr. Bidwell had had an Indian wife. Mrs. Bidwell told Henry to throw the letter away, and said she had a standard response for such comments, something to the effect that the General availed himself of the best that God had to offer, and that his Indian wife was the best that God had to offer prior to herself.

"Annie Bidwell also told Henry that when she arrived in Chico at the Bidwell Mansion for the first time, Nupani was introduced to her as the housekeeper. She soon realized that Nupani had been much more than a housekeeper. Nupani kept a large ring of keys to the mansion, and one day Mrs. Bidwell approached her, saying that she had been at the mansion for some time now, and wasn't it time she had the keys. Nupani drew herelf up and pointing at her chest said, 'me Mrs. Bidwell number one, you (pointing at Annie Bidwell) Mrs. Bidwell number two. I keep the keys.' And Nupani kept the keys until she died."

[3] Nopanny seems to refer here to a threat from someone in authority referring to the fifth item in Bidwell's 1885 proclamation, that Indians who did not work on Rancho Chico could not reside in the rancheria.

[4] Letter, Nopanny to JB, 6-12-1887. box 78, AKB Collection, Calif. State Library. Her spelling has been preserved.

[5] Annie Bidwell in a talk on Mechoopda Indians, 1906. MSS AKB Bidwell Collection, The Bancroft Library. Also reprinted in *Rancho Chico Indians,* writings and talks given by AKB collected and edited by Dorothy J. Hill, 1980. Bidwell Mansion Association.

[6] Letter, AKB in Washington to JB in Chico, 11-24-1876 (misdated by Annie 1877), AKB Collection, California State Library.

[7] Letter, JB in Chico to AKB in Washington, 10-3-1887. AKB Collection, CSL.

[8] Annie Bidwell talk, 1906, *Rancho Chico Indians.*

[9] Bidwell closely observed the lives of his children in the rancheria, although he made no overt attempt to have contact with them. In a letter to Annie written in December 1876, he mentioned seeing Amanda from a distance and that "she has grown a great deal since I saw her last."

[10] Letter, Nopanny to AKB 10-23-1909, box 32, AKB Collection, CSL. This reference to George Clements and his "putting in the name of Nopanny" as missionary is puzzling, for Clements rarely came to the rancheria at that time, and certainly had not seemed interested in mission work.

[11] Annie Bidwell's text for a talk on Mechoopda's, *Rancho Chico Indians.*

"Susan B. Anthony kissed me," pp. 229–234

[1] It can be argued that the existence of slavery has a longer history prior to remedy by the Amendment Thirteen to the Constitution. Considering the years that the U.S. was an independent democracy with a constitution as we know it now, slavery existed 1787-1865, a few years longer than the formal struggle for women's suffrage (1848-1920).

[2] Barbara Goldsmith, *Other Powers,* 1998, chapter 4, "My Long Accumulating Discontent."

³ JB diary, 3-30-1875.

⁴ For JB's high opinion of Anthony, read Gillis & Magliari's chapter "A Career in California Politics," in *John Bidwell and California,* pp. 247-48.

⁵ AKB's diary, November 1890.

⁶ AKB's diary, June 1895.

⁷ Letter, AKB in San Francisco to JB in Chico, 5-7-1896.

⁸ Letter, AKB in San Francisco to JB in Chico, 5-8-1896.

⁹ Ibid.

¹⁰ Letter, AKB in San Francisco to JB in Chico, 10-5-1896.

¹¹ Letter, Susan B. Anthony to AKB, 1-16-1901. "Your demand to be constable of your town is a worthy one and should be respected."

¹² AKB diary, July 1905.

¹³ Letter, Mary S. Anthony to AKB, 8-13-1905. AKB Collection, The Bancroft Library.

The old and the young, pp. 235–248

¹ During Annie's visit to Washington in 1885, she copied a number of her mother's recitations in her diary.

² AKB's diary, May 31, 1899.

³ Letter, Ella Gatchell to AKB in Washington, 3-19-1897. AKB Collection, The Bancroft Library.

⁴ Letter, SKA in Washington to AKB in Chico, 1-13-1904. AKB Collection, CSL.

⁵ Letter, Sallie Alexander in Washington to AKB in Chico, 11-7-1898. AKB Collection, The Bancroft Library.

⁶ Letter, Sallie Alexander in Washington to AKB in Chico, 1-29-93, AKB Collection, California State Library.

⁷ AKB's diary has full account for this period. It is hardly mentioned in JB's diary.

⁸ AKB's diary.

⁹ Letters, George Clements to AKB, 1884. AKB Collection, CSL.

¹⁰ JB diary, December 1885.

¹¹ JB's diary, 6-21-1885; 7-2-1885. In his diary, John Bidwell specifically identifies Clara as George Clements' wife. Yet Craig D. Bates, from his records on the Mechoopdas found no mention of a Clara. He wrote to the author on 10-24-2001, "… to the best of my knowledge [George Clements'] first wife was not Clara, but was Mary (Kelly, Kea'a'la) later Mary Azbill. I don't know the exact dates for their marriage and separation, but believe it was in the 1887-1891 period, between Mary's brief residences in Hawaii. After their separation, George married Jessie Holmes … . I do not have a record of George Clements marrying someone named Clara."

¹² The quotes as well as narration of facts are from AKB's diary.

¹³ Ibid.

¹⁴ Ibid.

¹⁵ Ibid.

¹⁶ The author has twice been told of a Clements family belief, based on information passed down from George Clements, that John Bidwell had asked if he might adopt Luther. Finding absolutely nothing in the Bidwell diaries or correspondence to substantiate this, the author has not incorporated it into the text of this research. However, after consider-

ing the matter and having some insight into the emotions that came to surface during the episode over George's arrest and trial for child abuse, it seems to me that this request to adopt may well have occurred. My reasoning follows:

(1) Indian oral tradition is generally based on fact. Like all information passed from person to person, it is subject to distortion, but there is usually a kernel of fact in any oral tradition.

(2) Although the author had thought no indication of communication existed between John Bidwell and George Clements, the author finds *Geroge Clemens* in Bidwell's diary entry for February 24, among callers to the mansion, four days after the trial and while Annie was making preparations to send Luther to the Greenville Indian School after she had been awarded custody in the local justice court. I know of no other time in his life that George came as the result of a summons from Bidwell delivered by another party, possibly Nopanny.

(3) John Bidwell was under stress. He must have worried over his decision not to show any recognition of his fatherhood of Amanda and George over the years. As long as he had had any hopes of having an heir through his wife, Annie, it would have been awkward to assume a father's role with the Indian children. Now he was an old man, he had no heirs. Within fourteen months of this episode he would be dead and buried.

(4) The argument that probably proved strongest with Bidwell was his recent observation of the obvious love and maternal devotion that Annie showed toward Luther as she bathed him, fussed over his clothing and found food that would tempt him. John Bidwell knew that in the past Annie's heart had gone out toward at least two motherless little girls. Within the few years preceding this incident with Luther, Annie's sister Sallie's adoption of a small boy not far from Luther's age had given both women delight—a pleasure that Annie had shared with her husband.

It seems uncharacteristic of John Bidwell to have broken with the resolve he had made years earlier as regards admitting parenthood, but greater contradictions in human behavior have certainly occurred. If anything could have moved him to act at this time, it would have been his love for his "precious, precious wife."

(5) George Clements could not possibly have granted Bidwell's request. As proud and stubborn as the man he knew to be his father, George could not give up his son. Luther could be taken from him; father and son could be forcibly parted; but George Clements' paternal right was something he could not be made to relinquish.

Another interpretation is possible for the visit George Clements made to the mansion. John Bidwell may have summoned him to give warning that George's presence would no longer be tolerated on the ranch unless he was willing to follow the rules.

[17] The Slaughter case was a notorious charge of sexual misconduct by a Baptist minister named Slaughter. He was defended by W. H. Schooler and Guy Kennedy. Mansfield's *History of Butte County, 1918*, pp. 382-83.

[18] JB diary, 3-11-1899.

[19] Annie herself seemed unsure that Maud was the name of Clements' new wife, for she uses quotation marks around "Maud" in her diary. Craig Bates has no records of a Maud as one of George's successive wives. According to diary entries George's new wife had "problems," over which Annie prayed with her.

Death comes to a pioneer, pp. 249–259

[1] Both JB and AKB kept diaries for this mountain roadwork period, both in considerable detail.

[2] AKB diary, 8-8-1899.

[3] Ibid., 8-5-1899.

[4] Ibid., 8-27-1899.

[5] Ibid., 11-7-1899.

[6] JB's diary in which AKB completed the year, 4-4-1900.

[7] AKB's diary, 4-9-1900; 4-11-1900.

[8] AKB Collection, The Bancroft Library, random entry with copies of her talk at time of Bidwell Park gift to Chico.

Also, letter, AKB to John Muir, 8-6-1905 on the occasion of a death in his family. John Muir Collection, Holt-Atherton Library, Univ. of Pacific, Stockton, CA.

[9] AKB's diary for 1900 covers her discomfort and illness of that year.

[10] AKB Collection, California State Library.

[11] AKB diary, 4-24-1900.

[12] AKB diary 4-30-1900.

The give and take of a successful marriage, pp. 260–280

[1] The author was brought into this conversation between two young Bidwell Mansion guides for her opinion.

[2] Letter, JB in San Francisco to AKB in Washington, 8-15-1869. AKB Collection, CSL.

[3] Letter, JB in Chico to AKB in Washington, 10-21-1887. AKB Collection, CSL.

[4] Letter, JB in San Francisco to AKB in Chico, 2-24-1869. Ibid.

[5] Letter, AKB in Chico to JB in Oroville, 12-24-68. AKB Collection, CSUC Special Collections.

[6] Letter, JB en route to San Francisco on steamer *Dana*. 1-2-1869. AKB Collection, CSL.

[7] Letter, JB in Chico to AKB in Washington, 8-9-1869. Ibid.

[8] Letter, JB in Chico to AKB in Washington, 7-22-1869. Ibid.

[9] Letter, JB in Chico to AKB in Washington, 7-17-1869. Ibid.

[10] Letter, JB in Oroville to AKB in Chico, 7-28-1870. Ibid.

[11] Letter, JB in Chico to AKB in Washington, 3-19-1872. Ibid.

[12] Letter, JB in Chico to AKB in Washington, 3-17-1897. Ibid.

[13] Letter, AKB in San Francisco to JB in Chico, 5-26-1873. Ibid.

[14] Letter, AKB in Chico to JB in San Francisco,10-9-1869. AKB Collection, CSUC, Meriam Library, Special Collections.

[15] Letter, JB in Chico to AKB in Washington, 6-26-1869. AKB Collection, CSL.

[16] Letter, JB in Marysville to AKB in Chico, 11-22-1871. Ibid.

[17] Letter, AKB in Washington to JB in Chico, 12-10-1874. Ibid.

[18] Letter, AKB in Washington to JB in Chico, 1-15-1875. Ibid.

[19] Letter, JB from train traveling westerly to AKB in Washington, 11-8-1876. Ibid.

[20] Letter, AKB in Washington to JB in Chico, 11-24-1876. Ibid.

[21] Letter, JB from Gibsonville to AKB in Washington, 7-2-1869. Ibid.

[22] Ibid.

[23] Letter, JB in Chico to AKB in Washington, 3-17-1872. Ibid.

[24] Letter, AKB in Washington to JB in Chico, 2-8-1875. Ibid.

[25] Letter, JB in Chico to AKB in Washington, 6-28-1880. Ibid.

[26] Letter, JB in Chico to AKB in Washington, 9-15-1887. Ibid.

[27] Letter, AKB in Washington to JB in Chico, 1-13-1875. Ibid.

[28] Letter, AKB in Washington to JB in Chico, 12-20-1874. Ibid.

[29] Letter, AKB in Washington to JB in Chico, 6-14-1880. Ibid.

[30] Letter, AKB in Washington to JB in Chico 12-5-1876. Ibid.

[31] Letter, AKB in Washington to JB in Chico, 11-4-1876. Ibid.

[32] Letter, JB in Chico to AKB in Washington, 12-2-1876. Ibid.

[33] Letter, AKB in Washington to JB in Chico, 1-11-1875. Ibid.

[34] Letter, AKB in San Francisco to AB in Chico, 5-2-1894. Ibid.

[35] Letter, JB in Chico to AKB in Washington, 2-16-1873. Ibid.

[36] Letter, JB in Chico to AKB in San Francisco, 8-31-1878. Ibid.

[37] Letter, JB in Chico to AKB in Washington, 12-8-1876. Ibid.

[38] Letter, JB in New York to AKB in Washington, 10-1-1876. Ibid.

[39] Letter, JB in Chico to AKB in Washington, 2-28-1875. Ibid.

[40] Letter, AKB in Chico to JB in San Francisco, 2-7-1876. Ibid. Also 5-17-76, from AKB in San Francisco to JB in Chico.

[41] Letter, AKB in Washington to JB in Chico, 3-14-1875. Ibid.

[42] Letter, JB in Chico to AKB in Washington, 6-21-1880. Ibid.

[43] This correspondence at Sutter's death was edited and published by Valerie Shearer Mathes, "The Death of John Sutter as Seen Through the Letters of Annie and John Bidwell." *Pacific Historian*, 26, fall 1982.

[44] Letter, JB in Chico to AKB in Washington, 7-13-1869. AKB Collection, CSL.

[45] Letter, AKB in San Francisco to JB in Chico, 11-1868. AKB Collection, CSUC Special Collections.

[46] Letter, AKB in Washington to JB in Chico, 12-20-1874. AKB Collection, CSL.

[47] AKB diary, 2-8-1888.

[48] Oral interview with Ruby Daily English, 6-8-1964 by James Neider. AKB Collection, CSUC, Special Collections.

[49] Letter, AKB in Washington to JB in Chico, 12-16-1874. AKB Collection, CSL.

[50] Letter, AKB in Washington to JB in Chico, 11-18-1876. Ibid.

[51] Letter, AKB in Washington to JB in Chico, 1-22-1877. Ibid.

[52] Letter, AKB in Washington to JB in Chico, 2-5-1877. Ibid.

[53] JB's diary, 8-30-1882.

[54] JB's diary, Feb. 24-March 12, 1890.

[55] Letter, JB in Chico to AKB in Washington, 9-11-1887. Ibid.

[56] Letter, JB in Chico to AKB in Auburn, 8-8-1888. Ibid.

[57] Letter, AKB in Washington to JB in Chico, 7-17-1869. AKB Collection, CSL.

Depression, pp. 281–287

[1] Letter, AKB in Chico to John Muir, 8-6-1908, after the death of his wife. John Muir Collection, Holt-Atherton Library, Univ. of Pacific.

[2] Annie's copy of the papers filed by Guy Kennedy, et al. are in the AKB Collection, The Bancroft Library. A copy of the brief filed by Thompson Alexander in rebuttal is also included.

[3] Statement by associate justice of the supreme court of the District of Columbia, A. B. Hagner, 6-3-1902. AKB Collection, The Bancroft Library.

[4] Sacramento *Bee*, March 11, 1918.

Widowhood—a review, pp. 288–293

[1] As usually was the case after his marriage, Eva, not Guy, bore the burden of family correspondence and wrote the letter to Annie thanking her for her help and reporting on Guy's defeat.

[2] AKB's diary tells of one occasion in which Annie asked a short term loan of $600 from Guy, who graciously refused interest until she persuaded him otherwise.

[3] This was common knowledge in Chico. It was told to the author by Lois Stansell, once secretary to Guy Kennedy, and by others.

[4] Letter, Joseph Kennedy to AKB, 4-4-1910, AKB Collection, The Bancroft Library.

[5] Letter, Joseph Kennedy to AKB 4-3-1912, AKB Collection, The Bancroft Library.

[6] AKB Collection, The Bancroft Library.

[7] AKB diary.

[8] Ibid.

[9] Letter, AKB to John Muir, 3-3-1905, John Muir Collection, Holt-Atherton Library, Univ. of the Pacific.

The urge to build, pp. 294–299

[1] AKB's diary is the source for all information of the Robin's Nest construction and occupancy.

[2] AKB diary, 8-22-1905.

[3] The architect was apparently clumsy or indifferent, for the windows in the addition did not line up properly with those in the main house, requiring Annie's insistence on alteration. The architect's lame excuse "I don't understand how that could have happened," was noted in her diary.

The war to eliminate alcohol consumption, pp. 300–314

[1] From a series by John S. Waterland, originally published by the Chico *Record* in the 1930s, reprinted in the Chico *Enterprise-Record* in 1987.

[2] AKB Bidwell Collection, The Bancroft Library.

[3] JB diary, 5-21-1882.

[4] WCTU materials, AKB Collection, CSL.

[5] Ibid.

[6] JB diary, Feb.-March 1900. AKB diary, 3-19-1900.

[7] AKB diary, 5-2-1900.

[8] AKB diary, 5-2-1909.

[9] AKB diary has numerous references to activities to raise money, find volunteer carpenters, etc. for this Chico Vecino WCTU. The school building was apparently moved and was purchased by the Chico Grange. It stands at 2275 Nord Avenue.

[10] AKB diary 4-20-1906. Eva Kennedy's sister Francis Mathewson may have been killed, for her small son Donald spent many of his growing-up years in the Kennedy household. Among refugees from the earthquake area to the mansion were Dr. and Mrs. Hirschfelder and another three persons.

[11] Eva Kennedy was secretary for this WCTU when she took part in its leasing.

[12] AKB diary, 5-14-1904 ff.

[13] In 2003 this building is no longer used for worship services but as a social hall by the Stirling City Local Assembly of God Church.

[14] AKB diary, 11-14-1904.

[15] See Mansfield's *History of Butte County, 1918* for brief description of Clough's role in the company, as well as that of his son, Frank.

[16] Letter, Carrie Brydon to AKB 1-1-1899, AKB Collection, CSL.

[17] AKB diary, 5-27-1899.

[18] The cornerstone was laid for the church by the Chico WCTU June 17, 1904, but subscriptions on the cost of building the church went so slowly that it was several years before the church opened for regular service.

[19] AKB diary entries over several years. Contract with McErney was signed 2-2-1904.

[20] AKB diary, 10-11-12, 1904.

[21] AKB diary, 2-29-1904.

[22] Mansfield's *History of Butte County, 1918*, p. 374.

[23] AKB diary, 1-16-1904.

[24] AKB diary, 1909.

[25] The Surface dispute is covered in Prohibition Materials, box 36, AKB Collection, CSL.

[26] A copy of Browne's campaign song. "We Will Make California Dry" is (as of this date) displayed in the Visitors Center at Bidwell Mansion State Park. The author first read of Browne in John E. Keller's biography of his grandmother, *Anna Morrison Reed*. Newspaperwoman Reed had editorialized Brown as a "pet pastor" of Mrs. Bidwell's who better belonged in the gutter. A news story featuring Brown's arrest and subsequent disgrace ran in the Chico *Enterprise*, 12-28-1914.

[27] This battle over this passage of Prohibition legislation in California in 1917 is reported by letters and in saved clippings in AKB's Collection, Prohibition Papers, CSL.

[28] Letter in Sacramento *Union*, 11-1-1916, from J. Curverez in response to a letter submitted by Annie.

[29] John E. Keller, *Anna Morrison Reed*, 1849-1921.

[30] Letter, JB in San Francisco to AKB in Washington, 12-31-1870. AKB Collection, CSL.

[31] In "An open letter to S. W. Odell and the Dry Federation of California" by Anna Morrison Reed, November 1915. From Keller book cited above.

Rancho Chico: The shrinking giant, pp. 315–322

[1] Lusk's letter of 3-14-1904, AKB Collection, The Bancroft Library.

[2] AKB diary, 3-8-1904.

[3] AKB diary, 3-14-1904.

[4] AKB diary, Ibid.

[5] Letter, AKB to Sen. George C. Perkins, 3-11-1904. AKB Collection, box 32 (Indians), CSL.

[6] Letter, Sen. George C. Perkins to AKB, 2-22-1904, Ibid.

[7] AKB's will, probate #3026.

[8] AKB diary 4-16-1904.

[9] AKB diary. Guy Kennedy mailed the check for her on March 9, 1904.

[10] These purchases are itemized in AKB's diary, March-April 1904.

[11] AKB Collection, The Bancroft Library.

[12] Ibid.

[13] Ibid.

[14] Ibid.

[15] Ibid.

[16] Ibid.

[17] AKB diary, August 1911.

[18] AKB diary, 8-9-1904. Of course, Lusk was getting older and not in the best of health. He died in February 1913. Mansfield's *History of Butte County, 1918.*

Loss of two loved grandchildren, pp. 323–339

[1] Quotes are from AKB's diary.

[2] Reported by Dorothy J. Hill in *The Indians of Chico Rancheria,* 1978. Hill's source was an interview of Amanda Wilson by Erminine Voegelin and published in *Anthropological Records 7, N. 2,* (1942). Apparently Amanda and Mrs. Bidwell never discussed this sensitive point.

[3] JB's will of 7-3-1897: the provisions given should he survive Annie. Recorded Butte County, Book C, pp. 381-383. Probate #1187.

[4] Letter, AKB in San Francisco to JB in Chico, 5-10-1894. AKB Collection, CSL.

[5] AKB's dairy entry of 4-11-1909 tells of her great joy at witnessing this event.

[6] AKB's diary, 11-8-1906. She notes that Hugh McErnery, 45, died the following month, thus bringing her Christian Men's Reading Room to a close.

[7] Letter, Elmer Lafonso in Chico to AKB in Washington, 9-26-1910. AKB Collection, The Bancroft Library.

[8] According to Henry Azbill's comments, the sweathouse would have automatically been destroyed with the death of its chief in accordance with Maidu custom.

[9] Letter, Maggie Lafonso in Chico to AKB in Chico, 11-1-1907. AKB Collection, CSL.

[10] Letter, Maud B. Camper of Chico to AKB, 11-19-1909. AKB Collection, CSL.

[11] See chapter "The Old and the Young."

[12] JB's diary mentions giving Nucholls permission to leave Bidwell's Camp in Big Meadows to visit his stepchildren in Greenville.

[13] The likelihood that Clara and Janey (or Jennie) were the same person, as suggested by Craig Bates, is given greater credence by the fact that Nucholls was married to the mother of George Clements' children.

[14] Letter from Edwin G. Paine to AKB, 2-23-1906. AKB Collection, CSL.

[15] AKB's dairy is source for this period.

[16] AKB diary, 10-13-1908.

[17] AKB diary, 1-27-1909.

[18] AKB diary, 2-13-1909.

[19] AKB diary entry, 4-11-1909.

A year of travel, pp. 340–346

[1] AKB's diary is major source for narrative and dates.

[2] Letter, William Alexander in Washington to AKB in Chico, 12-17-1903.

[3] AKB diary, 1909-1910.

[4] San Francisco *Call Bulletin*, 11-3-1899.

[5] Letter, Gladys Bingham in Los Gatos to AKB in Chico, 9-2-1909, AKB Collection, The Bancroft Library.

[6] Clippings, undated, and the newspapers not noted, are tucked within Annie's diary.

[7] AKB's diary.

Good-bye to Sallie, pp. 347–349

[1] Letter, AKB in Chico to Col. J. K. Armstrong of New York, 11-22-1914. AKB Collection, The Bancroft Library.

[2] Chico *Record*, 1-14-1912.

[3] Letter, AKB to Col. Armstrong, op. cit.

[4] Chico *Enterprise*, 12-28-1914. See also chapter "Rancho Chico: The Shrinking Giant."

[5] Chico *Record*, 10-2-1913.

And what of the rancheria? pp. 350–357

[1] Amanda's census was as follows:

Children: Sherman Wilson, Eva Wilson, Edward Wilson, Dewey Conway, Jodie Conway, Robert Silvers, Anita Silvers, Homer Silvers, Evelynne William, Viola Henry, Sweeney Henry, Margaret Henry, Henry Asbill, Johnnie Asbill.

Women: Mrs. Santa Wilson (Amanda), Mrs. Hacy Silvers, Mrs. Tom Frank, Mrs. Emma Cooper, Mrs. James Lanno, Mrs. Bessie Henry, Mrs. George Barber, Mrs. Mary Asbill, Mrs. Ellen Powell, Mrs. Ed Kern.

Men: Santa Wilson, William Conway, Cado Sparks, Dalbert Sparks, Pete Frank, Richard Cooper, Chico Tom, Lamma Young, Ed Kern, William Preacher, Frank Henry, John Richards, George Barber, John Asbill, Rufus Pulicy, J. C. Mitchell, Mike Jefferson, Jack Frango, Master Isaiah Conway, Master Burney Wilson, Master Earnest Young, Mr. Pablo Silvers, Elmer N. Lafonso. Source: AKB Collection, The Bancroft Library.

[2] Amanda's accounts have been largely incorporated into Annie Bidwell's talks and writing on the rancheria Indians as published by the Bidwell Mansion Association in *Rancho Chico Indians,* by Annie K. Bidwell, 1980.

[3] AKB Collection, The Bancroft Library.

[4] Annie Bidwell made note of the fact that she had discovered through years the pride of the Indian people and their preference to earn their way rather than to take charity.

[5] Letter, Elmer Lafonso in Chico to AKB in Washington, 8-26-1910, AKB Collection, The Bancroft Library.

[6] Letter, Elmer Lafonso in Chico to AKB in Washington, 9-20-1910. Ibid.

[7] San Francisco *Call*, 5-28-1911.

[8] Letter, Luther Clements in Lawrence, Kansas to AKB in Chico, 4-18-1915, AKB Collection, CSL.

[9] Chico *Enterprise-Record* story, clipping undated except as 1965. The association members receiving shares in the distribution or land titles were listed as: Carl Delgado, Delores Sylvers McHenry, Raymond Sylvers, Donald Sylvers, Homer Sylvers, Sr., Homer Sylvers, Jr., LeRoy Nucholls, Alfred Nucholls, Darwin Nucholls, Virgil Nucholls, Luther

G. Clements, Luther L. Clements, Earl Clements, Lillian Stubblefield, Barbara Beasley, Marie Van Sycle, Ruth Payne, Bud Bain, Ivan Conway, Vernon Conway, Jodie Lee Conway, Sherman Wilson, Thelma Wilson, Edward Wilson, Marvin Wilson, Elmer Aranda, Genevieve Aranda, George Aranda, Harriet Ramirez, Norma Ramirez, Jimmie Durant, Frances Potter, Bernice Rogers, Joyce Drenon, Donna Rickard, Juanita Simpson, Mary Pomeroy, Jon Azbill, Henry Azbill, Kenneth Azbill, Eva Pierce.

[10] Ibid.

[11] Ibid.

[12] Ibid.

[13] Chico *Enterprise-Record,* 7-3-1961.

[14] Annie Bidwell may have credited herself with the Indian's decision to destroy the sweathouse/dancehouse in the Mechoopda Indian village in 1907 after Holai Lafonso's death.

According to Henry Azbill, it was a custom to always destroy the sweathouse (Kum meh) of a chief so that the new chief (Yeponi) might build his own. The Chico sweathouse was not replaced as no new chief was ever chosen. The Mechoopdas did continue to participate in other dance societies if they were elected to do so. Author's source: Letter by Henry Azbill to Ruby Swartzlow, Paradise historian, 6-18-1966. Elmer Lafonso reported once that he was not admitted to the secret nature of some of the sweathouse ceremonies, apparently because he had become too Anglicized.

[15] Letter, Craig D. Bates, curator of ethnology, Yosemite National Park, to Lois H. McDonald, 10-24-2001.

Allies in the cause of education, pp. 358–364

[1] Sources on Mrs. Hearst include brief biographies of herself and U.S. Senator George Hearst in the *Encyclopedia Americana* and a research paper by Vonnie Eastham, "Aspects of the Life of Phoebe Apperson Hearst," California State University, Chico, Special Collections.

[2] From *Here Is My Land,* Butte County Pen Women, 1940.

[3] Both Bidwells in their diaries noted numerous contacts with public schools at all levels.

[4] AKB's diaries.

[5] Two instances noted in AKB's diary 12-23-1891; 10-2-1899. On one of these occasions when the speaker was detained, Annie Bidwell addressed the teachers' institute.

[6] Annie Bidwell's talk to Normal students on conservation can be found in the AKB Collection, The Bancroft Library.

[7] During April and May 1905, AKB visited the Forestry Station, U.S. Capitol, numerous times to get materials and to talk with Gifford Pinchot about the Mt. Lassen region and her interest in protection of the roadside shade trees. AKB diary, 1905.

[8] AKB diary, 1-25-1906.

[9] The testimony of a close friendship between the two women comes from Helen Sommer Gage in the NLAPW, Butte County Branch 1940 publication *Here is My Land.* Mrs. Gage is also the primary source for the belief that Annie had an entire wardrobe fashioned at Mrs. Hearst's request. Certainly Mrs. Gage was in a better position to have such facts than the author, but it should be noted that Mrs. Gage was a child through most of the years that she observed Mrs. Bidwell, scarcely a confidante.

[10] Letter, Phoebe A. Hearst to AKB, 3-9-1915, AKB Collection, The Bancroft Library.

[11] Interview with Ruby Dailey English, Special Collections, Meriam Library, CSUC.

Exit, pp. 365–382

[1] In a letter to Annie in Washington 12-21-1876, JB writes of the Irish maids breaking off whole branches of red berries and ordering the houseboy to assist in gathering more "to decorate the mansion for Christmas" while "the truth is the girls wanted them to decorate the Catholic church … the fact is Catholics think it is no harm to steal for their church!" AKB Collection, CSL.

[2] She signed the codicil to her will at the Hotel Ramona on January 25, 1918.

[3] He had also wanted some work done on his brother Thomas' headstone. Here, America would have to consent and the author has no information on this.

[4] John and Cora Kennedy's stone is set separately from the "friends," a bit closer to the Bidwell marker.

[5] Eva Kennedy was the first of the four to be interred in the vault. She died in 1934.

[6] The Sacramento *Bee*, 7-21-1963. On June 23, 1934, a sale of the reversionary rights on all property sold by the estate with Annie's reversionary stipulation, took place and was made to The Title Insurance and Guaranty Company of San Francisco. In 1948 this company conveyed its reversionary interest to Bidwell Park, the Children's Playground and City Plaza, so that if future action were taken against a property owner, any such property judged forfeited would go to benefit the people of Chico.

[7] It was the decision of the administrator to leave these bequests for the last. Funds had run low and most of the Indians received only half of what had been specified for them.

[8] Dan Reed, grandson namesake of John Bidwell's brother Daniel, also received a lot.

[9] BCHS *Diggin's*, special Bidwell Mansion issue, 1968, Frank Bidwell Durkee.

[10] Ruby Dailey English had insisted at this interview that Florence's last name was *Crowd*.

[11] The Prime Timers is a noncredit program of classes sponsored by California State University, Chico, for retirement age residents of the service area.

[12] Letter, Larry V. Richardson to Velma Butler, 1967.

[13] AKB diary, 12-13-1905.

[14] AKB diary, 12-15-1905.

[15] The author was privileged to read Annie L. Meriam's diaries, 1900-1920, by her son Ted Meriam. Notes taken on the diaries in 1999 were lost from her computer, so memory of the diaries' contents is relied on.

[16] AKB diary, 6-18-1906.

[17] AKB diary, June 18-21, 1906.

[18] A parallel situation is detailed in the recent book by Dr. Robert Cutler, retired Stanford University physician, who presents the theory, with evidence, that Jane Stanford, the co-founder and benefactor of Stanford University (with her husband, Leland Stanford), died by poison, possibly with the assistance (and certainly with the cover-up) of the university's first president, David Starr Jordan. Mrs. Stanford reputedly interfered in administrative decisions, including ordering the firing of a professor. Sacramento *Bee*, October 11, 2003, "The Mysterious Death of Jane Stanford." It is not suggested that such deep animosity ever existed between a member of the Chico Normal School administra-

tion and Annie Bidwell, but Annie believed that it was her moral duty to challenge decisions at the normal school as well as to often ask favors of its faculty and presidents.

[19] Chico *Enterprise*, March 8, 9, 12, 14, 19, 1918.

[20] The author has played with the notion that Annie had her pale blue wedding dress, which, so far as records show was not among the clothing she gave away before or at death, remade into a dress to wear for reuniting with her husband.

Bibliography

Primary References

The diaries of Annie K. Bidwell, 1888–1911.
    Original diaries, California State Library, Sacramento.
    Photocopies, Special Collections, Meriam Library, California State University, Chico.
    Photocopies, Bidwell Mansion State Historic Park.
    Typed copies and on CD-ROM, Bidwell Mansion State Park.
The diaries of John Bidwell, 1866–1900, located as above.
Annie Kennedy Bidwell Collection, California State Library, Sacramento.
    Correspondence between Annie Kennedy Bidwell and John Bidwell, 1866–1900.
    Correspondence to AKB from her mother, Catherine M. Kennedy; her father, Joseph C. G. Kennedy; her sister, Sallie Kennedy Alexander; her brother Joseph M. Kennedy; her brother John R. Kennedy; sister-in-law, Cora Wayland Kennedy; nephews Guy and Joseph Kennedy, and William Alexander; and numerous other persons including residents of the Rancho Chico Rancheria village.
    Papers concerning AKB's Indian school and membership in numerous organizations concerned with Indian welfare.
    Papers concerned with Prohibition causes and organizations.
Annie Kennedy Bidwell Collection, The Bancroft Library, Berkeley.
    Correspondence with family members and others.
    Papers concerning the Mechoopda Indians.
    Daughters of the American Revolution applications.
    Civil War era journals and miscellaneous letters from friends.
    Assorted legal papers.
    Clippings.
    AKB business accounts, 1901–1910, sketchy thereafter.
Annie Kennedy Bidwell Collection, Special Collections, Meriam Library, California State University, Chico.
    Assorted correspondence from early years.
    Oral interviews, transcribed: Helen Gage, Henry Azbill, Ruby Daily English, Rebecca French Bolt, and Freida Petersen Knott.
    Hector Lee Folklore Collection.
    Photographs of Kennedy and Bidwell families, Rancho Chico, and the Bidwell Mansion.
    Baz, Sara Stanley "Men and Women in the Nineteenth Century Prohibition Movement: John and Annie Bidwell as an Example of Complementary Roles,"

unpublished paper, 1998.

Goss, Virginia J. "Annie Ellicott Kennedy Bidwell," unpublished M.A. thesis. California State University, Chico, 1981.

John Muir papers, Holt-Atherton Library, University of the Pacific. Correspondence between Annie Kennedy Bidwell and John Muir.

Royce, Charles C. In Memoriam, John Bidwell: Scrapbook Compiled by C. C. Royce, 3 vols. California State Library, Sacramento. Partial copies, Bidwell Mansion State Park.

Books

Bidwell, Annie K. *Rancho Chico Indians.* Dorothy J. Hill, ed. Chico, Calif.: Bidwell Mansion Association, 1980.

Bidwell, Joan J. *Bidwell Family History,* 1587–1982. Baltimore: Gateway Press, 1983.

Crawford County History, California State Library, Sutro Library Branch, San Francisco.

Delmatier, Royce D., et al., *The Rumble of California Politics,* 1848–1970, New York: John Wiley & Sons, 1970.

Gillis, Michael J., and Michael F. Magliari, *John Bidwell and California: The Life and Writings of a Pioneer.* Spokane: Arthur H. Clark, 2003.

Goldsmith, Barbara. *Other Powers.* Alfred A. Knopf, 1998.

Gray, George Moses. *Reminiscences of the Life of General Bidwell.* From a series in *Sandy Gulch News,* 1938–1939. Chico, Calif.: Association for Northern California Records & Research, 1999.

Hill, Dorothy J. *The Indians of Chico Rancheria,* Sacramento: California Department of Parks and Recreation, 1978.

Hoopes, Chad L. *What Makes a Man. The Annie Kennedy–John Bidwell Letters, 1866–1868.* Fresno: California Valley Publishers, 1973.

Hutchinson, W. H. *When Chico Stole the College,* Chico, Calif.: Butte Savings and Loan, 1983.

Hutchinson, W. H., Clarence McIntosh, and Pam Herman Bush. *A Precious Sense of Place: The Early Years of Chico State.* Chico, Calif.: Friends of Meriam Library, 1991.

Keller, John E., ed. *Anna Morrison Reed.* Lafayette, Calif.: Privately printed, 1979.

Latour, Ira H. ed. *Silver Shadows, A Directory of Early Photographers in Northern California.* Chico, Calif.: Chico Museum and Chico Art Center, 1993.

Mansfield, George C. *History of Butte County, 1918.* Reprint with additions. Chico, Calif.: Association for Northern California Records & Research, 1996.

McGie, Joseph F. *History of Butte County, 2 Vols.* Oroville, Calif.: Butte County Board of Education, 1982

National League of American Pen Women, Chico Branch. *Here is My Land.* 1940. Essays:

Currie, Anne Helen. "General John Bidwell."

Gage, Helen Sommer. "Mrs Bidwell as Her Friends Knew Her."

Stansell, Lois. "Bidwell Mansion."

Hagen, Edythe. "From Normal to State College."

National League of American Pen Women, Chico Branch. *Ripples Along Chico Creek: Perspectives on People and Times.* 1992. Essays:

Hartsell, Lynn. "Annie Bidwell, Elegant Pioneer."

Levenson, Rosaline. "Bidwell's Relations with Minorities."

McDonald, Lois H. "The Bidwell Family."

McDonald, Lois H. "Years of Decision."

Shover, Michele. "John Bidwell: A Reconsideration."

Ramsland, Margaret. *The Other Bidwells.* Chico, Calif.: Jensen Graphic, 1972.

Linda Rawlings, ed. *Dear General: The Private Letters of Annie E. Kennedy and John Bidwell, 1866–1868.* Sacramento: California Dept. of Parks & Recreation, 1993.

Wells, Harry L., and W. L. Chambers. *History of Butte County, 1882.* Reprint. Berkeley: Howell-North, 1973.

Articles

Chandler, Robert "The Failure of Reform: White Attitudes and Indian Response in California During the Civil War Era," *Pacific Historian* 24, no. 3, Stockton, Calif., 1980. 284–294.

Currie, Annie E. "Bidwell Rancheria," *Diggin's* 4, no. 3. Oroville, Calif.: Butte County Historical Society (hereafter BCHS), 1960. 4–8.

Durkee, Frank B. "Saving the Bidwell Mansion." BCHS *Diggin's*, special publication 1968. 21–28.

Eastham, Vonnie "A Comparison of Two Lives [Phoebe Hearst and Annie Bidwell]," BCHS *Diggin's* 15, no. 4, 1971. 11–16.

Gillis, Michael J. "John Muir and the Bidwells: The 1877 Mt. Shasta Expedition," BCHS *Diggin's* 37, no. 4, 1993. 83–87.

———. "John Muir and the Bidwells: the Forgotten Friendship," *Dogtown Territorial Quarterly.* Paradise, Calif., spring 1995. 4–5, 18–23, 26.

Jones, William L., "A Naturalist's Vision: The Photography of Henry Wetherbee Henshaw," BCHS *Diggin's* 30, no. 2, 1986. 31–37.

Lenhoff, James W. "When the President [Hayes] Headed West." BCHS *Diggin's* 24, no 3, 1980. 55–69.

Levenson, Rosaline, "Chico's Jewish Residents and the Bidwells: Interactions and Relationships." BCHS *Diggin's* 33, no. 2, 1989. 27–53.

Magliari, Michael, and Michael Gillis, "John Bidwell and the Indians of Chico Rancheria: Was He Their Protector—Or Their Enslaver?" *Chico News & Review,* March 2, 1995.

Mathes, Valerie Sherer, "The Death of John Sutter as Seen Through the Letters of Annie and John Bidwell." *Pacific Historian.* Stockton, Calif., fall 1982. 40-52.

———. "Indian Philanthropy in California: Annie Bidwell and the Mechoopda Indians." *Arizona and the West.* Summer 1983. 153–166.

———. "Annie E. K. Bidwell: Chico's Benefactress." *California History.* California Historical Society. Spring–summer 1989. 14–25.

Neubarth, W. Wesley "The Neubarth Brass Band," BCHS *Diggin's* 12, no. 2, 1968. 14–16.

Ramsland, Margaret, "Nopani: Unsung Heroine." Butte County *Bugle.* Chico, Calif., March 1, 1973.

Slade, Martha "Bidwell Hall For Ever," BCHS *Diggin's* 27, no. 4, 1983. 79–95.

Stansell, Lois, et al., "Chico Women's Club and the Bidwell Mansion," BCHS *Diggin's*

15, no. 4, 1971. The entire issue of *Diggin's* was devoted to descriptions of articles obtained for the archives at the Bidwell Mansion for research use.

Correspondence

Henry Keaala Azbill, San Francisco, to Ruby J. Swartzlow, Paradise. June 18, 1966.

Craig D. Bates, curator of ethnography, Yosemite National Park, to Lois H. McDonald: November 1998, October 2001, December 2001.

Larry V. Richardson, Paradise, numerous letters to Lois H. McDonald; letter to Velma Butler, November 1967, re Chicoans' view of A. K. Bidwell.

Franklin Lusk to Annie K. Bidwell, 1901, 1904, copies, gift of Ted Meriam to Lois H. McDonald.

Newspapers

Butte County *Bugle.*
Oakland *Tribune.*
Philadelphia *Press.*
Sacramento *Bee.*
Sacramento *Union.*
San Francisco *Call.*
San Francisco *Chronicle.*
San Francisco *Weekly Examiner.*
Chico *Chronicle-Record.*
Chico *Record.*
Chico *Enterprise.*
Chico *Enterprise-Record.*

Miscellaneous

Annie Lund Meriam's diaries, loaned by Ted Meriam and returned.

Annie K. Bidwell's will and codicils to same (copy), gift from Ted Meriam.

John Bidwell's will (July 3, 1897) and probate papers, no. 1187, filed book County Recorder's Book C, 4-16-1900. Microfilm, Special Collections, Meriam Library, California State University, Chico.

Carllene Marek's index of Richard Schillen Collection of Historical Materials; collection in Redwood City Public Library; index to Butte County in Paradise Genealogical Society Library, Paradise.

Haskell McInturf's loan of an 1886 John Bidwell letter to John McKinstry Smith of Oroville.

John S. Waterland, 1930s Chico *Record* series on early Chico and its residents. Reprinted as Old Timer series in 1987 by Chico *Enterprise.*

Encyclopedia Americana.

Numerous conversations and interviews with knowledgeable Chicoans.

Index

A

B

D

E

N

O

About the author

*L*ois Halliday McDonald is a native of Illinois, growing up on a farm not far from the confluence of the Illinois, Mississippi and Missouri rivers. She graduated from Illinois State University, majoring in speech arts and English.

Teaching, homemaking, and working as a Butte County, California, social worker occupied her first thirty years after college, but then she met Clio on a blind date (her mother coaxed Lois into accompanying her back to New England to look for family beginnings!) and has never since left that muse's side. To cement the union she took a master's degree in history from California State University, Chico, in 1976.

Lois McDonald has three children and two stepchildren, adults, all California residents. (One son recently reminded her to include among her activities that of puppet master, one of her hobbies he and his friends enjoyed mightily as a boy.)

For fifteen years Lois served as a director of the Paradise Performing Arts Center. Other board memberships include the Association for Northern California Records and Research, Bidwell Mansion Cooperative Association, the Butte County Branch of the League of American Pen Women and the Paradise Branch, American Association of University Women.

Her previous books include *The Fur Trade Letters of Francis Ermatinger, Elsie Hamburger: I Never Look Back,* and *This Paradise We Call Home.* She edited and contributed to an anthology published by the National League of American Pen Women, *Ripples Along Chico Creek,* and edited other Pen Women publications. She has edited both a quarterly, *The California Historian,* and the local history semiannual journal, *Tales of the Paradise Ridge,* writing many articles for the latter. For over six years she contributed a weekly history column to the *Paradise Post.*